THE VISION OF A NEW CHURCH AND A NEW SOCIETY

Christian Heritage Rediscovered

The Series, as the name suggests, is meant to focus on Christian Faith & Living vis-à-vis topics like Literature & Poetry, Indigenous Philosophizing, Ethical response towards Agriculture, Health & Healing, Science & Technology, Ecofeminist Theology, Sociological approach towards Human Rights, Law & Politics, Arts, History of Ideas, Ancient Civilizations, Cultural Contiguity, Religious Cosmologies & Mysticism, Footsteps of famous Theologians, World Peace & Harmony, Global Capitalism, Network Marketing, Cybertheology, Population & Demographics, Epigraphic Studies, Contextualized Education, and many others. We welcome a Mss. on any topic/s mentioned, whether they are original works, scholarly monographs, collections of conference papers, revised dissertations, or translations of historical documents. Through the Series we, the Publishers, are striving to put forward published works that may help Institutions, Academic Bodies, Researchers, Scholars and the World at large in furthering their respective knowledge and understanding on the concerned subject. We welcome your comments on our efforts and further suggestions on how we can foster the upcoming thoughtful theologically grounded books.

Christian Heritage Rediscovered - 26

THE VISION OF A NEW CHURCH AND A NEW SOCIETY

A Scholarly Assessment of
Dr. Samuel Rayan's
Contribution to Indian Christian Theology

Edited by
Kurien Kunnumpuram, SJ

CWI
Christian World Imprints(TM)

First Published in 2016 by

Christian World Imprints(TM)
Christian Publishing & Books from India
H-12 Bali Nagar, **New Delhi-110015**
info@christianworldimprints.com
www.ChristianWorldImprints.com
Phone: +91 11 25465925

ISBN: 978-93-5148-083-9 (HB) ISBN: 978-93-5148-084-6 (PB)

Cataloging in Publication Data--DK
Courtesy: D.K. Agencies (P) Ltd. <docinfo@dkagencies.com>

The vision of a new church and a new society : a scholarly assessment of Dr. Samuel Rayan's contribution to Indian Christian theology / edited by Kurien Kunnumpuram, SJ.
pages cm. -- (Christian heritage rediscovered ; 26)
Papers presented at a national seminar held at Calicut in December 2014.
ISBN 9789351480839 (HB)
ISBN 9789351480846 (PB)

1. Theology--India--Congresses. 2. Mission of the church--India--Congresses. 3. Rayan, Samuel--Congresses. I. Rayan, Samuel, honouree. II. Kunnumpuram, Kurien, 1931-, editor. III. Series: Christian heritage rediscovered ; 26.

DDC 230.0954 23

Printed at D. K. Fine Art Press Pvt. Ltd.

The Book

Rev. Fr. Samuel Rayan (1920-) is an Indian Jesuit theologian who has contributed significantly to the Indian Church. Being a radical humanist, Rayan is convinced that the human person in community is the object of God's special love. Through his theological writings, Rayan pleads for care of the earth, concern for life and commitment to people. In the last week of December 2014 a National Seminar was held in Christ Hall, Calicut, in order to study Rayan's Theological writings and to assess his contribution to Indian Christian theology. Most of the twenty-two papers collected in this book were presented at the Seminar and they reflect on the significance of the Indian Church and its role in the lives of the ordinary people. These have been suitably presented under 4 parts, namely: Theological Themes, The Church and its Mission, Approach to the Bible, and Theologizing in India. It is our fond hope that the book will inspire the readers to study Samuel Rayan's writings and discover his vision of a new Church and a new Society.

The Editor

Rev. Kurien Kunnumpuram, SJ (born July 8, 1931) is a Roman Catholic, Indian Jesuit priest and well-known Christian theologian. Member of the academic staff of the Faculty of Theology at Jnana-Deepa Vidyapeeth, Pune (India) (Emeritus), he contributed in the field of ecclesiology, particularly with regard to Vatican II. He was the founder-publisher-editor of *Jnanadeepa: Pune Journal of Religious Studies*, from 1998 to 2010. He was also the founding editor of JDV's Encyclopedia of Indian Christian Theology, till 2009. He is the author of more than twelve books.

Introduction

In the last week of December 2014, a National Seminar was held in Christ Hall, Calicut, in order to study Dr. Samuel Rayan's Theological writings and to assess his contribution to Indian Christian theology. Nineteen of the twenty-two papers collected in this book were presented at the seminar. Three more papers were written specifically for this book. These papers are divided into four parts: Theological Themes, The Church and Its Mission, Approach to the Bible and Theologizing in India.

Included in **Part One** are six articles which deal with some important theological themes. The first one is by Jacob Parappally and discuses the Christological vision of Samuel Rayan. He begins by asserting that experiencing and interpreting Jesus in the Indian context was a passion for Rayan. He believes that Rayan's Christology is a Christology from below. His emphasis is on Jesus of Nazareth, the historical Jesus, a real human being who is recognized as the supreme revelation of God, the compassionate. The one single thread that holds together all Rayan's reflections on Jesus Christ is his insistence on the humanity of Christ and Christ's dynamic presence in the struggles of the poor and the victims of all forms of oppression.

The second paper by P. R. John deals with the Divine in the writings of Rayan. Schooled in the Sadhana of St. Ignatius of Loyola Rayan first speaks of God as a labourer. God labours in creation. Rayan believes that the *dynamics* of the Divine is present in the totality of creation, working for its wholeness and healing, and calling creation to its fullness. According to John, Rayan encountered the Divine in Jesus Christ. God was present and active in the world in and through Jesus for the salvation of humankind. For Rayan Jesus is the highpoint of God's self-manifestation. Under the influence of Indian thought, Rayan sought to understand the Divine as *Saccidananda* and *Antaryamin*. For Rayan the Divine remains hidden like roots and foundation, like wombs and sources.

The third paper by Mohan Doss is on Rayan's thoughts on the Holy Spirit. The author points out that for Rayan Spirit-experience is the starting-point of Pneumatology. This experience enriches one's personal life, offers a new vision of life and reality and urges us to build a new world. Mohan Doss calls attention to Rayan's discussion of the symbols of the Holy Spirit like water, fire and dove as well as prophets and other charismatic persons. For Rayan, Jesus is the unique symbol of the Holy Spirit. Rayan describes the neglect of the Holy Spirit in western theology and its disastrous consequences in the life of the Church. He mentions briefly the impact of the Spirit perspectives on Spirit Christology and Spirit ecclesiology.

The fourth paper by Francis Gonsalves discusses Rayan's theology of the Eucharist. He maintains that Rayan has carefully reread the Bible and creatively reinterpreted tradition in order to gain new insights into the nature and meaning of the Eucharist. As a result Rayan looks upon the Eucharist as an energizer of life. Gonsalves also refers to presence of the Eucharistic Lord in the lowly, the lost and the last as well as His reconciling and unifying work.

The fifth paper is by Kochurani Abraham who deals with Rayan's thoughts on women. Describing Rayan as a feminist theologian, she highlights his voice of prophetic protest. She points out that the process of asserting women's personhood involves protest as it entails challenging patriarchy as a system that privileges men's interests and desires above those of women. She is happy to note how Rayan finds the daughters of Zelophehad initiating a social revolution in their refusal to see themselves as destined to be passive victims of anatomy, history and fate, and in their readiness to question the traditional economic arrangements which in their view need to be changed (See Num 27:1-4). Kochurani believes that Rayan's idea of a 'dissident' God challenges us to engage in critical theology.

The last article in this part titled: "Mother Earth: A Spiritual Matter" is written by Shalini Mulackal. In this paper, Shalini discuses Rayan's thoughts on ecology. At first she examines Rayan's understanding of the ecological crisis and the factors which cause this crisis. She then goes to deal with his theological reflections on nature, the earth and life. She concludes the paper by highlighting the programme of action Rayan puts forward in order to respond positively to this crisis.

There are seven papers in **Part Two** which deal with the Church and its mission in India today. The first one is by Kurien Kunnumpuram and discusses Rayan's ecclesiology. The author describes how Rayan looks upon the Church as the Jesus movement, as a counter-cultural movement and as an event, a happening. Rayan also discusses the local church and inculturation as well as the structures of the Church. Rayan is aware that it is not possible to develop a complete ecclesiology, as the Church is not something ready-made, finished and set squarely on the ground. It is something still in the making, something still seeking for its face, its identity.

The second paper, titled "Mission of the Church according to Samuel Rayan", is by Joseph Lobo. It begins by highlighting eleven challenges to the mission of the Church today as perceived by Rayan. It then goes on to describe how Rayan questions some of the traditional understanding and practice of the Church's mission. It also discusses the Rayan's proposals for mission today. The paper concludes with a brief critical appraisal of Rayan's views.

In the third paper on "Rayan's Vision of a New Society", Charles Davis discusses Rayan's idea of a new society. Davis begins by examining Rayan's critique of capitalism and advocacy of socialism. He goes on to describe how Rayan answers the question whether the kingdom of God can serve as a blueprint for a new society. According to Rayan: "What faith in the kingdom can offer is an orientation and a vision, a sense of direction and of values, motivation and the assurance of a hope that wins.... But tools for analysis and action must come the sciences". Hence, a new society can only be the outcome of a joint venture of science and religion, technology and vision, human beings and God. Davis concludes the paper by asserting that the Church should not only work for the creation of a new society patterned on the kingdom of God, but also be in her life a mirror of the kingdom.

The fourth paper in this part is by George Pattery which discusses Rayan's views on peace and peacemaking. He underlines some of Rayan's ideas: that Jesus was a radical peacemaker; that peace that does justice involves conflict; that the cross is the price of peace as well as the inevitable consequence of following Christ; and that incarnation is the establishment of peace between God and human beings and among human beings. Pattery refers to Rayan's discussion of the models of peace and points out how Rayan prefers the Jesus model.

The fifth paper is on the social and liberative consequences of Samuel Rayan's theology. The author, Nicholas T. begins by exploring the main influence on Rayan's liberation theology. As a young boy he was affected by the national struggle to end the colonial rule in India and the struggles of the oppressed *Ezhava* community in Kerala for socio-economic liberation. M. K. Gandhi, Sri Narayana Guru and Kumaran Asan had a lot of influence on Rayan. This made him reflect on the role of religion and spirituality in the struggle for liberation. Rayan is convinced that liberation here is not the completion of salvation, but without it, there is no salvation. And God is actively involved in the struggle of the people and the Holy Spirit is guiding the process of liberation. And Rayan's vision of development as evangelising mission makes Rayan suggest that the Church in India has to incarnate itself in the culture of the poor and the down-trodden and their struggle for liberation.

The sixth article by Kuruvilla Pandikattu is titled: "The Missing Child: The Contemporary Relevance of Samuel Rayan's Reflections on Children". The article begins by referring to Kailash Sathyarthi and Malala Yousafzy who were jointly awarded the Nobel Peace Prize in 2014. It also calls attention to the brutal murder of 145 people, including 132 innocent children, in Peshawar on 16 December 2014. In 2014, hundreds of children around the world were kidnapped from the school or on their way to it, while thousands were forcefully recruited by armed groups. An estimated 230 million children are affected by armed conflicts in different parts of the world.After summarising Rayan's reflections on children and highlighting the main points of the speeches made by Malela and Kailash during the Nobel Prize ceremony, Kuruvilla concludes: "Only if we can listen to the cry of the child and pay attention to its smile can we celebrate Christian life in general and Christmas in particular".

The last paper in this part discusses the transformative spirituality of Samuel Rayan. The author Stephen Chunmdamthadam begins by pointing out that Rayan was not satisfied with traditional spiritualities which are focused on pietistic practices oriented towards life in the next world. Based on his experience and involvement in the struggles of people Rayan sought to develop a spirituality which would be an appropriate response to reality. Such a spirituality can sustain people in their struggle for the transformation of social structures. Openness to the mystery of God, the prophetic dimension of Christian spirituality and the need for a spirituality of compassion are aspects of the spirituality that Rayan proposes.

Included in **Part Three** are three articles which deal with Rayan's approach to and use of the Bible. The first article by Jacob Prasad discusses Rayan's approach to Scripture. He points out that one of Rayan's main concerns is to interpret the Word of God in the multi-religious context of India. Rayan is also interested in the development of a theology for the creation of a just and more humane society. Prasad believes that Rayan's efforts to interpret the Bible contextually accords well with the position of the Pontifical Biblical Commission which in 1993 stated that "the interpretation of a text is always dependent on the mindset and concern of the readers". Besides, Rayan is able to interpret Scripture creatively with a liberationist thrust because he systematically studies it.

In the second paper, Paul Raj seeks to understand how Samuel Rayan uses the Bible, especially the New Testament. Many theologians influenced by old scholasticism, tended to look upon Scripture as *ancilla theologiae* (maidservant of theology) rather than *anima theologiae* (the soul of theology). But, Rayan makes use of the Bible as the soul of theology in accordance with directive of Vatican II (see *DV* 24). Paul Raj highlights some of characteristics of Rayan's use of the Bible: Contextualised reading, inter-textual analysis, and the principle of priority. It is remarkable that in his reading of the New Testament Rayan remains faithful to its central message. Many of Rayan's theological insights are a fruit of his creative reading of the Bible.

The third article by Henry Pattarumathil seeks to make an appraisal of Samuel Rayan's biblical exegesis and hermeneutics.

Henry bases his comments on a careful examination of an article Samuel Rayan wrote in 1997 titled: "With Us – With Whom – is God?" Henry appreciates Rayan's sharp observation: "The beauty of Rayan's exegetical conclusions is that they are founded on his sharp observation of the text". He points out that Rayan has an interdisciplinary approach to his study of the Bible. Insights from the social sciences, Marxism, cultural anthropology, aesthetics, ecological studies and feminist studies are used to interpret the biblical text. Besides, Rayan applies synchronic approach and structural exegesis to interpret the Gospel of Matthew. Finally, Rayan's article invites us to recognize the presence of Immanuel in the poor and the downtrodden and to work with God in his project of human liberation.

There are six papers in the **Fourth Part**. The first one is titled: "Exploring the Realm of Implicit Theologies". In it the author P. T. Mathew reflects on Rayan's method of theologizing. Mathew begins by examining Rayan's understanding of theology since he believes that one's understanding of theology embodies one's method. For Rayan theology has to be at the service of life at all levels. In his own words "Our theology will be at the service of those who work, suffer and hope, those who struggle for justice and human dignity for all women and men". For Rayan, commitment is the first act of theology and methods are a guide to clarify our commitment and praxis. Method points to a direction, and liberation is or ought to be our direction. Mathew believes that latent theologies as important as academic theology.

The second article by Keith D´Souza is a critical examination of Rayan's contention that theology is more of an art than science. Keith investigates the nature of both art and science in some depth. He then goes on to point out that there is some ambivalence in the writings of Rayan with regard to the nature of theology. On the one hand, he seems to propose a programme of theological articulation which is clearly aesthetically oriented, thereby revealing that for him theology is an art. On the other hand, there is a strong critical theological agenda that he wishes to pursue, with many dimensions of social critique involved. Hence, it may not be wrong to say that for Rayan theology entails both artistic and scientific dimensions.

In the third paper Sebastian Painadath examines the impact of Indian thought on Rayan's theology. He finds that of all the classical sources of Indian thought it is Bhagavad Gita that has significantly contributed to Rayan's theological enterprise. Rayan has a great appreciation of the myths and symbols of India. He believes that as Indians our psyche should resonate well with the myths and symbols of this country. Rayan has been inspired by Bhakti literature. In his opinion, the Upanishads, Buddhism and the Gita are voices of dissent. Gandhiji, Tagore as well as the leaders of social movements in Kerala--Sree Narayana Guru, Ayyankali, Kumaran Asan and Sahodaran Ayyappan--have exerted a lot of influence on Rayan's theological thought.

A fourth article by Isaac Padinjarekuttu studies Rayan's understanding of history and its importance for Indian Christian theology. Rayan discuses three models of history – the cyclic, the linear and the spiral. In general, the linear is attributed to the ChristianWest and the cyclic to the other societies of Asia, Africa and America. Rayan is of the opinion that the linear view is not fully accepted even in the West. For a thousand years Christian theology was formulated with the help of Platonic and neo-Platonic philosophies which were basically philosophies of changeless permanence and the eternal return of the same. Isaac also points out that Rayan challenges the widespread opinion of thinkers, both Christian and Hindu, that India has no sense of history. According to Rayan, there are unmistakable evidence that people of India had a deep sense of history. For example, the historical dimension of the Gita is remarkably profound. The author of the Gita shows a keen awareness of history which is holy.

The fifth paper by A. Kulandaisamy discusses Rayan's articles on the dalits. The author points out that Rayan has systematically contextualized the word of God, the doctrines of the Church as well as its mission taking into account the situation of the dalits. The liberation of the subaltern people is the main thrust of his theology. However, Kulandaisamy feels that Rayan does not sufficiently lay stress on the dalits as agents of their liberation, the strength of the dalits and the dalit experience as the source of theory and action.

Hence, Rayan is a prime path-finder of the dalits but not the path of their liberation.

The sixth article by Victor Ferrao contends that Christians in India cannot just erase the memory of colonization and go about living and theologizing with no reference to colonialism and its aftermath. We need to recover the original grace that is given to us through faith which is entangled with the evils of colonization. Ferrao appreciates the noble effort Rayan makes to do this in his seminal article: "Decolonizing Theology". But, he thinks that Indian Christians in general have tried to suppress the colonial pain by keeping it under erasure. However, the complex and dynamic afterlife of colonization has come back to haunt us. Hence, we have an imperative of faith to disentangle Christianity from the colonial tangle and find a new way of theologizing in India today.

It is my fond hope that the articles collected in this book will inspire the readers to study Samuel Rayan's writings and discover his vision of a new Church and a new society.

Before I conclude, I wish to express my grateful thanks to all those who helped me in the editing of this book. And I sincerely thank A. Francis for his competent secretarial assistance.

Kurien Kunnumpuram, SJ

Contents

Part Three
Approach to the Bible

Part Four
Theologizing in India

PART ONE

THEOLOGICAL THEMES

1

Meaning of Jesus Christ in the Indian Context

The Christological Vision of Samuel Rayan

Jacob Parappally, MSFS

Introduction

Experiencing and interpreting Jesus in the Indian context was a passion for Samuel Rayan. His faith-experience of Jesus is the very warp and woof of his life and its theological articulations cannot be reduced to a theological treatise on Jesus Christ called Christology. One of his articles is titled, "Jesus had Imagination". Rayan too has imagination. A true theologian must have imagination. He or she must go beyond the text of dogmas and doctrines taking along what they signify and letting them enlighten, challenge and transform the context of the theologian. In this process, the theologian, the text and the context get transformed. It would, then, positively affect the work of the Spirit to shape the entire world into God's Kingdom and form everyone into humans like Jesus.

As a keen observer of the events of history with a prophetic mind and as a sensitive participant of the cosmic process with a poetic and mystic heart Rayan sees the Christic presence of Jesus of Nazareth in everything human and cosmic. Therefore, his understanding and interpretation of Jesus, based on the New Testament witness about the Person and Mission of Jesus and the Christian faith-tradition, are in constant dialogue with the context of his life, namely, the sufferings of the poor and the marginalized as well as the experience of divine in the Indic religious traditions. In order to make Jesus' tradition dialogue with the Indian context Jesus needs to be liberated from everything that has alienated him from the very purpose of the incarnation, namely, the historical identification of God with all humans, in his or her socio-cultural, economic and political situation. Therefore, though Jesus was born at a particular time and in a particular place in history he includes in himself every place and every time. He is particular and universal; he is limited by space and time as well as unlimited. He is historical and trans-historical at the same time. Therefore, he can be encountered in every culture and every nation, as a human being who can identify himself with all humans in every culture and as the divine who transcends everything and everyone but at the same time immanent in all as the only vivifying and energizing eternal power.

1. Liberation of Jesus from Various Alienations

If God was limited in space and time through his historical incarnation as Jesus of Nazareth, the Christological doctrines, both true and false, as well as dogmas which tried to encapsulate the meaning of the mystery of Jesus Christ limited him in such a way that it emphasized his trans-historicity and neglected his historical existence or over-emphasized his divinity neglecting his humanity.

Rayan refers to various heretical groups as well as theologians who contributed to the alienation of Jesus from his historical existence or devalued his human life in preference to his trans-historical existence. The first heretical group which tried to propose a false doctrine about Jesus was the Ebionites. It was a Jewish-Christian sect which followed Jewish practices and yet believed in Jesus and argued that "the body of Jesus was fashioned in some heavenly realm out of incorruptible star-stuff, and not in a woman's womb nor our human flesh".[1] There were other groups of Ebionites who claimed that Jesus was the natural son of Joseph and Mary. However, the Gnostic type of Ebionites separate Christ from the realm of the ordinary mortals. For all varieties of Gnosticism with their dualistic understanding of reality with spirit as good and matter as evil, Christ could not assume a humanity through incarnation because matter was considered evil. For Gnostics Jesus was divine and not human. The Docetics had the same problem of considering matter as evil. For them Jesus only appeared to be human and was not really human.

Among the Fathers of the Church, Clement of Alexandria, affirmed that Jesus was "entirely impassible" which means he could not really suffer. According to him, Jesus needed no food and was so perfect that he could not feel pain or pleasure. Jesus needed no courage, fear or zeal as there was no room for such emotions in this perfect man. He was, indeed, the perfect man of Stoic idealism of *autarchia* which means a person unaffected by pleasure or pain. Hilary of Poitiers also held such views because he taught that the humanity of Jesus was from God. The Scholastic Christology credited Jesus with beatific vision as well as the fullness of spiritual happiness and knowledge possible for humans and angels. Thomas Aquinas tried to reconcile this with Jesus' agony in the garden and his suffering on the Cross by advancing the earlier theory of two regions of the soul having upper and the lower soul. The upper region of the soul of Jesus enjoyed beatific vision and the lower region of the soul experienced suffering, pain and abandonment. It was further explained that his ignorance, or learning something is a way of teaching or giving us good example. Thus, philosophical, psychological and theological reasons are given to explain away the real human life of Jesus in order to highlight that he was divine.

The Christological dogmas and Christology itself tried to blot out the humanity of Jesus by emphasizing his Divinity. Jesus was presented as one who shares our essence but not our existence. He seemed only to possess our nature and not the problems and difficulties that historical humans experience every day of their lives. Even in 1943, Pope Pius XII taught[2] that in his historical life Jesus enjoyed beatific vision in a more excellent way than the saints in heaven did. Thus, the Jesus of the Christian teaching was not much different from the Docetic Christ, over spiritualized Christ in the clouds. "Super-humanized and angelized, Jesus is no longer one of us, a man among men with whom we can identify ourselves. The technique has been to make Jesus spiritual, heavenly and universal.

Take him out of the total reality and particularity of the moment in which he lived. Make him non-historical".[3]

The popular devotions and pious exercises centred around Jesus further alienated him from his historical life and mission. He was de-contextualized and made alien to our earth. Rayan says, "When Jesus came to be imagined and treated in this way, a beautiful and powerful fountain of authentic humanism dried up, and the emergence of a compassionate, free, creative, and warm social order got blocked and ground was cleared for abstract, rigid and cold socio-religious policies and authoritarian structures".[4] To recover his humanity Jesus must be liberated from these heretical doctrines as well as from the exaggerated theological reflections and magisterial teachings on Jesus' divinity at the cost of his humanity.

2. Christic Identity

The fundamental Christian confession is about the person of Jesus Christ that this man, this Jesus of Nazareth, is God. Any reflection on this Christian faith ends up in seeking and finding the identity of the person of Jesus. Therefore, the question of Christology or a systematic reflection on the Christian faith in Jesus Christ is, "Who is Jesus Christ?" It is not an academic question but the heart of a quest for meaning in one's life. After his resurrection from the dead the early disciples of the Jesus of Nazareth encountered him as the absolute meaning of their lives, the beginning and the end, the Alpha and the Omega. The articulation of their faith experience of Jesus is expressed in the NT writings. They had experienced him as a prophet, mighty in word and deed, however, different from other prophets because he spoke with authority hitherto unknown to his predecessors. He identified himself with the poor and the marginalized and stood against structures and systems that dehumanized and the God he revealed was different from the God proclaimed by the established religion and finally he was murdered for 'blasphemy'. However, his true identity was recognized by his disciples only after his resurrection. His identity was rooted in his Father. Rayan says: "Jesus is clear about his own identity. Clearer than we are. He persists in affirming that what he is, what he has, what he says, whatever he does is not from himself. It is all from another whom he fondly calls

Abba, dear Father. Jesus' identity is not known apart from his roots in the Father's heart".[5]

The early Church recognized this identity of Jesus after his resurrection from the dead. It is through the Pentecostal event, by the power of the Holy Spirit, that the early Church recognized who Jesus was and who Jesus is.[6] Otherwise, he would have been understood only as a prophet "mighty in word and deed" who was expected to redeem Israel from foreign rule as the disciples on the way to Emmaus thought about him (Lk 24:19f). Through the power of the Holy Spirit the early Church recognized that the identity of Jesus has its roots in his intimate relationship with his Father during his earthly life. Therefore, it affirmed and confessed that Jesus' words of compassion and caring, of forgiveness and reassurance were God's words. But not only Jesus' words and teaching, his deeds too and his services originate from God. According to Rayan, the early Christian community, therefore, "encountered Jesus as the Word of God, as something God was/is saying to them, a Word about God's own Self and about us humans and our world and history and destiny. They knew him as God's Word of love and forgiveness, compassion and peace, spoken into their hearts and lives. A life-giving Word at the foundational level of creation and the crowning Word at the level of redemption (Jn 1:1-3)".[7] Thus, for the disciples Jesus was "the Image of God" (Col 1:15) and "the exact Likeness of God's own Being" (Heb 1:3). He is the image of the One who loved the world so much and gave his Son (Jn 3:16) and the image Yahweh who comforted Israel (Hos 2:14-25; 11; Is 40:1-1; 54). Jesus represents God to creation and the entire creation to God. Jesus' life and ministry to redeem the fallen created order into obedience to God was the exercise of the true image and likeness of God. Rayan affirms: "Jesus then is the image of Him whom Paul blesses as the All-merciful Father, the God who gives every encouragement and supports us in every hardship, and helps us in all our troubles, and thus enables us to help and comfort those who have all sorts of trials and sufferings (2 Cor1:3-4). He is the image of the God who "raises the dead" (2 Cor 1:9). He is the comforting Hand, God's consoling Word, incarnate Compassion (2 Cor 7:4-7); Is 40:1)".[8] Thus, Jesus is God's compassion translated into the idiom of our flesh and blood, our vulnerability, freedom love-ability and our responsibility or the ability to respond to God, fellow humans and the entire creation. It is in the human life of Jesus in history that he manifested his Christic identity as the image and likeness of the God of compassion. In his humanity, the incarnate compassion of God becomes visible and experiential.

3. Jesus, the Human

The main thrust of the Christology of Rayan is to recover and re-affirm the humanity of Jesus so that the meaning of God becoming human and the consequences of it for every human being and the entire universe can be clearly recognized, accepted and celebrated. His critique of the traditional Christological formulations whether in the heretical Christologies or in the orthodox Christian doctrines on Christ is that they do not let Jesus be Jesus, flesh of our flesh and the bone of our bones, though he was divine.

> The Gospels give us certain information about the person and mission of Jesus. Though the narrations about his historical life is coloured by the faith-experience about him after his resurrection, they show that there is a real continuity between the historical reality of Jesus and the risen Christ. The Synoptic Gospels identify the historical Jesus with the risen Christ. At the same time it 'Offers a clear account of the kind of man he was. Through various representative events and sayings the Gospel narrations about Jesus give us a general impression about his person than about his achievements. Rayan says, "If the humanity of Jesus comes so well through these theological interpretations suffused with the splendour of the resurrection faith, that humanity surely was rich and memorable and of central significance".[9] This humanity of Jesus is not an abstract idea but a truly human life. Its greatest significance is that it reveals God. In Jesus, humanity and divinity do not constitute two realities but the divine and the human make one single mystery of faith. Therefore, Jesus the human is the expression of God. Jesus' human activity is his divine activity. Rayan says, "It is in the humanity and life-story of Jesus that God is revealed rather than in what we call 'divine' in Christ's life. Divinity is best disclosed at the most human of his humanity".[10] In fact, the divine and the messianic were embedded in his historical

life and the early Church discovered it after his resurrection and in the light of his resurrection. He was so radically human that he could not but be divine. Referring to Ignacio Ellacuria, Rayan reaffirms that distinct from Christology based on the *logos* of the Greeks we need a Christology based on Jesus' flesh and humanity. According to Rayan, "this flesh-and-history or humanity of Jesus is the place of revelation". We can reach what the Father has disclosed only following Jesus, the human, and by leading his life ourselves.

4. The NT Witness to the Humanity of Jesus

It is true that the Gospel narrations about the Person and mission of Jesus are coloured by the resurrection experience. Some of the Christological titles of Jesus as well as his miracles are presented from the perspective of the resurrection experience. However, if we take seriously our Christian confession that Jesus was truly human though he was divine, we can discern some remarkable human traits of Jesus.

Rayan observes that "Jesus strikes us as a man of rare freedom and fearlessness. He was a non-institutional and unconventional figure. Totally authentic and independent. Remarkable for the courage of his convictions and his positive insights. A man with no grudge against the world, no trace of fear of losing his reputation, or creating a scandal, or staking his life".[11] He was alive to everything around him. He was in close and respectful contact with the common, the small and the neglected. He had a style of his own in being human, probably, inimitable in his mode of being human. He affirmed and called forth the free and the unique in everyone who encountered him. With conviction, confidence and ease he handled hostile questions about the resurrection, the identity of the neighbour, tax to Caesar and re-interpreted the laws, the taboos and the traditions of his Jewish religion. He associated himself with social undesirables, ate with outcasts, publicans and ritually impure and welcomed the lowly, the leper and the prostitute. He debunked the establishment and its piety in favour of human beings and for him justice and mercy counted far more than the temple, priest and the Sabbath. Jesus did not flee the world but got totally immersed in it: its problems, difficulties, its joys, sorrows and anxieties.

Jesus did not fit into the power systems of his times as they were oppressive and dehumanizing. He resisted all values of the establishment, whether religious or political, that prevented the unfolding of humans or oriented away from the physical, social and spiritual welfare of women and men.

The humanity of Jesus finds its best faith-expressions in the witnessing of the Letter to the Hebrews. It explains how Jesus was 'an intimate participant in our lowly flesh and painful history'. There is not only no dichotomy between the saving mission of Jesus and his humanity but the very mission of Jesus depends on the authenticity of Jesus' humanity according to Hebrews 2:10-18. Since, Jesus was to be the leader of our salvation and our sanctifier, he was destined to be one like us. "Jesus' vocation was to be with God's children, a child among children: therefore he shared equally in the same mortal blood and flesh as children share. Jesus was chosen to be our compassionate and trustworthy high priest: therefore he had to be 'completely like his brothers'".[12]

Jesus' likeness to humans extends beyond his physical constitution and it affects the deepest reality of Jesus' human spirit. He is made perfect through temptations, struggles and suffering (Heb 4:14-16; 5:7-8). He is like us and we are like him. Rayan asks, "In his loud cry and tears before God don't we recognize ourselves? In his humble submission, in his godly fear, in the religious awe with which he prays to God, don't we touch the human at is most authentic, its deepest, its humanest? Throughout the letter Jesus' humanity is consistently kept in mind". Jesus is from the tribe of Judah. As mediator, he intercedes for us and he comes to the presence of God with the offerings of his own blood and human life poured out for his brothers and sisters (Heb 5:4, 7, 13-14, 24; 8:6; 9:14, 24-25; 12-24). Rayan argues that for the author of the Letter to the Hebrews, no emphasis on the humanity of Jesus was too much.

The Synoptic Gospels and the Letter to the Hebrews highlight the fact that Jesus was radically, deeply and authentically human. He was the flesh-translation or human translation of Divine compassion. In spite of the early communities' proclamation about his divinity which they experienced after his resurrection, by and large they emphasized his humanity, not in terms of Greek categories of thought as the Councils and doctrines later did, but in his relationship with his Father and other humans and nature as well as in his being a real human being.

5. A Christology of Christic Presence

According to Rayan, Jesus Christ is the Good News of God's presence and solidarity with the oppressed. While not denying or limiting the presence of God who makes his sun shine and his rain fall on the good and the evil alike, God's effective and transforming presence is with the poor and oppressed. Based on the critical study of the Gospel of Matthew from the perspective of the poor done by George Soares-Prabhu and others, Rayan develops a comprehensive and clear articulation of Christic presence especially in the poor and the marginalized and their struggle for liberation from everything that prevents them from becoming human.

How is God involved in the history of those who have no one but God alone to support and save them from the miserable situations of life that they are thrown into? The answer to this question can be found in God's self-revelation in Jesus Christ as Immanuel or God-with-us. Rayan says that Matthew's gospel is to be read from the beginning to the end as the good news of God's saving presence and solidarity with "us".[13] This is epitomized in the revelation of Jesus as Immanuel. Matthew expresses this liberative presence of God and his solidarity with us through the opening and the closing of the Gospel with a genealogy culminating in the birth of the son of Mary who has two names. The name *Jesus* refers to the mission of saving the people from their sins (Matt 1:21) and the second name, *Immanuel* which means God-with-us, expresses the presence of God with those who are open to God and need his presence (Matt 1:23). "The name Jesus discloses what Mary's child does while Immanuel reveals who Mary's child is..."[14] The Immanuel circle which begins at the birth of Jesus ends with the promise of the Risen Jesus to his disciples that his presence would continue to be with them "to the end of time" (Matt 28:18-20).

The reference to Immanuel at the beginning of the Gospel according to Matthew refers to Jesus' decisive significance for the salvation of Israel and at the end 28:20 shows his decisive significance for the salvation of the world though it is already alluded to in the genealogy beginning with Abraham in whom all the nations are blessed. The revelation of Jesus as Immanuel is to be understood as God's presence is where Jesus is and God's presence is where the Kingdom is. Matthew's story unfolds this liberative presence of God both in the person of Jesus and in his mission of proclaiming the Kingdom. Therefore, Rayan says:

The Immanuel theme implies more than a sort of static presence among us of God-in-Jesus. It is a dynamic presence, active to save, and involves solidarity. It affirms God's drawing near to share our human condition and make his own our experiences and concerns. God-in-Jesus identifies with us and renounces privileges and riches in order to serve us; and immerses himself in the realities of our life including our sufferings and struggles. He commits himself to our liberation and salvation, risking life and laying it down in solidarity.[15]

Jesus' liberative solidarity as Immanuel is with us. But Rayan raises the question who is this "us"? In the gospel according to Matthew, the reference to Immanuel is taken from Isaiah 7:14. In the historical context this sign was given to King Ahaz, Immanuel or God with us was not referring to the presence of God to the entire world or the whole of the Hebrew people but only to those threatened and frightened people of Judah who were powerless and in the shadow of imminent invasion and destruction. God's presence was with them who needed him and who were open to receive his protective and supportive presence. In Matthew, the context of the birth of Jesus is the fulfilment of this prophecy about Immanuel, God-with-us, because it was the assurance of the presence of God with those early Christian communities which were mostly comprised of poor people, who were powerless and oppressed for witnessing to Jesus as the Christ or Messiah, the Saviour who was crucified. In a hostile situation of their existence, the disciples of Jesus who were mostly publicans, so-called sinners, other outcasts and ordinary workers who encountered Risen Jesus as alive in their midst experienced his promise, "I-am-with-you" (Matt 28:20) or his being Immanuel sheltering and protecting them. Therefore, the "us", specifically refers to the poor, the marginalized and the oppressed. Matthew includes four women, Thamar, Rahab, Ruth, Bathsheba, besides Mary, the mother of Jesus in the ancestry of Jesus to show that Immanuel is in solidarity not only with men or the chosen Mary but also with women who belonged to other religions and those who were even despised and abused. Matthew also affirms the solidarity of God with the marginalized women when they are chosen to witness to the resurrection of Jesus and to mediate this truth to the men disciples!

The identity of the 'us' in God-is-with-us or Immanuel according to Matthew includes non-Jews to show its universality and also its specific presence away from the place of power. The revelation to the Wise Men from the East, extending the blessings of the Kingdom to the Canaanite woman, the recognition of Jesus' greatness by the Roman guard and so on expresses the presence of God beyond the borders of the chosen people, the Jews. The Immanuel is not with the powerful Herod but with the humble wise men, his presence is embodied not in the powerful but in the powerless who need him and in the unjustly killed or destroyed and the solidarity with them is total when Immanuel himself was killed by the powers that be. Matthew chapter 2 and 27 narrate the murder of the innocent children by Herod and the murder of the innocent Immanuel by the same political power supported by the religious power respectively. Rayan says: "God raised Jesus from the dead and gave him all authority in heaven and on earth (Matt 28). God is with him, vindicating him and revealing him as Immanuel. God's solidarity with the oppressed is established irrefutably for ever".[16] Jesus was killed in the children whom Herod killed. Jesus is oppressed and dehumanized in every woman and man all over the world at all times. He also rises in every movement towards securing human rights and dignity and every struggle to establish the values of the Kingdom, namely, justice, love, equality, fellowship, peace and reconciliation. He is present in those who take sides in the cause of justice and on behalf of the victims of brutal power. The "us" with whom God is, comprises the victims of the Herods of all times. "The 'us' is summed up in Mary's Child, powerless before Herod's sword but enveloped in the Rule of God who saves the oppressed".[17] In Jesus, God is with the poor, the persecuted, the disinherited and those disallowed to live. Jesus' solidarity with the hungry, the thirsty, the naked, the imprisoned, the homeless and those who struggle with them for justice and fellowship is total and is for all times. Not only did the historical Jesus identify himself with the poor, the outcast, the discriminated and the dehumanized but also the risen Christ continues to have his Christic presence with all those who suffer injustice, oppression and dehumanization.

6. Presence of Christ in the Indian Context

According to Rayan, the social order in Palestine at the time of Jesus has similar features compared to some of the characteristic traits of India's caste system. It has a hierarchical system of descending order with the sacred and secular ruling aristocracy, the upper class, the poorer masses of the peasants, pliers of despised trade, the unemployed, the debtors and the slaves. The patriarchal system discriminated against women. Much in the hierarchical system was determined by birth, profession and by notions of ritual purity and pollution. Even today, the socio-cultural, religious and economic situation of India is not very different from that of Palestine of Jesus' times. Jesus challenged this system of discrimination and dehumanization. He freely associated himself with the so-called ritually impure and the outcasts of every sort. He ate with him. His table-fellowship with them challenged every rule of purity and pollution, discrimination and inequality.

Jesus continues to be present in those who experience all kinds of discrimination in the name of caste, class or gender and all who struggle with and for the deprived, despised and rejected outcasts: the pulaya, the paraya, the chamar, the wankar, the kurava, the veda, the bhangi, the musahar, the dusadh (Lk 18:9-14; 14:11; Matt 23:12).[18] Paul refers to an early Christian hymn in Phil.2:6f which narrates how Jesus Christ was self-emptying his divine status and assumed the condition of the lowliest in the society. "In our language we would say, he refused to grasp at power, prestige, privilege, profit; he refused to side with the votaries of these. Instead he chose to be a Dalit, a Paraya, the lowest among the outcastes".[19] Matthew presents the situation of Jesus as a condemned one and a refugee from the beginning of his life. Luke expresses the poverty and rejection of Jesus when he refers to Jesus' birth in a manger, the poverty of his parents when he was offered at the temple and the prophecy of rejection by

Simeon. In his gospel, John presents the flesh-becoming of the Word and its rejection. According to Rayan, in the Indian context, John's witness about the Word can be expressed thus:

And the Word was made an outcaste, a çandala, a paraya; he lives in the jhuggis outside the village, and in the hovels in the slums of our city; we have experienced his presence and his greatness, the unique greatness of God's Son which consists in the authentic graciousness of identifying himself with the wretched of the earth and the judgment passed thereby on the power structures which so degrade the children of God.[20]

Jesus identifies himself with the powerless and the rejected outcasts and invites his disciples to do the same. Jesus would take food and water from the untouchable defying social traditions and religious sanctions. The most dehumanizing character of the Indian society is the caste system which discriminates against millions and does not let them live a dignified life as humans. According to Rayan, "As long as a single Indian is outcaste, untouchable, India sits in disgrace, untouchable and outcaste".[21] The caste system that discriminates against humans on the basis of their birth in a particular socially determined group is a human problem like racism, apartheid or war and it affects world history and touches the dignity of every woman and man. Jesus' spirit becomes visible in all those who stand against this inhuman discrimination, like Ambedkar, Gandhi, Tagore, Jotirao Phule, Periyar Ramaswamy Naickar, Ayyankali, Narayana Guru, Mangoo Ram and a number of movements. Rayan says that we cannot keep the memory of the Lord's death in the scriptures and *in* the Eucharist without participating in the pain of the outcastes. "For the untouchables are the passion of Jesus…They are the crucifixion of the Son of Man, the Son of God, today. No Christian faith is possible in India today without identification with them and commitment to their Resurrection from the tombs in which they are held guarded by the musclemen of the ruling castes and classes according to the law and otherwise".[22] We find Jesus in the huts of the Dalits, in the colonies of outcastes outside the village.

Jesus' presence is with the millions to whom life is scarcely permitted, whose 'bread of life' is daily taken away and are massacred and burnt alive if they show any sign of growth or dignity. He becomes the bread of life for them and also for those who struggle with them. His disciples are called to go to him outside the camp, sharing his insults while identifying themselves with his and his people's defenselessness, outcasteness, fleshness and with him and with them pour out their lives too in liberating action.[23]

Rayan discovers "a vital link between Jesus of Nazareth and peoples' struggles in India, in Asia, anywhere in the world, any time in history. It is meant to suggest that the struggles are inspired and sustained by him in mysterious and hidden ways. By him are they invisibly led, encouraged, blessed and given meaning and hope. He is present in them and is involved in their vicissitudes. In them he recognizes his own concerns for humankind, and his own dreams of healing and wholeness for the world".[24] Therefore, there is the hidden Christic presence in all people's movements for food, land, home, dignity, welfare and peace. He is present in people's struggle against all forms of domination, oppression, exploitation, poverty, exclusion, and discrimination based on race, colour, gender, caste, religion. He is present in the Dalit and Tribal struggles against all forms of social, economic and political enslavement. He is in the struggles of the Industrial working class for right wages and safe environment for work with dignity and he is present in the struggles for protecting nature and the eco-system which is threatened by the forces of globalization and market-economy. He is present in the struggles against the degradation and loss of productive land due to mining, industrialization, capitalist development projects of multinational companies, against deforestation, polluting of water resources, befouling of air through various ways etc. in order to protect nature and the eco-system. He is present in the struggles of women to regain their humanity and their right to live their vocation as human persons to the full. The Christic presence is to be found in all movements against any form of fundamentalism that creates division and exclusion, hatred and bigotry.

Jesus is related to the struggles of peoples to live in dignity as humans as they are the continuation of his action and passion for human wholeness. His solidarity is with the outcaste, the oppressed, the victims of history's slavery and untouchability system, of colonial plunder, accumulation on a world scale, globalization and greed. His promise to remain with the disciples is a reality. His Cross reveals a God who suffers as well as the power of the suffering of the oppressed as a whole to rise against all forms of exploitation. Rayan says, "We believe the Cross is the place where the new humanity begins to bud. It is the Cross of the outcaste that bears the promise of the new earth and the new India with a human heart, a heart of flesh, full of *karuna,* sensitive to the all-encompassing *Brahman* and realizing the *advaita* and brotherliness and sisterliness at all levels of life and relationships".[25] The Church needs to realize that solidarity with the downtrodden *is* an essential constituent of the Church. By choosing to be identified with them, the Church is recognized and encountered as the Kingdom of God and in sharing the suffering of the poor and downtrodden and in their struggles, Jesus is encountered in his contemporary life. The Christic presence in the struggles of the people challenges the disciples of Jesus to continue his liberative mission in the process of their becoming authentically human and thus divine.

Conclusion

Samuel Rayan's Christology is a *Christology from below.*[26] His emphasis is on Jesus of Nazareth, the historical Jesus, the real human being who is recognized as the supreme revelation of God, the compassionate. He is compassion enfleshed. As Rayan's Christological reflections are scattered in various articles he has written for different journals at different times, one may not find a progressive development of this theme. But, one single thread that holds together his reflections on Jesus Christ is his emphasis on the humanity of Christ and Christ's dynamic presence in the struggles and rising of the poor and the victims of all forms of discrimination.

Rayan's interpretation of Jesus Christ and his mission evolves from his basic conviction that God became man to reveal to us how God is involved in the struggles and sufferings of humans to become authentically human. According to Rayan, the way to know the truth of God's involvement in human history is by encountering, Jesus, the human. In and through Jesus we discover who God is and how Jesus is the revelation or enfleshment of God's compassion. Jesus' involvement in the lives of the poor and the marginalized, the outcastes and the sinners of his time continues through his Christic presence after his resurrection. Therefore, commitment to Jesus demands a commitment to struggle with and for the poor and the exploited and all victims of social, cultural, religious and political discrimination and oppression. The Church's orthodoxy in her proclamation of Jesus Christ as Lord and Saviour needs to be translated into her orthopraxis of commitment to the poor and the marginalized. This understanding of Jesus Christ is of the utmost importance to Christian commitment in the context of India where there are many poor people, many outcastes and many religions.

Notes

1. Samuel Rayan, *Selected Writings of Samuel Rayan, SJ, Vol. I,* K. Kunnumpuram, (ed.), (Mumbai: St. Pauls Publ., 2011), p. 197. Hereafter the *Selected Writings of Samuel Rayan, SJ* will be referred to as SWSR.
2. Pius XII, *Mystici Corporis Christi,* No. 46.
3. SWSR, p. 198.
4. SWSR, p. 197.
5. *Ibid.*, p. 90.
6. S. Rayan, *Breath of Fire. The Holy Spirit: Heart of the Christian Gospel,* New York: Orbis Books, 1979, p. 106.
7. SWSR, pp. 91-92.
8. *Ibid.*, 92.
9. *Ibid.*, p. 200.
10. *Ibid.* p. 200.
11. *Ibid.*, p. 203.
12. *Ibid.*, p. 201.
13. *Ibid.*, p. 158.
14. *Ibid.*, pp.159-160.
15. *Ibid.*, p. 162.
16. *Ibid.*, p. 170.
17. *Ibid.*, p. 172.
18. *Ibid.*, p. 280.
19. *Ibid.*, p. 285.
20. *Ibid.*, 288.
21. *Ibid.*, pp. 269-270.
22. *Ibid.*, 292.
23. *Ibid.*, 289.

24. *Ibid.*, p. 234.
25. *Ibid.*, p. 294.
26. See Cinthia Pinto, *Encountering Christ in the Suffering Humanity (Mt 25:31-46): Christological Contributions of Samuel Rayan and Raimon Panikkar and the Significance of the Suffering of the Battered Women of Maher from Christian and Hindu Perspective,* Wien& Berlin: LIT Verlag, 2009, pp. 91-92.

2

The Divine in the Writings of Samuel Rayan

P. R. John, SJ

In this paper, I shall speak of Samuel Rayan's perspectives on the Divine. Then, I shall look at three broad reflections of Rayan on the Divine: first as a *Labourer*, second in *Jesus Christ* and third as *Saccidananda* and *Antaryamin* (Indweller).

Samuel Rayan's Perspectives

Samuel Rayan's thoughts on the Divine are unusual, strange and creative. In my opinion, Rayan remains creative throughout his career not as a philosopher, theologian or exegete but as a sincere seeker of the 'Divine' - *Athato brahma jijnasa* (thirst for knowing the Ultimate Reality). He desires to explore both the sacred and the secular. Rayan's unlocking of creativity on the Divine translates into a cascade of theological reflections on the subject. At the same, it is closely intertwined with the Asian/Indian context which is one of an innate appreciation of beauty and the thrust towards the contemplative life.

In his many writings, Rayan articulates the 'Divine' as nature, energy, spirit, hope, truth, justice, love, beauty, artist, poet, peace, rice, anger, flesh-translation of divine compassion (Jesus), crucified (*dalit*), *daridranarayan*, *antaryamin* and *saccidananda*. In one of his articles, "Naming the Unnameable", Rayan discusses extensively his idea of the Divine saying that, "No single name exhausts the divinity. No name is the name of God". S. Painadath affirms, "It is true that an Asian seeker is reluctant to name the Divine. If named at all, that name will be withdrawn in the next breath, and it will be said: I do not know how to speak about it".

Rayan believes that humans are Divine-seekers. Thus, he says that we seek the Divine in the wonders of nature, in the marvels of history, in the cave of the heart, in hectic activity, in silence, in sacred ritual, in authority figures, in holy scriptures, in ascetics and saints, in prayer and *bhajans*, in *gurus* and guides, in temples, images, pilgrimages or in legal and dogmatic rigidities and pieties. To seek the Divine is to listen to the songs of the people and to their stories, cries and inner longings. Often words fail to express, as we flounder to discern the movements of the Spirit, or to understand and interpret the signs of the times to be able to proclaim our faith to the community. All this leads us to see that in such a context our theology must necessarily be dialogical. Nevertheless, human beings are conditioned by their particular time, place and culture, and we know that the vision of the Divine is not the same for all. The understanding of the One Divine reality may differ largely from person to person and from nation to nation. Rhetorically Rayan questions: But where is the Living God present and active on our behalf? Where does the Divine become accessible to us? Is the Living God present in the faces of the farmers and coolies who till the hard ground to earn a mouthful of rice? Is the Divine present in the midst of the pavement dwellers and the street children? Where are we likely to meet our God? Where should we be looking for our Lord? Our Master, where do you live?

Rayan's greatest strength is the re-reading (*dhvani-resonance*) of the Bible and his desire to emulate Jesus. Rayan is more a pilgrim in search of the Divine. He holds, "No one has ever seen God" (Jn 1:18). "God is Spirit" (1 Jn 4:12). We can encounter the Divine only in and through the created realities, historical events and our personal experiences. Without their mediation we can neither think nor speak about the Divine. The Divine can, of course, touch us immediately and directly. The Divine has access to depths within us which are inaccessible even to ourselves. Following the Indian tradition and method, Rayan stresses the indwelling of the Divine in humans (*Antaryamin*), the approach to the Divine in the realm of the Spirit, the desire to meet him (her) always and everywhere as the Universal Spirit, as the Self of the individual self.

The Divine is a Labourer

Rayan schooled in the *Sadhana* of St. Ignatius of Loyola articulates the symbolism of the Divine as a Labourer. St. Ignatius uses many images of the Divine in his *Spiritual Exercises* but within all of Ignatian thought we see God as both and at once immanent and transcendent. God is of the realm of the heart and thus God is a God of love. God labours in creation. For Ignatius, everything comes from God in Jesus Christ and everything returns to God in Jesus Christ. God invites us to have a part with Jesus Christ in that same cycle of creation and redemption. This is how God labours in creation, and we, who are sharers in the mission of Jesus Christ, are partners in that labour. God is the centre, the heart of creation, and from there God shares God's own glory with us. God is in all things, in every bit of our life experience. God is actively working in the details of our life (Sp. Ex. 236).

Speaking along these lines, a few years ago Steve Bevans began to realize that God – the God revealed to us by Jesus of Nazareth through the power of the Holy Spirit – might be best described as a *verb*, not a noun. What this means is that the God we know from revelation might be best imagined not as a static kind of "person" – who is sort of like us but wiser and more powerful and – who is "up there" or "out there". Rather God is a Movement, an Embrace, a Flow, more personal than we can ever imagine and who is always and everywhere present in God's creation. Thus, God is there in a way that is much more exciting and worthy of our adoration and love. The early Church writings leading up to the Council of Chalcedon echo the importance of *physis* in its dynamic sense:

If we take *physis* to mean 'essence', understood as fixed stock of characteristics, then it would be very hard to make sense of two natures concurring in one subsistence. However, here we may remember that the Greek word *physis* was originally a very dynamic term, with some such meaning as 'emerging'. The Latin equivalent *natura* had originally a similar dynamic meaning. It is formed from the future participle of the verb *nasci,* to be born, so that *natura* meant everything that might arise or be born out of something... So, the idea of the two natures concurring in the one person of Jesus Christ makes very good sense, if we conceive the language in a dynamic way.

Rayan holds that the *dynamis* of the Divine is present in the very warp and woof of creation, working for its wholeness and healing, and calling creation to its fullness. The earth is the Lord's and the earth is God's beloved daughter. God is calling the earth and creating it and it is an ongoing journey. Rayan says that God who bends over the earth in service: "Millions of years God bends over the earth adorning her with lights and flowers, celebrating her with bird songs and cascading life and loveliness. The earth is God's body, God's bodiliness, the love reality that is God become see-able and touchable and historically processive. The earth stands as a primordial sacrament of God. God reveals the divine self to us as life and the giver of life - *isavasyam idam sarvam*". What is even more amazing is that God invites women and men on a small planet in a minor galaxy in this vast universe – billions of years old, billions of light years in extension-into partnership in God's work. These women and men, whom Genesis calls 'us' (1.26-27), are created by God in the divine "image and likeness". God in God's deepest identity is a relationship, a communion. On the part of humans they too are called to reflect on the activity and the incessant work of God in all creatures.

This is what St. Irenaeus of Lyons believed that by becoming a human being, Jesus, God wanted to share with every human person his own, eternal life in such a way that our fragile, contradictory human nature would not be overwhelmed or crushed, but fulfilled utterly. Irenaeus wrote: "Life in man (woman) is the glory of God; the life of man (woman) is the vision of God." Another translation says: "The glory of God is a living man (woman); and the life of man (woman) consists in beholding God". What is so appealing in Irenaeus' writings is this notion of "life", because surely every human being wants to be truly alive and discover ways of living more truly and fully.

To reflect on the incessant work of God or the Divine as a labourer, Rayan provokes human persons to enter into a contemplative silence where they open themselves to listen to reality. Silence is related not only to the unspeakable reality of God, but to the inexplicable reality of the universe as well. The ultimate aim of silence is to love (embrace) everyone and everything in God:

> Let us be silent for a moment
> Silent before the awesome reality of Asia
> Before Asia's vastness, variety and complexity
> Asia's peoples, languages and cultures
> Asia's poor, their crises, tears and wounds
> The death of her babies by the millions and
> The humiliation of her women and men and their struggles
> Let us take Asia (Indian Culture) to our hearts;
> And see her and feel her within us.
> Embrace her
> In her wholeness and her brokenness
> And let her rivers and her tears flow through us,
> And her winds and her sighs blow within us.

Though Rayan deals with the theme of the Divine in nature still his paramount concern in God's creation is always the **human person**. Thus, he says, "We can't speak of the Divine without also speaking of humans". According to him, the human person is endowed with value and sacredness, rights and dignity. For Rayan, the human person seems to hold the centre of values and of concern. He does not talk of humans in the abstract but of concrete human persons, men and women as they live, love, toil, hope and die; men and women who relate and become community; a community whom God loves. He is truly fascinated by the love of his Master Jesus, and in the light of this revelation he looks at the human person as a pearl. For Jesus, a human person is great -- great in dignity and worth, in possibility and destiny, in capacity for creativity and response.

God is so fond of human persons that he gives his Son for humankind's life and wholeness (Jn 3:16). Rayan says: "God is world concerned and human concerned. Our history is his history and he is not an onlooker but a participant". "It is this divine search for a lost world and concern for a wounded humanity that became historically embodied in Jesus of Nazareth". God showers on all men and women without exception the gifts of sunshine and of rain. In *Contemplation on the Love of God,* St. Ignatius speaks of the limitless blessings of God that cascade down on our world like the rays of the sun. For Jesus, the human person would be the treasure and pearl that God has discovered and is buying at a great price. Therefore, every person is a pearl, independent of social status and public opinion. No human person and no human concern are too small or too trivial for his attention and esteem.

Rayan calls for a radical humanism. Thus, with Jesus, everything must orbit around the human person and serve his/her true and total well-being. To devalue the human person in favor of power, profit or prestige, be it sacred or secular, would be the ultimate evil, and the one thing Rayan would fight against to his last breath. The human person is the point on which the sacred as well as the secular should converge in readiness to serve. Thus, Sabbath is for human persons and not human persons for the Sabbath (Mk 2:28). For Rayan, the vital dimension of Jesus' philosophy of the human person is that the human person is not a closed, separate and solitary individual, going to God and saved by himself/herself. Human being is always a person, open to other persons and to a community. While society is a functionally organized human group, community goes far beyond and shapes humans through relationships of the heart like mutual understanding, acceptance, respect, appreciation, encouragement, forgiveness, love and tenderness.

To sum up, the God who labours calls human persons to a life of service (work). In serving God and serving one another we become/emerge as parts of the body of Christ. We collaborate with Christ in the work of redeeming and healing the world. "My Father is still working, and I also am working" (Jn 5.17).

The Divine is Jesus Christ

Rayan has a deep intimacy with and fascination for Jesus. Intimacy with Jesus is the central grace sought for in the Spiritual Exercises. Intimacy holds nothing back. The partners of a truly intimate relationship share everything. Rayan was constantly in touch with grass-root groups and social activists. His reflections on Jesus are embedded in bringing out the dark side of history, namely oppression and marginalization. To Rayan, Jesus is like one of the working class men/women, who lives with them amidst their problems and pains and their songs of hope and hopelessness. Peasant struggles, women struggles, *dalit* struggles, tribal struggles, industrial working class struggles, environmental struggles, migrant workers' struggles, pavement dwellers/children on the street struggles, the large number of prisoners comprising of dalits, tribals and women in Indian prisons -- these are the contexts of mass struggles in which Rayan presents the image of Jesus as the Friend of the Masses.

People's struggle for justice and freedom are suffused with God's will to human wholeness. They are the best historical embodiments or incarnations of God's word of human liberation and God's will to human completion. The struggles are theological events, and articulating the theology latent in them is to understand in-depth their nature and to see its affinity to ultimate realities and meanings. They sustain the hope of God's Reign on earth. According to Rayan, Jesus, in mysterious hidden ways, inspires and sustains these struggles. Jesus leads, encourages, blesses, and gives meaning and hope. Throughout history, the masses have struggled for life, food, home, for land, honor and happiness. They have fought for freedom, dignity, community and peace. People have battled against forces of domination, oppression and exploitation; against poverty, exclusion and discrimination based on colour, race, gender and religion; against egoism, greed, hatred, against adversities, suffering and loneliness. They have striven for meaning and truth as well as for fuller knowledge, finer skills and a human future. This vision invites us along with Jesus to unveil an economy of justice and sharing: give to anyone who asks; lend to those who would borrow; love as God loves. In the words of S. Arockiasamy:

> Participation in people's action for their liberation, with firm belief in God's presence in their midst and trust in his assistance, is also an integral dimension of the liturgy. Worship is therefore celebrated not only in rituals and sacraments, but also in the day-to-day work and struggles to attain fullness and to transform the human community into the household of

> God. In this perspective, baptism becomes the commitment to a God who commits himself to his people and their struggle, and the Eucharist becomes a celebration of this struggle and their victory.

Rayan says that it is to the ordinary people that Jesus spoke the divine language of the Kingdom of God expressed in agrarian terms: vine and vineyard, fig tree, sycamore tree, fruit and root, digging and pruning, seed, sowing, generation, barn, chaff, winnowing fan, the plough and the bramble are the agrarian images of the people. Camel, sheep, bird, dog, viper, wolf, dove, fish and the moth are images of the animal world. Stones, caves, sand and wilderness, the river, the sea, grass, reeds, foxholes, flowers, nesting, watering, sun, moon, stars, the clouds, the wind, the lighting and the rain are the images of the cosmic and natural world. He sought to share with them his vision of a New Humanity and issued the call to struggle for a New Earth. His stories upset the existing social order, questioned the moral basis of all systems then held sacred and provoked angry reactions. At the end, he was caught and killed. Therefore, he has become a song of revolt.

For Rayan, Jesus is the highpoint of God's self-manifestation. Jesus is the Word through whom the universe was made. God is speaking to humans through Jesus. God is ever present and active in Jesus to save humans. In Jesus, humans have the final coming forth of the Divine as the will to save humankind from within, by sharing in humans' existential condition of brokenness and sin. This profound mystery of the divine in Jesus breaks forth tangibly on the banks of the Jordan where Jesus meets God in a unique way – divine meets divine. "Jesus saw the heavens torn open", he saw "the Spirit descending upon him", he heard "a voice from heaven saying, thou art my Son, my Beloved, on thee my favour rests" (Mk 1:10-11).

Jesus met and felt God. God descended on him from above in a total invasion of his being, and emerged within him from below from the foundations of his heart. "Thou art my Son" was a creative word constituting, in an altogether new manner, what he already was, namely God's Beloved Son. Within this experience of his own dynamic Sonship, Jesus encountered God and received him anew, in an unprecedented way, as his loving Father. This bipolar experience of interpersonal relationship between God and the human being as between the Father and Son is the basis and axis of Jesus' life and work, especially his work of forging new human relationships with which to weave a new community of men and women.

The Jesus-community was to be created precisely through and within the sharing of this experience of God's Abbahood. To everyone who accepted Jesus, he would give power to become children of God, he would give his Spirit enabling him/her to experience God as dear Father and bestow on him/her the miraculous freedom to call him Abba ("Appa" in the languages of South India) in the intimacy of his/her heart. Jesus experienced God as God for men and women. Part of Jesus' experience is that God expresses his own greatness in serving man and woman. Jesus knew that in and through his own humble service, God was continually seeking to express this deep longing for humankind. Jesus' God-experience that developed from his baptism to his resurrection was more than enough to show how radical God was in his approach to the world, in his self-gift to humans, in his disclosure of love and his redemptive plans.

Rayan holds that Jesus, in the Eucharist, devised an entire community-building programme in which all are to become one loaf (bread), which is then broken and shared as the beginning and pledge of the fraternal sharing of all wealth and the large loaf (bread) of our earth. Fellowship implies identifying oneself with all men and women, especially the poor, the neglected and the downtrodden and in taking upon oneself the responsibility for the wholeness of the world. Through such solidarity, openness and concern, the human person forms community and the community forms human persons who care and are cared for. They grow together hand in hand becoming progressively human and deepening the humanization of the world. A person can only become truly divine and human by encountering other humans and giving himself/herself to others. His/her communion with God can be realized and expressed on earth in a community with human persons, since the love of God is inseparable from the love of a neighbour, who is God's visible image and sacrament on earth. The society and the individual are not partners on an equal footing. The human person is an end in himself or herself. Each person is a centre of the community circle, but he/she can only develop as a centre within the circle, in openness to and communion with other centres.

Therefore, Rayan's idea of the centrality of the human community is based on the dream of Jesus' – the dream of a new human community, built on freedom, meaning, and love and based on a personal experience of God. Jesus chose to be a dreamer and a seer of visions on behalf of the future of humankind. In this process, he was willing to pay the price to encourage people who would be strong and mature enough to enter the group and tread the path he trod in order to defend, rebuild and enhance humankind. With the freedom of the Spirit, he dreamt of people who would not give up in the face of opposition, persecution and suffering. To work for this dream will entail struggle. It will mean hungering and thirsting for justice; it will mean suffering and paying the price. Such a vision would flower forth into a New World and a New Humanity. Elsewhere he writes:

It is by dreams that people live and by visions that hope is sustained. Jesus is the first to receive the Holy Spirit, and he is the source of the Spirit for the rest of us. He is, therefore, the dreamer of humankind's dreams and the seer of our visions. We can aspire, we can look forward, we can hope, we can strive for the future because Jesus has dreamed dreams for us and opened up new vision, creating new horizons for our lives. His dreams concern people; they are about new men and women, about a fraternal society, about a community of love and joy and creativity. He calls it the Kingdom of God upon earth.

Rayan reflects further that the Divine is a *dalitaized* traveller. He was stripped, robbed, broken and left half alive on the roadside of history. The Divine suffers outside the walls where the untouchables are forced to live and suffer. "Jesus suffered outside the gate to sanctify the people with his own blood" (Heb 13:11-12). In Jewish worship, animal blood was brought into the sanctuary by the high priest for the atonement of sin, while the bodies of the slaughtered animals were burned outside the camp. The camp meant Jerusalem. Jesus' death outside the camp was meant to disclose, to proclaim and to affirm the inborn dignity and the native purity of all our castes. To join Jesus outside the camp is to discover in him a new, surprising Crucified-God. The Crucified-God sets aside the entire system of taboos, which is based on ideas of purity and pollution of races, contact and occupations. In the Indian context, taking food or water with or from untouchables is the worst contamination for a high caste man/woman. However, the Crucified-God challenges the out-castes to live in open freedom and to refuse every mode of enslavement. Jesus represents a new image of God as one dethroning the ruling classes and high castes and putting the *Dalits* (tribals) in charge of history. For such a vision, Rayan envisages *metanoia* as essential:

When we are converted and make the faith-commitment we shall discover that we are with the *Dalits*, the people of God, God's beloved Christ, crucified and buried outside the gate. Their tombs God is breaking open in the night when the non-dalits are sleeping. With the break of the day we shall see the wounds we have inflicted on crucified bodies and lives filled with light and life. We shall see them and touch them reverently and come to have faith in fresh depths, and come to express it in the cry, My Lord and My God. A cry in which all the crushed and crucified of history shall be affirmed as the body of Christ on whose unveiled face the glory of God shines and from whose heart streams the water of life in which non-dalits, if they change, may find cleansing and life.

Rayan, reflecting deeply on the healing stories of the Gospel, comes out with the image of the Divine (Jesus) as "A Flesh-Translation of Divine Compassion". Jesus' Passion is his compassion. His compassion is in relation to his understanding of the attitudes and approaches of people (Mk 1:4-9).

Rayan considers the symbol of the reign of God as compassion. Healing and feeding are privileged *loci* for the revelation of Jesus' compassion and thus to restore the sanity of the human person. Jesus' act of eating and sharing food with the poor are signs of compassion, indicating the expansion of his heart's warmth to radiate concern and compassion. The Eucharist, that Jesus gave us, is couched in the language of a mother, has maternal imagery and motherly gestures. This farewell supper invites persons to "take and eat, this is my body, my self, given for you". Its language is the silent idiom of motherhood and of maternal compassion. Therefore, Jesus is compassion. Compassion is his name. The compassion of God suggests that the most persuasive representation for a Christology for our times would be that of Jesus as the incarnate compassion of God. God is heart and womb. God's love is familial. God welcomes back the rebellious child, the faithless wife. He does so with overflowing yearning, forgiveness and love.

Food is one of the basic necessities of humans. Jesus called himself the Bread of Life, the true Bread and the Bread of God that comes down from heaven and gives life to the world (Jn 6:32-34): "Take eat, this is my body, myself" (Matt 26:26). Jesus further affirms, "I am the living Bread; my flesh is real food, my blood is real drink; whoever eats me will draw life from me" (Jn 6:51-7). Therefore, the Good News is Jesus himself as bread, rice, the food and the basis of life. Food is a sacrament of equality and friendship and a shared meal is a place of recognition and honour. Without bread (rice), there is no Eucharist. Without the earth and work, there is no bread. For the earth is a good and great loaf of bread baked over the fire in God's Heart and given to his family of living beings for their sustenance. "Wealth and bread are not for grabbing but sharing as a great sacrament of brotherhood. Therefore, upon the unbrotherly, unshared, selfish possession of wealth, even when it is legally not ill-gotten, there rests a judgment of God. The point of the story of the Rich Dining Man is not that the hungry have comfort beyond the grave, but that here and now men and women should listen to prophetic voices and the demands of the Gospel for a brotherhood and sisterhood realized and lived out within the concrete social, political and economic dimensions of existence". Rayan poetically sings that Jesus as the daily rice:

> Rice is for sharing,
> Bread must be broken and given.
> Every bowl, every belly shall have its fill,
> To leave a single bowl unfilled is
> To rob history of its meaning;
> To grab many a bowl for myself is
> To empty history of God.

People are drawn by the beauty of Jesus' words. It is this divine search for a lost world and concern for a wounded humanity that became historically embodied in Jesus of Nazareth. The Divine is tangibly sought in the neighbour (Matt 25:35f). God is Christ come to us in the victims of humankind's history and in his solidarity with them. As much as God is on this quest we as human beings are also on quest. The God-experience of Jesus was a personal mystery and a historical reality. Jesus' experience of God was marked not only by love's light, warmth and tenderness, but by its strangeness too and by the silence and darkness and terror of the divine. Jesus' experience of God (and of people) kept deepening and developing into something large and rich and beautiful until it came to final blossoming and total clarity in his resurrection.

The Divine is *Saccidananda/Antaryamini*

One finds two predominant terms in Rayan's approach which point to the transcendence, namely, the Divine as the *Saccidananda* the Divine as the *Antaryamin*, which are often used in Indian Christian theology. One of the richest Indian words incorporated into the Christian vocabulary is Sankaracharya's concept of God as "*Saccidananda*" to designate the mystery of the Blessed Trinity. Indian Catholic theologian Brahmabandhav Upadhyay appropriated these three words for God the Father, the Son and the Holy Spirit. The hymn is an adoration of the Trinity using throughout words from the early Indian tradition to describe first the Trinity as a whole and then, in separate stanzas, each of the three Persons. The hymn was sung before Pope Paul VI during the International Eucharistic Congress in Mumbai in 1964. The birthplace of the "*Saccidananda*" formula is the *Vedantic* meditation on *Brahman*: The Ineffable Mystery underlying all reality is simultaneously existence (*sat*), consciousness (*cit*) and bliss (*ananda*). The three components are not "qualities" of *Brahman* but point to its very nature or *svabhava*. The Indian context presupposes the basic affirmation that Brahman is *ekam eva advitiyam*, one alone without a second, and therefore ever *akhanda*, unbroken, in the oft-repeated expression of Sri Ramakrishna.

The Christian meditation observes appropriately *Sat* as representing the Father, the source of all existence, *Cit* as alluding to the Wisdom of the Father, his Logos, also designated as the Son, and *Ananda* as an appropriate designation of the Spirit so often associated with joy in the NT, who is meditated upon as the very Bliss of God. Christian faith regards these words as designating distinct "Selves": it even calls them, analogically, "Persons," but never forgets that the "Selves" are the same Reality, One Nature and One Essence. We experience the Divine also as the Spirit, who sweeps over the waters at creation (Gen 1:2), descends over Jesus at his baptism (Matt 3:16) and over the first community of men and women around Mary at Pentecost (Acts 2:1-4). The Spirit is also given to all of us for the service of the community (1 Cor 12:1-11). The Hindus experience the Divine as the *Antaryamin*, the indweller in humans and in the universe, the divine-human-cosmic energy. Gregory Palamas spoke about the energies of God. God who transcends is also the God within. It is this God who gathers and reconciles everyone and everything (cf. Eph 1:10, Col 1:20; 1 Cor 15:28) in a cosmotheandric harmony. This is the mystery of the *advaita*. We can therefore look for God in the world, in human lives, in history. We may find only 'traces', which will lead us, not perhaps to a conceptual-rational knowledge of God, but to an experience that may be as much darkness as it is light.

Rayan holds that the "mission of Jesus" reveals the identity of Jesus as *Antaryamin*. In his writings, the two natures of Christ are symbolized by his images of *Bread* (flesh-human) and *Breath* (spirit-divine). In this regard, he remains faithful to the councils in attributing to Jesus a twofold order of being, "according to the flesh" (*kata sarca*), i. e., as human and "according to the spirit" (*kata pneuma*), i.e. as divine (Rom 1:3-4). It is a way of combining (not mixing) the two natures in Christ, the immanence and the transcendence of God. Rayan proposes that the linguistic approach of speaking about the divine in an Indian context must begin with the indwelling Christ who is the real, best and deepest self. From there, he proceeds to the Christ who is in all and is the Self of all, the Universal Self and the *Antaryamin*. He further develops the idea of a new community, which experiences Christ as indwelling and loving and shares in his personal experience.

Finally, he sees this experience as an experience of being wholly from God, of being born of God, of belonging to the world of sin and death and of God's redemptive action which raises the dead and calls into existence that which is not. In the historical Jesus, with his awareness of the indwelling Father as his best Self, the circle is complete. In fact, the great theologians of the New Testament, Paul, Luke and John, explicitly link the sense of joy or bliss to the Spirit of God. This may seem to be new in the Christian theological tradition that has generally identified the Spirit with Love or as the One who is the mystery of the union of Father and Son (hence other theologians in India have called the Spirit the *advaita*, non-duality in God), but not explicitly with joy or bliss. And yet it is true that the Spirit is the Bliss in God.

Rayan enunciates that "Jesus is pre-eminently the man of the Holy Spirit, the giver of the Spirit, the dispenser of the gifts of the Spirit, and it is Jesus who makes it possible for us to share in the Spirit of God". "What God says to him (Jesus) is said to all humankind. The endearment that enfolds Jesus 'My Son, my beloved'. We are all God's beloved. His favour rests on us as it rests on Jesus. The Spirit's descent on Jesus includes and guarantees the coming of the Spirit on all of us and on our earth. God here commissions Jesus to service that is to lead up to the fullest outpouring of the Spirit on humankind". "God's Spirit of holiness and consolation, God's truth and salvation are not reserved for one people, but are given to all peoples. The Hebrew people are chosen, not in an exhaustive sense, but in a sacramental sense, as a sign, to point out that all peoples are chosen, all peoples are God's beloved. It is like shaking hands with a friend. When I take my friend's hand, I express my warm, reverent acceptance of the whole person of my friend, not just one part of him. Israel was the hand of humankind which God took visibly for all to see. But in the last days, in the days of Jesus, God takes not only the hand of humankind, but picks up humankind itself in his arms".

One of the profound insights of the *Upanishads* is that even in our personal lives we are not alone, a spark of existence floating for a moment in empty space. We have our roots in the Absolutely Real. Moreover, the Divine Reality is not only a Presence as the

Ground of our being, but also the Power that promotes and guides the conscious life that flows within us. There is an *antaryamin.* He is the "Inner Controller", the Ultimate Subject in all our subjective acts. Commenting on the *Brhadranyaka Upanishad,* Sankara points out that in all forms of awareness this internal guide or ruler is the *antaryamin.* God is Spirit; the life-giving Spirit (1 Cor 15:45).

In the biblical sense the 'Spirit' describes God's life-giving activity rather than defines his nature. God is Spirit in that He gives the Spirit as God in light and love (1 Jn 1:5; 4:8). This explains how and why the true worshipper of God must worship Him in spirit and truth. Thus, Chandogya Upanishad speaking of Atman, the Pure Spirit-beyond sorrow, old age and death; beyond evil, hunger and thirst, says: 'It is Atman, whose love is truth, whose thoughts are truth' (Chand. Up.8.1) and again: 'This is Atman, the Spirit that we must find and know; man must find his own self. He who has found, and knows his Self has found all the worlds, has achieved all his desires'. Thus, spoke Prajapati. After living with him for years –to seek this Spirit, Indra and Virochins were told: 'What you see when you look into another persons' eyes, that is Atman, immortal, beyond fear, that is Brahman'.

He is in us not as object but as subject and this is the way, we enter into deepest union with the Divine. St. Paul too spoke of the "inner Teacher", Christ, who is the ground or possibility upon which all human knowledge rests. "It is no longer I who live, but it is Christ who lives in me" (Gal 2:20) and "the mystery of Christ" is defined in a later writing as "Christ in you, the hope of glory" (Col 1:27). Christian devotional hymns and theologians in India speak of the *antaryamin* more with reference to the Holy Spirit "since the Spirit of God dwells in you" (Rom 8.9). Especially our life of faith is a life produced by the *antaryamin* Spirit: "When we cry, 'Abba, Father!' it is that very Spirit bearing witness to our spirit that we are children of God" (Rom 8:15-16). St. Augustine said, 'the Divine dwells where Man (woman) dwells'.

Contemplating the spiritual heritage of India, Rayan presents Jesus as the Risen Lord. This Risen Lord is the life-giving *Prana,* who is no longer known according to the flesh but who abides in the believer and is *Antaryamin* or the Dweller within, who bestows on human the divine *Prana* and commands unlocalised worship in spirit and in truth. This centres particularly on the indwelling Christ, whose body we are.

A genuine Indian Christology will have to centre on the Risen Lord who is Spirit and life-giving *Prana,* who is no longer known according to the flesh, who abides in the believer and is *Antaryamin* or the Dweller within, who bestows on man/woman the divine *Prana* and commands unlocalised worship in Spirit and in Truth. An Indian Christology could perhaps best begin here. The order would be (a) to start with the indwelling Christ who is my real, best and deepest self and (b) to proceed to the Christ who is in all and is the Self of all, the Universal Self and the Antaryamin; and (c) to go on to the new community which experiences Christ as indwelling and loving, and shares in his personal experience: and d) finally to see that his experience was an experience of being wholly from God and for God, and of being born of God; of belonging to the world of sin and death and of God's redemptive action which raises the dead and calls into existence that which is not. Here, in the historical Jesus, with his awareness of the indwelling Father as his best Self, the circuit is complete.

The authentic tradition of India shall seek and find Christ within (Holy Spirit), in our own self, and experience him as our true, real self, the Self of our self. Holy Spirit is the *Mahasaksti* or great Shakti that is especially operative in this world from the moment of Jesus' resurrection. It is through Her, the Spirit, that Jesus is leading humanity to the Kingdom of God, to be the sons and daughters of God.

To conclude, Rayan shows that the Divine is not an object of the senses, nor is Divine a concept of the mind. The Divine remains hidden like roots and foundation, like wombs and sources. But, from our depths he warms our hearts and feeds our freedom. In history, the Divine is beautiful, spirit and freedom. The Divine is small, hidden, almost wretched, contradicted, threatened, defenseless, silent and yet present, unforgettable and active in the power of his weakness. The Divine is imagination and creativity. Creation is a divine way of seeking and finding us in the first place. To be divine is to be open and responsive to reality, listening to the spirit. It is the divine sea of life in which we live and move and have our being. Our fleshly eyes have to be replaced by the Divine eye to experience the Divine. As to Arjuna in the Gita, God gave us the divine eye of faith, a *divya caksus* to 'see' God, to 'experience' the Divine, here and now (BG 15:16).To be Divine is to be open and responsive to reality and to the future.

> Little candle,
> I wish you would touch me
> with your fiery finger;
> clasp me in your blaze,
> and kindle at my centre,
> till I too glow and melt,
> and bear on my heart and head
>
> the searing sorrow of my people,
> and thaw in love and dissolve
> in service of light and warmth
> and fresh dreams and hopes
> spread out at their sacred feet.

However, a reader of Samuel Rayan can't ignore the element of 'curiosity' in Rayan's thoughts on the Divine. Rayan is creative and so he is curious 'just like a child' who explores the sacred and secular. Sometimes such a curiosity of Rayan is labelled as deviant. Let us not forget the glorious words spoken by George M. Soares-Prabhu: "Rayan's theology…has successfully completed the movement from alienation to inculturation and so remains an inspiration for all of us who are trying to theologize in India today".

3

The Spirit of Life
Rayan's Thoughts on the Holy Spirit

Mohan Doss, SVD

Introduction

Samuel Rayan's writings are poetry in prose and paintings in words. They are experiences expressed in ordinary and yet in captivating images, symbols, and metaphors. They spring from a heart that knows deeply the presence, pain and power of the Holy Spirit who has been journeying along human history and is actively involved in the contemporary life situations. The objective of this paper is to highlight some of Rayan's significant reflections on the Holy Spirit who is revealed in the Christian Scripture, spoken about in tradition, and experienced in the life of the people and in the contemporary history. The paper first presents Samuel Rayan's thoughts on various dimensions related to the Holy Spirit and at the end spells out his creative contributions in the realm of Indian Christian Theology.

1. The Starting Point is *Anubhav*

Spirit-experience is, for Rayan, the starting point of Pnuematology. The OT shows how women and men were transformed by the Spirit-experience and the NT presents Jesus as one who "is anointed, shaped, grasped and led by the Spirit (Lk 1:35; 3:21-22; 4:1; 14:18-19; 10:21; Jn 3:34)". The Spirit-experience was the foundation of Jesus' intimacy with the Father, of his unimaginable authority, his power to heal the sick, his energy to love others compassionately and relate to others gently, and of his life from Mary's womb to the empty tomb. The people of his time recognized him as a Spirit-filled person.[1]

The Holy Spirit was quite real for the first Christians. They experienced the Spirit "as new life, as power and courage, as liberation from scrupulous keeping of laws and prescriptions, as freedom from fear of elemental forces, as immediacy in their relationship to God like it is in a family, and as an exodus from known life, and as a dangerous adventure".[2] The Holy Spirit equipped them with her[3] power and gifts "for mission and witness, for action to renew the world and build a culture of love and a humane world community".[4]

The Early Church was radically pneumatic but from the third and fourth century, Rayan observes, "charisms and experience of the Spirit have not been held to be constituent of Church" and were perceived as "exceptional phenomena, individual cases unrelated to the nature of the Church or Christianity".[5] Later in the West, as the Church became clergy-centred and dominated, the Spirit was reduced to the Church. But in the present times, one finds "the upsurge of many and various forms of experience of the Spirit throughout the world".[6]

1.1 The Nature and Content of the Spirit-experience

In Samuel Rayan's theological horizon the Holy Spirit occupies a significant place. The experience of the Spirit is the starting point and this experience offers a new vision to orient oneself and urges the believers to work towards building a new society based on the values of the reign of God.

1.1.1 *The Spirit-experience offers a new vision*

The Spirit-experience enables everyone to see nature, others, and oneself in a new way. The Spirit enables one to see "the familiar in a new way", to discover suddenly "the fascination of the ordinary", be "struck by the hitherto unsuspected depths of everyday reality" and to realize that simple things around seem to have a message. The Spirit opens one's eyes to Christ, to one's fellow humans and those who are in need.[7]

The Holy Spirit, who possessed Jesus of Nazareth, enables the believers to wake up, open their hearts and become sensitive and responsive to the bubbling of life around them. The Spirit kindles faith and enables the believers to commune with God. It is in and through the Spirit that believers experience God as accompanying them. The Spirit makes them strong in dark moments, courageous to be different and even oppose accepted paths, and to deal with their failures. One experiences the Spirit in many ways, in the fellowship which inspires, in moments of personal and community prayers, and in nature. The Spirit-experience includes, in the words of Rayan, "God communicating God-self; God acting in Jesus, God making the world, God involved in the miracles of the earth, God giving the breath of life to animals and humans, God gifting freedom or love-ability to women and men". Therefore, the Spirit-experience "is common to all and special to each".[8]

1.1.2 *The Spirit-experience urges us to build a new world*

Rayan holds that the Spirit is "known in the concrete activity of building a new world", and She "works primarily by generating awareness and communion, by opening our eyes and establishing contact, by giving us vision and urging us to build community".[9] In the basic communities reading the Bible, prayer that rises from the routine of daily life, and celebrations, which consolidate and strengthen the community, and provide a base for community action are real Spirit-experiences.[10]

Experience of the Spirit is discernable in positive actions. These are experiences of an unexpected transformation. People feel themselves seized by new strength and that makes them do things they had never thought of doing. "Individuals and communities that had been disheartened, lacked in dynamism, resigned to the endless struggle for survival, discover themselves to be protagonists of history far greater than themselves. Their experience is one of conversion, the advent of a new life, an all-embracing experience, working on five main areas which include practically all aspects: action, freedom, speech, community and life".[11]

When, people who were objects of history and were excluded from the decision-making process, begin to assert themselves, take hold of their destiny in their hands and experience a new life and rebirth, their assertive action is an instance of an experience of the Spirit. When people who were enslaved and exploited for long begin to struggle collectively for freedom and risk their dear lives for dignity and equality, their experience of freedom is a "rebirth of humanity and reaffirmation of dignity", and an experience of the Spirit. When the voiceless begin to speak for the good of the community and relate spontaneously to God and proclaim the values of the Gospel, it is an experience of the freedom of speech, an experience of the Spirit. When the dispersed poor, deprived of their role in the community formation and collective action, begin to participate actively in the struggles for re-creating social life and mould their destiny discarding the dictates of the power structures, it is an experience of the emergence of community, an action of the Spirit. The violence of the past has intensified longing for life. Consequently, liberation struggles are more for improving the quality human relationships than material conditions. The way the poor accept their life is a spiritual experience and an experience of the Spirit.[12]

Rayan is of the view that these are "not five partial experiences but one overall experience of the Spirit. It is an experience of God in creation and of creation in God...The experience of the Spirit comes about with history, in the actions of subjects-agents-of their history...Experience of the Spirit is not an individual thing; it is tied to the building of community. Such experience of the Spirit is life and resurrection, newness of life".[13]

2. Symbols of the Spirit

Rayan reflects on the person of the Holy Spirit, who is "Subject, Activity and Relationship"[14] through the four biblical symbols: water, fire, wind and dove.

2.1 Biblical Symbols for the Spirit

2.1.1 *Water*

"Water is a primordial and miraculous element. It is the mother of life. It is bound up with our experience of freshness and newness. Biblical and Christian tradition in theology and piety relate water with the Holy Spirit". A medieval hymn speaks of the Spirit as "sweet refreshment here below" and as "grateful coolness in the heat" and prays: "On our dryness pour thy dew, wash the stains of guilt away".[15]

Commenting on Jn 7:37-39, Rayan says that "the Holy Spirit is the drink God gives to slate the thirst of our heart, which cannot be quenched with anything or by anyone less than, other than, the Spirit of the living God". Jesus, as John narrates (Ch. 4) "would accept a drink of water from our own wells and cups… and in turn "offers us the gift of God, the living water". The living water is the symbol of the Spirit of life. Rayan argues that the water Yahweh gave from the rock to Israel in the desert is also an image of the Spirit (Ex 17:11-17). "For Paul the rock is an image of Christ and drink is spiritual" (1 Cor 10:4; Ps 78:15-16). On Calvary a soldier struck this Rock with a lance and "immediately there came blood and water" (Jn 19:33).[16]

Rayan refers to the stream in Ezekiel 37 as a symbol of the Holy Spirit. The three biblical texts, Ezekiel 37, Revelation 22 and Genesis 2, in his view, share a common perspective: "The Spirit is…the river "whose streams bring joy to God's city".[17]

2.1.2 *Fire*

In the Bible God often appears in flames of fire, and speaks out of the midst of fire, and accompanies his people in or as a pillar of fire (Ex 3:2; 19:8; 20:7; 12:21-22; Deut 4:12; 15:33; 5:26; 10:4). In the Old Testament fire is the symbol of Yahweh. "Fire cleanses and purifies; it liberates gold from dross; it melts and thaws; it warms the home. Similar is the work of the Holy Spirit in the realm of the heart and of human relationships". John the Baptist spoke of Jesus as one who would baptize with the Holy Spirit and fire (Lk 3:16; Matt 3:11). At the Pentecost, the Spirit appeared as tongues of fire (Acts 2:2-3). The fire that Jesus brings to the earth is the Holy Spirit, the final promise and fruit of his sacrificial life and death. God's free and ultimate treasure offered to humans is "The divine fire which burns in the heart of God and flowers on the branches of the cross".[18]

In some Asian traditions, Rayan points out, "fire is priest; priestly hands that convey humans' offerings to God. It is also God's hands and mouth accepting and consecrating our gifts. A powerful symbol of the consecrating Spirit is the fire that consumed Elijah's sacrifice on Mount Carmel (1 Kings 18: 20-40)".[19]

2.1.3 *Breath and Wind*

On Easter day, the Risen Lord said, "As the Father sent me, I am sending you" and breathed on them and saying: "Receive the Holy Spirit" (Jn 20:19-23). Jesus, the one anointed with the Spirit and sent, now sends his disciples after anointing them with the Spirit. Rayan makes an insightful reading here, while saying that "Mission and Spirit are related" (Acts 8:12-13; 2:3; Mt. 10:19-20). To continue the mission of Jesus, Rayan asserts that the disciples "need to be energized by his Spirit and to live by his breath".[20] Reflecting on Genesis 2 and 1:12, Rayan says: "We become alive and human only when God blows the breath of life into the nostrils of what he has shaped from the soil (Gen 2). Without God's breath and Spirit we humans are no more than a cold lump of earth. The Spirit gives life and transforms chaos into cosmos".[21]

"In the beginning at the original creation, the *Ruach* of God swept over the waters (Gen 1:2). At the dawn of the new creation there is the hovering Spirit again." In the light of Acts 2:1-4, 2 Corinthians 3:17, and John 3:5-8, Rayan understands the Holy Spirit "as life-force and as creative freedom".[22] He interprets the 'low murmuring sound" that Elijah heard on the Mount Horeb, as the symbol of the Holy Spirit. Thus, the Holy Spirit is also "intimacy and peace, quiet depth and silent strength".[23]

2.1.4 *Dove*

The dove is "the most popular" image of the Spirit in Christian tradition and "the oldest image" in the NT for the Spirit. The reference to the dove in Mark 1:10 and Luke 3:22 "is to the beauty, gentleness and peace associated with the dove". Rayan also points out that it may be "a description of the coming down, a reference to the descending movement rather than the physical form", and adds that the point of the symbol of the dove could be "God's humanwardness, God's earthwardness".[24]

2.2 The Prophets

For Rayan, "the more telling symbols of the Holy Spirit are inspired women and men, poets and prophets, charismatic leaders, and their enthused deeds, words and movements". Therefore, for him, a significant way to experience the Spirit of God is "to identify with the cause of great poets, prophets, dreamers, visionaries, social critics and revolutionaries of the Bible as well as of all spiritual and cultural histories".[25]

Rayan considers the prophets, their prophecies and prophetic gestures as the powerful and dynamic symbols of the Spirit. Their uncompromising condemnation of all forms of injustice, their compassionate passion for justice to the poor and the oppressed, their protests against the oppressive and powerful mighty, their indomitable courage and fearlessness against the religious and political powers, their agony at the alienation of the people from the covenantal relationship, the fire of God that consumed their inner self at God's commission, their fiery words, the tenderness and concern of Yahweh they embodied and expressed – all these constitute the symbols of the Holy Spirit and the experience of the Spirit in history.[26]

2.3 Jesus: The Symbol of the Holy Spirit

The Holy Spirit was the way Jesus walked and lived his mission-existence. Jesus was the symbol of the Spirit in his defiance of the power structures of his time, in his compassion for the hungry, and in his daring cleansing of the Temple in Jerusalem. Jesus is "the harp of the Spirit as well as the music. He composes and plays on it".[27]

Rayan describes Jesus on the Cross as "the supreme symbol of the Spirit....If Jesus' life was the dance of the Spirit on our earth, Calvary was its culminating, crowning movement".[28] He describes Jesus on the Cross as a cosmic dance: "A cosmic dance, the rhythm of which reverberates in every fibre of the universe and keeps throbbing in the centre of every spirit and in the heart of every particle of matter". It is this dance that brought about "the birth the new age of freedom and abounding life and the outpouring of the Holy Spirit".[29] He interprets further that "the cross of Jesus blossoming into the resurrection is the supreme affirmation of life, freedom and joy, the ultimate dance which gathers the cosmos into the profound harmony and unity of the Divine".[30] The Easter stories are dances performed to a different music. The appearances of the risen Lord are "the dance of the Lord of the Spirit, the dance of the Holy Spirit".[31]

2.4 The Disciples

Rayan speaks of the disciples of Jesus, all those who walk the way of Jesus and continue his liberative mission, as the symbols of the Holy Spirit. The poor of the world and all who love liberty and uphold human dignity are also symbols of the Spirit. Thus, the world is "full of icons of the Holy Spirit and signs of her healing, new creating and gladdening presence".[32]

3. The Outpouring of the Spirit

The phrase, 'to pour out' is used, Rayan points out, in the context of worship, suffering and sin in the Bible. Its use in relation to the Spirit suggests "a sense of prodigality and abundance", and implies that the Spirit "is present and active liberally and lavishly in all ages, climes, among all peoples, in every culture and history, within every situation and in each human heart".[33]

Jesus is the recipient of the Spirit without measure (Jn 3). But the gifts bestowed on him are meant for humanity and the world (Rom 8:33, Jn 7:37-39; Acts 2:33). Isaiah 32:13-16, and 44:1-4, refer to abundance and prodigality of the outpouring of the Spirit. Ezekiel 39 indicates the thoroughness of the deliverance through the outpouring of the Spirit. Joel's vision of universal outpouring of the Spirit (2:18-27 and 3:10, "I shall pour out my Spirit on all humanity"), Rayan believes, is anticipated in the wish of Moses: 'Would that the entire Lord's people were prophets, and that the Lord would put his Spirit on them' (Num 11:29b). Moses' prophetic wish and Joel's vision find partial fulfilment at Pentecost when the Spirit is actually poured out on everyone present in the upper room (Acts 2:1-4, 15-21). Rayan says: "The Spirit transcends the barriers we build, and in a tidal surge dissolves the divisive walls we raise. The Spirit is not the possession, nor the monopoly of any church, religion, culture, race or epoch".[34]

Quoting St. Paul that the Holy Spirit has been given to the believers and God's love has been poured out into their hearts by the Holy Spirit (Rom 5:5), Rayan points out that the outpouring of the Spirit invites the disciples "to think out new styles of Christian living, new forms of religious life, new kinds of Church structure that will be expressive of the community the Spirit gathers and serve the brotherhood he builds".[35] The self-giving of the Spirit has always been greater, surprisingly more abundant, and generously boundless.[36]

Rayan gently asserts that the Holy Spirit does not confine herself to Christian churches, religions and believers; does not only live and act in the sacraments of the church, in sacred persons, sacred scripture and holy places, but "is present and active everywhere, in all ages, and places, cultures and religions. She is the atmosphere that envelops the earth, moves in the heart of every reality, and become the heart's gift to hearts across distinctions of caste, class, sex, race or religion. The Spirit outpouring is there on all struggles against oppression, on all movements for justice, equality and freedom, and on all strivings for a sane human and gentle history". The Spirit is the beauty of small things and dwells in the huts and hovels where the simple live, love and share their lives, food, hunger, tears, hope and a determination to change the world.[37]

4. The Grieving Spirit

St. Paul sums up his understanding of renewal in Christ: "Do nothing to sadden the Holy Spirit with whom you were sealed" (Eph 4:30). Rayan comments that Paul implies by that the lifestyles and behavior patterns that make the Holy Spirit sad and vexed should be parted with. Human selfishness, rebellion and forgetfulness of the very foundation of life sadden God. God's questions to Adam and Eve, "where are you?"; to Cain, "Where is your brother? What have you done?" speak of God's pain and anguish. Rayan interprets the story of the flood in Gen 6:5-13, not only as "the story of torrents of God's wrath", but also "of God's pain, the tide of his grief, the flood of his tears".[38]

Yahweh's words to Moses from within the burning bush (Ex 3:7-8) illustrate vividly that "the burning bush is Yahweh on fire with grief and anger. It is a picture of the heart of God". The burning bush is God's identification with a humiliated, oppressed and suffering people in Egypt.[39] However, it is "in the prophets and in relation to exile that the grief and wrath of God reach their most touching expression…The sorrowing mother and anguished father in God" is presented in many ways in the prophetic literature (Is 1:2-7, 40:1-2; Hosea 11:1-9, Is 54; Ezek 37).[40]

Jesus is the "finest symbol of the Holy Spirit". His "grieving and weeping, his pity and compassion…symbolize and point to the grieving Holy Spirit of God". Jesus felt sorry for hungry crowds, for publicans and sinners, for the victims of oppression (Mt 4:23-25, 9:35-37, 14:14, 15:32; Mk 6:34-38; Lk 7:13, 36-50). His identification with the victims of injustice and exploitation means that "the grief of the oppressed is now the symbol and sacrament of the grieving Holy Spirit of God". The occasions where Jesus wept (Jn 11:32-36; Lk 19:41-44) are other manifestations of the grieving of the Spirit. Rayan poignantly asks: "is not the grief of Jesus the grief of the Spirit made manifest?" and his "service to life, the touch of the living and life-giving Spirit?" and his "defiance of the law, the breath of Her who blows where She pleases in sovereign freedom?".[41]

Rayan says that the Spirit continues to grieve over even today "over all signs of a culture of death and decay, God weeps, his Christ sheds tears and his Spirit grieves and sighs". Rayan says that the disciples of Jesus are called "to share in the concerns of the Spirit" to stand on the side of the poor and the oppressed and "to join the struggle for a different, a new human world. The Holy Spirit leads the way, even as She grieves, to a new age in which nothing will be thought or done that could sadden the Spirit".[42]

5. The Oblivion of the Holy Spirit

Rayan explains, perhaps as no other Indian theologian does, the oblivion of the Spirit particularly in the Church of the West till the recent times. He admits along with other theologians that the difficulty concerning the theology of the Spirit arises due to the elusive quality inherent in dealing with theology of the Spirit, "because of the non-objectivity and hiddenness of the Spirit, and because the

Third Person, unlike the Father and the Son, has no proper name... The Spirit is fluid, mobile, mercurial".[43]

Rayan rightly assesses that the oblivion of the Spirit that one finds in the Church(es) of the West is in contrast to the experience of the first century Christians for whom the Holy Spirit was "the chief actor in the historic mission of the Church...the director of the whole enterprise". He adds further that the marginalizing the experience of the early Christians has marginalized the significance of the Holy Spirit and "relegated the Holy Spirit to the edges of our theology" in the Churches of the West.[44]

Rayan is of the view that the following reasons led to the neglect of the Spirit: (a) Lack of fully reflective teaching on the Spirit in the Scriptures. He admits that "in the biblical texts there are many open questions, but also much that is clear"; (b) The fascination of post-biblical writers and believers with the historical nearness and newness of the Jesus-event, and the preoccupation of the early Christological councils to get Christ recognized as the Son of God.[45] (c) The Greek philosophy examined the revelation from the category of 'substance', and its influence in theology made the Holy Spirit a stranger who "did not fit" in the realm of theology. The influence of stoicism from the second century moulded the Christian thinking to speak of 'God' rather than the 'Trinity of Persons'. Moreover, The Latin theology preferred to speak of 'divine nature' rather than of the three persons. (d) The separation between theology and spirituality since the Middle Ages also contributed to the oblivion of the Spirit.[46] Rayan agrees with Jose Comblin that the oblivion of the Spirit in the past has produced "historical distortions in theology and in the life of the Church". Consequently, the Spirit remained "the great unknown" for many Christians; this in a way contributed to the lack of interest in the Holy Spirit as shown by theology and liturgy.[47]

Rayan observes that the theology of the Spirit is a neglected treasure even in the Second Vatican Council which for some "did not exhibit any deep penumatological awareness". It is true that the Vatican II broke with the long tradition of the Latin Church and used Trinitarian language and mentions 258 times the Holy Spirit but did not do justice to the Spirit[48] and did not work out a real Pneumatology. Rayan makes also a justified critique *Dominum et*

Vivificantem (1986) by saying that although it gave a well-organized presentation of biblical texts in part I, it did not redeem the situation.[49]

Rayan has well documented - nearly 20 theologians, from Hilary of Poiters (315-367) and St. Augustine (354-430) to the recent ones like Emmanuel Clapsis (1989) and to John Ashton (1991) to present the backdrop of the Eastern Churches' accusation of the Western theology of its preoccupation with 'Christomonism'.[50] The West "evolved a theological construct in which Christ has no need of the Spirit" and subordinated the Spirit to the Word...Christomonism derives primarily from the imbalance between the missions of the Son and of the Holy Spirit in Western theology".[51]

Rayan notes that "there has always been a Christology but there has never been a parallel Pneumatology in the whole scholastic tradition till recent times... this Christology has virtually ignored the Holy Spirit" (and) that "the traditional Christology overlooked the presence of the Spirit in Jesus; Western theology in general bypassed the role of the Spirit in the world and in history". This has been true till recently because the Western Christological categories made the Holy Spirit as "an extra, an addendum" and was satisfied with decorating on the already constructed Christological categories with "pneumatological baubles, a little Spirit tinsel".[52]

Rayan concludes along with Clapsis that the excessive Christomonism that prevailed until recently in the Western theology neglected to give adequate importance to the role of the Spirit in the life of the Church and in history.[53]

5.1 Consequences of the Oversight

Rayan is of the view that the Spirit is "the distributor of diverse gifts within the Church and outside, the author of newness, and the initiator of radical changes" and hence there was a conscious "attempt to institutionalize the Holy Spirit in the life of the Church". He agrees with Tylor that the creative Lord is "treated as a thing – a force to be manipulated, an influence to be placed at the disposal of bishops and priests, and dispensed sacramentally and in no other way".[54] Rayan describes in a captivating style the institutionalization of the Spirit as: "an effort to cage the Wind (Jn 3:8), to silence the Storm (Act 2:20), to clip the Dove's wings (Lk 3:22), to dam the Stream (Jn 7:38), to cap the Fire (Acts 2:3), to stifle tongues and prophecies (Act 2:4, 11, 17), and to smother dreams and visions (Acts 2:17-18). With that the Church tended to become a power structure, a pyramid of graded power, over-organized and over-centralized. It came to hold and use patterns of power which Jesus had decisively banned from his movement, namely, the kill-power of the Caesars".[55]

Rayan gives a long list of consequences - 22 in all - of the neglect of the Spirit in the life of the Church: separation of Mystery from the institutional dimensions, of the believing people from the clergy; marginalization of women and their intuitions and insights into the Mysteries of our Faith; radical separation of spirit from matter; the division of the church into the ruling and the ruled, the speaking and the silent, teaching and learning Church; the obliteration of the unity/complementarity of the people's priesthood and ministry and those of the clergy; the imposition of the laws, customs and rituals of one local church (Latin) upon the world Church to the snubbing the Pentecostal Spirit of many tongues (Acts 2:4-12; 10:44-46); the growth in number and power of central bureaucracy which is preoccupied with formulations, abstractions, privileges rather than with life's realities; death of prophetism in the Church; devaluing and killing of creative freedom and personal responsibility; turning the Church into an establishment oriented towards the past and suspecting of initiatives; failing to be sensitive to the call of the Spirit in the Ecumenical Movement; alarming insensitivity to new perspectives in science, biblical studies, theology and methods of evangelization, neglect of the Spirit's presence and action in the world, history, and in the lives and hearts of people; and to a false supremacy of the frame of mind that is suspicious of mysticism and enslaved towards positivism and rational order.[56]

5.2 New Consciousness

Rayan rightly reads the signs of the times in the present and admits that there is "a new consciousness of the Spirit". He discerns the following as its causes: "the question of God in the context of modern atheism, the Charismatic movement, the ecumenical movement, renewed interest in Trinitarian theology, the event of second Vatican Council ('an epiphany of the Spirit'), and the people's own experience of the Spirit as they struggle for food and freedom, humanity and dignity". Consequently, there is a renewed interest in the person and work of the Spirit among the Christian Churches. The revival of interest in the Holy Spirit is greatly due to the Charismatic movement throughout the Church. Thanks to the above mentioned factors today there is "a resurgence of the Holy Spirit". It is a phenomenon unique in the history of the Church and a total inversion of the course that the Church in the West followed since the 3rd century.[57]

6. Pneumatology: The How and the Horizon of Theology

Rayan says that the experience of the Spirit has become "a major factor in the life of the Churches, as well as a basis for a renewed theology, (and) forces theology to reformulate its objectives and methods and to pay greater attention to the way the Faith is lived than to purely academic concerns".[58] He acknowledges that Penumatology cannot replace Christology, but it is at "the heart of Christian theology" as it touches all aspects of faith in Christ: the divinization of humanity by grace, the renewing and reconciling presence of God in history, the mystery of the Church, the celebration of the sacraments, and the exercise of Christian witness.[59]

6.1 The Comprehensive Horizon

The Spirit is "the point of entry into the mystery of Christ through which the mystery of the Father is attained". Hence, theology starts "with the historical experience (individual and collective) of the Spirit". It is 'in' the Spirit that any theological statement becomes possible. The Spirit is "that infinite theological horizon inside of which any theological reflection should be performed. That is why the Spirit cannot as such become an object of theological reflection like other theological matters".[60]

"Pneumatology is a universal horizon determining the interpretation of all reality", because the Spirit's sweep is co-extensive with the reach of Christ's work. Consequently, Rayan speaks of "a two-directional hermeneutical function to Pneumatology: i) it is both the point of entry and the hermeneutical principle for the interpretation of Christology and Trinity, and b). it is the point of entry and the hermeneutical principle for the interpretation of history and ecclesiology".[61]

According to Rayan, "Pneumatology is not a body of theological knowledge alongside Christology, because the Spirit is "not a second theological focus". The Spirit is interpretative perception which informs the whole of theology, operating at the centre of the Christological moment. Christ and the Spirit are both at the centre; one is the 'What', the other is the 'How', the Way.[62] "In Pneumatology the theological orientation must be Christological and Trinitarian; in this sense the doctrine of the Spirit is central". It "is a methodological (How) centre, not a material (What) centre". Rayan shares his theological conviction that "the doctrine of the Spirit must permeate the whole theological concern, not as dominant theme, but as interpretive perspective".[63]

The Spirit operates "at the interior of every statement about the Spirit (and) is the universal comprehensive horizon within which any and all theological reflection is possible". The Spirit makes any theological statement intelligible. "The Holy Spirit cannot be objectified and viewed from the outside". Therefore, "Pneumatology is to theology what epistemology is to Philosophy" and it "determines the 'rules' for speaking about God". The Spirit enables one to know Jesus, the visible image of the Father who sent him, to recognize the presence of God in history, and "the face of the Son in his Church, and a sacrament of God in his creation". Rayan concludes quoting K. McDonnell, "if Pneumatology is the point of entry into the world and the Church, and a portal to Christological and Trinitarian mysteries and theological hermeneutics, we need to know more clearly what a theology in the Spirit (in contrast to a theology of the Spirit) means".[64]

6.2 Effects of Pneumatological Perspective in Theology

6.2.1 *Spirit Christology*

Rayan illustrates briefly the impact of Spirit perspective in Spirit Christology and Spirit ecclesiology. Spirit Christology asserts that it is not possible to develop a Pneumatology separately from the Word. Pneumatological Christology emphasizes that Jesus is Christ and Lord only through the Holy Spirit, while Christological Pneumatology understands that there is a Spirit at all only if Jesus is Christ and Lord. In and through Christ the Spirit is revealed and hence, "to identify Christ is to find the Spirit". The relation between Penumatology and Christology can be perceived in the way Paul relates "in the Spirit' to "in Christ". The two interpret each other. Thus, for Rayan, "Every Christological statement has its Penumatological counterpart".[65]

Rayan sees the development of Spirit Christology in two stages: in the historical life of Jesus and in the life of the Risen Jesus. In the former stage, the Spirit is at work in him and in the latter "the Spirit is experienced in a new way as eschatological salvation poured out in abundance as faith, love, forgiveness, redemption, adoption by God, liberation, and charisms to serve the community".[66] Rayan spells out the difference between Spirit Christology and Logos Christology in the following way: "Spirit Christology functions in an inclusive way, open to other NT Christologies, ready to consider, interpret and appropriate them, while Logos Christology has tended to be exclusive, throwing other Christologies in a shadow". He assures that "God as Spirit working in the life of Jesus can form the basis for a multiple interpretation of him".[67]

Spirit Christology pays special attention, according to Rayan, to the following points:

i) It "affirms and safeguards the integrity of Jesus' humanity, his human subjectivity, personhood, freedom and obedience. He was a real actor in history, while Logos Christology has often obscured and undermined Jesus' humanity in an attempt to uphold his divinity".[68]
ii) "God as Spirit has been effecting salvation from the beginning of world history. Salvation did not begin with Jesus. Jesus reveals it, realizes it historically, and becomes its perfect exemplar, the new Humanity, planted in the body of history and offered for our taking through faith-praxis".[69]
iii) Jesus is unique in Spirit Christology also. He is unique as "normative manifestation of what God is and the pattern of what human existence should be". God as Spirit was active in Jesus "in a complete, fully effective, supernatural way in

> view of the specific mission entrusted to him. Since, no less than God acts in Jesus for the salvation of the world, this salvation is universally relevant for humankind. In this sense Jesus is normative for all. But Jesus is not exclusive though he is decisive and absolute for the Christian". Therefore, Rayan holds that "Jesus as symbol participates in God as Spirit, mediates God, and makes God present. Worship directed to the human being Jesus moves through him to its mediated destination, namely, God, who is not separate from Jesus, who is encountered in Jesus".[70]

6.2.2 *Spirit and the Church*

Traditionally it was held that "Christ founded the Church as a hierarchic society, and thereby provided all that was needful to the end of time. The Spirit only confirms what Jesus did". But the rediscovery of the role of the Spirit has led to a new balance towards the understanding the Church. Rayan goes along with Congar in affirming that the Church is founded on two events: the Christ-event and Spirit-event. The Spirit is co-constitutive of the Church. Christ's basic Church-founding act was the sending of the Holy Spirit who is the "guarantor of continuity" of his mission.[71]

Rayan is convinced that an Ecclesiology based on the Holy Spirit will be effectively aware that:

i) The Spirit "acts from within people and their decisions and actions. The Church does not originate at the top and filter down. It begins with people, drawn by the Spirit, coming together to form base communities… The Church does not start with power but with the communion uniting persons and communities".[72]
ii) The unity of the Church is protected by the Spirit by incorporating the believers into the Body of Christ. The Spirit brings them together in freedom and facilitates unity amidst greatest diversity.[73]
iii) Catholicity is experienced as the Church emerges anew in the Spirit on the basis of the past and the personality proper to each people. The Spirit helps these people to

be shapers of their own churches and these will "seek communion with the old churches on a basis of equality, having become a church without dependence on the West". Rayan raises accordingly pertinent questions: "Will the Churches of western origin recover their catholicity by breaking these (colonialism and conquests) links, and let Asian and African churches emerge without coercion in theology, liturgy, language and law? Could a Church take sides (of the poor and the oppressed) and remain catholic?".[74]

iv) "Apostolicity means that the Church is founded on the martyrdom-witness of the Apostles", and that the Church is here to proclaim the Word and bear witness to it, even by laying down her life. Therefore, "the whole Church is apostolic". But unfortunately, "since the second century apostolicity has been reduced to a question of Episcopal succession, a sort of a relay race".[75] Rayan is categorical in stating:

> The Word, Speech, is no preserve of the clergy, the elite or the powers. It is the Spirit that communicates the Word and discloses its meaning in each concrete situation. The sacraments,... are in the hands of the Spirit, and not under priest's power. The charisms proceed from the Spirit; they are many and diverse, and are distributed among all the people, and not concentrated in anyone place or time or person or group or movement. They too are nobody's preserve, and when the clergy seek to control them they destroy much.[76]

v) Authority in the Church is to be understood as "the power of increasing the faith of the community, of guiding prayer, of making the liturgy an experience of the Kingdom; of stimulating works of charity, of awakening all to a sense of responsibility... Authority is service and...comes from Christ the Vine and spreads to all his branches; it comes from the Spirit to the community and each member of it on whom the Spirit rests".[77]

vi) The Church is charismatic, because all her actions are really derived from the gifts of the Spirit. These gifts are to be recognized and respected, otherwise the Church would be a lifeless and hallow institution. Rayan says that hierarchy in the Church is "a regulating principle" and "not a source of life". Life is the gift of the Spirit. He affirms that the "action of the Spirit is not determined by the Church. It is not for the Church to tell where the Spirit should blow. The reverse is true: the Church ought to follow where the Spirit blows. Only by following the Spirit does the Church exist".[78] Rayan perceives the three realities – the normative documents (Scriptures), the sense of faith of the people of God, and the charism of ordained ministers – as a single whole. "They complete and in a sense condition one another. They should function together".[79] The Spirit is the coordinator and unifier of diversity.

Rayan agrees with Congar that the spiritual movements do have a vital role to play, because they "share a desire to escape from the establishment of power structure and to derive an evangelical way of life from the sources, not through the mediation of the clergy". Reflecting on the post-reformation era, Rayan raises significant questions: "Are not the new churches, movements, sects a revolt against rationalism in religion? Against a Christianity externally regulated and imposed by Western rationality or irrationality?" and "How should the dialectical tension between diversity and communion be conceived and put to effect?"[80]

Rayan rightly reads the present era that "with the new consciousness of the Spirit who is communion, we are beginning to change; we speak now of collegiality, lay participation, pastoral councils, lay ministry, witness and teaching, and the home-church", and that the new era of the Church will be "under the sign of the Holy Spirit and the aspect of experience will be valued more highly than ever since the second century".[81]

6.3 Pneumatological Cosmism

Rayan regrets along with Congar that "the cosmic aspect of the Spirit (revealed in Gen 1:2) has hardly been developed at all in Catholic theology". "The cosmos has been created in, through and for Christ Jesus, and Jesus is "the human expression of a radical orientation to the Father" (*pros ton Theon*). Consequently, the whole cosmos is "oriented Fatherward, while it is in process of transformation into the Body of Christ". Rayan affirms that it is the Spirit who "leads this pilgrimage, and shapes the Body of Christ in the womb of history".[82] Along with John Taylor, Rayan affirms that the Spirit is present "deep within the fabric of universe" and "in the inside of creation. And if God is really on the inside, we must find him in the process, not in the gaps… nature is all of a piece, a seamless robe…. If the hand of God is to be recognized in this continuous creation, it must be found not in isolated intrusions but in the very process itself…. (and) every particle and process of material existence is alive with the activity of God".[83]

The Holy Spirit is the author of dynamism and beauty in nature and holds the diversity of creation together, "weaving them into a cosmic harmony". The Spirit of life is at work in nature, in humans and renews, energizes and creates life and beauty out of chaos. Therefore, everyone is called "to stand with the Spirit and work together, respecting life, caring for environment, creating art and beauty, and moulding beautiful social relationships instead of building oppressive social pyramids and ugly conflicts and littering death".[84]

7. The New Creative Spirit

Rayan is convinced that the Spirit "never leaves us, never despairs of us, never gives up. She continues to hover over our chaotic, broken world, struggling to bring to birth afresh. But, She is given to us as first fruits, as hope. Hope is the first installment of renewal and salvation, of liberation and life…. all grief will be turned into joy", because, the Spirit is the promise of the Father, giver of hope which "guarantees a future beyond the present frustration and travail" (Lk 24:49; Gal 3:14; Eph 1:13; 2 Cor 1:20, 5:5), and makes our hope overflow (Rom 15:13). This hope rests on the very promise of God whose project is the creation of new heavens and a new earth.[85] The Spirit is a "principle of creation" in the transformation of chaos into the beautiful cosmos in the beginning, and so She is the Source of new creation[86]: "When the new creation takes shape in the womb of the old, the Spirit is there overshadowing Mary, the mother of the new (Lk 1). And when the Newness that is Christ Jesus begins to grow and develop into a social-historical ferment, the Spirit is there as the roar of a tempest and as tongues of fire, energizing the new movement and adding power to the explosive new wine of the Gospel (Acts 1 and 2; Mk 2:21-22)".[87]

The dramatic vision of the 'valley of bones' in Ezekiel 37 speaks of the intervention of Yahweh: "I am going to open your graves; I shall put my spirit in you, and you shall live". The Spirit, the power behind the resurrection of Jesus and the Indweller in all calls everyone to commit themselves to "the task of resurrecting the dead, of opening tombs of poverty and prejudice in which millions of people are forcibly interred and of assuring for all peoples an ever finer and fuller life".[88]

Jesus understood his mission as one of liberation of the poor. His mission began with the descent of the Spirit and was carried on in the Spirit. Thus, "freedom is the first and characteristic gift of the Spirit" and it is "the ability to love and love is what the Spirit is". Therefore, Rayan shares his conviction: "The decisive rejection of domination of every kind, and the determined bid for freedom by subjugated peoples, races and classes, as well as a global explosion of a sense of dignity and self-worth are unmistakable signs of the Spirit mightily at work in our history today".[89] "An option for the poor and the oppressed is central to the history of biblical faith". It is the work and gift of the Holy Spirit. This insight is explicit in the invocation of the Spirit in the medieval hymn: *Veni, Pater pauperum.*[90]

The almost identical descriptions of the life of the early Christian community in Acts 2:42-47; 4:32-35 indicate that the "pooling of resources in order to be shared" is a consequence of sharing the Word in the apostolic community that had experienced the Holy Spirit. Therefore, Rayan challenges the Christian communities of today: to reflect deeply on "the relation between the experience of the Holy Spirit and the radical renewal of the world in the direction the early

Christians have shown of an egalitarian community of sisters and brothers who work together and share everything in dignity and freedom and joyful creativity". Acts 10 and 15 narrate the "breaking down of ethnicity and parochialism, and the opening of the Gospel to the whole world" as "a special revelatory and revolutionary action" of the Spirit. Thus, the Holy Spirit is "revealed as the source of renewal and change, growth and freedom".[91]

Rayan attributes to the inspiration of the Holy Spirit Paul's advocacy of Christian community to be a law-free society but love-filled/reigning society and his call to "live in the boundless freedom of the Spirit".[92] The Spirit gives "new strength and courage to dissent and to resist dehumanisation and oppression". Therefore, it is the vocation of the believers, according Rayan, to "be sensitive to the new-creative, transformative presence and action of the Spirit in peoples, events and revolutions which mould and weave the history of our times". Rayan holds that "the criteria of transformative newness will always be greater freedom for more people – greater equality, greater justice, finer and fuller life, further growth in humanness and gentleness and the celebration of one another".[93]

8. The Holy Spirit: The Joy of God

The Holy Spirit, the giver of life, is "no opium meant to tranquilize us and provide us with escapes from life's harsh realities". The Spirit equips us to stand on the side of justice and freedom and "enables us to dissent and to resist, and become God's counterculture as She equipped Jesus for his struggle unto death, and enabled the martyrs, the seers of all traditions", and all those who struggled to uphold human dignity and equality. She is "God's energy and power", who recreates the world and resurrects the oppressed; She is the "power" through whom God raised Jesus and condemned the forces that destroy life; She is "Gentleness of God, God's tenderness and Affection, God's love and God's joy", therefore, humans' struggle is "a celebration of life, of God and of God's reign".[94]

Jesus shares his own joy with humanity and wants everyone to experience it in full (Jn 15:11, 16:20-24) and it is the gift of the Holy Spirit to him (Lk 10:21). Paul's description of the reign of God brings out the relation between joy and the Holy Spirit (Rom

14:17). The New Age and New Earth, the work of the Spirit, will be "a world of unclouded joy" (Is 65:17-22). "The whole dynamics of transformation/salvation is a transition from sorrow to joy, from death to life. The Spirit grieves in order to make...our pain the vehicle of her joy". In God's presence there is "fullness of joy" (Ps 16:11). It is not only that we rejoice in God but God also rejoices in us as Luke describes in Chapter 15, which is the heart of Lucan theology.[95]

One of the Indian traditions, Rayan recollects, speaks of the Ultimate reality as Brahman, and realization of Brahman as Ananda which "is the goal of all spiritual an intellectual quests". Rayan perceives creation as "the profusion of God's measureless joy". A dance "is the exuberance of life's joy, and life's celebration. That precisely is the Holy Spirit: the song, the dance, the joy and the celebration of God". The Holy Spirit is life, freedom and joy.[96]

9. The Spirit in the midst of the people

The Holy Spirit is most revealed and experienced in the resurrection of Jesus as the "Joy of God and the Power of God". This power of God "is put forth not merely on behalf of life, but on behalf ... of oppressed life, life crucified and held in tombs, life disallowed... (and) forbidden to grow or to flower".[97] Various liberative movements in the history of human society are the joy and dance of the Holy Spirit. Joy is in ferment in the upsurge of people for life, dignity, equality, fraternity, freedom and in the acts of care and concern for humans and nature. The dance of the Spirit is in progress "in people's rallies, protests and demonstrations, in their courting of arrest and courageous resistance, and in their insistent demand for justice and freedom and dignity for all".[98]

The Spirit is in the midst of people. She is active in human history. She continually renews human hearts and social structures through various events, committed persons, trials, sufferings, crises, creative insights and movements. Through it all the Spirit is "resurrecting the earth and fashioning the New Age; She is coming, ever coming with justice and freedom, challenging us to the more, the greater, the finer, more human".[99]

10. An Evaluation

Samuel Rayan has made a creative contribution in systematic theology by exploring the biblical insights into the person and work of the Holy Spirit in Christian life. He brings the doctrine of the Holy Spirit, which for long "has been the Cinderella of the theology" and was at "the edges of theology" to the very centre of Christian life and as the heart of theology.[100]

"The traditional Christology overlooked the presence of the Spirit in Jesus; Western theology in general bypassed the role of the Spirit in the world and in history",[101] whereas Rayan's reflections effectively highlight the presence and power of the Spirit in the world and in our contemporary history. His reflections on the Holy Spirit strongly emphasize that "the recovery of a full appreciation of the Holy Spirit in the Christian scheme is so vital for the Church".[102]

Rayan paints a comprehensive picture of the situation of Oblivion of the Spirit in the West and has pointed out that the Church of today has not been liberated from its unfortunate causes and sad consequences.

Rayan's exploration of Pneumatology is a matter of the heart for all theology and understands it as a horizon, methodology, as an interpretative perspective of the Christ-event, Church and her life and the history of humanity.

Rayan's reflections on the Holy Spirit implicitly give a clarion call to the academia to become consciously aware of the necessity that 'Spirituality of Theology' should run through the whole of theological formation.

Pope Francis' Christmas message of 2014 on the 'curial ailments' echoes Rayan's reflections on the Holy Spirit in many ways and one of them reads: "Indeed, the Church shows herself to be faithful to the Holy Spirit to the extent that she does not seek to regulate or domesticate it. The Spirit is freshness, imagination and innovation".[103]

Conclusion

Samuel Rayan in his writings on the Holy Spirit presents the Holy Spirit through biblical symbols and in and through them he has experienced the presence and power of the Holy Spirit. He interprets Jesus as unique symbol of the Spirit. Rayan explores the nature, content and goal of Spirit-experiences. He reviews the state of Pneumatology in Western Church till recent times, and considers some of the reasons for its neglect und underdevelopment; lists some of the consequences of the one-sidedness of the Western theology. He explains Pneumatology as a horizon, methodology for all theology, and as an interpretative perspective. He further looks at the way Spirit Christology, Pnuematological Ecclesiology and Pneumatological Cosmism are in the process of shaping up in the churches and their implications for the contemporary times. He has shared of his as well as of the believing community's experience of the Holy Spirit as a person, power, life, as One who journeys amidst the suffering people as one who grieves, as their hope, strength, joy and as the director of humanity from within. One cannot but notice the explosive insights in his gentle theological reflections and their revolutionary significance for a multi-cultural, multi-religious, and a socially exploitative context of India.

Notes

1. Samuel Rayan, SJ, *Collected Writings of Samuel Rayan Vol. III. God's Hope Becoming Visible: Indian Christian Reflections on Some Relevant Issues of our Times*, (ed.) Kurien Kunnumpuram, SJ. (Delhi: ISPCK, 2013), p. 90. Here after it will be referred as, Rayan, *CWSR – III: God's Hope Becoming Visible.*
2. Rayan, *CWSR – III: God's Hope Becoming Visible,* 90.
3. Since Samuel Rayan uses the pronoun 'She' for the Holy Spirit, in this paper feminine pronoun is used to refer the Holy Spirit.
4. *Ibid.*
5. *Ibid.*
6. *Ibid.*, p. 91.
7. *Ibid.*, pp. 92-93.
8. *Ibid.*, p. 92.
9. *Ibid.*, pp. 91, 92.
10. *Ibid.*, p. 93.
11. *Ibid.*
12. *Ibid.*, p. 94.
13. *Ibid.*, pp. 94-95.
14. *Ibid.*, p. 114.

15. *Ibid.*
16. *Ibid.*, pp. 114-115.
17. *Ibid.*, p. 116.
18. *Ibid.*
19. *Ibid.*, p. 117.
20. *Ibid.*
21. *Ibid.*, p. 118.
22. *Ibid.*
23. *Ibid.*
24. *Ibid.*, p. 119.
25. *Ibid.*
26. *Ibid.*
27. *Ibid.*, p. 120.
28. *Ibid.*
29. *Ibid.*, p. 138.
30. *Ibid.*, p. 120.
31. *Ibid.*, p. 138.
32. *Ibid.*, pp. 120-121.
33. *Ibid.*, p. 121.
34. *Ibid.*, p. 124.
35. Samuel Rayan, *Come Holy Spirit*, (Delhi: Media House, 1998), p. 23.
36. Rayan, *CWSR – III: God's Hope Becoming Visible*, p. 124.
37. Samuel Rayan, *Renew the Face of the Earth*, (Delhi: Media House, 1998), p. 32; Rayan, *CWSR – III: God's Hope Becoming Visible*, p. 125.
38. Rayan, *CWSR – III: God's Hope Becoming Visible*, p. 126.
39. *Ibid.*
40. *Ibid.*, pp. 127-128.
41. *Ibid.*, p. 129.
42. *Ibid.*, p. 130.
43. *Ibid.*, pp. 76, 78-79.
44. *Ibid.*, p. 79
45. *Ibid.*, p. 80.
46. *Ibid.*, pp. 80-81.
47. *Ibid.*, p. 80.
48. See, Luis Bermejo. *The Spirit of Life: The Holy Spirit the Life of the Christian*, (Anand: Gujart Sahitya Prakash, 1997).
49. *Ibid.*, p. 81.
50. Mohan Doss, *Christ in the Spirit: Contemporary Spirit Christologies*, (Delhi: ISPCK, 2005), p. xxii.

51. Rayan, *CWSR – III: God's Hope Becoming Visible*, p. 81.
52. *Ibid.*
53. *Ibid.*, p. 89.
54. *Ibid.*, p. 83.
55. *Ibid.*
56. *Ibid.*, pp. 83-86.
57. *Ibid.*, pp. 88-89.
58. *Ibid.*, p. 95.
59. *Ibid.*
60. *Ibid.*, p. 96.
61. *Ibid.*
62. *Ibid.*
63. *Ibid.*, p. 97.
64. *Ibid.*
65. *Ibid.*, p. 98.
66. *Ibid.*, p. 99.
67. *Ibid.*, 100.
68. *Ibid.*
69. *Ibid.*
70. *Ibid.*
71. *Ibid.*
72. *Ibid.*, p. 101.
73. *Ibid.*, p. 102.
74. *Ibid.*
75. *Ibid.*
76. *Ibid.*
77. *Ibid.*, pp. 102-103.
78. *Ibid.*, p. 103.
79. *Ibid.*, 104.
80. *Ibid.*, pp. 103-104.
81. *Ibid.*, p. 105.
82. *Ibid.*, p. 106.
83. *Ibid.*
84. *Ibid.*, p. 107.
85. Rayan, *CWSR – III: God's Hope Becoming Visible*, p. 130.
86. See, Juergen Moltmann, *The Source of Life: The Holy Spirit and the Theology of Life*, (London: SCM Press Ltd, 1997).
87. *Ibid.*, p. 131.
88. *Ibid.*

89. *Ibid.*, p. 132.
90. *Ibid.*, p. 132-133.
91. *Ibid.*, p. 133.
92. *Ibid.*
93. *Ibid.*, p. 134.
94. *Ibid.*, p. 135.
95. *Ibid.*, p. 136.
96. *Ibid.*, pp. 136-138.
97. *Ibid.*, p. 138.
98. *Ibid.*, p. 139.
99. *Ibid.*
100. *Ibid.*, p. 79.
101. *Ibid.*, p. 81.
102. *Ibid.*, p. 86.
103. Pope Francis's Christmas Message 2014, See, http://ncronline.org/blogs/roman-observer/francis-gives-roman-curia-officials-coal-christmas, accessed on 26.12.2014.

4

The Eucharist as Source and Summit of Abundant Life

Reflections on Samuel Rayan's Eucharistic Theology

Francis Gonsalves, SJ

1. Personal Preface: Rayan Exuding Eucharistic Exuberance

I am happy and honoured to share some reflections on Samuel Rayan's eucharistic theology, since, besides being my guru and colleague for close to twenty years, he has been a friend whose presence in Delhi's Vidyajyoti Jesuit community and around the Vidyajyoti College campus has been a great source of happiness, affection, serenity, laughter and inspiration to staff and student alike. Even during my student days in the early 1990s, Samuel Rayan came across to me not so much as a scholarly academician to be met by appointment only to discuss theology (although he certainly *is* very scholarly!) but as a knowledgeable elder, a wise confidant, and a humble, itinerant Christ-like guru who could be consulted on the road or in the garden, along college corridors, and across the dining table for the toughest or simplest of questions—for which he always had a practical, wise and revolutionary answer.

Besides the love for nature and poetry that we share, Samuel Rayan and I share the same birthday (July 23); and though exactly forty years separate our births, I've always felt close to him and at ease to address him simply as 'Sam'. With a twinkle in his eyes he'd reply: "Are you calling me '*sham*'?" In ways like this, his humour, cheerfulness, friendliness, approachability and childlike candour shine brightly. These enviable virtues of heart are matched by awe-inspiring qualities of mind—creativity, insightfulness, intelligence and wisdom—and steadfastness of spirit that have made Samuel Rayan a much sought-after theologian not only in India, but also abroad. At the outset, I mention these personal traits of Rayan, since his theology is but an outpouring and overflow of '*who*' he is. It's not uncommon to meet theologians whose personal lives are not fully consistent with their professed ideals, both spoken and written. Not so with Sam. His eucharistic theology is a radiant reflection of his eucharistic life that is lived in deep contemplation of, close communion with, and faithful commitment to, his Eucharistic Lord, Jesus, and the 'least' of his sisters and brothers.

This article, which briefly reflects upon the eucharistic theology developed by Samuel Rayan, is based upon two of his more recent articles compiled in a book edited by Kurien Kunnumpuram,[1] and an earlier article in a book edited by me.[2] I will quote extensively from these works and also add few fragments of personal reminiscences of eucharistic celebrations at Vidyajyoti College when Sam was the main celebrant, since *how* one celebrates the Eucharist clearly reveals *what* one believes in and is committed to. I shall divide this article into three parts: (a) Back to the Basics: Rayan's Rereading of the Bible; (b) True to Tradition: Rayan's Creative Fidelity to Church Tradition; (c) Eucharist as Energizer of Life: Rayan's Theology Today. To ensure that this article reflects Rayan's eucharistic theology and not just my thoughts, while quoting extensively from Rayan's works, I will put within inverted commas all his words so as to distinguish them from my comments and observations, which will be kept to the barest minimum.

2. Back to the Basics: Rayan's Rereading of the Bible

Since, theology is 'God talk' every theologian necessarily asks: Who is God for me? Who is God for my community in my concrete context? Rayan's God-image is drawn from his rereading and reinterpretation of Scripture always from the perspective of the *anawim*: the poor and the oppressed whom God preferentially loves and providentially cares for. Thus, for Rayan, God is *Jeevandata*: Life-Giver, Life-Sustainer and Liberator. He traces the origins of the Eucharist to the peak events of the Exodus in the First Testament. For those bearing the burdens of injustice and oppression, God was the Liberator who freed them from enslavement by the Egyptians. That was *their* Passover. "The Eucharist is *our passover*, a celebration of our political struggle full of tough hope and tender trust in the liberator God. The story of Exodus makes it clear that the faith of Israel could not be celebrated in Egypt in the midst of oppression: the people had to move out into the space and freedom of the desert in order to eat and drink with/before their God. So it is with the Eucharist: it cannot be celebrated except in freedom and as freedom, and as a struggle for freedom and dignity and life for all".

Since, God is Liberator and the One who frees all those who are oppressed and heavily burdened, God can never be captured in concepts, confined in any one creed, worshipped through only one cult and imprisoned in one church-community. For Rayan, this is a basic principle for worship. What Jesus said to the Samaritan woman (Jn 4) is significant for sacramental celebrations: "It is time that true worshippers worship the Father in spirit and truth". Rayan opines: "God is spirit and freedom. God is no localized thing. God is not bound to any mountain or temple or direction. Not to the east or to the west or the southwest. The Jews worshipped in Jerusalem or turned towards Jerusalem when they pray elsewhere, just as Muslims turn towards Mecca when praying." But, with Christ, things are transformed, since, "The risen Christ went north from Jerusalem and promised to meet his disciples in Galilee (Mt. 28:10,16; Mk 16:7). The risen Lord is with his disciples as they go in all directions speaking his Word among all the nations. And wherever two or three meet in his name he is there among them irrespective of the direction they face together, or whether they face one another (Matt 28:19-20; 18:19-20). In fact, Christ is in every starved man and deprived woman and hungry child; and in all the stripped, the despoiled and the broken, regardless of what the compass says".

The historical Jesus of Nazareth reveals the God of the covenant in even more radical and revolutionary terms. Just as God fed his hungry people with manna in the desert, Jesus *is* the new manna, the Bread of Life who comes to satisfy the hunger not just of some elite 'chosen people' but the hunger and thirst of all the nations. Rayan reiterates Park Jae Soon's view that the Jesus Movement is "a Table Community Movement that shared bread with the hungry; and a Serving Movement that proclaimed the principle of serving the oppressed; and a Life Restoration Movement that brought the cripples and the mentally ill to full and abundant life". Rayan writes: "Jesus chose table-fellowship with outcasts, sinners, peasants and fish-workers and marginal peoples as '*the new symbolic centre*' of the community. In place of the temple is a simple meal which represents participation in Jesus' body" (Mk 14:22-25).

Rayan's scriptural readings and reflections take us back to the basics. Jesus is portrayed as one who redefines centre and periphery, who throws overboard ritualism and legalism, who cleanses godless structures like the temple and its commercial cult, who critiques the Sabbath and its inhuman demands and who reiterates the supreme law of love—where love of God is sterile and futile if not overflowing into love of neighbour and even love of one's enemies. Rayan writes at length on scriptural passages that show Jesus as a prophetic subversive who ushers in God's Reign in favour of the poor, the hungry, the so-called 'sinners' and the 'least' of God's children. God so loves the world "as to give it his only Child for its salvation, to add heart to it, to rebuild its freedom, to broaden and clarify its visions, to share its wounds, to clothe it in tenderness and to give it wings" (Jn 3:16-17). And, in order to add heart to the world, to rebuild its freedom and give its' inhabitants wings, Jesus is drawn to prophetically challenge and condemn everyone and everything that goes against his Kingdom-vision.

"Jesus attacked formalism and verbosity in prayer and insisted on worship by praxis. Deeds, not words, are crucial. Sharing, not fasting, is the attitude that befits the newness of the Reign of God". Religion could not be divorced from social systems and political structures. "In Jesus' analysis, the temple was the central mechanism of the country's political economy. Instead of acting as a redistributive system to secure socioeconomic justice within the community of Israel, the temple accumulated capital, and directly oppressed the poor by cultic obligations they could not meet". For Jesus, "life is larger than temples, liturgies and rites; it is right to give life on the Sabbath, and lay cult aside in order to serve people in need" (Mk 3:1-6; Lk 13:10-17; Jn 5:1-18).

Just as table-fellowship with the *hoi polloi* becomes the '*symbolic centre*' of newborn Kingdom communities, "so does Jesus' Body, the Body of Christ, replace the temple as 'the *new symbolic centre*', the new place of encounter with God. This is indicated by the symbols of the last meal, and will be made explicit at the moment of Jesus' death when the 'destruction' of Jesus' body is juxtaposed with the 'destruction' of the sanctuary curtain.... The curtained Holy of Holies symbolizes the ideological justification of priestly elitism: in this order Yahweh is exclusive (reclusive?), dwelling 'apart from and above' the people, mediated by priests. That which divides the people from Yahweh also divides them from each other: the priest also lives 'apart and above'. Thus, the destruction of the curtain symbolizes the end of such an order".

Besides questioning traditional conceptions of Israel's hierarchical priestly establishment, Rayan exposes widespread patriarchal prejudices in scriptural interpretations which hold that only male disciples were present with Jesus when he celebrated his last Passover meal, his Last Supper. "So, when in the evening, Jesus reclined at table in the upper room in his friend's house, some of his other friends and close followers were with him: women and men. Some at least of the 'many women' who used to accompany Jesus as he travelled through Galilee, preaching the good news of the Reign of God (Lk 8:1-3), they may now have followed him to Jerusalem. In the upper room, with Jesus, were 'the many women' who would, the following day, stand on Calvary, watching Jesus' crucifixion, death and burial (Matt 27:55-6; Mk 15:40-1; Lk 23:49,55-6; 24:9-11). If the Supper was a Passover meal, it was a family celebration, and Jesus' family comprised all his disciples, women and men. If it was a simple farewell meal, Jesus would surely have all his friends on the spot present. Any suggestion that Jesus has the women wait outside the upper room while the men ate would be unacceptable. Nobody may lampoon Jesus as a bigoted misogynist".

Rayan's reflection on the Last Supper seems so simple, logical and direct; and yet, it takes the steam out of one of the strongest arguments for the non-ordination of women, i.e., on that night of the Last Supper when Jesus instituted the priesthood, no woman was present, and therefore, by extension, he wished that only males be ordained as priests for all ages to come. Rayan reflects on the proceedings of the Last Supper at some length: "At table, to Jesus' right, I guess, reclined his Mother... At the very start, Jesus said, 'I have eagerly desired to eat this Passover with you before I suffer' (Lk 22:15). In the course of the meal he took bread and cup, gave them to his family and said, 'Take, eat, this is my Body; and drink, this is my Blood poured out for you' (Mk 14:22-24). As he did so, Jesus travelled back in spirit to his boyhood and saw his Mother place before him his dinner, and heard her say through that silent gesture: 'Son, take, eat, drink, and grow up: this is my body, my energy, transformed through love's labour.' He realized that a similar vibrant message had been addressed to him much earlier, when he was a baby. When his Mother suckled him, was not her whole being saying to him in silent accents of milky sweetness: 'Take, my child, drink and live; this is my blood transformed through love and flowing for you'?... All this came to him in a flash as he reached his Body-Bread and Blood-Cup to his tablemates, beginning with his own Mother... He saw clearly that Mothers are eucharistic persons; that women in general are. It is they that trace for us the pattern of the Eucharist, and eucharistic words rich with significance. They are its finest symbol: their body feeds every human being that comes to birth and it is they that shed blood 'for the life of the world'.

3. True to Tradition: Rayan's Creative Fidelity to Church Tradition

Plaited together with Sam Rayan's refreshing reinterpretation of Scripture, are his readings and reflections on the two thousand years of Christian Tradition. Notably, much as Tradition provides an anchor for communitarian belief and practice, it also runs the risk of digressing and being domesticated so as to legitimize the options and actions of the powers that be—thereby purging it of its potential "to mould us and our world after the mind and heart of Jesus Christ". Aware of this risk, Rayan revisits the post-Pentecostal Catholic Tradition to decipher what the Eucharist meant to Jesus' friends: the firsthand witnesses of his life, death and resurrection. Launching out from there, on the one hand, he points out periods where the Church's creedal beliefs were truly consonant with their liturgical-sacramental practice and fruitfully overflowed into committed Christian practice, and, on the other, the historical digressions and regressions that must be remedied so as to be faithful to the ideals and praxis of our Lord and Liberator, Jesus.

Apostle Paul, points out Rayan, "not only bears witness to the eucharistic practice of the ancient Church, but seeks to interpret the Mystery and draw some practical lessons. A first comment by him throws light on the ecclesial dimensions of the Church. The Cup 'for which we give thanks' and 'the Bread that we break' are a participation in the Blood and in the Body of Christ. It means union with the Person of Christ in his Passion and Resurrection, in his complete giving of himself to us and to God. The Bread and the Cup we share mean being united to Christ and to one another, becoming one Body in the Lord, becoming the Body of the Lord, the Lord's community, the *Kyriake*, the Church (1 Cor 10:16-7)..... It follows that if there are factions among Christians, if, when they meet, the wealthy go ahead eating and drinking without waiting for the sisters and brothers to gather, and thus put the working people and the poor to shame, then God's assembly stands dishonoured, and the Body of the Lord left unrecognized in the Church no less than in the Eucharist. In that context, what they eat is not, cannot be, the Lord's Supper but judgement and condemnation" (1 Cor 11:17-22, 27-29).

Rayan reminds us that "Patristic and early medieval tradition, drawing on the Pauline image of the Body of Christ, spoke of a three-fold distinction of Christ's Body: (i) the historical Body, meaning the physical Body of Jesus; (ii) the ecclesial Body, that is the Church; and (iii) the sacramental Body, or Christ as present in the eucharistic elements. Both the sacramental Body and the ecclesial Body are *Communion*, the one calling to the other". Consequently, "The community's commitment to charity is the heart of the Eucharist. The original Lord's Supper was cradled in beautiful expressions of the Lord's love in his flaming exhortation to love another as he has loved us, to wash one another's feet in lowly, loving services, and to lay down our lives for our friends" (Jn 13 and 15). This is most powerfully seen in the narratives of the Acts of the Apostles (Acts 2:42-7; 4:32-7), which Rayan sees as, "the strongest affirmation, perhaps, and the clearest illustration of the social-economic dimensions and demands of the Eucharist.... The fellowship is communion in the Body of Christ; the Bread broken is communion in the same Body; and the sharing of goods is where the communion becomes historically enfleshed and visible".

Reflections on early eucharistic practice are backed by striking exhortations given by Church Fathers. For instance, "Ignatius of Antioch observed that: 'Those who have no care for love, no thought for the widow and the orphan, none at all for the afflicted, the captive, the hungry, or the thirsty, are also those who care not for the Eucharist". And, later, "Augustine, speaking to a group of newly baptized Christians who were about to receive their First Holy Communion said to them: 'Behold, your Mystery is here on this table. Receive what you are, namely, the Body of Christ".

The first three centuries—splattered with the blood of Christian martyrs, as they were—proved to be, as Tertullian prophesied, the seeds of a blossoming Christianity and the building blocks of a vibrant church-community. But, "with Constantine as Emperor of the Roman Empire and with the marriage of the sword and the cross began the process of steady Caesarization of the Church. Imperial values and mores competed with and overshadowed the newness of the Gospel and the radicalism of the Eucharist. Jesus' community of love and service became a pyramid of differential power, countering the Lord's stand". To illustrate his observations, Rayan cites the gospel passages pertaining to love, service, fellowship, equality, sacrifice, servanthood, etc., that gradually began to be watered down and conveniently forgotten. "In the process, the Eucharist moved out of people's homes to great Basilicas and Cathedrals; the emphasis shifted from its meal aspect to its sacrificial dimension; the table became the altar, and moved away from the people; the celebration became clergy-centred with people somewhat marginalized and forbidden to touch the sacred Bread and Cup. The vision of the Church as the Mystical Body of Christ got dimmed, and the dialectical relation between the Church and the Eucharist got obscured".

The Middle Ages were no better than Constantine Christianity: "Christian populations let society fall into a feudal mould, consisting of a few rich, powerful Lords and a mass of serfs controlled by the Lord. The Eucharist and the Our Father were muted and disallowed to have their say. The same could be said about the mercantile and capitalist eras that followed". In tracing the ups and downs of Christian Tradition, Rayan gives illuminating narratives that show the inseparable link between the celebration of the Eucharist and its demands for Christian living. For instance, when "Bartolomé de Casas—who arrived in 1502 in the West Indies as participant in and beneficiary of 'the blood and fire conquest of the Indians'—was gifted a batch of local slaves for his ordination in 1514—he discovered that the bread he was about to offer had been snatched from the poor … that to deprive the Indians of the fruit of their work was to murder them. He saw the relation (the contradiction) between the eucharist liturgy and the economic system of oppression. He saw the bread stained with blood." So also, "St. Francisco Solano, OFM, preached in Peru and Argentina in the 16th century. Once he was invited by some conquistadors to eat with them. He said the blessing, took a piece of bread, and squeezed it in his hands, and lo! blood began to ooze out of it. He then said, 'This is the blood of the Indians' and went to his convent without touching a mouthful, leaving the Europeans amazed and dismayed".

Rayan unearths scandalous inconsistencies between the eucharistic ideals and the daily living of Christians down through the centuries, worldwide, by raising probing questions which call for reflection and response: "How is it that people of the Eucharist and the Our Father have been ruthless imperialists, invaders, colonizers, slave traders, slave owners, exploiters and destroyers of civilizations the world over? Why do sharers in the Eucharist deprive the world's poor of land, food, freedom and dignity? How is it that they prefer pet dogs, liquor and cigarettes for a third part of humanity while the rest go hungry to bed? Why are dogs and bombs preferred to children?"

Rayan's critique of eucharistic belief and practice does not stop with bygone ages, but continues to our lifetime: "Vatican II has made change and reform possible. The only major reform has been the recognition of the people's right to worship in their own language, a right suppressed for centuries. But, recent Roman documents on the Eucharist do not seem to respect the right of the local Churches to be liturgically creative and to respond in faith to concrete situations as these evolve. The bureaux even demand that every local church submit to them its liturgical compositions and translations as if its faith were suspect while theirs is perfect, and as if they knew better than it does the local language, culture and concrete context". In this context, Rayan cautions about the reported saying of Pope Pius XI that the mission of the church is to get people to the Mass, as well as the statement of Pope Paul VI who said that the liturgy was not only the first subject treated in VC II but 'the first in intrinsic worth and in importance in the life of the church'. "This clearly is a church-centred, even a liturgy-centred, concept. and the perspective is dualistic. The church seems to see itself 'as collective subject of a sacred history' running parallel to or united to the world's secular history". Instead of a dualistic vision and a divorce between the sacred and the secular, Rayan insists on an inseparable marriage between liturgy and life, divine mystery and human history, the Eucharistic Body of Christ and the Cosmic-Ecclesial Body of Christ.

4. Eucharist as Energizer of Life: Rayan's Theology Today

With creative and constructively critical readings and interpretations of Scripture and Tradition, Rayan develops his current eucharistic theology, which, I think, is best explained in terms of the '*presences*' of the Eucharistic Lord in our midst, today. He accepts the popular pronouncement of Vatican II's *LG* 11 that: "The Eucharist is the source and summit of Christian life". However, this 'life' is something very concrete; and, the Eucharist can be called 'source of life' since: "Authentic liturgies spring from and lead to commitment and struggle for justice, freedom and human dignity. In a world that is essentially political, worship cannot be non-political and neutral. The only legitimate context of the Eucharist is an ecclesial community, solidarity with the efforts for the liberation of the oppressed, the dalits, women, fisher-folk, the landless, the bonded, the tribals, the handicapped." The joys and sorrows, the struggles and triumphs of all these should enter into liturgical and sacramental celebrations.

Let us briefly examine some of the '*presences*' that seem central to Rayan's eucharistic theology.

4.1. The Eucharistic Lord's Presence in the Lowly, the Lost, the Last

One of the striking aspects of Sam Rayan's eucharistic celebrations at Vidyajyoti College was his 'Introduction' that inevitably brought the celebrating community in spiritual solidarity with the lowly, the last and the least. He would usually begin the Mass by reading one of Rabindranath Tagore's poems, which would put the spotlight on the poor and bring to awareness the real focus of our worship: "*Leave this chanting and singing and telling of beads! Whom dost thou worship in this lonely dark corner of a temple with doors all shut? Open thine eyes and see thy God is not before thee! He is there where the tiller is tilling the hard ground and where the path-maker is breaking stones… Put off thy holy mantle and even like him come down on the dusty soil…Meet him and stand by him in toil and in sweat of thy brow*". Poems like this one, and others that Sam would read, frequently set the tone for worship. This would be followed up in the 'prayers of the faithful' where Rayan would set aside time for the community to mention societal concerns and historical events that were close at heart and required our reflection, prayers and committed interventions.

Rayan repeatedly reminds us that all eucharistic celebrations must be focused on the paschal mystery of our Lord, Jesus, which embraces the poor and the suffering in a very special way, today. "The Eucharist must be so celebrated as to help the community to deeper and stronger 'option for and solidarity with the poor and the oppressed in their struggle for justice', in their experience of the 'dark night of injustice, weariness, trials, torture, starvation and persecution'. This commitment to give the impoverished and the downtrodden a dignified life is in itself an experience of the death and resurrection of Jesus. It is a true encounter with the Paschal Mystery of Christ in the Eucharist. The struggle for justice itself becomes a celebration of the Eucharist".

4.2. The Eucharistic Lord's Presence as Reconciler and Unifier

Some years ago, when one of Rayan's interviewers inquired of him: "What is the 'central point' of the Eucharist?" he replied in two words: "unity and sharing".[3] No unity, no Eucharist. Unity always leads to sharing. "In the Eucharist we celebrate God's unifying presence. But how can we do that if our community is torn by injustice, discord and divisions? A community celebration of the Eucharist commits all Christians to struggle against everything that discriminates against and denigrates humanity… The Eucharist does away with all divisive categories in the community of faith—no rich, no poor, no Kannadigas, no Tamils… The celebration is the radical breaking down of all inequalities between people. The community is a community of friendship in which there is no rank and status… The Eucharist is the only historical context of human existence where the terms 'father', 'brother', etc., lose their biological exclusiveness, and reveal relationships of free and universal love". He adds: "Another corrective step demanded by the Eucharistic Communion is the abolition of caste hierarchy, preventing it from infecting the community of Jesus. The system comprises high, middle, and low castes and outcastes… If the Eucharist does not teach us to respect and welcome people irrespective of caste, culture, race, gender and status, we must realize that our participation in the Eucharist is defective, if not false".

The Eucharistic Lord, Jesus, is for Rayan a peacemaker and reconciler: "The Eucharist is communion with the Prince of Peace in whose Reign swords shall be beaten into ploughshares, in which the wolf will live with the lamb, and no hurt shall be done in all God's holy mountain" (Isa 2:4; 11:6-9). Calling for eucharistic oneness and hospitality not only in ecumenical circles but also within wider interfaith circles, Rayan supports Ched Meyer's proposal that, "Not only must the door be always open to the poor and the outcast, but non-Christians who do the work of justice and compassion must also be accepted". We seem a long way off from implementing these ideals in our Eucharist.

4.3. The Eucharistic Lord's Presence in His Word Related to Work and Life

The liturgy of the word is central to the Eucharist; for, Christ is present in His Word, read, reflected upon and responded to, by every member of the community. The idea of gathering around a table to be fed and nourished by Scripture is prominent in Rayan's thought. "The Eucharistic table could be restored to the people. People could gather around it, greet one another, pray together, listen to the word of God, meditate in silence, share their insights, discuss their problems and need, design ways to meet them and plan collaborative action for finer social, Christian living in deeper solidarity and love in the light of the word heard and in the warmth of the bread shared".

Rayan bemoans the present structure of the Mass of the Latin Rite that leaves so little by way of participation of the Eucharistic assembly. "Let the people be much more involved in the celebration that they are now: praying aloud for special intentions, naming needs and problems that call for immediate attention, sharing in dialogical homilies and bringing from their own land and labour the elements required for the Eucharist instead of using imported matter. And let no one presume to possess the power to forbid God's children to praise their Father with a resounding doxology".

4.4. Christ's Presence in the Cosmic 'Loaf of Bread' and in 'Bowls of Rice'

"Come, worship him with a loaf of bread; Come into his presence with a bowl of rice. Share out the rice and break the bread and hand it round and eat together in his company".[4] Among the prominent images that Rayan uses to capture the core of the Eucharist are certainly God's 'loaf of bread' and 'bowls of rice' referring to mother earth, her fecundity and her bounty. "The Eucharist is also a symbol of the earth which is a large loaf of bread baked by God over the fire of His Heart, to be broken among His children; not one of them is to be forgotten, overlooked or excluded. The Eucharistic table symbolizes the Earth-table God has lovingly and lavishly laid out for His family, with exquisite food and drink..... None of His children may be denied access to the table and not denied a decent share in this earth-bread." Here, one gets glimpses of Teilhard de Chardin's

'Cosmic Host': "The prophetic energy of Jesus is concentrated there [in the Eucharist], transforming everyone and everything in the cosmos into the Divine Milieu".

When Sam has presided over the eucharistic assembly at Vidyajyoti, Delhi, everyone has felt deeply drawn into the depth dimension of life. His words, gestures, prayers, pauses for silence, the little additions and personal phrases that punctuate prefaces and eucharistic prayers unfailingly call out the mystic, awaken the poet/artist/musician, and disturb the prophet dormant in each of the concelebrants and in the eucharistic community, at large. Consequently, on the one hand, one never loses sight of the bread, the loaf, the chapatti, the bowl of rice, the earth and the whole cosmic Communion, and, on the other, becomes aware of the injustice, selfishness and insensitivity of those who disgrace and disrupt this Holy Communion, ourselves included! The end-result is that every Eucharist leads to a heightened family/community consciousness where one feels that: "To celebrate the Eucharist worthily and meaningfully is to reorganize Christian communities on the model of a loving family – the family of God which together prays the Our Father and sees to it that the Father's gift of daily bread reaches every member of the family, every child of God in the locality".

4.5. The Lord's Presence in All His Priestly People

In his Eucharistic theology and through his personal practice, Rayan cautions us about the excessive clericalism that has crept into current celebrations. "There is a close unbreakable link between the Eucharist and the people. The Eucharist is the Bread Jesus gives for the life of the world (Jn 6:51). It is the body of Christ in 'mystery', and the people of faith are His 'mystical Body' (1 Cor 12:19-30). Saint Basil [330-379] reminds us that 'in ancient times the faithful, harassed by persecutions or living in solitude ... nourished themselves even daily receiving holy communion by their own hands when the priest or deacon was absent'. In a situation of persecution and danger, men and women developed a spirituality of equality, freedom and sharing, symbolized by and expressed in the Eucharistic meal. It was only later that 'the Eucharist and Christian spirituality began to be monopolized by the clergy and the monks." Coupled with a critique of clericalism is a questioning of the excessive focus on rigid rubrics, insistence on uniformity in liturgies, worldwide, the use of expensive and outlandish vestments for Mass, the payment of mass stipends and so on.

Urging us for a review of the marginal roles and responsibilities given to women in the eucharistic assembly, Rayan writes: "The community of Jesus is a 'Spiritual house' and a 'holy priesthood' to offer spiritual sacrifices to God through Jesus Christ'. They are 'a kingdom of priests', a 'holy nation' (1 Pet 2:5, 9; Cf. Rev 5:9-10). The Jesus-community is indeed the Body of Christ (Rom 12:3-5; 1 Cor 12-21; Eph 4:4-6). It is the Mystery of this Body and of this Royal Priesthood that the Eucharist represents. At this level there can be no discrimination on the basis of race or culture or status or gender—'for you are all one in Christ Jesus' (Gal 3:26-28)." He adds, "Despite the fact that women are deeply related to the mystical and sacramental Body of Christ, they have, for centuries, been excluded from priesthood and the responsibility concerning the Eucharist. Till recently they were even excluded from reading out the Scriptures during services, and from serving at the altar, and from distributing the Eucharistic bread. .... Concerning women, he [Jesus] took a radical stance. This therefore is one of the aspects in which the Eucharist has to be renewed today. Accepting women as equal persons before the Eucharist is a matter of justice and of fidelity to revelation".

5. Conclusion: Communion for Integral Liberation of All God's Children

It's impossible to condense Rayan's rich eucharistic theology within the confines of an article since, besides the articles that I've culled out insights and quotations from, he has written about, lectured on, and, most importantly, *lived out*, the Eucharist at many forums and in myriad forms over an exemplary life spanning over ninety years! Be that as it may, the greatest contribution of Sam is to see the Eucharist as "multidimensional". Like an expert embroiderer he weaves together many threads—religious, social, political, economic, aesthetic, poetic, mystical, familial, local, national, global, prophetic, priestly, pastoral, etc.—to bring to the Eucharist that richness and to evoke that response that Christ would've desired for all those who dare to be his disciples and build His Body.

The 'Holy Communion' Rayan dreams of and desires for all of Christ's sisters and brothers is not some sanctifying pill for personal solace or undisturbed contemplation of an uninvolved and isolated Christ, but a 'Cosmic Communion' made concrete in Christic unity, sharing, justice and commitment to struggles for building a "new heaven and a new earth". Like Pope Francis, who ceaselessly proposes 'horizons of hope' for Church and World, Samuel's theology is critical in order to construct, pointed in order to probe, and creative in order to build a Whole New Communion. In his words, "The Eucharist is a perennial energizer of Christian hope. The very purpose of the Eucharistic celebration is to enable us to have hope in an alternative community in which new human beings are born in Christ.... Every Eucharistic celebration is a prophetic call to live the Passover – passing through death to life – by transforming ourselves and our society in view of the Kingdom of God which is God's dream for humanity".

May we all, like Samuel Rayan, earnestly strive to build up this Whole, Holy Communion with our Lord Jesus, with the 'least' of all his sisters and brothers, and with Mother Earth, God's Great *Roti*, baked with the warmth of the Divine Heart!

Notes

1. See Rayan's articles entitled: "Worship in Spirit and Truth," and "The Eucharist Today," in Kurien Kunnumpuram (ed.), *The Selected Writings of Samuel Rayan, SJ, Vol. II, In Spirit and Truth: Indian Christian Reflections on Spirituality and Worship*, (Mumbai: St. Pauls, 2012), pp. 245-59 and 266-95, respectively.
2. See his "My Body for You," in *Body, Bread, Blood: Eucharistic Perspectives from the Indian Church*, ed. Francis Gonsalves (Delhi: Vidyajyoti & ISPCK, 2000), pp. 191-215.
3. See his interview in *Satyadeepam*, November 1-5, 2004, reprinted in Kunnumpuram (ed.), *The Selected Writings of Samuel Rayan, SJ, Vol. II*, pp. 296-305.
4. See the opening lines of his poetic work entitled "Worship Him with Bread and Rice," in K. Kunnumpuram (ed.), *The Selected Writings of Samuel Rayan, SJ, Vol. II*, pp. 260-5.

5

Mother Earth
A Spiritual Matter

Shalini Mulackal, pbvm

Introduction

I would like to begin this presentation by citing a few news items that came in *Times of India* (New Delhi) on 19 December, 2014. (1) The environment minister Prakash Javadekar informed the Rajya Sabha that 241 projects got environment clearance. Out of these 55 projects belong to Gujarat. All these projects got their clearance during the first six months of NDA rule. (2) India successfully tested the heaviest launch vehicle GSLV Mk- III weighing 630.5 tonnes, the heaviest rocket to be made by ISRO (Indian Space Research Organization). (3) Private and Chartered craft owned by corporate houses regularly ferry politicians. These *nethas* are accompanied by family, officials and corporate barons. (4) There is about 5.1 lakh shortfall of teachers in government schools in India. Millions of school children are growing up "functionally illiterate," unable to divide, subtract, or construct proper sentences even in the secondary school.[1]

After going through the five essays written by Fr. Samuel Rayan S. J. during the early 90s on ecology, nature and ecological crisis and other concerns related to planet earth, I felt that the above news items are somehow connected to the issue at hand. Even though environmental scientists and some theologians began to speak on these issues a couple of decades ago, the situation has not improved much. On the contrary, the ecological crisis is growing from bad to worse. Ecological issues are the burning issues even today. What has been predicted to happen a few decades back is already happening. For instance, we are already experiencing climate change, the impact of global warming and a gradual decline in the overall health of human beings, animals and plants. Our Mother earth is wounded beyond repair. Therefore, it is significant and relevant to study Rayan's contribution in this area besides his contribution in other areas of theology.

In order to have a clear understanding of his perspective on environment, ecology and planet earth, I thought of presenting his thoughts in four parts. The first part will deal with the context, how he perceives the ecological crisis and other related concerns. The second part will dwell on some of the factors he has identified as causing this problem. The third section will deal with his theological reflection on nature, earth, life, etc. In the fourth and final part we will identify some action plans he proposes in order to respond positively to this crisis.

I. The Context

As is obvious, the context of his theological reflection is the Earth and what is happening to it today. He identifies three major areas of concern which contradict the biblical and Christian view of the Earth and its mystery. These are (i) the commercialization of Earth, (ii) the global imbalance in land/population proportion, (iii) the ecological crisis.[2]

(i) The commercialization of Earth

Over the centuries, humans have made the Earth a market commodity for sale. This goes counter to God's intent and purpose as it is expressed in all primal societies. For instance, the Pacific Peoples have been reminding us that it is the land that possesses us, not we possess the land. Rayan brings this aspect very clear by citing what the Chief Seattle (Sealth) said in 1854:

> The great chief in Washington sends word that he wishes to buy our land... How can you buy or sell the sky, the warmth of the

> land? The idea is strange to us. If we do not own the freshness of the air and the sparkle of the water, how can you buy them? Every part of the Earth is sacred to my people. Every shining pine needle, every sandy shore, every mist in the dark woods, every clearing, every humming insect is holy in the memory and experience of my people.[3]

It is clear that the world-view shared by all primal societies affirms that the Earth is God's family; she is our Sister and Mother; our partner in life and worship; co-pilgrim with us. Its reduction to the state of a commodity is a fundamental aberration. Rayan identifies the vestiges of these early convictions enshrined in the Bible especially in the book of Leviticus where we find, "The Land shall not be sold in perpetuity, the land is mine" says God (Lev 25: 23).

He makes a historical analysis of how this world-view of the primal societies changed over the years. According to him the condition of merchandise began with the advent of class societies, and got perfected in ancient Rome and its laws, passed into feudal societies, became the ethos of capitalism, and spread over the world during the centuries of colonial subversion of ancient cultures. He asserts that the Earth needs liberation from this commercial culture and needs to get back its dignity as the sacrament of God and source of our shared life.[4]

(ii) The Global imbalance in land/population proportion

The second concern Rayan deals with is the global imbalance of land. A cursory glance at the world will make us aware of this injustice. Today West Europeans occupy North, Central, and South America, Australia, New Zealand, and parts of Africa. They made colonies of the whole of Asia except China, Japan and Thailand. The East Europeans (the Russians) on the other hand expanded their empire to the Pacific and the borders of China. Thus, the Europeans have appropriated to themselves a lot of space on the face of the earth and have built a world system aimed at perpetuating their domination for the benefit of Euro-American peoples.[5] It is also good to remember how the indigenous peoples of America, Australia and other countries were mercilessly wiped out by the White settlers.

This imbalance becomes very clear if we look at the following facts: The population of India, China, and Japan, comprising forty percent of the human race, is confined to ten percent of the Earth's surface, while Canada, Australia and New Zealand, with one percent of the world population occupy thirteen percent of land space. Brazil, slightly smaller than China, sustains a mere tenth of China's population. Bolivia which is three times the size of Japan has only five million persons as compared to Japan's one hundred and fifteen million. Bangladesh which is only half the size of New Zealand supports a population twenty-five times that of New Zealand.

This induced and unjust imbalance has racist dimensions as well. The different racial groups are allotted separate and unequal spaces in which they have to live.[6] Such a system is perpetuated by the present day immigration laws. For example, Australia advertises to get whites to settle there and will readily take 250,000 whites from Zimbabwe, but only grudgingly admit 25,000 Asians, and that too on condition that these have skills, education and financial backing. "All the under-populated countries- USA, USSR, Canada, Brazil, Argentina, Australia, New Zealand -- have immigration laws that discriminate against Asians".[7] This imbalance in the distribution of population has resulted largely during the European expansion that took place from 1500 to 1950 wherein the Europeans occupied most of the habitable parts of the Earth.

(iii) The ecological crisis

Among the concerns raised so far, the ecological crisis is better known and spoken about. Rayan deals with this in three of his essays. He says,

> ...our development processes and technological practices have become a threat to life on this earth and to the earth itself. The threat is constituted by large scale devastation of the environment, damage to water, air and soil, and to genetic diversity; by the destruction of rain forests, extensive soil erosion and desertification; by massive use of pesticides, insecticides and herbicides which deplete and poison the soil; by the squander and destruction of sea resources, mangrove swamps and coral reefs; by anarchic and profligate industrial

> production and over-consumption as well as overuse and waste of nature's scarce and non-renewable treasures; by the ambiguities of nuclear technology, the horrors of nuclear weaponry and the hazards of radioactive waste, the disposal of which is already a major intractable problem...[8]

He further describes the crisis in terms of acid rains, death of lakes and rivers, extinction of species; the depletion of the ozone layer, the greenhouse effect; diseases and death from chemically and radioactively contaminated food, air and water.[9] He also describes some of the major disasters that have come upon humanity in the name of development like Minamata in Japan (1953), Seveso in Italy (1976), Three Miles Island in U.S. A. (1979), Bhopal, India (1984), Chernobyl, Ukraine, USSR (1986), and Sandoz, Switzerland (1986).[10]

Today's ecological crisis is not only a question of Christian or other viewpoints and theologies but it is a question of human survival on this planet. Nuclear, radioactive and other fatally toxic wastes which are being dumped in the oceans or on islands and continents of the poor and the powerless seem to be the most life threatening signs of the crisis.

Talking about pollution as one of the concerns, Rayan does not limit pollution to physical level alone. He takes a broader view of the environment which includes the social, economic, political, cultural and the moral spheres. He says that the cultural environment, the political atmosphere, the social ecosystem can also get polluted and poisoned. Contaminated and degraded, they can cause disease and death for the earth, and everything it holds.[11] The four types of pollutions he mentions are:

A) Physical pollution

Physical pollution includes the poisoning and debilitating, followed by disease and death, of the earth, air and water, and of living things that depend on them. Toxic chemicals used excessively as pesticides, sprays, additives and fertilizers, undermine the health and vigour of the soil and cause diseases directly through inhalation and contact, and indirectly through consumption of contaminated plants and animals. Modern society has produced some 70,000 kinds of chemicals. Some of these are known to cause a serious threat to life. The ozone layer is seriously damaged by chlorofluorocarbons, used as refrigerants, propellants and solvents. The greenhouse effect is on the increase since a large amount of carbon dioxide is released into the atmosphere through the burning of fossil fuels like oil, gas and coal.[12]

B) Social pollution

Social pollution manifests itself in the existence of massive poverty and destitution with their degrading and destructive consequences together with the enormous wealth and affluence of the rich who indulge in unbridled consumerism. The gap between the rich and the poor is increasing day by day. For instance, the 'developed countries, with 26 per cent of the world's population, consume 80 per cent of the world's paper, metals, and commercial energy, and eat fully half of the world's food, and feed a quarter of the world's grain to their animals. At the same time millions of people elsewhere are chronically undernourished, and a quarter of a million young children die every week.

Other major aspects of social pollution are the colossal military spending; the growing debt crisis and the debt trap in which the poorer nations get caught; human rights violations; the death of children to the tune of 1500 every hour from hunger-related causes; the attempt of advanced countries to dump toxic and hazardous waste, both chemical and nuclear, on southern lands or Pacific islands where the poor live; the maintenance of racism and caste divisions; sexist oppression and marginalization of women; and the mounting nuclear threat.[13]

In our country, social pollution may be illustrated by untouchability, caste fragmentation of society, organized prostitution, system of child and bonded labour, the depressed conditions of women and communal conflicts.[14]

C) Cultural pollution

First and foremost, cultural pollution is represented by the large-scale illiteracy of the masses. This is the result of the indifference of the ruling block towards the ruled block. The colonial and elitist devaluation of people's cultures, experiences, achievements and their wisdom too is an indication of cultural pollution. Today under the free market economy, the corporate and economically powerful are pushing their world-view and seek to impose their ideologies and priorities on weaker sections of society and poorer nations of the world. Western technological culture is at the moment rampant; in the face of it, the diversity of local cultures tends to fade, is overwhelmed, and may eventually disappear. In the process, we may even lose much of life's poetry and some of the finest creations of the human spirit like old tribal ideals of life in close communion with one another and with nature.[15]

D) Spiritual and moral pollution

Finally the spiritual and moral pollution erupts as greed, competition and consumerism. These are often held up as ideals that humans can aspire to. Its contamination becomes fatal and dehumanizing. People who are under these pollutants suffer from short-sightedness. They look for immediate gain and overuse scarce resources, some of which are non-renewable and irreplaceable. They are unmindful of the long-term effects for the earth and for future generations of humans and other living beings. This scheme of things degrades everyone and everything to the level of tools for market commodities.[16] Moreover, degradation of moral environment is seen in the cult of violence, contempt and discrimination against the poor, the rural population, the dalits, the tribals, systematic killing of emergent tribal leadership, malpractices in public life and the distortion of political processes.[17]

II. Analysis of the Context

Going through the above it is clear that our life and the life of the earth are in peril. Before taking any action to improve the situation it is important that we understand what causes the present ecological crisis and the various pollutions as enumerated above. Rayan identifies seven causes for the present degraded situation of our planet. Some of these include biblical religion, science and technology, capitalism, etc.

1. The Christian Religion

The Christian religion has contributed towards the ruthless exploitation of nature. According to the Genesis account of creation stories, human beings are given dominion over the rest of creation, and all things are put under their feet (Gen 1; Ps 8). The literal interpretations of these texts have given rise to an anthropocentric philosophy of the human person, according to which the human person is superior to all other creatures. Nature exists to serve his/her needs. Since, Christianity preached an 'other-worldly' salvation for many centuries, it has desacralised nature in the process. This has paved the way for the brutal exploitation of nature leading to the present crisis. God too is imaged as transcendent and away from this world. Moreover, Christianity fused with Greek philosophy and rationality saw nature as a mechanical system for manipulation.

2. Science and Technology

Science and technology are the major cause of environmental destruction. Scholars like Claude Alvares, Shiv Visvanathan, Vandana Shiva and Ashis Nandi point to this fact. For instance, Alvares says,

> Pollution is the first indicator that modern science ill fits nature. And because the scientific remedies suggested for pollution are all technological fixes, we arrive at a notion of circular-science...In cases like radioactive wastes, even the talk of technological fixes is abandoned for all that has been recommended by science are sophisticated means of dumping the problem on future generations.[18]

According to Vandana Shiva, the Reductionist science, though it presents itself to be the saviour of the ecosystem, is in peril too grave to be ignored. There is nothing more ironical than the claim of the destroyer to be the saviour.[19] Claude Alvares argues that rationalist, one-dimensional, abstract "science and technology constitute two major oppressions of our time," and that the scientific method itself has become "anti- rational, culturally and socially oppressive, ecocidal and anti-life".[20]

3. The Ideology of Development

The ideology of development is another major factor for environmental degradation. It is linked to science and technology and also to the state. In the name of development ordinary citizens are asked to sacrifice even the means of their livelihood. In the words of Samuel,

> In its name forests are destroyed, toxic wastes are released into river and sea, nuclear reactors are multiplied, enormous dams are built, all against the peoples' will, disregarding their real interests, evicting them from ancestral land, disrupting the total texture of their life and culture, crushing their spirit and letting them wither and perish, all this is done at great cost to the state and health risk to the population.[21]

4. The Modern State

Another contributing factor comes from the modern State. The State too acts as an ecocidal agent with its commitment to total development as defined by rationalist science and colonial technology. In the name of development, the State bulldozes peoples and cultures into technological uniformity and conformity and uses the police, the gun, and torture to compel the submission of those who stand against it. According to Nandi,

> Science has become a new reason of State, the State and its various arms can kill, maim or exploit in the name of science. Science in turn…can inflict violence in the name of national security or development and increasingly under its own flag and for its own sake.[22]

5. Capitalism

The above mentioned are not independent factors, nor are they ecocidal, totalitarian, destructive and terroristic by nature. They have become such because they are historically the products and tools of the global economic system called capitalism. While the mercantile phase of capitalism developed through world conquest and subsequent mass destruction of people and their cultures, its industrial phase saw ecological deterioration and threat to life.

The capitalist system needs for its survival ever-expanding production and consumption, and ever larger profit and power. It is the competition between insatiable capitalist appetites that gave birth to the modern science and technology, and shaped the modern State. These are not marked by concern for human life, dignity, liberty or creativity, but by the cult of commodity and consumerism. The entire system is shortsighted. Often the long-view of economic and human costs is not taken into consideration. Alvares observes that:

> Diseases caused by polluted water, the victim's medical bills, the loss of cattle or sheep, the decline in agricultural productivity, the overall reduced quality of life - none of these costs figure in profit-and-loss accounts or business theories.[23]

6. Imperialism

Samuel considers all the above factors as instruments in the hands of imperialism which he sees as the ultimate source of pollution both physical and social. It is a pervasive system of control in the social, economic, political, cultural and military spheres. It concentrates power in the hands of a small group and disregards the priorities and well-being of the people as a whole. Its international economic, political and military policies are implemented through repressive national governments and corporate structures.[24]

7. Loss of a sense of the Sacred

Samuel identifies the lossof a sense of the sacred as the profoundest cause of today's ecological crisis. Because of this loss, nature is seen as a mere mechanism and an object to be conquered with no sense of nature's dignity, mystery or depth-relationship to life, to the human reality and to the Divine. The so-called civilized and modern people have lost the sensibilities of the peasants, artisans, villagers who sense the Divine in nature and consider nature as sacred. According to Shiv Vishvanathan, "rationalist science has no conception of the sacred. As a result, ecology becomes a managerial science, mopping up the ecological degradation after industrialization, rather than a cosmic view of the world".[25]

III. Theological Reflection

In the five essays which Rayan wrote on the issue at hand, what is outstanding is his faith based reflection on the present-day crisis wherein the focus is our planet earth. He gives an apt reflection on the earth keeping in mind the way the earth is wrongly perceived as an object to be controlled, manipulated and used in today's globalized capital system. Through his reflection he also tries to inculcate a sense of the sacred in creation.

1. The Earth belongs to God

In his long reflection on this theme,[26] Rayan brings home the message that the Earth and all that it contains belong to God. This is the jubilant proclamation of Psalm 24. This faith confession keeps recurring in the Bible: in the book of Psalms, in the Prophets, and in the Torah.[27] The land is the Lord's (Lev 25:23) and so are the gold and the silver; its wine and its grain; its wool and its flax (Hos 2:10-11). God called the earth into being and loved it into existence. God fashions it and names it. The word, Earth is mentioned more than fifteen times in the opening chapter of the Bible.[28]

The Earth is central to God's purposes. It is significantly placed at the heart of the prayer which Jesus taught his disciples, "Your will be done on Earth..." Great things should happen on the Earth. The Kingdom of God should happen to it. Thus, transformed, the new Earth sums up, in the closing chapters of the Bible, the outcome of a long history of God's saving action and passionate concern.[29]

The Earth is God's cherished bride from the beginning till the end when she will be "coming down from God, out of heaven, adorned and prepared for her husband (Rev 21:2). God establishes the Earth in justice. It is also the foundation of God's own throne and reign (Is 54:13; Ps 89:15). God warms, renews, and refreshes daily and seasonally God's Earth-bride. God waters the land and cares for it, enriching it with natural resources; God drenches the furrow, levels the ridges, softens the soil with showers and blesses it with crops. It is God who turns the deserts into pasture land and clothes the hills with gladness...This is the way God deals with Her precious Earth (Ps 65:7-14).[30]

God makes His Earth-Bride inexhaustibly fecund. At God's command the Earth brought forth every kind of plant and tree, and cattle and reptile and wild animal. Then God's Breath and bits of Earth united to give birth to human beings.

The Earth is God's betrothed. God has covenanted her to Himself. The covenant covers Noah and his posterity and every living creature on the earth (Gen 8:21-22; 9:8-12). The pact is that never again will the Earth be cursed because of the evil-doing of humans. God's rainbow set in the clouds is the sign and sacrament of the covenant, the everlasting covenant between God and the Earth (Gen 9:13-17).

The Earth is the Lord's, for it is the Lord's self-manifestation. It is the place for God's ongoing revelation, the unfolding of the word of God in which God's thoughts and heart are disclosed and much of God's attitude to us is conveyed. The Earth then is a revealed Word of God; always alive and fresh. The earth and everything in it are the loving and saving words addressed to us. "God says it all with rainbows and flowers, with rice and wheat, and the glory of sunsets, the charm of children, the beauty of brides, the innovativeness of youth and the prayers of trees, the mystery of silent things and the joy of friendship".[31]

The Earth is the Lord's Table laid with care for God's children. "A feast of rich food and choice of wines" (Is 25: 6). God lays this table with flowers every morning. The Earth is also God's Body, God's Bodiliness. God becomes seeable and touchable. In this Earthiness of the Divine, we may encounter God. We have no way to take the touch of God but through the touch of the Earth.[32]

As mentioned above, the Earth is the Lord's in many ways. It is God's creation and self-expression, God's word and image, symbol of His presence and power, of Her beauty, love and strength. The Earth is where God abides and comes to meet us. The Earth is sacred.

2. The Earth is Our Home

Psalm 115 speaks about the heaven as belonging to the Lord and the Earth as given by God to human beings. According to the Bible and the teaching of many early Christian thinkers, the Earth and its resources are God's gift for the whole of human family. It is meant to serve the need and creative possibilities of all God's children. Earth is our common home. It is a place of creative engagement. The earth is our Mother, the abiding source of life for all living things.

Humans enter into multiple relationships with the Earth as it is interior to our existence. Our self-understanding and all our mental and physical activities and movements are bound up with these relationships. Ultimately we are Earth-bits of earth which have come to develop a mysterious interiority, the capacity for reflexive thought and for freedom and love. The Earth is our common Body. We share this Body not only with all humans but also with all living things and with the entire cosmos. That's why mystics like St. Francis of Assisi felt a sense of equality and shared dignity within a cosmic Sisterhood/Brotherhood which gave birth to the well-known canticle of Francis of Assisi.[33]

The relation between humans and the Earth needs to be one of respect and love. To the Aboriginal Tribes of Australia and to Tribal peoples everywhere, Earth is Earth Mother. This is true for many Asians as well. If Earth is our Mother how do we relate with her? The Earth and the things it holds are not to be taken for granted, nor treated as dead; nor merely 'used'. They deserve to be recognized, acknowledged and respected.

Earth is matter. God made matter and gave it to people, used it in revelation and redemption. The Earth deserves a greater theological respect. Earth is indeed a theological category. In Jesus Christ the Earth does become the Face of God and the place of saving encounter. In His resurrection, the Earth, that has seen and borne so much death and dying, finally transcends death and attains abounding and endless life. In Jesus Christ the Earth has become supremely honoured.[34]

3. The Earth is precious to God and Humans

The Bible bear witness to the preciousness of the Earth and all Tribal traditions as well. It was God who first appreciated the worth and the wonder of the Earth in the opening chapter of the Bible. "God saw that it was good" (Gen 1:10, 12, 16-18, 20-21, 24-25, 31). The Earth is precious in itself. It is unique and one of its kind. It is beautiful beyond words and it invites us to its contemplation.[35] The

Chief Seattle bore witness to tribal understanding of the preciousness of the Earth about a century and a half ago:

> Every part of this Earth is sacred to my people. Every shining pine needle, every sandy shore, every mist in the dark woods, every clearing, and every humming insect is holy in the memory and experience of my people... Our dead never forget this beautiful Earth, for it is the Mother of the Red man. We are part of the Earth and it is a part of us. The perfumed flowers are our sisters...the ashes of our fathers are sacred. Their graves are holy ground, and so these hills, these trees, this portion of the earth is consecrated to us... The air is precious to the Red Man, for all things share the same breath; the air shares it's (the land's) spirit with all the life it supports. Our God is the same God. This earth is precious to Him.[36]

The Earth is a symbol that sums up all the gifts of life and love which God shares with humankind and all living beings. Therefore, it is necessary to prevent the grabbing and monopolizing the Earth and its resources by individuals and groups. They must remain common to humankind. Early Christian thinkers therefore considered the concentration of land in a few hands as unjust and contrary to the Earth's God-given nature and purpose. It must always remain a Eucharistic Mystery: the Bread of God, the Body of God given for the life of the world.[37]

4. Theology of Nature[38]

Besides the above reflection on the Earth, Rayan makes further reflection on nature making use of some poets in addition to the texts of the Bible. He finds the theology of nature implicit in some poetic intuitions. He gives us the clue how to harvest the sense of the sacred from the biblical approach to nature. He also reflects on the Christic dimensions of the universe and how to look at nature from the side of the new-creative Spirit and her transformative action.

A. The Poets

Rabindranath Tagore (1861-1941) sang: "Silence, my soul, these trees are prayers". The trees are the earth's prayers, the lifting up of her spirit to God, her hands raised in worship. The trees are Earth dancing out her praise and thanks...

Richard Crashaw (1612-1650), contemplating on the wedding at Cana (John 2), sings of how "the chaste waters saw her Lord and blushed". To the poets, nature is not dead mechanism; it is alive and responsive: responsive to one another and to God. There is a deep, secret, intimate closeness and exchange, understanding and affection between the Creator and every one of his creatures.[39]

Hildegarde of Bingen (1098-1178) describes the mutual love that binds nature and her Maker.

As the Creator loves his creation
So creation loves the Creator.
With the love of the Creator:
The entire world has been embraced by his kiss.[40]

Reflecting on the above poem Rayan says, "God's kiss is on every stone and grain of sand, on every leaf and bee and bird, on every ray of light and speck of dust, on the forehead of every child, woman and man, and on the forehead of the earth".[41]

Elizabeth Browning (1806-1861) makes a cosmic translation of the Moses' experience of the burning bush and reminds us that every bush is aflame with God; he who sees takes off his shoes; the rest sit and pick blackberries. This is a devastating picture of those who have lost the sense of the Sacred.

William Blake (1757-1827) invites us to educate our hearts and eyes

To see a world in a grain of sand,
and a heaven in a wild flower;
Hold infinity in the palm of your hand,
and eternity in an hour (Auguries of Innocence)

For Blake, the smallest and lowliest particles of the cosmos represent the whole of the universe. They symbolize, signify and carry in their heart, in some mysterious fashion, realities which are ultimate, heavenly, infinite and eternal.

The Poets of both East and West perceive nature as a mystery. They experience nature as a variegated liturgy in which all are invited to join in.[42]

B. Biblical Perspectives

1. The perspective of creation

The Earth is presented in the Bible as something God loves and cares for, and adorns and enriches and invites us to be co-creators with himself (Gen 1; Ps 65, 104; Job 38- 41). As God's creature nature has a dignity of her own, which ought to be recognized.

In the biblical view nature is something God is doing, loving into existence and calling by name (Gen 1). A powerful and beautiful description of God's affectionate relationship to earth and sea, star and cloud, rain and thunder, mountain goats and wild donkeys and sea monsters can be found in Job 38-41. Not everything in nature is for humans' use or humans' manipulations. Much is there to be contemplated and admired.

Bible sees nature as God's self-revelation and self-witnessing. Not only do the heavens declare the glory of God; but the whole created world makes visible what can be known about God's deity and power (Rom 1: 19- 20). Through nature God is saying something to us. Nature therefore is a word of God making faith encounter possible for us.[43]

According to philosophers, nature as creation is something of God, and is somehow in God. Creation is a participation in the Divine. In that measure and manner nature is sacred. It has in it a touch of the Divine. In this sense "this universe is pervaded by the Lord" (*iisaavaasyam idam sarvam*). Not only God is in everything, but everything is in God. It is in him that we and all creation live and move and exist (Acts 17:28; also Gita 6. 30-31).

The earth is the primordial sacrament of God. She resembles God in many ways: we come from her and return to her; she is the ground of our existence and the rock of our life; she is the giver of bread and breath and is, like God, endlessly resourceful. She is never far from us.

The Bible also views the earth as somebody God has covenanted and betrothed to himself in everlasting love (Gen 9). All creation, the entire nature, stands clothed in the holiness and tenderness of God's covenant.[44]

2. Christic Dimensions[45]

A fundamental confession of Christian faith is that all creation exists in, through and for Christ (Col 1:15-17; Jn 1:3, 18; Heb 1:2). A profound re-interpretation and deepening of the biblical tradition of creation is found here. This re-interpretation brings creation and redemption together in the body of Christ. The two are inseparable: creation is the beginning of salvation, the first divine act. From the beginning creation is planted and rooted in Christ. Nature therefore is radically Christic. In Christ nature is God's child.

Nature is of the family of God because it comes from God, is rooted and held together in Christ. The whole creation is nourished along with humans at the table of God's heart. Therefore, we share a brotherly/sisterly relationship with nature as Francis of Assisi shows us in his Canticle of Brother Sun. We belong together as one family. We are to love one another and pray together. They invite us to join in their cosmic liturgy and we invite them to be with us to praise the name of the Lord (Ps 148; Dan 3:57-82).

Christ in his teaching and action bans every kind of oppressive power and domination. Every sort of lording over including lording over nature is prohibited. In the Kingdom proclaimed by Christ, the first shall be last and the servant of all. If we humans have primacy over nature, we will realize it in service to nature and in the defense of its integrity and beauty. The Christian call is to serve, even to serve nature in its needs, promises and possibilities (Cf. Jn 13; Mk 10).

Moreover, in the incarnation the material universe's evolutionary pilgrimage attains the unexpected culmination and fulfillment. In Christ all matter and all its forms and processes have been drawn into the sphere of the Divine and endowed with a new sanctity and dignity. All matter is sister to the Body of Christ. The whole of Nature is the Mother of the Son of God. Ronald Rolheiser says, "The real trump card of Christianity is not just that we believe in God. The mystery we are about is much more than that: It's that the material and the spiritual coexist. It's the mystery of the Incarnation".

The parables of Jesus reveal nature as symbolic embodiments of the mystery of the Reign of God. For instance, the paschal mystery, the paradigm of death-unto-life, is symbolized in the grain of wheat which has to fall and die in order to give a rich harvest (Jn 12:24).

Every seed dies to rise; the *agarbathi* burns to release its fragrance; the day dies to give way to a new day. There is a profound affinity between Christ and nature. It is interior to his life and spirituality and is the language of his revelation (Matt 5:23, 25-27; 6:26f; Lk 21:29, 12:54-55; Jn 15:12-24).

The passion of Christ continues when the earth is being stripped and tortured. Humiliated and crucified, both of them are victims of a criminal assault on the part of power and greed. To be disciples of Jesus is to stand with him in resisting the destruction of the little ones of nature and of the small people. To have faith is to work for the re-greening of the earth and the uprise of the oppressed. Fishes and birds die, and rivers languish, the whole creation groans, and grieve with Mary at the foot of the cross. Though we grieve and groan, we do not give up hope; the earth too does not despair. She clings to life and protects it. She nurses in her heart the hope of a cleaner, greener and saner tomorrow. In the midst of environmental decadence and the sufferings of the poor, the earth stands on tiptoe straining to catch a glimpse of the newness and the freedom and the life that is coming over the horizon (Rom 8:18-24).

3. Spirit's Transformative Actions[46]

The Ruah of God that moved over the primal waters has been understood as a symbol of the Spirit of God who presides over creation and the emergence of life. The Creed refers to the Spirit as Lord and Life-Giver, the life imparting Power and Energy of God. All the beginnings, all fresh stirrings of life in particular, all creativity and development, all lushness and blossoming is associated with and attributed to the action of the Holy Spirit.

Our Christian faith enables us to discern the work of the Spirit wherever life starts, or creation is renewed, or baby leaps in the womb and joy throbs in the heart of man/woman, beast, sea or tree (Ps 103; Lk 1:10, 11) or wherever seed sprouts, but bursts into blossom or fragrance wafts in the air; where tenderness wells up in motherly breasts and compassion floods life as waters cover the sea.

Prophet Isaiah tells us that Israel's faithlessness grieves the Holy Spirit of God; and Paul pleads with Christians not to grieve God's Holy Spirit. The Spirit grieves whenever she sees her beloved people destroy themselves or defile her dear earth (Is 63:10; Eph 4: 30). The ravages suffered by the earth, the diseases and death caused by industrial poisons, and the social pollution of dire poverty produced by our economic system are the grief of the Spirit.

The Spirit also works to befriend us and bring about a cosmic reconciliation of people with people and with the earth and with God in the Body of Christ which was broken in order to break down dividing walls (Eph 1:10, 2, 4; 2 Cor 5). The Spirit is pleading with us to let ourselves be befriended by God and by nature. Nature itself is pleading with us through the eroded soil and the dying rivers not to grieve the gentle Spirit of God but to collaborate with her to green the earth, to open the buds, to create the beautiful, both physical and social, to enhance life and make the joy of God fill the earth and the justice of God flow like a river.

The Spirit is the supreme Gift of God and every gift is also a task; we receive in order to rear, develop and help to flower and fruit. The Spirit is the power energizing the whole process. She new-creates and transforms. Nature like all other blessings is a gift and a task. Nature is not only to be contemplated and thanked for; it is also there to be transformed. Wood and stone can, through human mediation, embody and express the human spirit, human thoughts, feelings and fantasies, and the human sense of the beautiful, the tragic, the celebrant, even as they already are embodiments and symbols of the thought and spirit and fantasy of the Divine. Earthly realities can enter more closely into and participate in human relationships, in human search for truth and human endeavours to make this planet homier, more humane, and more revelative of the grace and glory of God.

4. Theology of Life

Rayan is convinced that a theology of the earth is best set within a theology of life. He identifies three factors namely, a new awareness, a new perspective and a new lifestyle within which a theology of life can grow. In order to get this new awareness we need to ask certain questions and try to answer them honestly. Rayan poses a number of questions: What does it mean to be a human being along with other human beings and to live among millions of other living things and to share the earth with them? What does it mean to be genuinely happy?

For Rayan, humanness does not consist in the endless production of goods and their consumption and the maximization of profit and power. But it consists in conviviality. It means living together and giving life to one another. It means sharing the sun, air and the earth with all living beings. Humanness consists in solidarity with the whole of creation, ensuring that the basic needs of everyone are met. It means that everyone has a share in the existing resources and opportunities to develop their creativity and giftedness. It consists in building and becoming a community of women and men walking, working and celebrating together. Only such togetherness can constitute happiness.[47]

We also need to develop a new perspective so as to look at nature as a mystery. Nature is something beyond our comprehension, awe-inspiring, unfathomable in its wisdom and love. It is a mystery because it is a sacrament of God's presence and love. It is a life giving Eucharistic reality. It is God's temple, a place where we encounter God. Besides being a mystery, everything that exists in nature constitutes the Web of life. There is interconnectivity and interdependence between humans, plants, animals and the elements. It is an organic community. Its resources are meant for all women and men and for all other living beings.

A fourth dimension of this new perspective consists in the recognition of the rights of all people including generations yet to be born, as well as of all creatures other than human. In the words of Rayan, "The right of all to be, to grow, to act and to create, each according to its own inner dynamism; their right to clean air, water, earth and light, to space, freedom, affection and respect; and to everything that would enable them to be fully themselves and to come to completion".[48]

The third factor that would enhance the theology of life is the adoption of a new lifestyle. It calls us to critique and challenge the super-affluent and over-consumerist and wasteful ways of living adopted by the rich nations and some sectors of the population in most countries. According to Rayan, "A spiritual and theological approach to life can enable us to live free of consumerist fetters, to travel light, squander less, spare more for sharing; and multiply compassion, love and care; and make life a thing of joy and celebration".[49]

Rayan sees the Bible as a book of life. It contains God's life-giving acts. Th Bible tells us that it is God who initiated life, accompanied its growth and development against all forces of death. In Jesus Christ God enters the world in a unique way so that all may have life. Jesus set aside life negating and life restricting religious traditions in order to heal and create space for life. He goes beyond the conventions of asceticism and fasting so as to defend and encourage life's spontaneity and celebration. Thus, he brings hope to the poor, healing to the sick and life to the dead.[50]

IV. Action Response

What response one needs to make in the face of the overwhelming scale of ecological destruction? What response one needs to give in order to bring back the sacredness of the Earth and give back to her the dignity and respect that is duly hers? Rayan proposes a few action plans. He says, "To meet the planetary crisis we need (among other things) a different kind of relationship to nature, a different view of the earth, a different perspective of its meaning for and before God, a different estimate of nature's role in the salvation of the world and an adequate vision of the destiny of the cosmos".[51]

1. A call to Conversion

Spiritual writers and others have been calling all to conversion. They demand that we pause to rethink and refeel our attitude towards the Earth. We need to shed our "orthodox Christian arrogance" towards God's creation. Balasuriya reminds us that "to want to dominate the Earth without respect for its own laws, needs, rhythms, and limits is clear proof of a lack of love of God, the author of nature".[52]

We need to develop a respectful concern for the Earth and the nature around us. A poetic approach to nature must balance and correct the reductionist scientific-technological approach. Like Jesus we need to learn how to look at the flowers and contemplate the birds and encounter the Mystery. Like Francis of Assisi, we need to recognize the equality of all creatures and the sisterhood/brotherhood which integrates all women and men, sun and moon, water and fire, into a single rainbow reality. We need to develop a feel for the mystery of life in all its forms and for the mystery of the Earth as the Bearer of Life. We need to recognize ever more deeply that this mystery is bound up with the Ultimate Mystery, the Womb of all reality.

2. Re-reading the Bible[53]

Since the interpretation of Gen 1 has contributed much towards the ecological crisis, Rayan strongly feels that we need to go back to the Bible and re-read and interpret the Bible. He says that the biblical view of nature and nature's relation to human is not confined to nor exhausted by the single Genesis word about dominion. There is much more and much else in the Bible.

3. Re-Allocation of land

A planned and peaceful re-allocation of land to people is a basic necessity… this should be on the world agenda. This will decrease pollution and waste.

Concluding Remarks

There is no doubt that Fr. Samuel Rayan has done an excellent work on this topic of ecological crisis. Even though most of his articles have been written more than a decade ago, his ideas are still relevant and significant. He was much ahead of his time in his reflection on issues concerning ecological and environmental crisis. His ideas regarding pollution go much beyond the physical to include other forms of pollution. He has analyzed the causes of the present ecological concern well and in detail. His use of poetic language and theological depth are admirable. However he has not spelt out the concrete ways by which individuals and communities needs to respond to this crisis.

All of us are aware of the seriousness of ecological crisis we are facing today. But we are not ready to take steps that would counter today's consumer culture. For fear of losing our comfort and convenience we continue to lead a lifestyle that is destroying our Earth. Fr. Samuel Rayan's reflection is putting a challenge before each one of us. What steps can I take in order to make our Earth greener and healthier? How can I restore her lost dignity and glory?

Notes

1. See *Times of India*, New Delhi, 19Dec. 2014.
2. See Samuel Rayan, "The Earth is the Lord's," in Kurien Kunnumpuram, SJ(ed.),*Collected Writings of Samuel Rayan SJ, Vol. I: Nature, Woman and the Church,* Delhi: ISPCK, 2013, pp. 3-23 at p. 6.
3. *Ibid.*
4. *Ibid.*, p. 17.
5. See Tissa Balasuriya, *Planetary Theology*, New York: Orbis books, 1984, pp. 24-25, as referred by Samuel Rayan, "The Earth is the Lord's," p.18.
6. The yellow peoples have China, Japan, and the adjacent islands. The Blacks have Africa. The Brown people are allotted India, Pakistan, and South East Asia. The rest of the world is largely reserved for Whites. See Balasuriya, pp. 28-29 and Rayan, p. 18.
7. *Ibid.*, pp. 26, 94 and Rayan, p. 18.
8. Samuel Rayan SJ, "Ecology and Theology: A theology of Nature, a theology of Life," in *Collected Writings of Samuel Rayan, SJ, Nature, Woman and the Church*, pp. 46-77 at 46.
9. *Ibid.*, p. 47.
10. Steve Ellsworth, *A Dictionary of the Environment. A Practical Guide to Today's Most Important Environmental Issues*, London: Paladin Crafton Books, 1990, as quoted by Samuel Rayan, "Ecology and Theology: A theology of Nature, a theology of Life," pp. 47-48.
11. See Samuel Rayan SJ, "Seek First God's Kingdom and His Justice," in *Collected Writings of Samuel Rayan, SJ, Nature, Woman and the Church*, pp.37-45 at 39.
12. See Samuel Rayan SJ, "Theological Perspectives on the Environmental Crisis," in Collected Writings of Samuel Rayan, SJ, *Nature, Woman and the Church*, Vol. 1, edited by Kurien Kunnumpuram SJ, Delhi: ISPCK, 2013, pp. 78-97 at 80-81.
13. *Ibid.*, p. 82.
14. See Samuel Rayan SJ, "Seek First God's Kingdom and His Justice," p. 39.
15. See Samuel Rayan SJ, "Theological Perspectives on the Environmental Crisis," p. 83.
16. *Ibid.*
17. See Samuel Rayan SJ, "Seek First God's Kingdom and His Justice," p. 39.
18. Claude Alvares, "Science, Colonialism and Violence: A Luddite View" in Ashis Nandi (ed.*), Science, Hegemony and Violence.A Requiem for Modernity*. Delhi: Oxford University Press, 1988, p. 103. As quoted by Samuel Rayan SJ, in "Ecology and Theology: A theology of Nature, a theology of Life," p. 49.
19. See Vandana Shiva, "Reductionist Science as Epistemological Violence" in A.Nandi (ed.), *Science, Hegemony and Violence.A Requiem for Modernity*,

p. 119. As quoted by Samuel Rayan SJ, in "Ecology and Theology: A theology of Nature, a theology of Life," p. 49.

20. Claude Alvares, "Science, Colonialism and Violence: A Luddite View," pp. 92-93. As quoted by Samuel Rayan SJ, in "Ecology and Theology: A theology of Nature, a theology of Life," p. 50.
21. Samuel Rayan SJ, in "Ecology and Theology," p. 50.
22. Ashis Nandi, "Introduction: Science as a Reason of State" in Ashis Nandi (ed.), *Science, Hegemony and Violence.* 10. As quoted by Samuel Rayan SJ, in "Ecology and Theology," p. 51.
23. Claude Alvares, "Science, Colonialism and Violence: A Luddite View," 108. As quoted by Samuel Rayan SJ, in "Ecology and Theology: A theology of Nature, a theology of Life," p. 52.
24. See Samuel Rayan SJ, "Ecology and Theology," p. 52.
25. S. Visvanathan, "On the Annals of the Laboratory State" " in Ashis Nandi (ed.), *Science, Hegemony and Violence,* pp. 276-277. As quoted by Samuel Rayan SJ, in "Ecology and Theology," p. 53.
26. For a detailed reading see Samuel Rayan, "The Earth is the Lord's," pp. 3-9.
27. See Ex 9:29; 19:5; Lev 25:23; Deut 10:14; 1Sam 2:8; Ps 2:8; 8:6-9; 47:8; 65:6-14; 50:10-12; 89:12; 95:4-5; Acts 14:16; 17:24-30.
28. see Samuel Rayan, "The Earth is the Lord's," p. 3.
29. *Ibid.*, p. 4.
30. *Ibid.*, pp. 4-5.
31. *Ibid.*, p. 5.
32. *Ibid.*, p. 7.
33. *Ibid.*, p. 9.
34. *Ibid.*, pp. 10-12.
35. If the Earth were only a few feet in diameter, floating a few feet above a field somewhere, people would come from everywhere to marvel at it. People would walk around it, marveling at its big pools of water, its little pools and the water flowing between the pools. People would marvel at the bumps on it and the holes in it and they would marvel at the very thin layer of gas surrounding it and the water suspended in the gas. The people would marvel at all the creatures walking around the surface of the ball, and at the creatures in the water. The people would declare it precious because it was the only one, and they would protect it so that it would not be hurt. The ball would be the greatest known wonder known, and people would come to behold it, to be healed, to gain knowledge, to know beauty and to wonder how it could be. People would love it, and defend it with their lives, because they would somehow know that their lives, their own roundness, could be nothing without it. If the Earth were only a few feet in diameter! (Author Unknown).
36. Chief Seattle (Sealth) Speech delivered in 1854. As quoted in Samuel Rayan, "The Earth is the Lord's," p. 13.

37. See Samuel Rayan, "The Earth is the Lord's," p. 14.
38. See Samuel Rayan SJ, "Ecology and Theology: A theology of Nature, a theology of Life," in *Collected Writings of Samuel Rayan, SJ, Nature, Woman and the Church*, pp. 53-69.
39. *Ibid.*, p. 54.
40. Meditations with Hildegarde of Bingen, Uhlein Gabriele (Tr.), Santa Fe: Bear and Co., 1982, 56. As quoted by Samuel Rayan in "Ecology and Theology," p. 55.
41. Samuel Rayan in "Ecology and Theology," p. 55.
42. *Ibid.*, p. 56.
43. *Ibid.*, p. 58.
44. *Ibid.*, pp. 59-60.
45. *Ibid.*, pp. 60-63.
46. *Ibid.*, pp. 64-69.
47. *Ibid.*, p. 70.
48. *Ibid.*, p. 72.
49. *Ibid.*, p. 73.
50. *Ibid.*, pp. 73-74.
51. Samuel Rayan, "Ecology and Faith: The Mystery of the Earth," in *Collected Writings of Samuel Rayan, SJ, Nature, Woman and the Church*, pp. 24-36 at 29-30.
52. T. Balasuriya, *Planetary Theology*, p. 153. As quoted in Samuel "The Earth is the Lord's," p. 21.
53. See Samuel Rayan, "Ecology and Faith: The Mystery of the Earth," pp. 28-36.

6

Caring to Protest
The Prophetic Voice of a Feminist Theologian

Kochurani Abraham

> "It is not that we are bereft of people who think autonomously and can ask relevant questions. But frequently where there should be voices, there is silence. Are we all being co-opted too easily by the comforts of conforming? Are we fearful of the retribution that questioning may and often does bring?"
>
> ***Romila Thapar***

The reputed Indian historian Romila Thapar, in her critical reading of the role played by different agencies in shaping Indian history, speaks of 'the question': "To question or not to question?"[1] Dr. Samuel Rayan as a theologian, in his determination to question, seems to be of a category different from the one whom Thapar is addressing. He is not co-opted easily by the 'comforts of conforming' and certainly is not fearful of the 'retributions that questioning may bring', as he challenges even the basic tenets of theology which are life-negating. For this reason, I have titled my paper *Caring to Protest: The Prophetic Voice of a Feminist Theologian.* Rayan expresses concern that very few faithful 'care to protest' when he writes about a highly clericalized Church in India.[2] Anyone familiar with Rayan's theology would certainly recognize him as a prophetic voice that has relentlessly challenged the different expressions of oppression we encounter in the Church and in society. What I want to focus on in this paper is his voice of protest as a feminist theologian, and so I begin with an anecdote that illustrates this point.

In the year 2002, while the Indian Theological Association (ITA) was celebrating its silver jubilee at NBCLC in Bangalore, the late Fr. Arockiadoss, SJ and I were asked to prepare the liturgy. While we were engaged in this task, Fr. Rayan came there, and on hearing about the text we had taken for the Gospel reading, the story of Jesus straightening the bent woman, he insisted that a woman should read it at the inaugural Eucharist. He stressed its importance considering the fact that ITA was celebrating 25 years of engaging critically in theological conversations with the Indian culture and its wider social context. We took note of Rayan's concerns, but unfortunately his desire could not be realized on that occasion as the main celebrant happened to be a Bishop who was petrified at the thought of a woman reading the Gospel at a mass that he officiated. However, Rayan's feminist theological concerns to straighten the 'bent woman' of the Indian socio-religious and cultural setting has continued unabated, as is clear from his writings and other critical interventions he has made thus far. In this paper, I would like to situate Rayan's feminist theology within the broader framework of his ecclesiology, particularly the way in which he envisions the emerging Church in India.

Why Protest?

Protest expresses voices of dissent, and it is seen negatively within a system where power is exercised as control, and conformity is expected of those on the lower rungs of the ladder. However, protest becomes theologically significant when it is a sign of a resistance or a refusal to bow down to the unjust dictates of any social order in a given society. Social theorists term resistance the 'weapon of the weak', as it enables the weaker sections of a society to confront power structures that are oppressive.[3] Since women come under the 'weaker' category in a social setting marked by patriarchy, voices questioning their marginalization or enabling them to resist oppression have a tremendous theological significance from a feminist standpoint.

Perhaps it is important to clarify here the term 'feminist' as different people attribute different meanings and connotations to it. Generally in the Indian context, when Church personnel address women's concerns in a seminar, they express it as the 'feminine' perspective of the issue under focus, and if I am invited to speak, I resist that for the obvious gendered associations of the term 'feminine'. However, since the organizers of this seminar have explicitly asked me to make a feminist reading of Dr. Samuel Rayan's theology, clarifying what is implied by a feminist positioning becomes necessary. Though feminism defies a single definition, as the nuances of its meaning vary according to its context, the underlying principle of a feminist stance is the assertion that women are fully human persons just as men are: persons with capacity to think and have opinions; persons with feelings, desires and interests; persons who need mobility, choices and opportunities for growth and for productive engagements in society; and finally persons who have a spiritual agency, who can mediate God and be in partnership with men in articulating the knowledge of God, and in the task of safeguarding the integrity of life.

This process of asserting woman's personhood involves protest, as it entails challenging patriarchy as a system that privileges men's interests and desires over and above those of women. Feminist thought critiques patriarchal power relations that deny women and other marginalized groups their rightful space, however 'sacred' that system be. This is where feminist theology emerges as a critical and prophetic voice. It functions as a double-edged sword, questioning on the one hand the hegemonic codes of a religion that legitimize women's subjugation, while, on the other hand, reconstructing a theology that is inclusive and liberative, in the way God is imagined and experienced, human relationships are defined, and human engagement with the rest of creation is interpreted. For that matter, a feminist theologian need not be a woman, and it is all the more striking when it is a man. In taking a stand for gender justice even when he is not personally affected, his voice becomes a prophetic challenge to the system from within. Besides, he can testify with greater authenticity that feminism is not about women entering into a rivalry with men -- as many people tend to think -- but about addressing systems of power that distort women's dignity as human persons in their own right. It is within this framework that I assess the contribution Rayan has made to feminist theology.

Prophetic Protest in Rayan's Feminist Theology

The feminist sensibilities of Rayan come to the fore in his critical awareness of women's experience of oppression in society, particularly within the precincts of religion. He expresses concern about cultures that take women as insignificant, where they are passed over in silence or worshipped and cuddled as dolls. As Rayan observes, this idolization of women "is but another way of edging them out of decision-taking and history- making processes".[4] He addresses the deep-seated prejudice against women in India which cuts across class, creed, age and profession, rampant not only in the secular world of economic activities, power relationships and cultural realities, but deeply entrenched in the structures and mores of the churches and religions. In Rayan's words: "Oppression runs deep indeed when religion steps in to reinforce it by taking a grip on our conscience and persuading us from within, to kiss our chains and cherish the lashes".[5]

Like the prophets of old, Rayan is sharp in questioning and denouncing the tyrannical exercise of religious power in his critique of what he terms the 'biblical illustrations of naked patriarchy'.[6] In conjunction with this critique, he identifies some feminist voices of prophetic and liberative protest. He presents five girls who ask 'Why' and a woman who says 'No' as examples of women with a striking sense of self-worth, whose courage becomes instrumental in challenging and dismantling even the hardened structures of patriarchy. The five girls who ask 'why' are Mahlah, Noah, Hoglah, Milcah and Tirzah, the daughters of Zelophehad, who demand property rights in a society where inheritance was strictly the privilege of sons.[7] As Rayan observes, 'woman could not lay claims to property, because she was herself property. She could not possess because she was somebody's possession'.[8] Rayan finds the daughters of Zelophehad initiating a social revolution in their refusal to see themselves as destined to be passive victims of anatomy, history or fate, and in their readiness to question the traditional economic arrangements, while demanding change. In his words:

> These girls are different: they raise questions, they dissent and make demands. They have a new vision of things, and a new understanding of themselves... They are not afraid of the powers that be... They are forcing a reconsideration of, and a change in, accepted laws and customs. They are asking for a new social order.[9]

Lamentably, this social revolution set off by the daughters of Zelophehad does not seem to have reached the Indian soil yet. On the property issue, Indian society has not changed much from the Mosaic times, as daughters are still denied the right to inherit property. If we are to take the case of Kerala, even though women can stake claims to intestate parental property after the much celebrated Mary Roy case of 1986, they come under the deprived lot, puppeteered by the strings of dowry. Even within the Church, women making claims to property rights is considered anathema, and anyone who dares to question the structural and gendered malpractices of the system are branded among the 'wicked' and cast 'out'. The case of Njarakkal sisters,[10] gives evidence of this in the Kerala Church.

The element of protest in Rayan's feminist theology is further accentuated in the character he presents as the embodiment of resistance, the woman who says 'No!'-Vashti, queen of the king Ahasuerus of Persia, who refused 'to display her beauty' before the king's guests.[11] She did it at a cost to herself as she was divested of her royal status and banished from the king's presence, for fear that following her example, women of the empire may disregard the husband's role as 'master' of the house. Rayan finds in Vashti a woman of incomparable clarity of mind, courage and personal dignity, and in her refusal to become a show piece, a toy in the hands of the king, ... a pleasure-object for the gratification of male-eyes, who 'debunked patriarchy'.[12] Applauding Vashti, Rayan invites his readers 'to draw light, inspiration and strength from her courageous resistance to humiliating male whims, masquerading as authority'.[13]

An obvious question that can be raised here is how Vashti can be a role-model for Indian women today? Since, patriarchy is a major cultural trait of the Indian society, male-gaze having a say on women's beauty and sexuality continues to be a defining factor of women's destinies. In this context, women becoming conscious of their self-worth and taking a stand to defend it, becomes fundamental to their dignity as persons. Active resistance and having the courage to protest becomes all the more imperative when male-gaze becomes a tool of outright abuse and sexual violence within the Church.

A recent case in which the Forum of Religious for Justice and Peace has been asked to intervene by the victim, a religious sister working in a northern diocese of India, lays bare the issue. The concerned sister found a camera fixed on the ventilator of her bathing room, while taking bath at a diocesan centre where she had gone to attend a meeting in the month of August 2014. The offender was caught at once and identified as a student of theology in Rome who had come on holidays. Even though the concerned Church authority promised her justice, no concrete action has been taken thus far. Instead, the criminal has been protected and sent back to Rome for his theological studies. On being pressurized by the FORUM, the concerned Church authority has informed the sister through her congregational leadership that the scholastic will be asked to discontinue his priestly studies, but she should give in writing that the issue will not be taken further.

In this case, the Church authorities have succeeded in silencing the sisters, making them believe that this is a problem that has affected one of their sisters personally and that it will be sorted out. The intervention of the FORUM has been seen spitefully by the Church authorities and even the congregational leadership. But as acclaimed in the feminist slogan, 'personal is political', the gravity of the situation calls for greater resistance and protest by women and men of goodwill, so as to bring to effect the gender policy of zero tolerance on issues of sexual violence in the Church. Certainly as Rayan has envisioned, queen Vashti has indeed become a role model for those who dare to question such perverse and abusive practices in the Church.

Dissent - An Essential Component of Gospel Politics

Rayan presents Jesus as 'a dissident',[14] whose practices are critical and subversive of the establishment, turning upside down the tables of power. It is within this framework of the politics of the Reign of God that Rayan decisively attests early Christianity as a counter culture. The logic of Jesus's practice transmitting the egalitarian vision of the Reign of God actively contradicts the logic of the religious and political system of his times. As Rayan observes, 'Jesus and his movement would make no distinction between women and men disciples. The breaking down of divisive and discriminatory walls was central to Jesus' revolutionary ministry. In fact, in a history of women's marginalization, Jesus decided to give women primacy of place in matters concerning the foundation of faith'.[15]

Rayan names 'freedom' the trademark of Jesus, freedom from the yoke of suffocating religious laws and social conventions, freedom from fears and the numerous mechanisms of self-depreciation. It is freedom that calls a new social order into being where the poor and the excluded find their pride rebuilt, and their right to social existence affirmed in defiance of all ideologies, taboos and laws. Jesus freely goes against the many conventions which discriminated against and exploited women and enhances their contributions to life by affirming their dignity and equality. From these observations, Rayan concludes that if Jesus was a social and religious dissenter and if the Reign of God he announced meant a different culture, then, 'the God he revealed is a dissident God.' The God of Jesus disagrees with the accepted ways of this world and its canonized values and rules and disowns a social order built on injustice and inequality.[16]

The idea of a dissident God is very appealing to women and other subordinate groups today because it energizes them to resist the hegemonic social formations and strategies of domination that deny them human dignity. Through resistance women reclaim their subjectivity and agency, cast away the robe of victimhood, refusing to remain 'inert and passive objects of defining discourses as people without any control over their lives'.[17] Even though passivity has for long overshadowed the traditional imagery of Indian woman, the expressions of voiced struggle and dissent being on the increase is indicative of an emerging consciousness that is liberative. Narratives of 'subterranean resistance' offered by ordinary women in their daily lives, and stories of 'staunch resistance to dominating regimes'[18] like that of Irom Sharmila, are all signs of the subversive powers at work in Indian feminist politics. And in this struggle, it is very consoling to know that the 'dissident God' is on their side.

The 'Dissident God' and the Church Today

I think it is important to examine the implications of this theology of the 'dissident God' for the Church, for its ecclesiology and praxis, from a feminist viewpoint. If the 'dissident' God disowns a social order built on injustice and inequality, how are we to address the exclusion and gendered subordinations which women continue to experience in the Church?

Let us begin with women's experience of exclusion in the Church. I come from a parish, where women are not expected even to enter the *Madbaha* or the space taken to be the 'holy of holies', set apart clearly by railings. Women do not go into this space to do the readings or even to receive the ciborium for distributing communion. While this may not be the practice everywhere, women's outright exclusion from ministering at the altar - though this ministry is in memory of the One who defied to the core the theology and structures of levitical priesthood -- continues to be an interrogation that calls into question the very identity of the Church. While the Catholic Church seems to be worried about the sex of God in its assertion of who can represent Jesus Christ, Esther Bharati, a transgender person from Chennai -- to be ordained soon -- stands as a striking witness of the inclusive politics of the 'dissident God', her very life becoming an interrogation to what or whom we consider a human being, and a challenge to the very foundations of the theology built on male/female gender binaries.[19] Rayan's feminist theology does not address the issue of women's ordination directly, but his open critique of the hierarchism, clericalism and sexism that mark the Church and his assertion that Jesus initiated a 'unity of free and equal persons', echoes the prophetic voices that have challenged the domineering systems of religious power.

The politics of exclusion works in more subtle ways, the Church being mostly an all masculine space particularly in the sphere of theological knowledge-making, policy making and leadership. As scholars observe, masculinisation of space means an access to and control over resources of various kinds – material, socio-cultural, political and ideological...Circulating ideals of gendered separateness, they make the presence of males and the absence of females seem "natural".[20] Masculinisation of the Church's knowledge making spaces[21] and leadership roles ought to be seen in relation to the notion of the 'dissident God'. And so, the question is: How can the Church address gender inequality in the outside society, when it is so deeply marked by 'gendered separateness' within its own structures - eclipsing women's agency, domesticating their contribution, and silencing the many questions raised from a growing critical feminist consciousness in the official documents and pronouncements of the Church?

The significance of the theology of a 'dissident God' comes to the fore more sharply on the question of sexual violence and the Church. Generally, the Church does not raise voices of protest unless its property, personnel or interests are challenged, assaulted or violated by external forces. When India raged in the wake of the Delhi gang-rape, the silence on the part of the official Church was conspicuous, and it was interpreted as the Church losing an opportunity once again "to intervene in and change the national discourse on issues of grave concern to the country, its democracy and its people".[22]

Analysts point out that political imagination in India has come to a standstill, aiding and abetting the construction of a homogenized cultural and political sphere.[23] In this context, the increasing incidence of different expressions of gender violence and the reporting of sexual violence is a matter that calls for critical attention. The obstinacy of the crime goes hand in hand with the breeding of impunity fostered partly by the State and partly by the class and caste inscriptions of patriarchy on gender, based on the identity of the offender and that of the victim. Dalits and tribal women have been routinely subject to rape by landlords and contractors but these remain unrecorded because the police, the village councils, the media and government officials reflect the biases of the caste system, and crimes against those on the margins get normalized as part of the accepted social order.[24]

The problem of impunity gets acute because the law and the legal institutions are socially embedded. The interpreters of law and upholders of the social order follow the same patriarchal dictates and are subject to the same biases and prejudices as the larger social world. For this reason, the interventions of *Khap Panchayats* which take law enforcement into its hands continue unbridled, though they have become infamous for the legitimization of honour killings and the marriages of the victims with the rapists.

The gender question continues to be an unresolved issue in the Indian context, and time has come to go beyond the conventional notion of women empowerment to new responses like re-thinking gender, particularly masculinity as this will help address issues of violence and facilitate bridging the gender gap within the Church and in the wider society. Besides these, new situations have emerged in the recent past -which is not foreseen by Rayan in his writings- like the assertions of transgender persons and people with different sexual orientations, claiming their dignity, space and inclusion into the mainstream. It is against the backdrop of this wider genderscape that I see the prophetic and political impact of the theology of the 'dissident God" as presented by Rayan, and the 'prophetic criticism' he speaks of, as 'a service the Church must give to society'.[25]

In the light of these observations, we need to examine the nature of interdependence between the Church and society, particularly in India. Has not the parameters of the Church's social engagement narrowed to an institutional presence which is seen as self-promoting rather than becoming a prophetic cutting edge? Would the Church dare to dismantle its power structures that are exclusive and patterned after the class/caste/gender hierarchy of the Indian society and engage in a counter-cultural politics that is inclusive and modelling the Jesus movement?

The Church has a long way to go, in order to become counter-cultural in the sense of freeing itself from the feudalistic and patriarchal cultural mire in which it is deeply entrenched. Becoming counter-cultural embodies a critical freedom, observes the reputed biblical theologian Lucien Legrand, as it represents the fundamental prophetic protest against the falsehood and injustice lurking in the most brilliant and most solid civilizations. This cultural confrontation is as fundamental as the holiness of God, whose transcendence shames human meanness.[26] In imagining a counter-cultural gender politics, Rayan's envisioning of the Church not as a finished and ready-made reality, is appealing. In his opinion, the 'Church is a process',[27] a subversive community which comes into being by responding prophetically to the changing times, but founded on a vision of being fraternal, equal, without social hierarchies or master-slave relations.[28]

Rayan's notion of the 'dissident' God is also an invitation to engage in critical theology. As Gregory Baum would say, "[C]ritical theology is the critical application of the various theories of alienation to the self understanding in faith of the Christian Church. This critical method may lead theologians to discover elements of false consciousness in their perception of reality and thus produce a significant change of mind and heart".[29] Further, it is the task of critical theology to discern the structural consequences of religious practice, to evaluate them in the light of the Church's normative teaching, and to enable the Church to restructure its concrete social presence so that its social consequences approach more closely its profession of faith. For what must be in keeping with the Gospel is not only the church's teaching and practice, but also and especially the actual, concrete effects of this teaching and practice on human history. Critical theology enables the Church to assume theological responsibility for its social reality.[30]

Rayan's feminist theology is a critical theology. In presenting the daughters of Zelophehad and queen Vasthi as role models, he invites women in the Church to engage in critical theology by daringly asking 'why?' and confidently asserting 'no' when situations call for such interrogations and responses. It is also an invitation to articulate a 'critical theology of culture', that which treats culture more as a critical praxis, a dynamic activity, a process rather than a content or substance. It is a praxis that interrogates, contests, negotiates and weakens the hold of hegemonic traditions, systems and structures which maintain an oppressive hold on the subaltern people,[31] and this dynamic opens up new and liberative ways for subalterns to move from the politics of domination.[32]

Conclusion

Rayan, in caring to protest, has opened up new horizons for ecclesiology and feminist theology. His critical and prophetic voice as a theologian serves as a challenge and a reminder. It challenges the hierarchical church of its fixations and the hegemonic manner of functioning. It is also a powerful reminder of the politics of the Reign of God as a liberative and inclusive politics, denouncing any form of oppression while announcing the freedom and dignity of God's children and the earth.

For me, discovering the feminist theologian in Rayan is a sign of feminist theology coming of age, as it is an attestation that women's concerns are becoming human concerns. It is heartening to find men addressing the women's question, in view of the fact that only those who are being freed of the shackles of patriarchy can actually let go of the many privileges accompanying male status in the Church and Indian society. Rayan's prophetic voice as a feminist theologian is an invitation for other men to join in this task of confronting and overcoming the "unnatural distinctions"-- borrowing an expression of Mary Woolstonecraft, the mother of the feminist movement-- who names as unnatural, the distinctions that are not inherent, but historically and socially constructed, legitimizing the subordination of one group of persons to another. Only by confronting these unnatural distinctions can we initiate a 'change in mindset' as observed in the Verma Commission Report of 2013, which will help counter the deep undercurrents of patriarchy in the Indian Church and society.

I would like to conclude with an appeal that Rayan makes to those who would take his work ahead. In speaking about the significance of women's awakening in the Church, Rayan points out with a sense of urgency: "There is much Gospel work for the Church to do…much oppression to criticize and subvert and many movements for human rights, freedom and solidarity with which to collaborate. Jesus needs all of us, women and men alike to accompany him and cooperate in his project of liberating people and making the world human and whole".[33] Only when women and men work in greater partnership, can we initiate a new social order which is inclusive, egalitarian and liberative as envisioned in the Jesus movement. This is the challenge put forward by Rayan's feminist theology.

Notes

1. Romila Thapar, "To Question or Not to Question? That Is the Question", *Economic & Political Weekly*, Vol XLIX, no 50, December 13, 2014, pp. 33-39.
2. Samuel Rayan, "The Ecclesiology at Work in the Indian Church Today", in Kurien Kunnumpuram (ed.), *Nature, Woman and the Church: Indian Christian Reflections on Ecology, Feminism ad Ecclesiology, Collected Writings of Samuel Rayan SJ,* Vol. I, New Delhi: ISPCK 2013, p. 163.
3. Cf. Scott James, *Weapons of the Weak: Everyday Forms of Peasant Resistance,* New Haven, Yale University Press, 1985.
4. Rayan, "In Christ: The Power of Women", in *Collected Writings of Samuel Rayan SJ,* Vol. I, p. 110.
5. *Ibid.*, p. 112.
6. Rayan, "Five Girls Ask Why? And a Woman says No!" in *Collected Writings of Samuel Rayan SJ,* Vol. I, p. 103.
7. The daughters of Zelophehad are mentioned in the Book of Numbers 27:1-11.
8. Rayan, "Five Girls Ask Why? And a Woman says No!..." p. 102.
9. *Ibid.*
10. In the Njarakkal case, a group of religious sisters got into conflict with the local Church on the property issue which continues to be unresolved, and their stand was judged as defiant by their own religious leadership and other church leaders.
11. Cf. the book of Esther, chapter 1.
12. Rayan, "Five Girls Ask Why? And a Woman says No!..." pp. 104-105.
13. *Ibid.*, p. 108.
14. Rayan, "Early Christianity as Counter-Culture", in *Collected Writings of Samuel Rayan SJ*, Vol. I, p. 210.
15. Rayan , "In Christ: The Power of Women", p. 110.
16. Rayan, "Early Christianity as Counter-Culture", p. 229.
17. Haynes Douglas and Gyan Prakash (eds), *Contesting Power: Resistance and Everyday Social Relations in South Asia,* Berkeley and LA: University of California Press, 1992, p. 2.
18. Feminist scholars are increasingly unearthing stories of resistance by unassuming Indian women, giving expression to the liberative dynamics of gender discourses. See Anindita Ghosh (ed.), *Behind the Veil: Resistance, Women and the Everyday in Colonial South Asia,* Ranikhet: Permanent Black, 2007.

19. BRAVOH (Bringing Adequate Values Of Humanity), a movement initiated by Olga. B. Aaron, another transwoman from Chennai, for the upliftment of Transgender persons, shares in this interrogation raised by Esther Bharati.
20. Prem Chowdhry, "Masculine Spaces: Rural Male Culture in North India", *Economic & Political Weekly*, November 22, 2014, Vol. XLIX, No 47, pp. 41-49.
21. The recent Synod on the family had a mere token representation of 24 women from across the globe, even though the 2013 document *Evangelii Gaudium* spoke of the need "to create broader opportunities for a more incisive female presence in the Church" (*EG* 104).
22. John Dayal, the General Secretary of the All India Christian Council and a member of the Indian government's National Integration Council, made this observation. See J. Dayal, 'A silent Church is a dead one: Why has it not spoken out on the Delhi gang rape?', ucannews, 8 January 2013, accessed on 20 January 2013 http://www.ucanews.com/news/a-silent-church-is-a-dead-one/67046.
23. Cf. Ajay Gudavarthy, Nissim Mannathukkaren, "The Politics of Secular Sectarianism", *Economic & Political Weekly,* Vol. XLIX , No. 49, December 6, 2014, pp. 16-19.
24. For more explanations on the question of impunity in addressing the issue of sexual violence in India, see, Kochurani Abraham, "The Saga of Sexual Violence in India", in Regina Ammicht-Quinn, Louis Carlos Susin and Lisa Sowle Cahill (eds) 'Corruption', in *Concilium,* SCM Press 2014/5, pp. 40-47.
25. Samuel Rayan, "Sociological Factors and the Local Church as an Eucharistic Community", in *Collected Writings of Samuel Rayan SJ*, Vol. I, p. 176.
26. Lucien Legrand, *The Bible on Culture*, Bangalore TPI, 2004, p. 171.
27. Samuel Rayan, "*The Church-The Jesus Movement*", in *Collected Writings of Samuel Rayan SJ*, Vol. I, p. 187.
28. Cf. Samuel Rayan, "Early Christianity as Counter-Culture", p. 230.
29. Gregory Baum, *Religion and Alienation: A Theological Reading of Sociology*, N. York: Paulist Press, 1975, p. 194.
30. Ibid., p. 195.
31. G. Patrick, *Wings of Faith: Towards Public theologies in India*, New Delhi: ISPCK, 2013, p. 235.
32. Sathianathan Clarke, "Dalit Theology: An Introductive and an Interpretative Theological Exposition" in Sathianathan Clarke & Others (eds.), *Dalit Theology in the 21st century-Discordant Voices, Discerning Pathways,* New Delhi: Oxford University Press, p. 287.
33. Samuel Rayan, "The Significance of Women's Awakening in the Church" in Kurien Kunnumpuram (ed.), *Collected Writings of Samuel Rayan SJ,* Vol. I: *Nature, Woman and the Church: Indian Christian Reflections on Ecology, Feminism and Ecclesiology,* New Delhi: ISPCK 2013, p. 148.

PART TWO

THE CHURCH AND ITS MISSION

7

The Beauty of the Church
An Investigation of Samuel Rayan's Ecclesiology

Kurien Kunnumpuram, SJ

It is difficult to do justice to Samuel Rayan's thoughts on the Church in a short paper like this, since he has written eleven articles on ecclesiology.[1] And some of these articles are quite long. Besides, there has been some evolution in Rayan's understanding of the Church. The earliest of his articles comes from the year 1969. And the latest one was written in 2004. How have Rayan's ecclesiological thoughts changed? What is Rayan's final idea of the Church? It is not at all easy to answer these questions.

Hence, all I seek to do in this paper is to highlight what I consider to be Rayan's original contribution to ecclesiology. I know that there may be some arbitrariness in my selection of Rayan's ecclesiological ideas. All the same, such an approach can help us to appreciate his original insights.

1. The Church as the Jesus Movement

1.1. The Church in the Acts of the Apostles

Rayan is convinced that the Church is the Jesus movement and believes that he can find a brief description of this movement in the Acts of the Apostles.[2] He refers to Acts 2:44-47 and 4:32-37:

> All who believed were together and had all things in common; they would sell their possessions and goods and distribute the

> proceeds to all, as any had need. Day by day, as they spend much time together in the temple, they broke bread at home and ate their food with glad and generous hearts praising God and having the goodwill of all the people. And day by day the Lord added to their number those who were being saved (Acts 2:44-47).
>
> Now the whole group of those who believed were of one heart and soul, and no one claimed private ownership of any possessions, but everything they owned was held in common. With great power the apostles gave their testimony to the resurrection of the Lord Jesus, and great grace was upon them all. There was not a needy person among them, for as many as owned lands or houses sold them and brought the proceeds of what was sold. They laid it at the apostles' feet, and it was distributed to each as any had need. There was a le'vite, a native of Cyprus, Joseph to whom the apostles gave the name Bar'nabas (which means "son of encouragement"). He sold a field that belonged to him, then brought that money, and laid it the apostles' feet (Acts 4:32-37).

We need to read these texts in the larger context of the Acts. According to the Acts the early members of the Jerusalem community thought of themselves as Jews. They worshipped in the Jewish temple; they kept the Jewish law; and they looked upon the Old Testament as their Scripture. So it is not religion that distinguished the disciples of Jesus from the Jews who were not his disciples. "What distinguished them, what was specific to the Jesus Movement, was their meeting in the homes around four shared realities: shared faith, shared prayer, shared or broken bread (which many think was the Eucharist) and finally shared material resources".[3]

These four elements are interrelated and each follows or leads into the other. There is no Jesus movement if any of these realities is missing. The experience of faith leads to thanksgiving; gratitude is expressed in the Eucharist which is a ritual sharing of bread. The sharing of the Eucharistic bread is the expression of a commitment to share all bread and wealth. By this sharing of all wealth the Christian community becomes God's family - "a family in which God can be meaningfully called our Father. In those early days an earnest effort was made to ensure that no one was marginalized or left in need".[4]

What is quite remarkable was that this sharing of their wealth was done by the early Christians under no force or compulsion "except the pressure upon their hearts of the love God had given them in Christ Jesus; and the pressure from the deep experience of a sense of fellowship and of a mutual responsibility which also sprang from the deep experience of Jesus and of the love that came from the Father".[5] In the Eucharistic celebration, the faith factor and the social factor are inseparably intertwined. The sharing of wealth necessarily follows the ritual celebration of salvation through the breaking and sharing of bread. As Rayan sums it up:

> The Eucharist and the Brother/Sister are one and the same reality. Both are the Body of Christ and the Sacrament of God's love. Faith acceptance of the Kingdom in the heart results in a community of equals who share bread and wealth. That is the earliest picture of the Church we happen to have.[6]

It is true that some people have suggested that the Church depicted in Acts 2 and 4 is an idealisation by Luke. However, "historical studies have begun to show that this teaching on the community of earthly goods was an essential part of early Christian catechesis. And the communities tried to realize that as fully as possible. It is not claimed that they fully succeeded, but that they strove to move in this direction for more than five centuries. Therefore, Luke's is not simply an idealistic picture".[7]

In any case, "it is within the Eucharist that the mystery of his (Jesus') life and redemptive action is enshrined. And it is by distributing this in a brotherly way that the new community is symbolised and realized".[8]

1.2. The Church of the Beatitudes

The beatitudes must be understood in the socio-economic and political context of Palestine at the time of Jesus.[9] Then Palestine was a colony of the Roman Empire which highly taxed and oppressed the people in a variety of ways. They had to pay for the maintenance of the Roman army stationed in Palestine to control and oppress them. Besides, the temple also exploited the ordinary people. It is in the context of the poverty and oppression which the bulk of the population experienced that Jesus proclaims the beatitudes. As Rayan points out:

> In the beatitudes we begin to discover something of Jesus' own conception of his community and something of Church's self-understanding. The Church is a movement of mercy, of protest against oppressive structures, of struggle against inertia by which the human tends to drift backwards on the path of evolution and return to the state of the brute in the jungle, where the big swallow the small and the strong prey upon the weak. The Church is a movement, supportive and representative, of planned, forward evolution towards complete tenderness, that greatest and finest of human inventions (Eric Fromm), that ultimate norm by which the human is defined and recognized.[10]

In the light of the beatitudes, the Church is a movement of people who seek justice, promote peace and are against every kind of oppression and exploitation. It is also a movement of people who make a single-minded commitment to bring the good news of salvation to the poor and to enable the oppressed to experience liberation and joy. This activity would bring the Jesus Movement into conflict with the powers of domination and oppression. "The beatitude therefore is that the disciples of Jesus must be prepared to face calumny, persecution and death. But such grim prospects should not deter them from their prophetic task, for there is a blessing on their struggles, there is happiness in dying meaningfully, for within such struggles and death a new humanity is being realized, affirmed and revealed, a new humanity that is free, loyal and solidary, one that cannot be dictated to and manipulated by the powers that be; one that lives from within and throbs to the pulse and rhythm of the glad tidings which have come to the world in Jesus Christ".[11]

1.3. The Church and the Trinity

There are two other great symbols of the Jesus Movement – the Trinity and the Our Father – which define the newness indicated by the Sermon on the Mount and try to point out the direction in which the transformation is to be effected. According to Rayan:

> The Trinity is the symbolic expression of a Divine Mystery which means that the ultimate reality is a community. It is a community in which everything is held in common and no private property exists; in which everybody lives for the others and there is no competition; in which the identity of each consists in living and being for the others, and all individualism is excluded. A community in which freedom, power and achievements are all collective and corporate; in which there are no class divisions, no privileged persons, no oppressed, miserable underdogs. If such is the shape and structure of Ultimate Source Reality then human life on earth and Church life above all will be authentic and true only in the measure in which it participates in the ultimate truth, that ultimate model.[12]

The other great symbol is the Our Father. In the Our Father the concern is that increasing numbers of people should experience God's love which comes in Jesus and thus become God's family on earth so that they meaningfully can call God "Our Father". "The Church is essentially conceived as a family in which all have the same dignity and the same share in the inheritance that comes from God. Humankind's inheritance from God is the earth and the wealth that we produce by transforming the earth through common toil".[13]

The first part of the Our Father is a version of a Jewish prayer. Here, the basic concern is that God's kingdom should come on earth, that God's will must be done on earth and thus the name of God be perceived as meaningful on earth. The three petitions mean practically the same thing. The second part is from Jesus.

> "What Jesus adds to this (Jewish) prayer to make it concrete and pointed and give it teeth to bite into the texture of human history, is the second part. God's name is experienced as meaningful and his reign keeps coming when everybody who is hungry has bread to eat, when everybody who needs forgiveness and acceptance is already given and bread is made abundant. It is our task to make both bread and forgiveness, symbols of the new community, available to everybody. The Lord's prayer is, therefore, not merely a good model prayer; it is above all a

> programme of action, which is very concrete, and has to do with the acceptance of people and with bread for the breadless, security for the threatened and honour for the dishonoured. To say the Our Father is to commit ourselves to such action. To live the prayer actively is to become the Church".[14]

2. The Church as a Counter-Cultural Movement

There is no doubt that Jesus was cruelly murdered by the powerful of his society, the representatives of the dominant classes. First of all, the Pharisees. As Mark points out: "The Pharisees went out and at once began to plot with the Herodians against him, discussing how to destroy him" (Mk 3:6). The Pharisees were seen again to act in collusion with the Herodians (see Mk 8:15; 11:27; 12:13). In a Lukan passage, certain Pharisees came to Jesus and said: "Go away. Leave this place. Herod means to kill you" (Lk 13:31). The scribes, the elders and the chief priests also sought to kill Jesus. As Rayan observes:

> It was this group that confronted Jesus and questioned his authority after he had expelled the "robbers" from the Temple (Mk 11:27). They wanted to arrest Jesus but desisted for fear of the crowd (Mk 12:12). As the Passover approached these men "began to look for a way to arrest him by some trick and kill him. Yet they pointed out, Not during the festival, or the people may riot" (Mk 14:1-2). It was finally the same group that sent armed men with swords and clubs to arrest Jesus (Mk 14:43), and handed Jesus to Pilate, and stood accusing Jesus and inciting the crowd to demand the execution of Jesus, and continued mocking the man as he lay nailed on the cross (Mk 15:1, 3, 11, 31).[15]

But the definitive sentence of death was given by Pilate, the Roman Governor (see Mk 15:2, 9, 12, 18, 26).

But why did these people kill Jesus? Because "the adversaries of Jesus experienced Jesus as a threat. Jesus was a dissident. His practice was critical and subversive of the establishment. The establishment was made up of three strands: the Romans, the Jewish authorities and the Pharisees".[16]

The Romans during the years of their occupation of Palestine humiliated the people by subjugation and military presence. "They oppressed the people by collecting taxes: a personal tax, a land tax, an annual tax to maintain the Roman garrison, and various indirect taxes and duties. 25 percent and upward of the product of Palestine was thus drained off for the benefit of Rome".[17]

The Romans ruled Palestine with the help of Jewish authorities: the chief priests, the scribes and the elders. These constituted the Sanhedrin to which a large measure of internal autonomy was given. The members of the Sanhedrin cooperated with the Roman rulers in the oppression and exploitation of the poor people of Palestine. Besides this, they had their way of oppressing the people. The Temple was the symbol of their oppression.

It was in this context that Jesus announced the advent of the kingdom of God. The announcement was a threat and a challenge to the kings, the lords and the wealthy aristocracy. But it was the dawn of hope for the poor. As Rayan says:

> Read the sequences in Mark 2:1 to 3:6: Here Mark is systematically presenting Jesus' practice as subversive of the symbolic field of the entire Jewish system of law and order. There is healing and forgiveness contrary to the canons of the scribes. There is the admission of polluted and polluting people to the inner circle of Jesus' followers and friends. There is a deliberate commensality with unclean and despised outcasts, publicans and sinners, tax collectors and harlots. The whole purity-pollution system is blown up. And there is a spirited defence of the subversion, and a vigorous affirmation of the new counter-culture... Jesus' hungry disciples plucked grain, the provision for the poor, and were accused of law-breaking; Jesus risked the narrow line between poverty and outlawry. In that decisive pronouncement, "The Sabbath is made for humankind and not humankind for the Sabbath", there is a symbolic reversal of the world of his day.[18]

In a deliberate opposition to avarice and greed, Jesus stood for a different kind of society in which humanness would prevail. This alternative was presented not in abstract theory, but in the practice of the kingdom he announced, the practice of freedom, justice and equality. In the economic sphere, he advocated the logic of giving, sharing and the community of goods in opposition to the prevalent ideology of exclusive accumulation. As against poverty and misery and the humiliation which goes with them, he brought in the logic of abundance. "We remember the plentiful wine of Cana, the extra basketful of bread in the desert and the saying about the fullness of life as the purpose of his coming".[19] In the political sphere he refused the kingship offered to him. To accept it would have meant that Jesus subscribed to the existing order and aligned himself with the oppressors. Jesus understood authority in terms of service. "He laid the foundations of authority not in hierarchy but in the equality of power and the ability to help grow".[20]

All this had a great impact on the movement that Jesus began. As Rayan has observed:

> Some sociological interpretations of the New Testament have come to the conclusion that the earliest, Palestinian, Christian communities came into being as a social protest. Conscious or unconscious protest was the social dynamic that "helped bring the Church into existence and that gave it the particular shape it took in those earliest years". Protest meant that the movement rejected "the assumptions of reality upon which the establishment bases its world". It also meant "the creation of a world with different assumptions: Counter-culture". As a consequence, the movement was egalitarian in character. It was marked by a glowing love and mutual acceptance. Commitment to it was voluntary, and therefore total.[21]

According to Rosemary Radford Ruether, in the Christianity reflected in the gospels and in Paul, "the Church functioned as a counter-cultural community which claimed priority in the lives of its members and dissolved the primacy of one's commitment to the family".[22] Ruether mentions some of the significant dimensions of this counter-cultural movement. Christians affirmed their right to hold the Christian faith, to belong to the Church and to worship according to their perceptions. Freedom of conscience and of religion was upheld against the claims of the family and the State. For those times, such radical, dissenting positions were innovative and dangerous. They gave birth to Christian martyrs, women and men who refused to toe the line, and became red and flaming affirmations of human dignity and freedom.

Many Christians left the natural family and joined a new community which was brotherly/sisterly and equal without social hierarchies and master-slave relations. There was a variety of experiments in communal living. "A new family, a new humanity, defined by Christ, was emerging. Christianity, appealing to individual and personal responsibility, disrupted the socio-religious ties in the old family structure. To depart from the family religion was to leave the religion of the ancestors and the State. This was subversion, which would be looked upon as treason. To follow Christianity was to strike at the heart of the social order of both the family and the State. Hence, early Christianity easily invited persecution".[23]

However, in the communities reflected in the later books of the New Testament, we notice a tendency to make compromises and to give up the radicality of the counter-cultural movement. Ruether notes how the First Letter of Peter enjoins the strictest conformity to every human institution: to the emperor, the governors and slave-masters, "even those who are harsh". Wives are directed to be completely submissive to husbands (I Pet 2:11 to 3:7; Eph 5:22-24). The original vision of equality too begins to be basically discarded. "The radical vision of an egalitarian Christian counter-culture is institutionalised in monastic Christianity" where women and men continue to claim that faith takes precedence over State and family. But, this was for the elite, not for all. Already in the New Testament household and later in the political theology of the Constantinian State, patriarchal family patterns are given Christian recognition. The husband-wife hierarchy is given theological respectability.

Is the counter-cultural movement of Jesus completely lost? Rayan believes that at present we are witnessing the re-emergence of the movement:

> Then suddenly the poor spoke up. In their voice the words of Jesus' challenge sounded again. The accent of protest was heard once more, and the call to freedom rang out. Dissent is back on the scene. It is criticism once more of prince and priest, temple and bank. It defies death again and refuses to conform. The culture of life is gaining ground, its streams flow. The struggle

> against death is starting afresh: in Africa, in Latin America, in Asia, in the communities of the poor the world over.[24]

3. The Church as an Event

The Church of Christ is not a finished product, a ready-made reality. It is a process. Jesus did not establish a fully structured Church with constitutions, dogmas, rituals and hierarchy. These things emerged and evolved gradually in the course of history. As Samuel Rayan observes:

> What Jesus started was a Movement of freedom and fraternity; and the source of this Movement was His own experience of God's unconditional love for the world. The Church has been a process, it has gone through many shapes and has taken many forms. It is still in process, it is becoming now. It happens not necessarily where theological systems are elaborated and theories are built, not necessarily where great edifices, with altars and crosses, are put up and decorated with art pieces; not necessarily where symbols of power are in evidence or elaborated liturgies are performed, or the rich and the powerful are catered to. It happens rather where men and women, who have experienced Jesus and are enthused by His memory, act to uphold the dignity of the people; where they say no to the forces of oppression, and to the authority of the dollar and the gun; where men and women are liberated from fear of every kind. Liberated from self-contempt, liberated from interiorised oppressor values, liberated from consenting to be the shadow of the high and the mighty and from crippling social and religious fear, men and women can work with God to create a more just and humane world.[25]

The Church also happens when people take steps to bring bread to the breadless, to offer acceptance and recognition to the marginalized and to enable the silenced to find a voice. One of the remarkable events in the Gospel is the healing of the deaf-mute. "Those who have been silenced are given back their speech. God always speaks in order to enable us to speak the liberating word to one another". But oppressive systems would have them remain deaf and mute: work more and talk less! Jesus goes against these systems.

"Participating in his work of enabling people to understand and speak up is a way of becoming Church".[26]

The Church happens when people work hard to prevent the strong hands from snatching the bread from the mouth of hungry children; when steps are taken to rebuild broken hearts with the assurance of God's unconditional love and the total pardon God has already given to the world; where efforts are made to destroy structures and traditions which break people; and when men and women respond positively to the demands of the basic symbols given by Jesus – the Eucharist, the Trinity and the Our Father, all of which signify community. According to Rayan:

> The Church is happening, thus, in villages, slums, factories, in small groups with a concern for justice, in workers' movements. Perhaps in the guerrilla camps; in the barrios, within the peasants' struggles, among radical priests and sisters, among committed bishops, among students. Wherever the memory of Jesus becomes a ferment in hearts and hands, vision and action, the Church begins to shape up, for Jesus is with the people.[27]

4. Local Church

The Church, called and gathered by God in Christ, realizes itself in a variety of communities. The smallest unit is the believing family. Vatican II speak of it as "the domestic Church" (*LG* 11), as 'the domestic sanctuary of the Church" (*AA* 11) and as "an initial seminary" (*OT* 2). In this little church the faith communion is intimate and intense; and the communication of the faith is singularly effective and profound. The Home-Church witnesses to the faith and transmits it, in all its beauty and richness, in the idiom of daily life and love, and of example and experience, rather than in abstract formulations and legal prescriptions. As a teaching authority, the family is fundamental and indispensable.

A local church is a communion of many domestic churches. In Rayan's words:

> These come together to express and celebrate, in the Eucharist, their own Mystery as the real Body of Christ; and to bear collective witness to the faith before the wider world; to show their love for one another and for the people among whom they

> live and whose needs and sufferings they wish to understand, share and alleviate. In such a wider group, blood relationships which characterise the Home Churches are both respected and transcended in recognising 'the others' as sisters and brothers in Christ in the larger family of God. The local church is truly Church in the full sense of the word: people called and gathered by God to continue on earth the life and work of Jesus under the guidance of the Spirit. It is not a fragment or a department of some larger ecclesial reality.[28]

Every local Church can be described as One, holy, catholic and apostolic. It is catholic and apostolic because of the faith it shares with the Apostles and with the other churches of the past and the present. It is holy because it is animated by the Holy Spirit who makes it the body of Christ. And it is one since it is united in a loving commitment to the cause of the Rein of God on earth. "No local Church, however, may lay exclusive claim to be the one, Holy Catholic and Apostolic Church. The One Holy is the communion of communities of faith, become the one Body of Christ, knit together by the Spirit and held in the Father's Hands".[29]

The origin and growth of local churches call for inculturation. As Rayan points out:

> Local churches shape up in the process of inculturation of the faith in the people's life and of the people in the faith. The process of inculturation and the process of faith are inseparable from people's commitment to the kingdom, to justice for all and to the liberation of the oppressed... The overarching concern is for the transformation of society and the creation of a new earth through involvement in action to take down structures that alienate and oppress, and to set in motion a process of freedom, justice and equality for all. The churches refuse to absolutise existing cultures and systems of death, and seek to identify and side with the historical signs of eschatological possibilities. Such questing, discerning, culture-creating commitment to liberation is the road to the local church. That road and that church carry a universal dimension as well, and a reference to the world church precisely because the concern is profoundly human and is bound up with the project of the coming kingdom.[30]

Local churches will be different in ethnic identity, in cultural sensitivity, in the experience of the Divine and in spiritual depth. That is why the Spirit speaks a different word to each of them (see Rev 2 and 3). "The Churches, all of them, are pilgrims of faith, learning to walk the Way that is Christ Jesus, under the guidance of the Spirit. Every church is a developing organism, a branch grown upon Christ, the true Vine" (Jn 5).[31]

By way of conclusion Rayan states:

> Local churches are therefore to be treated as others, as equal partners and witnesses, as co-responsible for the gospel, and surely not as objects of directives and controls from one local centre. As in ancient times local churches should be exchanging letters of witness and warning, exhortation and encouragement. What Paul VI told the United Nations Organisation in 1965 is a rule also for the churches: 'Never one above another'. The struggle for first place and dispute about ranks may be quite 'original' and 'apostolic' (Mk 9:33-37; 10:35-45; Matt 18:1-5; Lk 9:46-50; 22:24-27). But 'It shall not be so' among us. The local churches will be sisters to one another, eager to serve in gladness. They will not be established realities, finished and ready, but established possibilities, which realise themselves through liberative action and response to reality which is in the process of historical becoming.[32]

5. An Indian Church

Rayan stands for a radical incarnation of the Church and the Christian life in the culture of the people of this country so that it becomes the "flesh of India's flesh". To understand this process of the incarnation of the Church we need to examine Rayan's view of the incarnation of the Son of God. As he explains:

> The ultimate incarnation and definitive revelation of this Word of redemptive creation is Jesus. Jesus was not simply God's eternal Word in a particular cultural clothing. He was a deeply historical, densely human reality, a sharer in our bodily existence and earthly conditions, flesh of our flesh, man among men and women, like us in all things though never sinning, never closing himself to God. His body was of this earth, fruit

> along with us of its evolutionary process. It was not made of incorruptible star-dust in heavenly places and then imported. It sprang from the depths of our earth and from the depths of a woman, a dear sister of ours. In coming to dwell among us Jesus was not adapting or accommodating anything to anything. He was not inculturating or indigenizing. He was just being himself in his own country and among his people; he was being himself there as the concrete saving presence and self-giving of God to them. When he spoke Aramaic, or used the familiar phrases of the Bible or of rabbinic catechesis, when he played with children, or considered flowers and birds and seeds and trees and women and leaven and labour for his parables, when for his Eucharist he picked up bread from the dinner table, he was not planning or practising inculturation, but just being himself, being human and honest, present and loyal to the here and now in which God had placed him.[33]

The logic of the incarnation applies to every church, every Christian community. "The Church is Jesus' Body in the measure of the density of its incarnation in concrete local history. The first disciples of Jesus were Jews. Their experience of him was coloured, qualified and shot through with their Jewish religious culture, ethos, hopes, sentiments, world-view, self-image and understanding of God and his ways with people. What emerged was a Jewish Christianity. It took time and challenges from the outside for the Jewish Christians to realize that their Christianity has to undergo a paschal transformation if it has to fulfil its wider mission".[34]

The New Testament bears witness to the intense struggle of the early Church to decide whether the Gentiles have to become Jews first in order to become Christians (see Acts 15 and Galatians 2); whether Church membership has to opened up to non-Jews like the Romans (see Acts 10); and whether the gospel is to be preached to people beyond ethnic and national boundaries.

Christian faith and Christian life need to undergo a paschal experience of dying and rising. According to Rayan:

> The faith falls like a seed into the folds and furrows of every new historical situation - a new culture, a new age, a new society, and new religious conceptions and sensitivities. There it dies

> and rises to new existence; and the sapling draws sustenance from the *milieu,* builds itself up with the human and the religious that is there, and waxes strong in God's light and air without let or hindrance. The faith will bear its own flower and fruit, but in terms of the light, soil and air with which it builds itself, in terms of the situation and the needs, possibilities and experiences of the people whose faith it is. No living thing grows according to rules written down in a book or orders given from far or near. Life develops from within according to its own inner dynamism.[35]

As a result there will be a "splendid pluralism": a wide variety of Church-structures, spiritualities, theologies, dogmas, "all springing from and giving expression to the one mystery of God in Christ Jesus".

It is necessary for every Church in every continent to die and rise again if it is to be living and relevant. "A faith or a church which does not grow from seed or sapling, which does not pass through the risks and pains of growing up, but is ready-made and imported, is likely to remain static and sterile".[36] This is what has happened to the Churches in India for many centuries.

What is quite clear is this: When we speak of inculturation of the Christian faith and Christian life we are not dealing with a few minor adjustments or peripheral accommodation. We are concerned with something which is far more vital and deeper. As Samuel Rayan explains:

> It is with the insertion of the faith into the life-stream of peoples, and the expression of faith-life in terms of their concrete historical existence, as well as the insertion of the peoples' life into the faith at levels deeper than any of its particular expressions. We are committed to the incarnation of the Gospel and of Christian discipleship in the Indian human situation. The Christian experience that forms the heart of the Gospel should be assumed into the religious experience of our people, and their religious experience assimilated into our central Christian experience, resulting in a single incarnate faith with its own vibration, colour, tonality and sensitivity, its own voice, symbolism and imagery in each place, open at the

> same time to the vibrations and voices of the embodied faith everywhere, willing to be corrected and completed by other realizations of the Gospel and to contribute to the correction and completion of others, knowing that every historical reality has its poverty and its wealth and that both are there for the service and growth of love.[37]

6. A Structured Church

Rayan does not discuss the structures of the Church at any great length. But he makes several significant observations. First, Jesus' main concern was that people should meet God and make their own free decision.[38] There is no substitute for their encounter with God: no doctrinal formulations and no organisational structures can replace the real meeting with and conversion to God. Secondly, the basic Christian call is to serve; "service defined discipleship; and the fundamental service and discipleship consisted in (readiness for) self-sacrifice and suffering on behalf of justice to the needy and liberty to the oppressed".[39] The Son of Man came to serve and to give his life (Mk 10:45). Jesus demands that his disciples follow his example. "To seek to dominate over others is an act of unbelief. Among the unbelievers the great ones make their authority felt. "This is never to happen among you.... anyone who wants to be the first shall be the slave of all" (Mk 10:42-45; Lk 22:24-26).

Thirdly, the Church is meant to be a community of brothers and sisters gathered around the one and only Father, God, and the only Master Jesus Christ (Matt 6-12; 8:29). In the family of God all are responsible adults and have to be treated thus. "This experience of brotherliness, expressed in personal attitudes and built into ecclesial structures and practised in the sharing of resources, can equip the Church to bring to the world a service of universal brotherliness, and educate it for the further stage of cultural evolution which is the socialism envisaged and projected by our Eucharistic practice. We may even go further and describe the Church as a circle of friends and a movement of and for total global friendship. To Jesus we are not merely daughters and sons and disciples. He would have us be friends to himself and among ourselves and, I guess, with God as Abraham was. Friendship is a free, equal, independent, permanent relationship. It is at this level that we should envisage the structures of the Church which derives from Jesus".[40]

Fourthly, the church is a community of fundamental equality and freedom. While there are differences of gifts and talents as well as differences that come from nature, "a basic equality of dignity, rights and duties is affirmed and realized in the Church. Freedom as the foundation of faith and as the possibility of love is a factor so essential that without it no Church could be the Church of God or of Jesus Christ".[41]

The members of the community have a variety of charisms which blossom into services. Any ability, talent or training when called upon by the Spirit to be at the service of the community becomes a charism. Charisms are not rare or sensational but ordinary and abundant and given to all at all times for the common good. According to Rayan:

> The mission, ministry and authority that is diffuse in the whole community can and does, through the work of the Spirit or the inner dynamism of the Spirit-filled community itself and through socio-religious factors, gather to a focus and come to concentrated expression in some individual members of the community or in some of its structures... Thus, there develop points of leadership at various levels of the community (local, regional, global), or in various areas of life (teaching, interpreting, coordinating, administering the sacraments). These foci are usually indicated and recognised through ordination. They exercise socially a function which basically belongs to the community as a whole. The concrete organisation and shape of the ministry of leadership should remain flexible but, from the earliest days and all through history, the three offices of bishop, priest and deacon have been recognised and found meaningful.[42]

The communion of all the local churches the world over is the universal Church. The universal church has the Pope for spokesman, leader and sign of unity. This is the Catholic view. But right now most churches would be glad to acknowledge in the papacy a global ministry to secure, maintain and symbolise the unity of all Christians and Christian churches and the unity and effectiveness of the universal

Christian witness. "They would admit a primacy of leadership that is integral to the structural social existence of the Christian movement. It will be a leadership of pastoral concern for fuller commitment of the Church to the Gospel, and for the progress of justice, freedom and peace in the world".[43]

It is sad to realize that for a long time the papacy has been a major cause of the division in God's Church and the main obstacle to the rebuilding of unity. "What can greatly help would be a voluntary renunciation by the papacy of what has accumulated around it through the play of circumstances, and a restructuring of itself in terms of service to the people at the global level in fraternal collaboration with all the serving Churches of the world and all the movements for justice and peace".[44]

7. A Fallible Church

Vatican II has honestly admitted that "the Church, clasping sinners to her bosom, is at once holy and always in need of purification" (*LG* 8). Why does she need to be purified? Because she is a sinful Church.

Samuel Rayan, too, believes that the Church is fallible, because she makes mistakes and commits sins. He has written a very perceptive article titled "I confess", in which "I" stands for the Church.[45] In fantasy Rayan sees the Church making a sincere confession to the Lord of all the sins she has committed down the centuries.

In another article Rayan points out that the secular society has had a significant impact on the structures of the Church and the values she has come to cherish.[46] The experience of the early Christians of the Church as the Jesus movement (see Acts 2: 44-47) and their faith in the Triune God and their celebration of the Eucharist were not allowed to shape the structures of the Church. In the words of Rayan:

> If these truths and celebrations of our faith were allowed to touch, shape and lead the evolution of Christian society, it is unlikely that socio-economic strictures should have developed along sub-Christian, capitalistic and exploitative lines within Christian communities. The fecundating power of our faith has somehow been prevented from reaching its full social

> fruitfulness. Instead, sinful structures have been allowed to shape and secure a place within the Church. Studies seem to show that from the time secular powers took the Church under their patronage, the initiatives reflected in the Acts have been curbed. The government of the Church at various levels, many church policies, the Church's material arrangements and the economic life of the brotherhood/sisterhood have been reflecting the class structure of society under the control of the privileged.[47]

Jesus and St. Paul spoke highly of freedom (see Jn 8:31-36; Gal 5:1 and 13). The Second Vatican Council has clearly affirmed that "freedom is an exceptional sign of the image of God in man and woman" and that "God willed that humans should be left to their own counsel" (*GS* 17). Besides, freedom is central to modern people's self-understanding. People speak of an explosion of freedom in our times. And yet freedom does not seem to be a cherished value in the Church. As Rayan observes:

> In societies aspiring after democracy and an egalitarian or communitarian style of life, free discussion, the creation of public opinion and popular election of office-bearers are cherished values. These have not found their way into the Church though the Church should have been their birth-place and their home. Or, is it that they were born in the Church but had to leave home to survive and to grow?
>
> A way of growth in freedom and truth, which human groups are coming more and more to appreciate, is *criticism.* Developing a critical ability is an essential part of education, since education is to create the future and not merely continue the past. Criticism is important for the advance of science, the health of literature and art, and sanity in politics. It can be used to destroy both what is good and bad, but if responsibly used, it can prove a blessing, not the least for the Church. The Church, to be alive and relevant as the voice and sign of the living God, needs to keep examining and evaluating its traditions, positions, assertions, formulations and fears. There will always be things to be discarded, corrected, adjusted, newly acquired. Prophetic criticism is a service the Church must give to society. But a service of criticism needs to be developed within the Church

> itself. It should be an honest criticism, one born of love and genuine concern. We shall do well to begin with a criticism of the fear the Church seems to have of criticism.[48]

8. A Spirit-led Church

Rayan has written a thought provoking article titled "Hear and Heed What the Spirit Says to the Churches".[49] Rayan is here drawing inspiration from the book of Revelation, Chapters 1, 2 and 3. As he states:

> The Risen Jesus is addressing John, the seer, and is disclosing to him the messages which the Holy Spirit is directing to various churches (Rev 2 and 3). Seven distinct churches in seven different places are named: seven local churches, each of them rooted in God's call and in the local people's faith-response. Each local group is recognised by the Spirit as an authentic church, as a faith-community, commissioned to bear witness to God's saving love made manifest in the crucified and risen Jesus; to witness to love by a life of love rather than by mere words however sublime. In the cultural context of John, the seer, the number seven, like the number twelve too, signifies completeness. The reference then may be to all the faith communities in a region or to the Church at large. The number may also be pointing to the unity of the many congregations, despite their racial and cultural diversity.[50]

Rayan believes that the Spirit can speak to the Church through the inspired words of the New Testament. According to him this is one of the things the Spirit says to it through Paul:

> For as in one body we have many members, and not all the members have the same function. So we, who are many, are one body in Christ, and individually we are members one of another. We have gifts that differ according to the grace given to us: prophecy, in proportion to faith; ministry, in ministering; the teacher, in teaching; the exhorter, in exhortation; the giver, in generosity, the leader, in diligence; the compassionate, in cheerfulness (Rom 12:4-8).

> Now there are varieties of gifts, but the same Spirit; and there are varieties of services, but the same Lord; and there are varieties of activities, but it is the same God who activates all of them in everyone. To each is given the manifestation of the Spirit for the common good. To one is given through the Spirit the utterance of wisdom, and to another the utterance of knowledge according to the same Spirit, to another faith by the same Spirit, to another gifts of healing by the one Spirit, to another the working of miracles, to another prophecy, to another the discernment of spirits, to another various kinds of tongues, to another the interpretation of tongues. All these are activated by one and the same Spirit, who allots to each one individually just as the Spirit chooses (1 Cor 12:4-11).

Rayan makes the following reflections on these texts:

> Every faithful heart, then, is a centre from which and through which God's Spirit acts for the benefit of all. The same could be said of every domestic church, of every local congregation of the Lord, as well as of the world communion of the assemblies of faith. All these are inter-dependent ecclesial centres bearing witness to God and His Christ in the Holy Spirit.[51]

Rayan is convinced that the Spirit can speak to the Churches through the words of Matthew and Mark:

> But you are not to be called rabbi, for you have one teacher, and you are all students. And call no one your father on earth, for you have one Father –the one in heaven. Nor are you to be called instructors, for you have one instructor, the Messiah. The greatest among you will be your servant (Matt 23:8-11).
>
> So Jesus called them and said to them, "You know that among the Gentiles those whom they recognize as their rulers lord it over them, and their great ones are tyrants over them. But it is not so among you; but whoever wishes to become great among you must be your servant, and whoever wishes to be first among you must be slave of all. For the Son of Man came not to be served but to serve, and to give his life a ransom for many" (Mk 10:42-45).

Commenting on these texts Rayan says:

> Within each local church, then, the personal charismas and functions are complementary. The Spirit expects the members of the community to listen to, learn from and enrich each other and collaborate in love for the good of the entire community and the advancement of God's Reign on earth. All the members are basically equal in human and Christian dignity, and in the vocation they have to love and serve. So are all the local churches too that dot the globe. This central truth and basic vision are threatened with neglect and oblivion in a world of caste, class and power hierarchies, or of domination and subjugation. The temptation to exalt ourselves and depress others and build socio-religious power pyramids is never far. That is why Jesus steps in time and again to urge us to hear what the Spirit says to all the churches and all their members.[52]

In order not to grieve the Spirit we need to reshape our life according to the word addressed to us, and put away,

> "all bitterness, fury, anger, shouting and reviling", and instead "be kind to one another, compassionate and forgiving" as God has forgiven us in Christ. (Eph 4:25-32).

Rayan has the following reflection:

> The Spirit, speaking through Jesus, makes it clear that not everyone who says 'Lord, Lord' will enter the Kingdom but only those who do the will of the Father. Those who hear the word and act on it are like a wise man who builds his house on rock. Rains may fall, floods may come, and buffet the house, but it will not collapse. But everyone who listens to the word and does not care to act on it will be like a fool who built his house on sand. When the floods came and the wind blew, the house collapsed and was completely ruined. (Matt 7:21-27). We are warned against following the example of hypocrites who "preach but do not practise" (Matt 23:3). This would apply to ecclesial circles, personal, familial, local, global. We have perhaps been accenting doctrine and ritual far more heavily than practice and life.[53]

Rayan is quite convinced that the Spirit can speak to the Church through poets and prophets who are not Christians. He believes that the Spirit is speaking to the Church though Rabindranath Tagore:

> Leave this chanting and singing and telling of beads!
> Whom dost thou worship in this lonely
> dark corner of a temple...?
> Open thine eyes and see thy God is not before thee!
> He is there where the tiller is tilling the hard ground
> And where the path maker is breaking stones.
> He is with them in sun and in shower,
> And his garment is covered with dust.
> Put off thy holy mantle and even like him
> Come down on the dusty soil.
> ... Our master himself has joyfully taken upon him
> The bonds of creation; he is bound with us all forever.
> Come out of thy meditations and leave aside thy flowers
> and incense.
> What harm is there if thy clothes become tattered and stained?
> Meet him and stand with him in toil and in the sweat of thy brow.[54]

Rayan also refers to a few modern prophets through whom the Spirit is speaking to the Churches. I shall not mention them here.

By way of conclusion I wish to make two comments:

1. In this paper I have not dealt with all the elements of Rayan's ecclesiology. He has many more things to say about the Church. I have just highlighted some of his original insights: the Church as the Jesus movement, the Church as a counter-cultural movement and the Church as an event. I find these insights both inspiring and challenging.

2. Rayan is quite aware of how difficult it is to describe the Church. There are several reasons for this. As Rayan explains:

> For one thing we are too close to this reality, we belong to it, are within it, we are it. For another, the Church in its long and complex history has taken on many roles and it is not easy to

> see what is its proper function as distinct from the accidental which could be taken up or left alone. It is difficult also because, sometimes we say one thing and do another thing. This gap between orthodoxy and orthopraxis also results in obscuring the face of the Church... But the profoundest reason may be that the Church is not something ready-made, finished and set squarely on the ground. It is something still in the making, something still seeking for its own face, its identity, its heart; though it knows what it is. It has still to find itself.[55]

Hence, Rayan will not claim to have developed a fully adequate ecclesiology. What he has said about the Church is necessarily tentative and incomplete.

Notes

1. See K. Kunnumpuram (ed.), *Collected Writings of Samuel Rayan, Vol I: Nature, Woman and the Church*, Delhi: ISPCK, 2013, pp. 155–343.
2. See S. Rayan, "The Church – The Jesus Movement" in K. Kunnumpuram (ed.), *Collected Writings of Samuel Rayan*, Vol. I, pp. 181-189.
3. *Ibid.*, p. 182.
4. *Ibid.*
5. *Ibid.*, p. 183.
6. *Ibid.*
7. *Ibid.*
8. *Ibid.*
9. *Ibid.*, p. 184.
10. *Ibid.*, pp. 184-185.
11. *Ibid.*, p. 185.
12. *Ibid.*, p. 186.
13. *Ibid.*
14. *Ibid.*, p. 187.
15. S. Rayan, "The Early Christianity as Counter-Culture" in K. Kunnumpuram (ed.), *Collected Writings of Samuel Rayan*, Vol. 1, p. 209.
16. *Ibid.*, p. 210
17. *Ibid.*, pp. 2109-211.
18. *Ibid.*, p. 214.
19. *Ibid.*, p. 215.
20. *Ibid.*
21. *Ibid.*, pp. 229-230.

22. *Ibid.*, p. 230.
23. *Ibid.*, pp. 230-231.
24. *Ibid.*, p. 232.
25. Rayan, "The Church – The Jesus Movement" in K. Kunnumpuram (ed.), *Collected Writings of Samuel Rayan*, Vol. I, pp. 187-188.
26. *Ibid.*, p. 188.
27. *Ibid.*
28. S. Rayan, "Hear and Heed What the Spirit Says to the Churches" in K. Kunnumpuram (ed.), *Collected Writings of Samuel Rayan*, Vol. I, p. 191.
29. *Ibid.*
30. S. Rayan, "Inculturation and the Local Church" in K. Kunnumpuram (ed.), *Collected Writings of Samuel Rayan*, Vol. I, p. 238.
31. S. Rayan, "Hear and Heed What the Spirit Says to the Churches" in K. Kunnumpuram (ed.), *Collected Writings of Samuel Rayan*, Vol. I, p. 192.
32. S. Rayan, "Inculturation and the Local Church", p. 241.
33. S. Rayan, "Flesh of India's Flesh" in K. Kunnumpuram (ed.), *Collected Writings of Samuel Rayan*, Vol. I, p. 243.
34. *Ibid.*, p. 244.
35. *Ibid.*
36. *Ibid.*, p. 246.
37. *Ibid.*, p. 249.
38. S. Rayan, "Theology of the Church" in K. Kunnumpuram (ed.), *Collected Writings of Samuel Rayan*, Vol. I, p. 309.
39. *Ibid.*
40. *Ibid.*, p. 310.
41. *Ibid.*
42. *Ibid.*, p. 311.
43. *Ibid.*, p. 312.
44. *Ibid.*
45. S. Rayan, "I Confess…" in K. Kunnumpuram (ed.), *Collected Writings of Samuel Rayan*, Vol. I, pp. 261-283.
46. S. Rayan, "Sociological Factors and the Local Church as an Eucharistic Community" in K. Kunnumpuram (ed.), *Collected Writings of Samuel Rayan*, Vol. I, pp. 172-189.
47. *Ibid.*, p. 173.
48. *Ibid.*, p. 176.
49. S. Rayan, "Hear and Heed What the Spirit Says to the Churches" in K. Kunnumpuram (ed.), *Collected Writings of Samuel Rayan*, Vol. I, pp. 190-207.
50. *Ibid.*, p. 190.
51. *Ibid.*, pp. 193-194.

52. *Ibid.*, p. 194.
53. *Ibid.*, pp. 198-199.
54. No. XI *Gitanjali*, Delhi: Macmillan, 2000, 46th edition.
55. S. Rayan, "The Church - The Jesus Movement" in K. Kunnumpuram (ed.), *Collected Writings of Samuel Rayan*, Vol. I, p. 181.

8

Mission of the Church according to Samuel Rayan

Joseph Lobo, SJ

Introduction

The integral approach of Samuel Rayan to the understanding of the mission of the Church typically comprises his thoughts on Christology, Ecclesiology, Social analysis and other religions. In this concise essay the focus will be mainly on critically appreciating his thoughts on the mission of the Church. Remaining faithful to Rayan's own fundamental theological rationale, I shall present and critically comment on his missional considerations in relation to their significance for the contemporary Indian situation. Therefore, this essay begins with presenting eleven challenges to the mission of the Church today as perceived by Rayan. I shall then briefly present Rayan's challenges to some of the traditional understanding and practice of the Church's mission and finally his proposals for mission today. I shall conclude with a brief critical appraisal of Rayan's views.

Challenges to the mission of the Church today

1. The lack of clarity in understanding the mission

Despite some success of *Ad Gentes* in integrating the two main missiological thoughts prevalent in the history of the Church, still a more comprehensive and systematic understanding of the mission of the Church is yet to see the dawn. The two missiological schools referred to are: (a) Christo-centric and personal that emphasize the "proclamation of the Gospel, conversion and salvation" and (b) Ecclesio-centric, whose focus is on "the planting of the Church, the establishment of hierarchy and the organization of young Churches".[1]

Added to the lack of clarity is the realization that every human heart longs for God whether or not it is acknowledged as such (*LG* 16; *GS* 22). Traditionally it was called 'implicit faith'. Rayan affirms that "all activities, movements and relationships which tally with God's wishes and plans as God knows them are implicit, existential, lived faith-responses to God's word, love and reign".[2] If so, what can the mission of the Church add to such authentic faith found in all people across religious traditions, even though it may be 'implicit'?[3] Is the Church as such ready to accept the fact that "situated as it is in the flux of history" she has to "understand herself and her task only progressively in confrontation, dialogue and involvement with the changing, growing, questioning world?"[4]

2. What constitutes mission?

Traditionally the mission of the Church was understood as ministry of the Word and sacraments. However, in recent times developmental and conscientization work is also seen as part of the mission; and sometimes even as the only possible mission.[5]And so, how to carry on the traditional mission in and through its new modes?

3. Mission ad Gentes?

The mission of the Church is faced with a special challenge in a multi-religious context. "How indeed are the Church and her mission related to other religions and cultures? Is Christianity the only true expression of the unique Gospel of Jesus?...Could it be that it is Christ that all the religions tell of and show forth, though it is in the Church alone that his face and name are recognized and acknowledged?"[6]

But, the more intricate issue regarding the mission of the Church is to ask whether "it is in God's saving plan that we seek and secure the victory of Christianity to the abolition and replacement of all other religions? What indeed is the role of religions in the plan of salvation? That is, what significance do they have for their followers with regard to salvation, and what meaning for us? What about the meeting between the missions of the various churches and Christian groups?"[7]

In this context, the decline in conversions leads us to perceive the background against which it is taking place, namely, "1) the resurgence and renaissance of ancient religions contrary to missionary expectation; 2) the love Asian Christians have developed, particularly after the Council (Vatican II), for the religions of their land and for a national and spiritual-religious heritage; and 3) the end of the imperial era which demands that missions be much more than cultural and theological colonies and closed ghettos".[8]

In the contemporary theological discourse a few theologians speak of the convergence of the religious traditions; their death and new rising in this convergence. In such a discourse, no particular religion as such is given a lasting importance. Much attention is given rather to "God's purpose for humankind, or God's kingdom, as this may be perceived from the collective history, common search and corporate experience of humankind as a whole".[9] If so what unique role can be claimed for the mission of the Church?

4. A renewed historical consciousness in the Church

Vatican II exhibits a profound historical consciousness in its understanding of human reality, the nature and mission of the Church and her relationship to the world today. Hence, it is duly acknowledged that history, sacraments, traditions, economics, politics, the human person etc. gain importance in experiencing and understanding God's ways with us humans. Indeed incarnation makes history the preferred way of God to communicate life and love to us.[10] Such considerations have consequences for the understanding and practice of Church's mission: mission cannot ignore life in its entirety here on earth. It means the 'spiritual' has to be served in and through the 'historical' and the 'material'. Indeed Jesus could not rest after a seemingly successful preaching on the mount until he fed the crowd.

5. Baptism: A water rite or drinking from the cup that Jesus drinks?

A careful reading of the 'great mission command' of Mt 28:18-20 unearths the fact that the text prioritizes 'discipling' above 'baptizing' – indeed an arduous task. Even then, baptism as such is understood more as the participation in the painful and challenging ministry of Jesus (Mk 10; Lk 12) than as a water rite. Indeed "the baptism which makes us disciples is not a baptism Jesus gives, but participation in the painful baptism he undergoes".[11] Such an understanding of the Matthean mission command places an unprecedented challenge for the mission of the Church. For it demands a life of discipleship as a necessary pre-requisite for water baptism.

6. A conquering Christianity with freeing baptism: A blatant contradiction

The colonial era saw a Christianity that conquered and exploited peoples in Africa, Asia and the Americas and at the same time baptized the conquered people. Such practices directly contradicted the truly and integrally liberating nature of the sacraments such as Baptism and the Eucharist. Under such circumstances the Gospel got de-historicized and sacraments became focused on other worldly realities. Today in the light of the documents such as the BEM document of Lima, the radically challenging and liberative character of the sacraments has to be retrieved afresh.[12] When that happens, the mission of the Church cannot remain silent about the atrocities of the neo-colonialism of our times.

It is noteworthy that the West's betrayal of the Gospel in the colonial and neo-colonial contexts proved and continues to prove a great block to the spreading of the Gospel. This could be one of the reasons why the Gospel of Jesus Christ did not send deep and widespread roots in Asia and Africa.[13]

The conquering and enslaving colonial forces could not accept a truly liberating Christianity. It is in this context that missionaries preached an otherworldly, a-historical and sterile Christian faith bereft of any reference to the here and now. "They had to distinguish sharply between the sacred and the secular, preach an individualistic eschatological salvation, and a vertical, a-political, a-social, innocuous, supernatural Gospel. Churches born of such missions have as a rule remained uncreative and sterile".[14] A similar critique is made of the Jesuit educational apostolate in India, which according to Rayan, for the most part has remained uncritical of social and structural oppression, and hence is busy preparing men and women of upper rungs of society for jobs.[15]

7. The challenge of the Eucharist

Rayan has special references to the Eucharist. Eucharist is seen no more as a mere ritual and much less as a cosy devotion. It is rather historicized by relating it to the challenging historical realities. And so "no broken bread can be remembrance of the death of Jesus if it is divorced from the brokenness of the people, from the death of their children for lack of bread, and the suffering meted out to the masses with whom Jesus identifies".[16] In Jeremiah's phraseology (Jer 1:10), the Eucharistic praxis needs to be related to pluck up and to pull down; destroy and to overthrow all that is exploitative and discriminating; thereby to build and to plant truly human and humane communities. It can never remain a private devotion, and much less, as in the colonial times, spiritual nourishment to the armies whose job was to kill, rape and loot.[17] Indeed "Without bread there can be no Eucharist; in the bosom of the hungry family and in the midst of an un-free and shrunken spirit there is no felt sign of God's presence and concern…Food and drink, then, and freedom and opportunities for creative life, are part of the justice, peace and joy the Holy Spirit gives (Rom 14:17; Gen 1 and 2; 2 Cor 9). That is why salvation does not occur in an spiritualization of the human person, but in the Incarnation of God's Son. People are not taken out of the world, but Jesus is sent into the world".[18] Indeed, despite his deep conviction that humans do not live by bread alone, Christ concerns himself occasionally with feeding the hungry crowds.[19]

Eucharist in Rayan's view is both a gift and a task in the life and mission of the Church. Just as in classical theology, deteriorated bread cannot receive or retain sacramental consecration, so too a deteriorated state of life within dehumanizing system cannot be a symbol of the Kingdom, unless in the living out of the Eucharistic reality the concerned community definitely work towards the healing of such states of life.[20] And hence "if ... the Eucharist is a sign of unity and a sacrament of community, how could it be shared equally at the same table by the oppressor and the oppressed, the black-marketeer and his victims?"[21]

Indeed, if Eucharist is intrinsic to the mission of the Church then such a mission receives unprecedented challenges from the Eucharist.

8. Local cultures are a means and a medium for the Gospel

The story of Jesus, if it has to be transformative, needs to be told in the local cultural idiom. Effective evangelization is possible only by such means. While maintaining the essentials of faith intact, expressing it in local cultural categories has been one of the most challenging and at the same time very fulfilling tasks of all times in the history of the Church.[22]

9. The challenge of the practical atheism

The biblical prophets lay a clearly higher emphasis on justice over cult. Since, as they say in various contexts, to do justice is to know God, it follows that practice of injustice is practical atheism, even though often such structures of atheism are couched with religious garb.[23] "Where the question of justice is downplayed, no authentic sharing in Jesus' faith-commitment is possible".[24]

10. Challenge of the revolting exploited masses

There is a definite shift from a passive fatalism towards rising in revolt against oppression among the Indian populace. Although, it has not reached the magnitude of a full-fledged bloody revolution, the passivity seems to be disappearing fast. Such a situation poses a serious challenge to the Church in India: how shall we participate in such protests?[25] This calls for adopting certain models of participation. Should they be Leftists (Russian, Chinese, Cuban) along with certain adoption of Latin American Liberation theology, or Gandhian? It is not easy to discern.[26]

Whatever may be the model(s) adopted, the task is to facilitate the Kingdom in the lives of our people; for the Church is the sacrament of the Reign of God. Such sacramentality necessitates that the Church community becomes a "social expression" as well as a pointer towards a future "from where the Kingdom comes and to which it leads".[27]

In this context, Rayan acknowledges the tremendous service rendered by the Church institutions especially in the educational and medical fields in addition to other works of charity for the poor and the downtrodden. A lot of middle and upper class people are also served by such institutions. However, as he sharply observes, such service has not really addressed the core and fundamental structures of injustice and exploitation which are causal to poverty, to any adequate degree.[28] In fact "given the Church's present setup, given its institutional ties, its economic base, its consequent political alliances, and its sociologically automatic mass membership on the basis of minimum demands, it is difficult for the Church as it exists today to do more or otherwise".[29] A radical re-structuring the nature and mission of the Church both in theory and practice seems to be the only option.

11. The enormity of the challenges

The enormity and the complexity of the challenges of our times have made it clear that any adequate response has to be a broad based one, which necessitates collaboration with different groups across religious, cultural and ideological traditions. The only uniting factor for such groups, at times, can be their commitment to integral human welfare. In this context, Rayan finds that a "rigid institutional-societal understanding of the Church will find it difficult" to elicit such a collaboration. The Church should understand itself more as a movement than as a rigid structure. A core of committed believers and many others who can be "associated with its goals in various ways and different densities" can labour together towards such liberational goals.[30]

The mission of the Church in Rayan's perspective

The nature of the Church

Rayan's understanding of the reality of the Church is intimately linked to his Christological views. The Church as a visible sign is the blossoming of the saving mystery that Jesus is. "As Jesus is the

Kingdom at the point where it emerges as personal history, so the Church is the kingdom at the point where it develops into a social history. Therefore, in and with Jesus she is the sacrament of all the religions of humankind".[31]

The sacramental character of the Church can be lived out only in terms of such praxis in which the Kingdom is served in its historical as well as eschatological dimensions. Hence, while the ultimate mission of the Church is to point beyond the history, nevertheless it cannot ignore the anti-Kingdom realities of history that dehumanize the children of God.[32]

Gaudium et Spes makes it clear that the Church does not exist for itself, but to serve humankind in working for its total liberation and integral well-being. In this sense the Church is naturally missionary. *Ad Gentes* further accentuates such a missionary character in terms of relationship with the world and especially with other religions.[33] In this context, the Church particularizes "the scope of a universal saving history into the scope of a particular saving history, which is the life of Jesus". For Rayan that defines the essence of Church's mission in the world.[34]

It is on the basis of this understanding of the reality of the Church that Rayan makes a critique of some of the traditional ways of understanding and practising the mission.

Some traditional theories and practice of mission challenged

1. Rayan strongly argues for well inculturated liturgical celebrations. That is because "in a celebration people express their faith and life, and life's joys, pains, frustrations and commitments. As cultural expressions of faith and life, celebrations cannot be exported, imported, imposed from outside or fixed forever. They have to be created and recreated by the people in every age and every cultural context".[35] The mission of the Church in India has to seriously consider these issues as of paramount importance if the Gospel of Jesus Christ is to be made responsive to people's aspirations.
2. He sharply critiques all the tendencies to isolate the developmental activities from evangelization or of naming them 'indirect evangelization', because the name of Jesus may not be

mentioned in such activities. Human life is one integral whole; and so the evangelization has to address all the dimensions (including physical) of the human reality. Citing the example of the early Ranchi Jesuit mission of setting the Tribals free from the clutches of the landlords, Rayan quite rhetorically asks whether a failure to seek instruction in faith and baptism on the part of some of these people are to be seen as "insensitivity to a God-given sign." Whether "peoples' acknowledged experience of God's justice and love, mediated through Christian action, always leads to and expresses itself in visible and social membership of an institutional Church".[36]

3. However, he makes it clear that the development programmes that keep the helpless perpetually dependent on the Church institutions certainly go against the very nature of the mission of the Church. Hence, he asks, "should not relief remain strictly an emergency measure which may not be institutionalized and perpetuated? Is it right to give the impression that the task of the Church is to pick up year after year those whom the system breaks and throws out and to enable them to die loved for an hour or two, but never to call a halt to the process that is destroying women and men by the millions?"[37]
4. Lack of integration between the 'this worldly' and the 'other worldly' in the mission of the Church has led to many a misgiving. Rayan cites the examples of the Church's lack of official critique of and resistance to issues such as slave-trade and slave labour. Pious missionaries rather tried to catechise and baptise the victims of slavery in order to send them to heaven rather than offering an effective and prophetic critique of the entire system itself.[38] It is remarkable how representatives of Andean Indians were sharply aware of the instrumentality of the Bible in destroying their culture and civilization. In an open letter addressed to the visiting Pope John Paul II, they asked him to take back the Bible and give it to their oppressors.[39]
5. Incarnation unites the 'secular' with the 'sacred'. This is seen so vividly in the Eucharistic reality. "In the absence of bread there is no Eucharist... In the Eucharist we have a divine affirmation of the human dimensions of life before God. We see once

more that it is within human relationships and within their material, social, economic basis that God's redeeming presence is indicated and salvation offered for humans' taking".[40] Indeed what God has put together in creation, incarnation, resurrection and sacramental practice no human being should separate![41] To take a leaf out from Gandhiji's own 'experiments with truth', his struggle for India's liberation from untouchability and from foreign domination were an essential part of his loyalty to God and to Truth; indeed a 'spiritual' quest (satyagraha).[42]

6. Hence, in a world that highly values what depends upon technological advancement, the Church can advocate for the use of technological innovations in the "service to the needy masses, [to contribute] to the cause of justice and human dignity [by functioning] within a different, humane, conception of economics and of production relationships".[43] The Church need not be reactionary or archaic in her perception of technological advancement; but must provide an ethical horizon for its development and functioning.
7. In Rayan's perception the survival and progress of the Church as an institution is clearly made subservient to the progress of the Kingdom. Hence, a meaningful self-survival for the Church is only by participating in Christ's crucifixion and death, so that she too could rise; but "rise not necessarily as Church, but as something greater, something transformed as the Kingdom of God in the wider context of human history".[44]
8. Any sort of political conquest theories and ideologies that informed the mission of the Church in the past have no place today. Rayan perceptively points out how the theological justifications for one race being chosen over the others, which are found in the Bible, are not historical records; but are "reconstructions of the past in terms of the people's religious and political ideologies around the close of 7th C BCE".[45] He builds on the Vatican II's unambiguous positive attitude towards religious freedom of all. From the age-old position of "error has no rights" to the current positive attitude it has been a long way in the history of the Church. The acknowledgment on the part of Vatican II that "in the life of the people of God as it has

made its pilgrim way through the vicissitudes of human history, there have at times appeared ways of acting which were less in accord with the spirit of the gospel and even opposed to it" (*Dignitatis Humanae*, No. 12) should in all circumstances, after the example of Christ himself, remind us that the missionary praxis of the Church can never afford to bear even the slightest traces of coercion on the people of other religions.[46]

9. The biblical texts that reflect a blanket devaluation of the non-Jewish religions and their adherents have to be understood as attributions done "in general from the viewpoint of the Jewish ethnic religion, and from within limited acquaintance with the people and religions of the world".[47] However, exceptions to such a view are also not lacking in the biblical texts. In Romans 1 and 2 despite his awareness of the existence of idolatry among the Greeks, Paul acknowledges the existence of obedience to the demands of the law written in their hearts (conscience) among all peoples (Rom 2:13-16). The Jews and the gentiles are further put in the same boat, as it were in being guilty before God and needing His mercy (Rom 3:9-29).[48]
10. Rayan is critical of the usual suspicious attitude of the Roman Church towards local theologies and liturgies in general. Such attitudes advocate a rather blind and universal applicability of ideas produced at the centre, whose viability at the periphery is taken for granted. Further, such a practice does not do adequate justice to the spirit behind the Church's own stand on universal religious freedom or for that matter freedom of conscience. In fact, it does not even take into cognisance the fact of God's presence and revelation in the local situations and in the experience of the local faith-communities.[49]
11. The above consideration leads Rayan to inquire into the epistemological bases of the Church's speech on any matter. He points out how for the biblical tradition the "spiritual is the historical that participates in and contributes to the coming of the Reign of God, and to the growth of love and the enhancement of humanness." Bereft of such participation the Church's discourse can only be a type of ahistorical 'gnosis' that would be satisfied to deal with the 'spiritual' separated from the historical.[50] And

the Church in such circumstances would grossly be unfaithful to the biblical tradition. In a similar way a spirituality that does not invite us "to join God where He opens prisons, smashes fetters, pulls down the mighty from their thrones and lifts up the lowly" though can be valuable and precious, has also been favoured by "colonialists and dominators, TNCs, generals and racists".[51] Indeed a spirituality that does not empower us towards a liberative praxis actually needs to be suspected for its tendency to make us inert – a situation of sin in the biblical perspective.[52]

12. Today we need to understand the Kingdom as a deeper, wider and more profound reality than what can be called 'Christian', which in turn is a "fairly small, limited and particular movement within and at the service of human history in a process and of the Kingdom which keeps coming into this history of realizing itself socially".[53] For indeed, "what is foundational to the Christian reality, namely the Kingdom, is more than 'Christian'".[54] It is this fact that sets a Christian free for the task of discerning the presence and budding forth of the Kingdom in many a truly liberation struggle and movement, however 'secular' they might appear to be.[55]

Rayan's proposals for the mission of the Church today

Rayan's Christological presupposition behind his understanding of the mission of the Church in relation to other religions is well articulated in the affirmation that "the revelation operative in the religions is always the Word of God made flesh in Jesus (the very human-wardness of the Word and its actual communication to humans being integral to the one historical event of the enfleshing of the Word), that grace imparted is the Paschal grace, that the (implicit) faith born in them (other religions) is a self-commitment of God in the dying of Christ, that their (adherents of other religions) obedience is a share in the submission of the Crucified One...There is only one Mediator of humankind and God, of creation and redemption, the Man Jesus. It is by his health that all men and women are healed. His friendship with God shared is salvation for the world".[56]

Though the Vatican II does not say that the other religions are valid ways of salvation for their respective adherents, Rayan takes the cue from the absence of any such denial in the conciliar documents to affirm that the other religions can be salvific means to their adherents. "It is not in spite of their religions but in them and in fact by means of them that men and women are saved by God. For the God who creates and saves through His Word in the Spirit is present in the world and in human realities".[57]

If so, religions have been giving varied expressions to their 'core' experiences of the Kingdom, all of which are imperfect and limited due to their obvious human character.[58] Indeed the "other is sign and guarantee that there exists one greater than I and they".[59] Among these Rayan acknowledges the special sacramental character of the Hebrew history, wherein "grace became national history and God's intervention began to be seen and consciously accepted".[60] In such an understanding of the basic character of religions the mission of the Christian Church attains a very 'catholic' dimension: "to appropriate, safeguard and to preserve for generations to come the spirituality God has been nurturing in this land down the centuries, even if Hindus themselves were to neglect it or forget it altogether (Matt 5:13)".[61]

One cannot deny the fact that the challenge that Hinduism in India faced at the arrival of Westernized Christianity was more on the social realm than at the levels of fundamental doctrines and spirituality. Correspondingly, most of the reformist movements focused on the social and political dimensions of Hinduism.[62] This opens up the possibility for the Church to consider the spiritual treasures of these traditions for mutual enrichment in the context of an interreligious dialogue. However, the 'mission *ad gentes* should not make the Church ignorant of a mission to herself, geared towards her own "conversion from the idols of casteism, sexism and hierarchism, of power and mammon" – a mission that needs to be spearheaded by the victims of such oppressive practices.[63]

In the death-resurrection event Jesus has made peace and united in himself all hostile factions, thereby creating a new humanity, in which are included all who are reconciled to God. The 'other' can no more be called 'dog', untouchable, or unbeliever, but fellow-citizen, brother and sister. Christianity, then, as the reconciled community by its very nature needs to work against all that divides the children of God, including religion and offer the world a spirituality of concern and compassion, offering a 'theology of the other' and a 'spirituality of mutualness.[64] It is in the practice of such compassion that is concretely lived in the "sharing of bread and breath", in the sharing of "resources, spiritual experience, money, personnel and organization, in supporting the struggles of the poor" that the adherents of various religions are invited to discover their own deeper and truer selves and ultimately God.[65] While such collaboration can be rightly called the service of the Kingdom, the Kingdom as such remains beyond what human efforts can bring about and beyond the grasp of any religious tradition.[66]

In such praxis the human person and communities gain preference over religious structures built by human hands. Such structures and buildings, however sacred and magnificent they may be regarded to be, can be dispensed with; for human persons have become God's dwelling place, and the true worship transcends all 'sacred' space and time and is identified as that which takes place in spirit and truth. In this perspective, any conflict related to the 'holy' places and times becomes absolutely pointless as far as their spiritual significance is concerned. They can be merely political and economic and hence can be treated as such by all those who are concerned about authentic spirituality. A religion that teaches to hate the 'other' destroys itself by destroying its very liberative core.[67]

And so, one remains open to another not by skirting one's own faith, but precisely by being led by one's own faith to embrace the other. This is because authentic faith that opens us to God also creates openness in us to the other. Authentic faith is as much 'horizontal' as it is 'vertical' in this sense.[68] But this does not mean that one needs to negate the specific character of various religions. In this context one can ask whether religions are humans' ways to God or God's ways to reach humans! In either case truth and unity cannot be had by ignoring the distinctness of each faith.[69]

One thing becomes clear that a meaningful spreading of the Church cannot be understood in terms of the number of the baptized, but rather in terms of the germinating and flowering forth of the Kingdom in the hearts of people and in societal relationships. Indeed it has to be seen in the "living out of the Our Father in human history".[70] That is why biblical prophets emphasize just relationships over cultic performances.[71] In the new dispensation the Church should understand her mission along similar lines. NT speaks of the parabolic yeast, mustard seed, salt and light in portraying the Kingdom. These metaphors effectively and evocatively bring out the character and mission of the Church as well. Sure enough, the mission of the Church in history remains symbolic. But because it is symbolic, it is also prophetic and contains a force within it to give energy and direction to many a liberational process, both in the present and in the future.[72]

Falling back on the Lima text, Rayan affirms the basic mission of the Church in terms of the living out of the baptismal reality, namely participation in the mission, life, death and resurrection of Jesus. It amounts to offering new life and hope to people.[73] Hence, the Great Mission Command for him is "Love one another as I have loved you" (Jn 13:34-35), which is concretely shown by the "dalitized" (Samaritan) traveller who serves the one "stripped, robbed, broken and left half-dead on the roadside of history".[74] In this way, the Great Mission Command in Matthew's gospel to disciple and baptize is to be understood in its reference to nations, cultures and religions and not merely individuals. Such a mission goes beyond mere water baptism and focuses on the metanoia of the masses to Jesus' concerns.[75]

A daunting mission of this type needs equally empowering supportive theologies and spiritualities. Rayan is convinced that they should be developed from the experience of God's liberating presence especially in the lives and cultures of the victimized people in history.[76] Such empowering theologies and spiritualities essentially consist of the story of Jesus told in diverse local contexts, so that its transforming potential may be made fully operative in them. Such an exercise demands a discerning heart to perceive how the Word is functioning in the histories of various peoples. It would necessitate deriving grace and inspiration from "all the sacred texts of all communities as far as they are humanizing, meaning (as far as they) help humans to walk the right path of justice, love and solidarity, and rejecting what is dehumanizing, meaning what degrades humans".[77]

The Church, Rayan confirms, has the duty to discern and announce God's salvific ways in all religions, which of course get a special meaning, significance and depth in Jesus.[78] And so the fundamental invitation in the mission of the Church is to turn to God and not for baptism, yet the Church community invites all to join her and be sharers of the 'treasurers' that she has in Jesus Christ.[79] Such treasures are not to be understood exclusively in a spiritual sense; they stand for the participation in the mission of Jesus of uplifting the downtrodden. This invitation of the Church to all people indeed is her evangelization – the planting of the cross.[80]

The template for Church's mission today (and always) is so vividly portrayed in the biblical narratives: In the case of Zachaeus, for instance, the salvation experienced by him is simultaneously articulated in terms of justice and fairness in societal relationships; in the narrative of the rich man and Lazarus, the point is not that the poor can hope for a 'pie in the sky when they die', but rather that the rich should listen to the prophetic voices of the poor and to the demands of the Gospel to live justly (Jn 5:24-25; 4:23; Lk 16: 1-12; Mt 5:42; 16: 19-31). The full flowering of the Kingdom indeed is eschatological, but the eshaton is already here with us in the Risen Jesus.[81] It is such narratives that sketch out some of the essential dimensions of the mission of the Church.

The mission of the Church is also to formulate liberative liturgies and thereby make the freeing presence of God experienced among people. This is possible only when liturgies are made to bridge the 'here' and the 'hereafter', 'earth' and 'heaven'.[82] In other words, liturgies should function to abolish any alienation that is brought about by reducing the living God to dumb and inactive idols and life-giving spirituality to empty religiosity. Indeed "Gods who have eyes but only for the splendour of temples and liturgies…and not for the affliction of the people are dead gods, idols. Gods that have ears, but only for the chants of fulsome praise and not for the cry of pain arising from among the masses of the earth, are senseless things to be rejected. Gods that have feet but only to walk the velvet halls of palaces and the marble floors of basilicas, and not the squalid, slimy slums of India's cities and her...villages, are worthless myths..."[83]

Basing himself on God's revolt against the oppression of his people which results in the liberation of, say, the Hebrew slaves, and on 'the song of high revolt' that Mary sang (Lk 1:50-53) Rayan endorses the insurrectional violence as the last resort in the mission of the Church, provided it is a "well-thought-out and adequately prepared political act and no mere impulse, (and is) minimal and full of promise of success in terms of a better social order".[84] The use of such violence needs a prior discernment. Rayan opines that it is the victimised group that should be the discerning party and not an unaffected outsider and much less the direct or indirect contributor to the oppression.

While the mission of the Church is to serve the cause of faith, it cannot be done without a radical commitment to the cause of justice. Indeed prophets like Jeremiah would insist that to know God is to do justice. An effective mission of this type needs the knowledge of the social, economic, political and cultural processes operative at local as well as global levels.[85] This indeed is an enormous task, which demands collaboration at all levels among all people of good will and across religious and ideological traditions, to the extent these have the genuine liberational potential in them. The collaboration envisaged here in not despite the differences, as if to come together by forgetting them, but by drawing out inspiration and energy from them. In the process these traditions also stand a chance to be purified of their humanly originated non-liberative facets.[86]

The mission of the Church consist very importantly in the Church itself becoming a beacon of light, by taking initiatives in the works for and with the poor and the downtrodden; not so much by doing some charitable works as by organizing and empowering them, by being an example of a society that shares its resources justly and with a special love for the poor.[87]

In this process the Kingdom, along with its eschatological dimension, understood also as "all human progress in justice, love and peace, in brotherhood, sisterhood, dignity and freedom",becomes the blueprint and action programme for a new society.[88] Such a project is geared towards a three-fold realization: firstly, acknowledging the parenthood of God, which in concrete terms provides survival and security for all; secondly, faith in God who is a community of equals, having everything in common, sharing everything in love becomes the model for the human society; thirdly, a human community that shares its resources and struggles to overcome all structures of domination and discrimination.[89] It is important to perceive the unfolding of the Kingdom in history in these terms, because without a related historical praxis faith becomes 'a harmful ideology'. Therefore, "all transcendent hope must have roots in the soil of realized historical hopes or of struggle for their realization".[90]

And finally, in the vision of Rayan, the Church remains provisional and hence should get merged into the Kingdom when Christ hands over his rule to the Father and God becomes all in all. The Church exists for serving the Kingdom. Indeed, she is "one of the servants and sacraments of the Kingdom on our earth". All religions and non-religions that play such servant roles in history too should "transcend their provisional symbols of cult, creed, and organisation, and merge into their own ultimate meaning which is the definitive reign of God on our earth, which is Eternal Life".[91]

A critical appraisal

1. Rayan is never tired of emphasizing the role of a genuine liberational struggle as intrinsic to any meaningful mission of the Church. With this key insight he bridges the traditional gap between 'this worldly' and 'otherworldly', 'sacred' and the 'secular', 'direct' and 'indirect' evangelisation etc. Although, eschatological dimensions of the Kingdom are not to be reduced to the historical, nevertheless any neglect of the historical liberation in understanding and serving the Kingdom is strongly and consistently rejected.
2. The 'historical' is the sacrament of the 'eschatological'. Hence, liturgies, the celebration of the sacraments, the proclamation of the Word, to be true to their fundamental rationale cannot afford to ignore the historical issues that plague human communities. Hence, the mission of the Church, while having eschatological horizons, becomes concretely responsive to historical issues.

3. There is a definite envisioning of a convergence of religions into the Kingdom of God in Rayan's thought. Religions to the extent they are truly and integrally liberative are seen as expressions of a core liberative or salvific experience, the source of which is God alone. Hence, clearly they are not only varied paths to God – their ultimate goal, but also are varied ways of facilitating the Kingdom in human history here and now. However, beyond such general considerations, Rayan has not worked out in adequate detail either a theological edifice or practical guidelines for interreligious relations and dialogue.
4. In Rayan's perspectives the entire identity of religion as such gets almost reduced to being an agent of promoting justice. Indeed, one cannot deny the inseparable link between religious experience/consciousness and ethical imperatives. However, the phenomenon of religion or religious consciousness is more complex and wider than a mere ethical consciousness. That is why in relation to religious traditions, what looks to be abhorrent for an 'outsider' can be highly meaningful and even perfectly moral to an 'insider'. Under such circumstances it may not be much fruitful for the outsider to brand it as immoral or oppressive in a simple and direct manner. In the early centuries of the Christian era the Eucharistic celebration was abhorred by some and was called cannibalism! Interreligious dialogue needs a much more sophisticated, sensitive, complex and maybe even experiential understanding of the religions than what Rayan seems to be exhibiting in some of his writings.

Notes

1. Samuel Rayan, "Mission after Vatican II Problems and Positions", International Review of Missions, Vol. 59, Oct. 1970, pp. 414-426, in Kurien Kunnumpuram, SJ (ed.), *Selected Writings of Samuel Rayan: The Mission of the Church, SJ,* Vol. III, St. Paul Society, Mumbai, 2013, 30. (Henceforth this work will be referred to as *Selected Writings*).
2. Samuel Rayan, "Faith Commitment and Commitment to Justice", *Ignis Studies*, Bombay, 1/1, Nov. 1983, pp. 5-23, in *Selected Writings*, p. 102.
3. "Mission after Vatican II Problems and Positions", in *Selected Writings*, p. 20.
4. *Ibid.*, p. 31.

5. *Ibid.*, p. 20.
6. *Ibid.*, p. 21.
7. *Ibid.*
8. *Ibid.*
9. Samuel Rayan, "The Lima Text and Mission", International Review of Mission, Vol. 72, April 1983, pp. 109-206, in *Selected Writings*, p. 44.
10. "Mission after Vatican II Problems and Positions", in *Selected Writings*, pp. 27, 31.
11. Samuel Rayan, "A Vision of Mission for the New Millennium – A Dalit Perspective", presented at the Research Seminar on *A Vision of Mission for the New Millennium*, Thomas Malipurathu and L. Stanislaus (eds), Mumbai, St. Paul's, 2001, pp. 115-122, in *Selected Writings*, p. 37.
12. "The Lima Text and Mission", in *Selected Writings* p. 47.
13. Samuel Rayan, "Telling the Story of Jesus in Asia – Theme of Asian Mission Congress", The New Leader, Vol. 119, 22 (11/6/2006), in *Selected Writings*, p. 62. Also Samuel Rayan, "Evangelization and Development", Mission Trends, No. 2, Gerald H. Anderson (ed.), 1975, pp. 87-105, in *Selected Writings*, p. 75.
14. *Ibid.*, p. 76.
15. *Ibid.*, p. 79. Also Samuel Rayan, "Human Well-Being on Earth and the Gospel of Jesus", Jeevadhara, Vol. 2, No.7, 1972, pp. 35-46, in *Selected Writings*, p. 86.
16. "The Lima Text and Mission", in *Selected Writings*, p. 49.
17. *Ibid.*, p. 48.
18. "Human Well-Being on Earth and the Gospel of Jesus", p.95, also Samuel Rayan, "Asia and Justice", Vidyajyoti Journal for Theological Reflections, 50/7 (1986), pp. 356-364, in *Selected Writings*, p. 157.
19. Samuel Rayan, "Christian Participation in the Struggle for Social Justice", P. Melenessia (ed.), The Church and the Future, No. 1, 1978, pp. 37-54, in *Selected Writings*, p. 142.
20. *Ibid.*
21. *Ibid.*, p. 143.
22. "Telling the Story of Jesus in Asia – Theme of Asian Mission Congress", p. 63.
23. "Faith Commitment and Commitment to Justice", in *Selected Writings*, pp. 116, 118.
24. *Ibid.* p. 120.
25. Samuel Rayan, "The Challenges of India Today: An Indian Christian Response", *Human Liberation in the Indian Context*, Students' Council, Jnana-Deepa Vidyapeeth, Pune, 1983, pp. 162-173, in *Selected Writings*, pp. 307, 308, 309.

26. *Ibid.*, p. 309.
27. *Ibid.*, p. 313.
28. *Ibid.*, pp. 314, 315.
29. *Ibid.*, p. 315.
30. *Ibid.*, p. 317.
31. "Mission after Vatican II Problems and Positions", pp. 28-29.
32. "Asia and Justice", p. 149; "A Vision of Mission for the New Millennium – A Dalit perspective", p. 35.
33. "Mission after Vatican II: Problems and Positions", pp. 17-18.
34. *Ibid.*, p. 30; "Evangelization and Development", pp. 83-84; "Human Well-Being on Earth and the Gospel of Jesus", p. 85.
35. "The Lima Text and Mission", p. 45.
36. "Evangelization and Development", pp. 73, 78, 79, 80. Indeed, "Developmental service is love and therefore a saving experience to engage in, which is to evangelize", p. 82
37. "Asia and Justice", p. 151.
38. "Human Well-Being on Earth and the Gospel of Jesus", p. 85.
39. Reference is made to M. Prior, *The Bible and Colonialism: A Moral Critique*, Shefield Academic Press, Shefield, 1997, p. 260 in Samuel Rayan, "Peace: Biblical Perspectives", *Jnana-Deepa: Pune Journal of Religious Studies*, Vol. 4/2, 2001, pp. 103-119, in *Selected Writings*, p. 193.
40. "Christian Participation in the Struggle for Social Justice", pp. 137,142; "Evangelization and Development", pp. 81, 82. In fact "a pattern of society is disclosed and experienced within the Eucharist when it is celebrated appropriately. It is this vision we are to pick up and make into a force for social transformation." – Samuel Rayan, "Your Kingdom Come", National Christian Council Review, Vol. 100/5, 1980, pp. 247-253; in *Selected Writings*, p. 253.
41. "Asia and Justice", p. 148; Samuel Rayan, "The Kingdom of God: Blueprint for a New Society", KristuJyoti, Vol. 1/3, 1985, pp. 22-36; in *Selected Writings*, p. 232.
42. "Human Well-Being on Earth and the Gospel of Jesus", p. 89
43. "Asia and Justice", p. 152
44. *Ibid.*, p. 160. Paradoxically Paul lived his freedom by making himself everybody's slave in love, and in being all things to all people (1 Cor 6:12-14; 9:19-23; 10: 23-24; Gal 5:13-15). Indeed freedom is for sacrificial love, and is defined in terms of it – see Samuel Rayan, "The Call to be Free", Jeevadhara, Vol. 3/15, 1973, pp. 217-221; in *Selected Writings*, p.265.
45. "Peace: Biblical Perspectives", pp. 205, 206. The following citation from *Bible and Colonialism* makes the point clear: "The archaeological evidence points in an altogether different direction from that suggested by Joshua 1-12. It suggests a sequence marked by a gradual and peaceful coalescence of diaspora peoples

into a group of highland dwellers. The Exodus-Settlement account reflects a particular genre, the goal of which was to inculcate religious values rather than merely present empirical facts...Israel's origins were within Canaan, not outside it. There was neither invasion from outside nor revolution within. The legendary account of Joshua 1-12 offers no legitimizing paradigm for land-plunder in the name of God. Indeed the extra-biblical evidence promotes a respect for the evolution of human culture rather than for a process that can deal with change only by a war of violent destruction." pp. 251-252; in *Selected Writings*, p. 206.

46. "The Call to be Free", pp. 257, 258.
47. Samuel Rayan, "He is Our Peace", in David Emmanuel (ed.), *Approaches, Foundations, Issues & Models of Inter-Faith Relations*, ISPCK/HIMI, Delhi, 2001, pp. 347-357; in *Selected Writings*, p. 177. Rayan particularly cites the Ephesian text, which enumerates five types of alienation of the non-Jewish people: i. they had no part in Christ; ii. They were excluded from the community of Israel; iii. They were strangers to the covenant and its promise; iv. They were without hope; and v. they were without God in the world (v. 12).
48. *Ibid.*
49. Samuel Rayan, "Instruction on Christian Freedom and Liberation", Jeevadhara, Vol. 16, No. 93, 1986, pp. 228-250; in *Selected Writings*, p. 281.
50. *Ibid.*, pp. 282, 283.
51. *Ibid.*, p. 291.
52. *Ibid.*
53. "The Challenges of India Today: An Indian Christian Response", p. 312
54. *Ibid.*, p. 311.
55. *Ibid.*, p. 313; Samuel Rayan, "Communalism in India: A Christian Response", in S. Arockiasamy (ed.), *Responding to Communalism – The Task of Religions and Theology*, Gujarat SahityaPrakash, Anand, 1991, pp. 107-137; in *Selected Writings*, p. 335; "Your Kingdom Come", pp. 252, 253.
56. "Mission after Vatican II: Problems and Positions", pp. 27-28.
57. *Ibid.*, p. 27.
58. *Ibid.*, p. 29. The principles underlying the religious plurality are (a) the utterly free and personal nature of divine self-communications. (b) the unfolding historical character of our perceptions and experiences and (c) the richness of both the Divine and the Human. See "Communalism in India: A Christian Response", p. 344.
59. "Communalism in India: A Christian Response", p. 338.
60. "Mission after Vatican II: Problems and Positions", p. 29.
61. "A Vision of Mission for the New Millennium – A Dalit Perspective", p. 36.
62. "Human Well-Being on Earth and the Gospel of Jesus", p.87.

63. "A Vision of Mission for the New Millennium – A Dalit Perspective", pp. 37, 38.
64. "He is Our Peace", pp. 180, 183; "Communalism in India: A Christian Response", p. 348.
65. 183-4; "Communalism in India: A Christian Response", p. 347.
66. 231
67. "Communalism in India: A Christian Response", pp. 341, 343.
68. *Ibid.*, pp. 344-345.
69. *Ibid.*, p. 345.
70. "A Vision of Mission for the New Millennium – A Dalit Perspective", p. 35.
71. "Faith Commitment and Commitment to Justice", p. 116.
72. "Asia and Justice", p. 156.
73. "The Lima Text and Mission", p. 46.
74. "A Vision of Mission for the New Millennium – A Dalit Perspective", p. 37.
75. "The Lima Text and Mission", pp. 47, 48.
76. "A Vision of Mission for the New Millennium – A Dalit Perspective", pp. 38, 39.
77. "Telling the Story of Jesus in Asia – Theme of Asian Mission Congress", pp. 55, 56.
78. *Ibid.*, pp. 58, 59.
79. *Ibid.*, p. 59.
80. *Ibid.*, pp. 61, 62.
81. "Human Well-Being on Earth and the Gospel of Jesus", pp. 94, 95, 97.
82. "Asia and Justice", p. 157. "Liturgy cannot be taken, ready-made and frozen, from the pages of books. It must come warm and fresh from life, which it will sum up, re-express and celebrate. It will have the throb and smell of the people and their earth… The Eucharist must become an education in the celebration of the new, egalitarian social order, the world of justice, love and of the primacy and centrality of human beings." *Ibid.*, p. 158.
83. "Faith Commitment and Commitment to Justice", p. 111.
84. "Christian Participation in the Struggle for Social Justice", pp. 138, 139.
85. "Asia and Justice", pp. 154, 155, 157.
86. *Ibid.*, p. 159.
87. *Samuel Rayan*, "The Justice of God", in John C. England (ed.), *Living Theology of Asia*, SCM Press, London, 1981, pp. 348-355; in *Selected Writings*, pp. 171, 172, 177.
88. "The Kingdom of God: Blueprint for a New Society", p. 233.
89. *Ibid.*, p. 245.
90. "Your Kingdom Come", p. 253.
91. "The Challenges of India Today: An Indian Christian Response", p. 319.

9

Rayan's Vision of a New Society

J. Charles Davis

1. Introduction

Society for Samuel Rayan means the whole humanity without discrimination of class, creed, colour or nationality. The story of Jesus as established by God must involve all the people. The disciples of Jesus are therefore entrusted with the task of preaching and witnessing to create a harmonious human society, where justice and peace can dance together. Without justice, there is no genuine peace. In a world where there is injustice and oppression, the ideal society after the story of Jesus has to necessarily strive for justice. Christian faith is not an individualistic spirituality but necessarily has to promote justice and peace in the world elucidating the inseparable connection between faith commitment and commitment to justice. Faith must be translated into praxis.

Human wholeness and salvation is at the heart of Christian faith, respecting the dignity and destiny of every human person and human community as a whole. The foundation of human society is God, in whose image and likeness humans are created. Every person without exception reflects this image. A humane society must therefore be of free and equal people who embody the Reign of God. In a world where there are poor and the oppressed struggling for justice, Rayan wants a change and proposes certain directives for a new society where there is equality, freedom, love, justice and peace.

For Rayan, "to dispense justice is to know God, then to do injustice is to have no knowledge of Him and to thus be in a situation of atheism. Unjust structures are indeed structures of atheism."[1] He says,"God makes His salvation possible and available in some way to *all men and women everywhere throughout history*".[2] This statement gives clear evidence that Rayan's idea of humanity includes everyone in history. It includes all. He advocates the Kingdom of God as the ideal project, to which he evokes in everyone a sense of "solidarity with the whole human race in a common destiny and responsibility".[3]

Rayan thus proposes the Kingdom of God to be an ideal symbol or project of a classless, non-oppressive and just society. In this effort, Rayan criticizes capitalism and partially advocates socialism. The Kingdom of God, for Rayan, is not an abstract idea of future but a historical project in a concrete historical context evoking a commitment to build an egalitarian and just society.

2. Rayan's Critique of Capitalism and Advocacy of Socialism

Rayan points out the inadequacy of capitalist economic liberalism. While strongly opposing capitalism and its tenets of maintaining status quo in society, Rayan appreciates the socialist principles in building up of an egalitarian society on earth, but immediately notes that the earthly society is not the ultimate goal for the humanity. The egalitarian society begins primarily from one fundamental principle, namely, God, who is also the end of humanity. Therefore, the Kingdom of God is the foundation and the end that motivates the Church to take up the responsibility to create a society based on love, freedom, justice, and peace. The foundation is not therefore mere humanism or Marxism, but Kingdom of God that has to come already now in concrete situations.

2.1. Rayan's Strong Opposition against Capitalism

The human person is central to the social question. Love and respect for the human person is the starting point of the social question. God´s love for humans and human´s love for others are intrinsically related. That is why, even the enemy is to be loved and liberated. Rayan says, "The reality of enemy is not denied; contradictions in society and class struggle are not overlooked. But they are to be striven against and overcome in order to help emerge a classless brotherly/sisterly community of people in which production is ruled by need and love and not by profit motive and competitive greed; an economy in which wealth is for the human person and not the human person for wealth".[4]

In critique of Capitalism, Rayan says that the economics of the Gospel defines wealth as a means and medium of friendship. It is for human use and free giving, not for grabbing and hoarding. Wealth is an interpersonal reality and a relationship with a human face. In the systems, it becomes an impersonal faceless thing which rolls on for the benefit of the few who control it. It causes unmindful suffering to the majority of humankind. The Gospel values put pressure on us to strive to break the power of wealth and shape an economic system which is at the service of people.[5]

In sharp opposition to capitalist ideologies that drive their economy on competition, profit and claim the right to private property, whereby the vast majority of humanity suffers due to man-made unjust structures based on false ideologies, Rayan points out that Christian economy is not based on competition and profit, but on restoring the human person in all its aspects including the whole human race. God himself joins in the struggle to restore the rights of human persons. Rayan explains:

> Struggle is necessary to restore the human person to himself/herself and to restore the rights of which he/she has been robbed. By original divine will and gift, the earth is commonwealth and belongs to the human race. Its common purpose therefore must prevail over all private claims. But this purpose has been effectively thwarted for the vast majority of people. The situation is unjust and calls for subversion. The revolt is led by God Himself; of subversive activity He is the leader and model.[6]

2.2. Rayan's Appreciation of Socialism

Rayan advocates the Old Testament God of Yahweh as God the liberator of the oppressed and the downtrodden. Rayan says that "social action…mean[s] struggle for liberation from conditions, systems and structures which perpetuate and consolidate underdevelopment, unfreedom and alienation. It will mean struggle for the destruction of all the forces that oppress and diminish the human person and for the generation of viable structures of freedom, creativity and communication at all levels, economic, political, cultural and human".[7] In other words, liberation means active participation of the oppressed in socio-economic resources, in decision-making processes, in the profits, in the management of production and in economic power.[8] According to Rayan, liberation expresses three interrelated levels of meaning, all of which must be held together:

The first is to be become aware of and take seriously the reality of conflict, within the economic, political and social processes, between the oppressed peoples and exploited classes on the one hand, and on the other the oppressors and exploiters; the masses seek their identity, freedom, dignity and rights and demand justice. At the second level liberation expresses a person's conscious assumption of responsibility for oneself, for one's world, for one's destiny and one's future. "The gradual conquest of true freedom leads to the creation of a new person and a qualitatively different society". And finally it expresses the heart's unfettering from selfishness and sin of which is born all injustice and ruin of fellowship. At all levels liberation involves struggle and contradiction; it can come only through free and intelligent human activity.[9]

It might appear that Rayan's proposal of liberation and development is not different from socialism. Therefore, at this juncture, it is important to see the differences between socialist class struggle for liberation and Christian faith action for comprehensive work of building the Kingdom of God on earth. Rayan says that:

> ...liberation and development, earthly well-being and human justice are not the kingdom of God. They are ambivalent, and often lead humans away from God. In the emphasis on social justice, there lurks the danger of neglecting God to serve people and the danger of diverting the Church from its task of preaching Jesus Christ. That is why the gospel keeps its distance with regard to material things. Eschatology and the perspective of eternity relativize and de-emphasize the world and temporal prosperity.

> Involvement in social action and political struggle can scarcely be called a Christian apostolate. No priest may enter politics, not at any rate the spiritual leaders of so small a religious minority from abroad. Even if political action were feasible, we would have to be careful to avoid all semblances of horizontalization, desacralization and secularization. Social concern clearly smacks of these. Temporal prosperity is of limited value, and seeking riches' sake can also bring about repression and alienation.[10]

Therefore, Rayan rightly says, "We make matters of justice our concern not out of fear or revolution, …Nor are we interested lest communists take over and India go the way of China… We are interested because *the question of justice is intrinsic to human wholeness and salvation, intrinsic to the Gospel Jesus announced and the kingdom he brought, intrinsic to his incarnate person and his risen life*, to God's plans and concerns, to the love that lies at the heart of the Christian reality and to the rights, dignity and destiny of every person and the human community".[11] In other words, as Pope Francis said, Rayan would hold that the Church is not an NGO that works for a mere social change but an eschatological movement that works for the coming of the Kingdom of God.

2.3. Socialism is nearer to but Capitalism is Incompatible with Kingdom of God

While discussing on the use of violence to bring about social justice, Rayan points out that there are two types of violence: institutional violence and insurrectional violence. Rayan points to capitalism driven by economic liberalism as institutional violence and socialism driven by class struggle to bring about a classless society as insurrectional violence. Rayan says, "One that opposes and exploits the helpless with a view to profit under cover of legality, another which strives against this system to achieve liberation and humanity for people".[12] The former is destructive violence and the latter is creative violence. Combating violence can also become destructive, as the power may only change hands and may not promote a better social order with ever fuller participation of the people at all levels of decision-making.

The two types of violence cannot be equated, for they are qualitatively different. It is very clear from Christian perspective that institutional or destructive violence must be stopped or at least avoided. But what about the creative or insurrectional violence, should we be allowed to use as an act of love and a creative and liberative service of people? Rayan seems to accept it, when he says, "the unjust social situation which now exists is radically incompatible with the coming of God's kingdom while liberating violence is not".[13]

Liberation precedes salvation. The former makes the latter concrete in history. Rayan defines salvation as "human wholeness, meaningful human existence, the communion of humans with God and with one another".[14] Sin is a breach of this communion brought about by people's attitudes and actions, by their decisions and omissions. Saving action consists in the struggle for the abolition of these. Action for liberation and justice merges with salvation and becomes an integral part of the movement of restoring all things in Christ to God. In this sense, too, Rayan could be seen as someone who accepted socialism as precondition to Christian salvation.

The early Christian community experimented with "communism" and "held everything in common", not in order to taste the mystique of material poverty, but with a view to abolishing poverty from their midst, so that "they had never a needy person among them", and on this account "they were all held in high esteem" (Acts 2:32-46; 4:32-35). Poverty has meaning only in a commitment to action for the abolition of poverty. It appears from such sayings that Rayan had not only appreciated communism/socialism but also drew some parallels with the early Christian community. It may also indicate that Rayan is against the claim to private properties because the earth is commonwealth.

3. The New Society

The idea of a new society according to Rayan has to be based on gospel values primarily making the Kingdom of God here on earth as a foretaste and concrete reality in history, how imperfect it might be. An absolute classless society depicting equality as a determinant factor predicted by Marxism and its different variants is not possible. It is only a one-sided story. The Kingdom of God is much more.

The Kingdom of God is not a profit making economy, but rather it includes spiritual, social, economic, political and cultural liberation leading to the human wholeness of every person. This would tell us that capitalism with its economic liberalism will never be able to make an egalitarian society, since wealth corrupts human mind.

Making a larger "cake" for a better distribution does not happen either. The question is centred on the "sharing of the cake", how big or small it might be. A new society of the Kingdom of God looks into the basic needs of all adequately. When there is a needy person, the rich has no right to possess more than what is necessary. A fair distribution is a must in creating a new society of peace, justice and love. This struggle is not just political, but much more spiritual; it is not just about economic system, but much more about human wholeness.

Rayan poses the question: "Could, then, the Kingdom of God of the Christian Faith be (among other things) a blueprint for a new society? … Could it serve as a plan for the building of an earth without war, torture and destruction of life, without poisoning of life's sources, without greed and domination and distortion of visions and values?"[15] His answer is affirmative. While saying that the Kingdom may not provide us with "detailed plans of action, concrete strategies, practical decisions, social analysis and organization in the spheres of economics and politics",[16] Rayan affirms, "What faith in the Kingdom can offer is an orientation and a vision, a sense of direction and of values, motivation and the assurance of a hope that wins. It can enable us and sustain our courage. It can commit us to sustained efforts to bring about transformation in a particular direction. But, the tools of analysis and action must come from the sciences. The new world can only be the fruit of a joint venture of science and religion, technology and vision, human beings and God".[17] According to Rayan,

> Earth is commonwealth.[18] [Earth] is the primordial sacrament of God's presence…To destroy the earth would be to practise godlessness. To plunder it wantonly, to waste its resources in feeding a consumer culture, to disfigure its face and litter it with plastic abominations, to pollute its water and air, are not only irrational and criminal acts, but acts of unbelief, refusal

> of commitment to God... Far worse an act of injustice and unbelief is to grab and fence off the best part of the earth and its wealth for the exclusive benefit of a few individuals or groups or corporations or ethnic circles or armed bands. Rigid privatization and exclusiveness in regard to land and material resources to the disadvantage of the masses of the people make void the meaning of the earth and cancel our faith-commitment at levels deeper than verbal confessions. In such situations faith means not a fresh recitation of creeds but action for justice..., for a redistribution of wealth and reorganization of society.[19]

It is clear to us from the above statements of Rayan that he seems to be partially on the side of socialists while strongly opposing capitalists. I do not know about his clear stand on private property, since he has not spoken it explicitly though he seems to advocate categorically that earth is commonwealth. Interpreting him from what is implied in his writings, I can however say that he seems to be against the claim of private ownership of land and material resources. Such thinking seems to be right in a world like ours where even natural resources, like water, are privatised driven by market economy. What is privatised needs to be made common again.

4. Concluding Remarks

The Kingdom of God is larger than the Church, and the Church needs to walk and work along with other religions and the people of good will to make peace possible locally and globally. Rayan is more than right in saying that the Church cannot be a lone agent of bringing about change and building the Kingdom of God. It is not lone or exclusive business of the Church either. God is God of everyone and Father of all. So, we cannot make boundaries in any sense, even in our mission of liberation and salvation.

The Kingdom of God is a concrete historical event and not an abstract future idea up there in heaven. Jesus' mission was concrete and historical. The Kingdom of God as a project of a classless and non-oppressive society can make significant contributions to the planning and programming of a new society. The Kingdom of God has one Father for the whole human family. It is an earth-reality, a community of equals that holds everything in common and shares everything in love; it counters class ideologies and unjust structures and supports liberation struggles for justice.

Jesus has directed us to seek the Kingdom first. It is a gift received in history. It implies the re-establishment of justice in the world.[20] The Kingdom of God is surely eschatological, but the coming of the kingdom has to begin here. It has to begin with liberating historical events. To this task, the Church cannot be a mere teacher and actor, but she must mirror the Kingdom of God. The re-establishment must begin right there in the Church.

A capitalist Church cannot authentically proclaim a society of equality, love, freedom and justice.In the Kingdom of God, there cannot be inequality; it disfigures the image of God. A capitalist or caste practising Christianity will be self-contradictory. If there is any preference, it is for the poor, the outcast, the little ones, the unlearned, the despised, the condemned, the hungry, the lowly, the downtrodden, the crippled, those who labour and are burdened, and the masses who are harassed and dejected like sheep without shepherd. It is apt to end the significant contribution of Samuel Rayan with Jesus' own manifesto, which reflects his too.

> The Spirit of the Lord has been given to me,
> for he has anointed me.
> He has sent me to bring good news to the poor,
> to proclaim liberty to captives
> and to the blind new sight,
> to set the downtrodden free,
> to proclaim the Lord's year of favour (Lk 4: 18-19; Isa 61-1-2).

Notes

1. Samuel Rayan, "Faith Commitment and Commitment to Justice," in Kurien Kunnumpuram SJ, (ed.),*Selected Writings of Samuel Rayan SJ, Vol. III: The Mission of the Church – Christian Reflection on Evangelization in India Today*, Mumbai: St Pauls, 2013, p. 118.
2. Samuel Rayan, "Mission after Vatican II: Problems and Positions," *Selected Writings of Samuel Rayan SJ, Vol. III*, 18. Italics mine.
3. *Ibid*., p. 19.
4. Samuel Rayan, "Christian Participation in the Struggle for Social Justice," *Selected Writings of Samuel Rayan SJ, Vol. III*, p. 136.

5. *Ibid.*, p. 137.
6. *Ibid.*, pp. 137-138.
7. *Ibid.*, p. 126.
8. *Ibid.*
9. *Ibid.*, pp. 126-7.
10. *Ibid.*, p. 131.
11. *Ibid.*, p. 132. Italics mine.
12. *Ibid.*, p. 138.
13. *Ibid.*, p. 139. Cited from Rene Laurent, Liberation, Development and Salvation (New York: Orbis Books, 1972), pp. 164-165.
14. *Ibid., Selected Writings of Samuel Rayan SJ, Vol. III*, p. 140.
15. Samuel Rayan, "The Kingdom of God-A Blueprint for a New Society?" *Selected Writings of Samuel Rayan SJ, Vol. III*, p. 231.
16. *Ibid.*, p. 231.
17. *Ibid.*
18. Samuel Rayan, "Mission after Vatican II: Problems and Positions", *Selected Writings of Samuel Rayan SJ, Vol. III*, p. 138.
19. Samuel Rayan, "Faith Commitment and Commitment to Justice," in *Selected Writings of Samuel Rayan SJ, Vol. III*, pp. 106-07.
20. *Ibid.*, p. 132. See Gustavo Gutierrez, *A Theology of Liberation* (New York: Orbis Books, 1973), p. 269.

10

"Peace and Peace-Making - A Christian Imperative"

Samuel Rayan's Contributions

George Pattery, SJ

The title of my presentation – 'peace and peacemaking' – invites the question: Is Rayan a peaceable person? Yes and no. His appearance certainly is that of a very peace-loving person and he always emitted a serene and peaceful smile. He engages any one in attentive and loving conversation. However, that smile and conversation often implied a severe critique of the existing system and an invitation to think differently. He wants peace that does justice.

1. The problematic

Let us problematize 'peace and peace-making'. Karen Armstrong in her book 'Fields of Blood' argues that through most of history, people mixed up religion and secular activities, not because of god-men, but because they wanted to endow everything with significance. Secondly, such involvements in socio-political activities have often been tied with violence: crusaders, conquistadors, Jihadists, VHPs and many more. But, she argues that violence almost always originates with the state and spills over to religion, rather than vice versa. This, she says, is because any governing body, democratic or tyrannical, peace-loving or expansionist, "was obliged to maintain at its heart an institution committed to treachery and violence", and because "violence and coercion . . . lay at the heart of social existence". The earliest states required force to maintain systems of agricultural production; mature ones found that the threat of violence — by police within their borders, by armies between them — was, sadly, the best way to keep peace. Thirdly, she argues that citizens face the dilemma of controlling violence carried out in their name by the state, without blaming religion for it; nationalism is far more productive of violence than religion. Hence, religions face the dilemma of whether to accept the protection of a state, and the threat of violence that necessarily entails, or to live in hermetic isolation. (Cf. NYT 141210 bkrw ArmstrongK Fields of Blood. http://www.nytimes.com/2014/12/14/books/review/fields-of-blood-by-karen-armstrong.html?emc=edit_bk_20141212&nl=books&nlid=50019937).

Karen's study challenges the Girardian thesis that violence and the sacred are intimately related and that all sacrifices were originary ways of containing and diffusing violence. Sacrifice and all religious institutions contain violence.[1] In the present political and religious scenario in India, the issue of violence and religion is very critical. Rayan's insights, I believe, are relevant to this debate.

2. Rayan's Apologetic Style

Rayan does not enter into this debate whether the state or religion is prime player in violence. He focuses on presenting his thesis that religion is fundamentally peace-building and that Jesus is our peace. To prove his point Rayan often uses an apologetic approach in this theological writings, - apologetic in the sense that he would present the point of view of the other or opposing camp and present it fully and then try to refute or disprove it with his own arguments. This is also true of his writings on peace.

In his article on 'Human well-being on earth and the Gospel of Jesus'[2] Rayan begins by arguing that Jesus was a pacifist: that he did not think of liberating his people from the Romans, submissively told them to give to Ceasar his due, declined the offer to become king in the Davidic line and help people, did not say a word against slavery, discussed no social problems, no programme for the transformation of structure, or raising the standard of life, proposed just relief work or almsgiving, advocated patience and abnegation. The hope he advocated pointed to heaven: do not worry about food or clothing, when someone beats you up, show the other cheek, and finally he let himself be stripped and murdered. His kingdom was not of this world. He told his disciples not to resist; no permanent city here, let the married live as though they were not married, in an eschatological perspective.[3] Such perspectives seem to be far from liberative.

Having travelled thus far with his apologists, Rayan moves on to establish the true credentials of Jesus and his vision and mission. In the event of feeding the hungry, Jesus chose to feed them. "What Jesus sought to do was to lift the people out of difficult situations and put them on their feet so that, free and strong, they could go their way".[4] Similarly by his healing ministry, he freed people from the control of demons. "What Jesus did was but a beginning and a parable; it is for us a lesson, an example and a commandment. We are to continue his work, and today it is entire societies that need to be lifted up, and whole political systems and economic situations that have to be exorcised and healed".[5] In this way Jesus sought to establish a society that is just and peaceful, according to the mind and heart of his Father.

Jesus was not a passive pacifist, but a radical peace-maker. "The transformation of society requires the release, at the same time, of people's souls from taboos, traditions and fears, which serve only to constrict the spirit, pin down its elan and snub its creative powers... with calculated precision he undermined the most ancient and sacred traditions, the Sabbath law, for instance, which loomed large in the Jewish system and constituted the heaviest of fetters on the soul and the trickiest of snares".[6] Jesus' breach of the Sabbath law is for reinterpreting the law, to shatter the oppressive structures and narrow view to lead people into the large expanse of God's freedom and peace.

3. Peace that does Justice involves conflict

Jesus' perspective on peace inevitably implies and includes right relationships with God and with one another. Peace is the fullness of grace and friendship. Right relationships are produced when wealth and bread are not for grabbing but for sharing. Each of the parables and deeds of Jesus seems to talk about a new kind of relationship based on the fatherhood of God. Wealth is to be made a medium of friendship and fraternity, of a new kind of relationship. While food, clothing, economics and politics do not constitute the kingdom of God, it is through these realties one experiences the joy and peace of the kingdom. It is in and through material things that we reveal and give ourselves to one another, that God gives himself to us. "Food and drink, then, and freedom and opportunities for creative life, are part of the justice, peace and joy the Holy Spirit gives" (Rom 14:17; Gen 1 and 2; 2 Cor 9).[7]

Rayan interprets the theology of incarnation as God's way of bringing about peace and joy. "The incarnation is God's reaffirmation in tenderness of the world in the power of love, and a reaffirmation in mercy of human existence He had set within the world. Work for human well-being will correspond to this divine 'Yes' to the world. It will be our way of making our own, gratefully, this gift of God, and our way of affirming Him who affirms the world and us".[8]

Peace implies the justice of God that includes tenderness and mercy. God's justice calls into question human notions of 'respect and hierarchy'. Working for true peace in right relationship, therefore, implies interrogating the existing system and law. Hence, to work for true peace entails conflict.

4. Cross as the price of peace and freedom, of being human

Jesus paid the price of affirming the human, for holding up right relationships with God and with one another as supreme values. He refused to accept the social and religious discriminations; he sought after true peace. One who works for peace and the dignity of the human will come into conflict with the powerful and the mighty. It is this conflict that was inevitable in working for his Father's kingdom that brought him to the cross. Rayan concludes: "Jesus was there on the cross because he had declined merely to be a conformist, and a thing that fits into a system and lets itself be used. He rather chose to be a *man*, unafraid and free; free to love, and to be loyal to his conscience and to his God, free to honour men and women, to think his own thoughts, to call in question accepted and established concepts and values, to speak out the truth and to live and die with dignity".[9]

Rayan asserts that the cross is an inevitable part of following him in discipleship. "The Cross, therefore, which he asks his disciples to carry is not a recommendation of passivity and feebleness. It is the courageous suffering, like his own, native to the conflict that is inevitable if people begin to love and live for others; the conflict that is inherent in any firm stand taken for justice, dignity and freedom for the common people. With Jesus abnegation is not for starvation but selfless action (Jn 12:24; Mk 3:21-22; Jn 7:1-9; Matt 4: Mk 8:31-33)".[10]

5. Kingdom as the horizon of peace initiative

One would inevitably think of initiating peace when one thinks of the kingdom of God as the horizon of one's life. Kingdom of God is God's concern for his people and their wholeness. This concern is manifested in three phases of revelation of God in creation, in the event of liberation in Exodus, and in the event of Christ. This concern forms the horizon of peace for us.

In this perspective, creation is not just an act of power of a mighty God, but is the manifestation of '*the tenderness with which God creates the universe*', the care with which he makes the earth, and the affection with which He calls into existence, one thing after another, all that the earth bears'.[11] God loves creation into existence.

Referring to Ps 65:6-11 and Ps 104:1-10, Rayan explains beautifully the importance of the earth. He says it so poetically: "The earth is God's beloved daughter. He takes her from his heart and puts her down at a distance from himself and calls and beckons to her to walk upto Him, growing with every step taken, with every step sharing more deeply in what He is, waxing in awareness, waning in determinisms, becoming freer and freer, ever more capable of love, until in the human reality it reaches out and touches His feet, and looks up into his face wonderingly, adoringly, and begins in Jesus Christ to speak to Him directly and call Him Abba, Father. It has been and still is for the earth a journey into its own depths, and towards its own centre which is life. And the centre and depth of life is freedom and love; of these the depth is Jesus and his depth is God. This pilgrimage of the earth continues in human inventions and creations, and in the march of history with all its twists and turns and vortices, as well as in the explosion of cultures and freedom. It continues in all the symbols with which men and women love, communicate and worship. It is thus that God loves His earth, enables it and enriches it and makes it beautiful and fecund. And He places it in our hands so that we too may join Him in caring for it, may till it and keep it, humanize it, and make it our home and our extended bodily self. God gives it to His human family as their inheritance, as a token of His love, as a shared medium of fraternal existence, as a great loaf of bread or bowl of rice for them to give to one another in love. (Gen 1: 2:4-15)".[12] Our faith response implies fidelity to the earth. This is the first phase of the horizon of kingdom that implies peace.

6. The concerned God

Second phase of this horizon is that God who revealed to Israel is wholly different from the gods of the nations of those days. God is disclosed as one deeply concerned about justice to the oppressed (Ex 3:7-9), as liberator of the down- trodden. This is the touchstone of all divinity and spirituality. Not a God who has eyes to see the splendor of temples, ears to hear the chanting of praises, have feet for walk the velvet halls of palaces and marble floors of basilicas but to hear their cry, to see their suffering and to walk them into freedom. God challenges them to revolt (Ps 115:4-8). "The historical event and the spiritual experience which founds Israel's religion and nationhood reveals a God who appears in a flaming bush; *who burns with anger and concern in the face of injustice meted out to the powerless*; who speaks from within a burning socio-political situation, and from within the blaze of suffering and wrath in the heart of a man involved and active".[13] Prophets invite Israel to remember that to know God is to do justice.

7. Jesus is our peace

The third phase of the horizon of the kingdom is the event of Jesus Christ. It is worth our while to listen to Rayan in his own words. "Jesus is revelation in his person, in his life, death and resurrection, in his word and his deed. He is also the embodiment and pattern of perfect faith-commitment. His openness and surrender to God includes a beautiful commitment to the earth, to life and to people. His loving look discovers the Father at work in the grass of the field and its tiniest flowers. His eyes discern the Father's provident care in the life of the bird and beast (Matt 6:26-30). With a touch of his word he loves to open up the deeper significance lying hidden in the simple realities of daily life and in the commonest of human experiences. Sprouting seeds and growing plants, morning and evening skies, salt and leaven, a lamp in the house, houses built on sand, children at play, wedding feasts, shepherds looking for lost lambs, and brides looking for a missing piece of ornament, forgiving fathers, women in travail, nightly thieves, fisher folk, and farmers, camels, moth, fox, sun and rain – all figure in Jesus' thought and parables. Jesus' approach to things and life is full of respect and sympathy, not untouched by a hint of humour. He sees his mission as a service of life. It is to give his life in ransom for the liberation of people in bondage that he comes. He comes that the masses who, down the centuries, have been fleeced and victimized by brigands, marauders, hirelings and wolves, may finally have life and have it in abounding fullness (Jn 10:10). Hence, he makes it his concern to feed the hungry, to heal the sick and rebuild broken selves and lives".[14]

'Because of the option God makes in Jesus, *all acts of justice and mercy*, all respectful concern and love, all restructuring of the socio-economic order to make it responsible to the dignity and destiny of all men and women, and all the new relationships built thereby *are acknowledged by Jesus*'.[15]

8. Peace is the abiding theme

In Hebrew thought, 'the Messiah, the friend on whom Israel relied and reposed all its hopes for a free and prosperous future, is named the Prince of Peace (Isa 9:5-6). Commenting on this notion, Rayan says that the symbol of the peace-prosperity brought by the Messiah-king is a river in spate or a nursing mother with abundant breasts, fondling her baby in her lap (Is 65:10-13).[16]

The two 'Prince of Peace' texts in Isaiah 9:1-6 and 11:1-9 are clearly focused on saying that the reign of peace is established and sustained by liberating people from oppression. Liberation is made available through the destruction of wars and hostilities (vv 1-4), bringing justice (v 6b) and peace (vv 5-6a) for all. The Exodus experience is the benchmark and this is celebrated in Psalm 85 that narrates the process of restoration, forgiveness, justice and peace. In Chapter 11, Isaiah speaks of the Messiah as a royal person, who will liberate the oppressed, bringing justice to the poor and thus effecting reconciliation and peace. Significantly this reconciliation is cosmic. The reference in Isaiah to beasts – leopard and lion – lying together shows the radical transformation that is intended, still more significantly that we humans learn from the beasts and end all warfare in the name of religions.

Against this background Rayan elaborates on Jesus as peace. He bases his arguments on St. Paul (Eph 2:11-22). The Pauline passage, according to Rayan, speaks of human alienation and the way in which Christ has overcome such alienation. Alienation is of different kinds: psychological, social, economic, political, religious and ecological. This alienation began long ago in Genesis – the elder one who killed the younger one and asked the perennial question of humankind: am I my brother's keeper? God's response to this question is to become a brother, especially to the weak and the small. In that way Christ is our peace – the place of reconciliation.[17]

Genesis 3 & 4 talk about the fate of the human being, who by excluding God falls into the stupid state of an ox and an ass. In Hosea this alienation pertains to Israel as a nation, rejecting the loving Yahweh. In the New Testament, the cumulative term for alienation is death and devil. Estrangement from God, from the origin, leads to all kinds of alienation. They lead to worship without justice. Jesus embodies true reconciliation and that implies reconciliation with one's neighbor. One can't love God without loving one's brothers and sisters (1 Jn 3:20). For Paul, then, authentic social reconciliation leads to integrity in all.

While the Letter to the Ephesians speaks of five-fold alienation and attributes them to non-Jews, the Letter to the Romans implies that Jews and Gentiles are both in bondage to sin (Rom 3:9-20). In both the failure of Israel to live up to its call is clear. The obvious example is the divisiveness shown within the Temple in Jerusalem, the lines of separation among the priests, males, gentiles and women etc.

The biblical account of war and peace, on the other hand, should be seen against the development of polytheism, and monotheism centred around Yahweh; the interest of the tribe is considered to be the interest of Yahweh. The very presence of the enemy can pollute the earth. Hebrew monotheism developed fully during the post-exilic period and perhaps under the influence of Zoroastrianism. The theological justification of war should be seen against this background. Hence, in the Old Testament, human life is cheap and even the best of believers had no qualm of shedding blood. The OT texts pose the fundamental problem of Yahweh mandating invasion, occupation and pillage and killing of people. This is problematic. Looking at the war texts in the OT Rayan concludes in the words of M. Prior: "In the light of history, one must question whether the values of the Torah can be relied upon to promote justice and peace, and underpin the imperatives of human rights".[18] However, the greatness of the Hebrew Bible lies in linking peace with righteousness and justice.

Jesus enters the scene to break down the barrier of hostility that kept Jews and Gentiles apart. Rayan is quite emphatic when he explains the role of Jesus in breaking down the barriers. "In his own flesh, that is, in his life of poverty, lowliness and rejection, in a life of freedom, of critical non-conformity and dissent, of solidarity with the oppressed and fidelity to their cause even unto death, Jesus abolished not the Jewish Faith, not the Faith of Abraham and the prophets, but the Jewish religion with its anti-life rigidities".[19] He abolished the prescriptive laws that distorted true faith and presented a different face of God. He praises the finer faith of the soldier than that of all of Israel. He declares that many will come from the east and the west, south and north to his kingdom (Matt 8:10-13). His table-fellowship with publicans and sinners (Mk 2:13-17) is his way of welcoming the outcast and of setting aside the purity/pollution laws of the Jewish religion in favour of the sick and the hungry and demolishing the divisive walls of religion.

9. Jesus' reconciling pedagogy

The story of the woman caught in adultery becomes a pedagogical teaching on reconciliation and peace-making. He makes the judges judge themselves: a necessary first step towards reconciliation; then he exposes the accuser's exclusive focus on the past (the deed of the woman, the letter of the law) and shows a future in God: forgiveness. Legalism offers to the sinner only death; Jesus offers life through his forgiveness. God's pardon meets with human needs and exhibits God's way of doing justice. Commenting on the Samaritan Woman's story, Rayan says: "The pride of religion, priest and temple, is deposed from its throne, and honest human compassion is lifted up as the spirituality of the New Age. The priest-religion of the temple worship and purity laws, in the measure of its lack of human concerns, is set aside as irrelevant".[20] In Matt 25:31-46 Jesus discloses his values and concerns beyond the preoccupations of religions, where in a spirit of compassion and peace all can meet. Similarly Jesus' ministries – eating with the outcasts, neglecting the Sabbath laws and prescribed fasts, healing on the holy day (Mk 2:13-3:6) are his ways of 'breaking down religious walls in order to unite people into a new community and to reconcile them to the Father'.[21] Jesus' Father loves the world and the cosmos and the entire reality has to be reconciled and only then will peace reign.

"Jesus stood for complete non-violence not only of the hand and the outward deed but also of the heart as well and inward dispositions. He radicalized the old commandments, you shall not kill. He deepened it: you shall not be angry with your sister or brother, nor hurt them even with an abusive word, not even if they are unfriendly, hostile or oppressive. Rein in every instinct to hit back, and reverse all traditions and philosophies of revenge and retaliation. Meeting stench with stench only fouls the air the more and that for everyone. Jesus wants our response to every situation to be positive and creative, capable of transforming it for the better: love your enemies; pray for your persecutors; offer the other cheek; let go your tunic too; offer to carry the baggage a second mile; forgive seven times seventy times, endlessly; recognize the primacy of reconciliation with your sister/brother over the worship of God; and know that what God wants is mercy, not sacrifice. In short, "set no bounds to your love as your heavenly Father sets no bounds to His" (cf. Matt 5-6). Such a gentle relationship is the Temple of the God of peace...the entire framework and horizon of his ministry, traced by healings, feedings and the raising of the dead and befriending of outcast, spell life and peace".[22]

The Peaceable way of Jesus is fully manifest on the cross and it is the final phase of the peace-making pedagogy. Rayan puts it succinctly. "Jews and Gentiles conspired to kill Jesus (Jn 18:3). By that very fact their religions have condemned themselves as anti-justice, anti-human, and anti-God, and thus they abolished themselves within the event of Calvary. In the cross of Jesus the old religious enmities have been put to death. Jesus thus made peace and united in himself hostile factions, creating out of them a new human reality. This new humanity, united beyond the ken of hostile religions, is then reconciled to God. Those who were far and apart have been brought nearer in Christ through his lowly and innovative life. The 'other' shall no longer be referred to as 'dog', untouchable, unbeliever, or sinner, but fellow-citizens, and sister".[23]

10. Radical shift in Jesus and a new perception of Peace

"By uniting people in his lowly life poured out in service, Jesus brought about a radical shift from religion to faith, from power structures to spirituality, from sacrifice to mercy, from cult to justice, from the clerical to the human, from the temple to relationships at the level of the heart, from the water of religious purification to the wine of human celebration".[24] The people became his major concern. The Samaritan and the non-religious will bend over the dispossessed even when the religious pass by in anxiety to get to the temple or to remain ritually pure.

The gospels are calling forth a vision of 'sisters and brothers reconciled among themselves beyond religions and their divisive symbols but within a spirituality of compassion'. Hindus, Muslims and the Buddhists are no strangers to one another. Ephesians 2:19-22 portrays God's new society. It is God's kingdom and our Commonwealth of which we are fellow citizens. Such a reconciled community alone brings about peace and the glory of God.

11. Incarnation as re-establishment of Peace

As the Fathers of the church interpreted, incarnation is the reestablishment of peace between heaven and earth. "The body of Christ is the bond that holds God and human beings together in an indissoluble union. In the same vein of thought the Fathers of the Church spoke of the Incarnation as an ever-lasting marriage in which the Creator and His creation became one flesh. In the flesh of Christ, then, reconciliation emerged; it only remains for it to blossom fully, and unfurl its petals in human history as a history of reconciliation".[25]

Rayan argues that peace and reconciliation is the flowering of this bond in resurrection. In and through the resurrection of Christ, the human race and the cosmos are forgiven and reconciled once and for all with God. The Church is the historical unfolding of the mystery and the meaning of Incarnation and resurrection. Church is the gathering of the many and the diverse to share the one bread in order to become one body. "To offend against unity by despising the poor, or by not waiting for the working people to arrive, to go ahead with eating and drinking without the community is to fail to discern the Body and disqualify oneself for the Mystery. For the Eucharist is the sacrament of unity and peace. (1 Cor 10:16-17; 11:17-33)".[26] In the Eucharistic Jesus, there is a deeper and universal sense of Christ as our peace and unity. Everyone participates, as the source and structure, in the sonship and filiation of Christ. This brotherhood and sisterhood penetrate all creation and bind them together. "We are bound up with one another at the most radical level in God, in Christ and in the Spirit".[27] "Jesus is peace also in the profound sense that it is his breath that provokes, inspires, and animates all creative activity, all holy living, all reaching out in love towards one another. The Spirit pervades the universe and is, in His uniting and life-giving role, like the air we breathe".[28]

12. Peace-Makers

Rayan is forthright in elaborating on the role of Christians in peacemaking. "Our historical vocation is to transform religion from the historical role it has played of dividing people and threatening life, into a spirituality of concern and compassion for God's suffering human family on earth".[29] Such concern and compassion should enable us to fight against poverty, to join in the struggles of the poor. In our sharing of bread and breath we shall discover each other's deeper and truer self, and in the process discover God and thus find peace.

"Jesus is peacemaker. His life and death were a peacemaking ministry through which he reconciled alienated groups among themselves, and an estranged world with God. Peacemakers therefore resemble him, and share in his special relationship to God, and will be called God's own children, God's daughters and sons (Matt 5:9).... Jesus' peace is not born of the sword but of the unspeakable love that led him to lay down his life for his friends and to pray for his killers (Lk 23:34; Jn 15:9-16)".[30] The early Christians understood Jesus' message as 'the Gospel of peace' (Acts 10:36). The God of peace, the Spirit of peace and the memory of peace-makers pervade the whole universe.

Rayan rightly concludes that the teachings of Jesus i) provide only 'highly questionable grounds for a theology of war'; ii) repudiates all wars of extermination; iii) lays foundation for a theology of spiritual warfare; and iv) eschatological wars are symbolic.[31] The political wars of conquest and extermination were fought by the Hebrews from a narrow and fierce henotheistic religion. Exclusive choice of one tribe and extermination of the rest are incompatible with moral monotheism; any kind of legitimization of wars in the name of the one true God is incompatible with a loving and compassionate God. However, it is true that Christian history betrayed the one creator God, the Father of all through its slave trade, the crusades, the World Wars, the Auschwitz, and the Vietnam wars etc.[32]

The prayer our Father welcomes us to be part of His reign; his will is our peace; sharing with all the blessings of the earth. To live the our Father is to live His Peace. The protection and liberation of creation and the realization of more justice among people is peace. It is a social reality, love made visible in this world, among peoples, communities and nations. Psalm 85 speaks of *shalom* = integrity, wholeness of a community; well-being, security and trust; it is the expression of the reign of God; it is *shanti* = peace with all and every element of creation. It entails fewness of desires and simplicity. It is a creative process in which we are invited to co-operate imaginatively.

13. Models of peace

Rayan traces the development of peace in our times by listing the different ways and models of peace that emerged, especially in western history. He begins with the *Pax Romana* model (it is armed peace: violent peace imposed by conqueror, with continual dispossession of peoples with taxes) and lists many such institutions that were promoting or meant to promote peace such as *Pax Britanica, Pax Americana* (colonial peace), Peace through partitioning of land (Big powers do this in order to further conflicts), Military intervention (Indian peacekeeping force in Sri Lanka), Peace through war (if you want peace, prepare for war), and deterrence theory etc. Much more positive signs of peace were the end of the feudal system, the establishment of the International Arbitration Tribunal, League of Nations, UNO, ILO, FAO, WHO, and UNESCO etc. The other set of peace initiative had religious tone: the prophetic models, (Is 2:3-5; Micah 4:4); Peace through Kings (Cyrus – the non-Israelite king becoming God's anointed one - Is 41:1-3; 44:28; 45:-12). The Edict of Asoka (rulers to tour villages and teach them *dharma*), *Satyagraha* model (Gandhiji), Peoples' Movements (centre-periphery model), the cosmos model (through deep understanding of evolutionary process and miraculous moments through which we are brought to this point after billions of years of historical and cosmic process), and the Holon model (Universe is a living organism, dynamic and intelligent). We – the entire universe- are part and whole at the same time - communities of communion, and not violent rivalries. The earth does not recognize national boundaries. Rayan proposes "Jesus model" as ideal and explains its features as identifying with the victim and forgiving and reconciling all in him (Eph 2:14-17). Jesus' model envisages one body, one earth, one history of suffering, one forgiven family, and all are called to one destiny.[33]

Peace entails a vision of the global human unity and of the earth as one that belongs to all, moving creatively to greater depth.

14. Concluding note

In poetic and descriptive style Rayan treats comprehensively on peace. With prophetic zeal he traces the link between justice and peace. As a permanent student, Rayan studies the evolutionary insight of science and finds new opening in Holon model. He remains embedded in the Jesus model that is premised on the kenotic path of identifying with the victim, forgiving and reconciling all, diffusing infinite and non-diminishing love and peace.

The contemporary evolutionary thinking moves in the same direction. Vimala Thakur says: "The challenge now is to create an entirely new, vital revolution that takes the whole of life into its sphere. We have never dared embrace the whole of life in all its awesome beauty; we've been content to perpetuate fragments, invent corners where we feel conceptually secure and emotionally safe... Today... we can no longer go on with this game of fragmentation" (as quoted by Cannato).[34]

"The other is not really other, but simply a simultaneous and concomitant expression of grace itself. The new human is a 'we,' but one grounded in a whole 'me'. In the mystery of the communion experience – as 'me' and 'we' come together in sacred space - duality falls away and we find ourselves part of the sacred unity that is the heartbéat of the universe".[35]And the result is peace and peace-making.

Notes

1. Cf. Girard Rene, *Violence and the sacred*, The John Hopkins University Press, 1972.
2. Kurien Kunnumpuram (ed.) *Selected Writings of Samuel Rayan, Vol. III, The Mission of the Church*, Mumbai: St.Pauls, 2013, p. 85.
3. Cf. *Ibid*, pp. 90-91.
4. *Ibid.*, p. 91.
5. *Ibid.*, pp. 91-92.
6. *Ibid.*, p. 92.
7. *Ibid.*, p. 95.
8. *Ibid.*
9. *Ibid.*, p. 96.
10. *Ibid.*, p. 97.

11. *Ibid.*, p. 105.
12. *Ibid.*, p. 106.
13. *Ibid.*, p. 112.
14. *Ibid.*, pp. 118-119.
15. *Ibid.*, p. 122.
16. *Ibid.*, p. 173.
17. *Ibid.*, p. 176.
18. M. Prior, *The Bible and Colonialism*, Shefield: Shefield Academic Press, 1997, p. 260.
19. K. Kunnumpuram (ed.) *Selected Writings of Samuel Rayan, Vol. III, The Mission of the Church*, p. 178.
20. *Ibid.*, p. 179.
21. *Ibid.*, p. 180.
22. *Ibid.*, p. 201.
23. *Ibid.*, p .180.
24. *Ibid.*
25. *Ibid.*, p. 182.
26. *Ibid.*, p. 183.
27. *Ibid.*
28. *Ibid.*
29. *Ibid.*
30. *Ibid;* p. 202.
31. Ibid; p. 204.
32. *Ibid;* pp. 205ff.
33. *Ibid.*, pp. 212 ff.
34. Judy Cannato, *Fields of Compassion*, Notre Dame, Indiana: Sorin Books, 2010; p. 161.
35. *Ibid;* p. 165.

11

The Social and Liberative Consequences of Samuel Rayan's Theology

Nicholas Tharsiuse

Introduction

India is a developing country. In the process of development, India is confronted with massive poverty, hunger, death, discrimination against women, the humiliated untouchables, the unemployed youth, the exploited *tribals*, the workers swindled of their rightful wages, the oppressed bonded labourers, forced rag-pickers (who are mostly children), those denied the possibility of any education (almost two thirds of the Indian masses is illiterate). They are mute but eloquent witnesses of the range of oppression and injustice that plagues every realm of the country. In the face of all this it becomes evident why liberation is a pressing challenge in India today. Rayan's theology not only meets the demands of the intellectual order but also other dimensions of human reality such as the divine, the cosmic and human. This paper has two parts. The first part sketches the theology of Rayan whereas the second part speaks about the relevance of his theology today.

I. The Theology of Samuel Rayan

Rayan's major focus is on the exploration of the social dimension of Christian faith for life and freedom within the context of the poor Indian masses. Rayan produces a theological vision relevant to his objective, i.e., liberation. This is done in an analytical-critical fashion. What is the understanding of the poor in Rayan's thinking? The poor are a 'social class or category', "through whom God shapes our salvation history".[1]

The substance and basic mood of Rayan's liberation theology springs from the national struggle to end British and other colonialisms, and from the struggles of the oppressed *Ezhava* community (in the 1920's and 30's) in the State of Kerala. The *Ezhava* community's struggle was and is for socio-economic liberation from age-long discriminations and humiliations, based on caste prejudices and class realities. As a student he took part in the above stated struggles. When he was 9, he came into contact with Kumaran Asan's poems.[2] They influenced his language and thought. These struggles brought him into critical contact with domination and oppression, unjust treatment of people,[3]people's resistance, people's organised power, the crucial nature of political and socio-cultural freedom and made him reflect on the role that religion and spirituality (in the persons of Sri Narayana Guru and of M.K. Gandhi) could play in liberational struggles.[4]The perceptions, insights, attitudes, and sense of values developed in the context of these prolonged struggles lie at the basis of Rayan's theological options made years later. As the years passed, he became much more sympathetic to socialism, to an egalitarian social order. Added to that there were a host of social, political, and economic disabilities from age-long discriminations and humiliations based on caste prejudices and class realities. His contact with AICUF students for 12 years and their questions and concerns led to the discovery that the meaning of Christian faith has to realise itself socio-politically. Living and searching with honest youth helped him to make his theology earthly-historical, rendering the Bible open-ended, unfinished. This is the basis of his theology of liberation. Rayan is concerned with the despised world of the poor, and thus tries to see what the divine plan is with regard to the poor.

To be sure, though he is critical of Marxist analysis, Rayan emphasises the economic analysis of society, the existence and operation of structures of economic power etc. However, Rayan goes beyond Marxist categories by honouring the value of the human person (in the Christian perspective), thus maintaining a critical distance from Marxist philosophy. And he supports a critical collaboration with Marxism in the measure that Marxism responds to gospel values enshrined in the Our Father, in the celebration of Eucharist and in the symbol of the Trinity.[5] Humanistic analysis, for Rayan, consists of socio-religious-cultural spheres which includes caste and gender analysis.[6] This is somewhat extra-Marxian. Rayan's understanding comes from Narayana Guru[7] and Kumaran Asan[8] and their fight for human sisterhood and brotherhood which reflects God's relationship with all God's children. He analyses society in reference to persons, groups of people, places and events in them. This gives a lot of concreteness to his theological methodology.[9] Rayan is convinced that the stories, myths and sagas of people often carry not only the messages of freedom, a quest for fullness and hope for liberated life, but also contain elements for analysing society. This is an innovative approach and a contribution to the use of social analysis in Indian Christian Theology. Rayan maintains that Yahweh's action for liberation is also found in the history of the *Ezhavas*, the *Shanars* (*Channars*), *Pariahs* and the *Pulayas* of Kerala; and also in the resistance of *dalits* and *tribals* and marginalised peasants and women all over India, and elsewhere.

Rayan's approach to social reality leads him to 'read' the Bible in dialogue with socio-political realities and the questions posed by them. Besides the Word of God and the Christian Tradition Rayan also makes ample use of the rich and varied human experiences of Asian people's, especially Asian women, their different religious and sacred texts, their folklore and stories. Asian and Indian traditions, according to Rayan, contain an affirmation of the value of the person as well as compassion for the poor. He points out that their scriptures, stories, and hopes reveal that even in armed struggle and costly revolution there is a struggle for justice. For example, the famous story in *Ramayana* has been reinterpreted to serve the cause of women's liberation and the conscientiousness of the villagers. The personality of *Sita* has been reinterpreted as that of a woman with a will of her own. She registers firm and well-argued protests against the ways and values of her husband. She subjects him to searching criticism, and condemns his ambiguous attitude of courting intrigue, to which both of them fall victim.[10] Rayan brings out the fact that women should regain their dignity in the patriarchal society. They have a right to a decent life, to defend their cause and establish justice against male discrimination.

The epics stand for a human cause and concern. *Rama*, for example, is a type of righteous person in society and *Ravana* the unrighteous. *Rama* struggles to overcome the evil one. *Krishna* stands for the struggle on the side of the oppressed. Any event taking place in society is interpreted by the people with reference to a similar situation in the epics; to every human type there is a corresponding character in epics. Given this, a villager is able to analyse his village pinpointing who is *Rama*, who is *Ravana*, *Krishna*, and so on.[11]

Another example in the *Bhagavad Gita* work, action and historical involvement are emphasised to transform an unjust situation for the sake of the well-being of all creation.[12] In the *Bhagavad Gita*, Krishna explains to Arjuna that

> Every selfless act, Arjuna, is born from the eternal, infinite Godhead. God is present in every act of service. All life turns on this law, O Arjuna. Whoever violates it, indulging his senses for his own pleasure and ignoring the needs of others, has wasted his life. But those who realize the God within are always satisfied. ... The ignorant work for their own profit, Arjuna; the wise work for the welfare of the world, without a thought of themselves... Perform all work carefully, guided by compassion.[13]

Rayan's hermeneutics aims at a 'life-giving', committed and transformative reading, and a hope-generating reading, in search of the promotion of humanity, life and dignity. He adopts a basic hermeneutical stance in asking how far the scriptures are life-giving to the struggling people, to build up a just and participatory community.

This consideration of a person-centred analysis of society and the creative reading of the sources in favour of the well-being of humanity leads to Rayan's concept of praxis. 'Praxis', in Rayan, refers to the real, active living out of faith in God in the here and now, particularly, within the experience and history of the marginalised. Here too he makes a methodological option for an egalitarian economy, an egalitarian social order that comes from his acquaintance with the Bible and his understanding of the Christian faith. For Rayan, then, praxis for change in the structures of society should inevitably go together with a change of heart--not one before or after the other.

According to Rayan spirituality is intimately linked to the way one lives one's life. Therefore, the church in India has to reshape the classical theological questions about the meaning of life and activity and the nature of God. This impels Rayan to reinterpret the heart of the mystery of Christian salvation within the religio-socio-historico-cultural context of India. Rayan interprets God as one who actively involves Godself and liberates people in history.

For Rayan, history is about humans and the meaning of history depends on human choices, decisions and actions in favour of the poor. In history, the salvation of God, both as a gift and a task, and as symbolised in the kingdom of God, demands human efforts to build up this kingdom through justice. As such, the kingdom grows in history in co-operation with people, as far as they are committed to the historical project of God's liberation. Liberation here and now is not the completion of salvation, but without it there is no salvation. According to him, God is leading this struggle of the people and Holy Spirit is guiding the liberation process.

In this regard, it is particularly interesting to notice how Rayan discovers that there are new ways of looking at the Hindu world-view of cyclic time. The cultural and religious climate of India, in Rayan's view, is sensitive and open to the historical dimension of human persons, and has a new appreciation of history due to the actual historical experiences of freedom. What is important in history, for Rayan, is whether a growth process is taking place and a destination is achieved. Thus, Rayan holds that the Christian view of salvation is relevant to socio-religious and cultural climate of India and therefore all religions, especially Hinduism, have to work together for the liberation of the people.

Rayan's theology of salvation and wholeness serves as the conceptual framework for his ecclesiological reflections. It necessitates a "theological re-evaluation" of the "commercial and colonial context in which Indian Churches originated".[14] The Church is a community of the poor of Jesus reflecting God's unconditional love for the world. It is not a ready-made reality; it has been and still is a process. The Sermon on the Mount and the Our Father are meant to shape all relations to the earth and to one another. In the Lord's Supper the poor of the church are equals. Nobody is excluded from sharing in Food and Drink. Rayan works out evangelisation in terms of human liberation and well-being within God's liberating plan in history. For Rayan, the human person is at the centre of the entire process of evangelisation. This leads him to locate evangelisation within a wider process which encompasses the total plan of God. Thus, evangelisation concerns one's development as co-creator with God. Development, as relationships of love and life-giving interchange, leads to an understanding that Christian mission and development have a common human design. Thus, the mission of the church in India is 1) liberation from all tastes and tendencies to manipulate human beings and the earth, and manipulate God and his people from all religious and ecclesiastical and political traditions; 2) development of the human person and societies; 3) to serve social justice for all; 4) empowering the people.

The vision of development as evangelising mission makes Rayan suggest that the Church in India has to become incarnate in India's flesh: its culture of the poor and down-trodden and their struggle. The church in India which claims its roots in God who liberates in history, in the historical person of Jesus who is friend of the outcaste, needs to drastically change its life and mission.[15]

Social-liberative Consequences

We propose that the social-liberative consequences of a Rayan-inspired theological framework to address the problems of the people in their life situation of poverty, oppression and suffering will help local communities to develop theological frameworks appropriate to the life-struggles in their own contexts.

1) **Towards an Inclusive Theology**: Rayan's theology has these consequences: a) the critique of Marxism that religion is an opium of the people; b) Gandhism which viewed the existing social (caste-*varna*) and economic (land-lordism-trusteeship) order as being due

to *karma* (his metaphysical belief in the law of *karma*). This view led Gandhi primarily to offer an ethical solution to the problems of India; c) those who are professing faith but at the same time ignoring the implications of Christian faith in doing justice; d) to re-examine the Vatican's scholastic analysis of society in view of the poor and from their cultural ethos and e) the institutionalised church which side-steps the poor.

2) **Christian Faith: A Liberative Praxis**: Rayan's praxis emerges from and is shaped by critical involvement in and critical reflection on lived Christian faith. Praxis is not meditation (critical reflection) alone, for that only changes reality in a small way. Praxis is thought emerging in deed; and deed evokes thought. As such, true justice requires both contemplation and action, prayer and action, to probe and engage the concrete realities of living our Christian faith.

Rayan's praxis emphasises and underlines the historical and socio-economic-political location of faith. Faith is embedded in social justice. His powerful intuition is that justice is not an alien theme to the God of contemplative life. For Rayan, faith is more life-transformative than an intellectual assent. Theology is not "tied up with philosophical speculations but with people and their quest for meaning and their will to freedom".[16] Rayan asserts that he does theology:

> not only with the analytical brain, but with the emotional intuitive heart as well. The analytical mind stands as an observer, deals with facts and their order, works with verbal imagination, becomes self-aware and seeks awareness of awareness, while the intuitive heart works as a participant, deals with experience and value perception, wonders with creative imagination, and develops awareness of the other.[17]

Theology is done with "passion and compassion". Theology is itself, in Rayan's view:

> an act of witnessing; and the theologizing process remains, from start to finish, rooted in the theologian's faith. Reason, elevated to a new level continues indeed to be reason, but in the arms all the while of the elevating faith-grace. It is only as a believer and a witness and as one committed to the demands of

God's love and justice in history that one can be a theologian, reasoning, discoursing and criticizing.

Rayan's praxis provides a common platform for religions, NGOs and ideologies to come together, refraining from arguing and claiming superiority over one another, by making a 'dialogue of life' in view of liberative praxis.

3) **From Imported Theology to Incarnated Theology**: Rayan's theology challenges the traditional *practice of theologising* (first enunciating a theory and then applying it), which is the hidden assumption of much of Theological Education in India. Rayan's model of praxis proposes that *theological education in India* should foster and promote social transformation toward a truly human world. In view of this, theological education in India has to initiate a methodology of action- reflection- action. This challenges theological education in India which was/is for all practical purposes imparting a traditional Western theology with its classical methodology.

4) **Secular/Sacred Theology:** Empirical studies prove that in India communalism and fundamentalism threaten human life. Rayan's theology discerns a liberative cultural ethos and humanistic values and visions of the poor and the oppressed from their non-Christian and scriptureless religions. Hence, his praxis challenges us to an inclusive critical examination and interpretation of them in view of the poor.[18]

Rayan emphasizes the coincidence of a spirituality of the struggle for justice, a commitment to liberation and a method in theology in his project of liberation. This coincidence of spirituality and method leads Rayan to the eco-concerns. The theological reflection should flow from the real situation or human experience arising from ecological threat and its issues. Indeed an inter-disciplinary and scientific approach is needed to indicate the significance of Rayan's theological methodology to the people of India.

5) **Theology of Religions**: Rayan's theology demands the rethinking of the missionary service of the church, and redefines the mission of the church in view of the kingdom for the poor, irrespective of caste and creed. He places the human person at the centre of the process of evangelization. He identifies evangelization

with the wider process which encompasses the total plan of God. Life and work interact and witness to and contribute to Word- witness. Rayan-inspired theological framework for an evangelizing mission towards human liberation and well-being will help the people of India to come together and interpret religious traditions with a view to establishing justice.The Second Vatican Council's openness to dialogue with other religions and ideologies, and its emphasis on justice, provides wider horizons to develop Rayan's theology of liberation especially in the areas of the theology of religions and the theology of dialogue in the life-context of India.

6) **Substituting the Colonial Umbrella with a Praxian Umbrella?:** In 1988 Rayan did not advocate approaching every religion from the perspective of the Bible.[19] What he does is incorporate the liberative potentials of other religions in view of human liberation. But, the ultimate criterion in making out which God is liberative, as pointed out in recent years, is taken from the God of the Bible. This is certainly justified in the multi-socio-religious cultural context of India.

However, it seems that Rayan is also doing 'injustice' to other religions. His theological approach provides a 'praxian umbrella' which brings other religions and ideologies under Christian faith. It is with this specific intention that he seems to use the notion of "implicit faith". As Rahner called the non-Christians 'anonymous Christians', Rayan also considers the non-Christians and atheists to be Christians. It seems that Rayan appropriates other religions under his praxian umbrella. But as Chethimattam asks, "can any one simply deny the uniqueness of one's own religion?"[20] Any scripture is an "'objectification' of the faith-experience of a community during the period of its constitution(.)" Every faith-experience should be considered unique. Such a faith-experience cannot be shared by others unless they also partake of that background (in all its dimensions).[21]

7) **Salvation through Liberation**: Rayans' theology of salvation is attuned to the religio-historico-cultural context of India which is not only sensitive and open to the historical dimension of human persons, but also appreciative of the historical experience of freedom. Rayan's approach to history, as Wilfred evaluates: 1) "calls for a re-examination of Western presumption to possess historical

sense, contrasted with its presumed absence in India";[22] 2) Rayan has proved that the theology of Christian salvation can be well understood in the religio-historico-cultural climate of Hindu India. No Indian ChristianTheologian has questioned Rayan's view on history up to now. Rayan's interpretation of salvation helps Indian ChristianTheologians to grow in its soil and Rayan's contribution, in this respect, deserves appreciation.

8) **Towards an Indian Theology of Liberation:** Rayan's critical appropriation of the Christian and non-Christian texts shares similarities with Latin American liberation theology in terms of socio-economic concerns. However, it keeps its own Indian specificity, such as its stress on personal (not just structural) liberation from aggression, fantasy and greed (dvesa, moha,lobha) as well as the recognition of the prophetic elements found in the Indian religious traditions. Independently of the Latin American liberation theology, from early 60's Rayan has consistently articulated the connection between faith and justice.

9) **Person Oriented Analysis:** Rayan, though critical of Marxist analysis, emphasizes the economic analysis of society, the existence and operation of structures of economic power. He goes beyond Marxist categories to the humanization perspective by honouring the value of the human person, thus maintaining a critical distance from Marxist philosophy.

Who are the historical subjects standing at the centre of Rayan's thought? Unquestionably, the answer, as articulated elsewhere, is the poor and the "... questions posed by their poverty and experience of domination".[23] Their questions are already theological; they are doers of theology by interpreting the Divine in terms of freedom and justice. For Rayan, the kingdom is offered "precisely to the poor, the downtrodden and the ignorant." It is the poor who hold the key to the truth of the kingdom as well as to a theology adequate to that truth.[24]

Conclusion

In short, Rayan's theology has the consequences for a) decolonisation, de-ideologisation of Indian Christian Theology from the influence of Western water-tight compartment rationality (especially of the epistemology); b) decolonisation, de-ideologisation of the church in India from its life-style and its administrative set up; c) the church must have a learning attitude from the perspective of the poor; d) moving from 'conquering'/'ecclesio-centred' mission to 'discerning'/'kingdom-centred' mission (the church of the poor with a liberating mission); e) moving from the culture of elites to the culture of dissent; f) struggling for justice and inculturating itself in the 'flesh of India's flesh;' g) exercising authority in the church within the faith community.

Notes

1. A. Pieris, *An Asian Theology of Liberation*, New York: Orbis Books, 1988, (120-124); G. M. Soares-prabhu, "Class in the Bible: The Biblical Poor as a Social Class," in *VJTR* 49 (1985) pp. 320-346; Rayan, *Development & Evangelization A Theological Sketch*, p. 29.
2. Rayan, "The Mystery of the Earth," in A. P. Nirmal (ed.), *Ecological Dimensions of Our Faith: To Care for the Earth – Towards a Theology of Nature,* Gurkul Lutheran Theological College and Research Institute, Madras, 1991, (1-14), p. 3.
3. The term 'people' in Rayan's writings mean the common people, the mass of the community as distinct from the nobility, the ruling or official class, and the clergy. Rayan, "The March Has Begun," in *JD* 9 (1979) pp. 161-88, p. 163.
4. "Interview with Rayan;" Rayan says "... theological reflection on the phenomenon and the challenge of men like Sri Narayana Guru and Mahatma Gandhi is a must." Rayan, "Theological Education in the Social Context of India Today," in F. Wilfred (ed.), *Theological Education in India*, (12-32), p. 29.
5. Rayan, "Asia and Justice," in *VJTR* 50 (1986) pp. 352-364, p. 363. Rayan notes that the Vatican document in 1986 employed a scholastic theological analysis which is elementary and historically debatable. The document did not analyse the global capitalism which is the dominant economic system and cultural pattern. This is the fundamental weakness and ambiguity of the document. Rayan, "Instruction on Christian Freedom and Liberation: Some Reflections on the Document," in *JD* 16 (1986) pp. 228-250, pp. 248-249.
6. Rayan, "Sociological Factors and the Local Church as Eucharistic Community," in *VJTR* 40 (1976) pp. 307-314, pp. 309-310.
7. Rayan, "People's Theology," in *JD* 22 (1992) pp. 175-202, pp. 185-86.
8. *Ibid.*, p. 186.
9. *Ibid.*, pp. 175-202; Rayan, "The March Has Begun," in *JD* 9 (1979), pp. 161-188.

10. Rayan, "Reconceiving Theology in the Asian Context," in V. Fabella & S. Torres (eds.), *Doing Theology in a Divided World Papers of Sixth International Conference of Ecumenical Association of Third World Theologians January 5-13*, 1983, Geneva, Switzerland, Orbis Books, Maryknoll, 1985 (124-142), p. 134. For the original see K. Asan, *Cintavistayaya Sita* [Sita in the Reflective Mood], (A Malayalam poem), Thonnackal, 1920.
11. Forexample, Rayan presents the film *Nisant* ["The End of Night"]. The film presents the revolt of an entire rural population against a landlord and his family who had been cruelly oppressing them for years. The revolt is provoked by the memory of *Rama*, the object of popular devotion, who had waged war against the organised forces of oppression. 'What did *Rama* do when his wife was abducted?" asks the temple priest whose social consciousness had been awakened by the rural school master whose wife had been kidnapped by the landlord's brothers. "*Rama* fought and did away with the abductor," replied the villagers. "And what do you do when your wives and fields are taken away?" The villagers begin to see the significance for them here and now of the religious story. Their insight is forthwith translated into action, and they set themselves free. Rayan, "Reconceiving Theology in the Asian Context," in V. Fabella & S. Torres (eds.), *Doing Theology in a Divided World*, (124-142), pp. 134-135.
12. Rayan, "Indian Theology and Problem of History," in R. W. Taylor (ed.), *Society and Religion Essays in Honour of M. M. Thomas*, CISRS/Bangalore, CLS Madras, 1976, (167-193). Rayan, "Development Process & Its Religio-Cultural Dimensions," (1-13), p. 10.
13. *Bhagavad Gita* 3:10-26. "What the (*Bhagavad*) *Gita* presents in the form of a dialogue between Sri Bhgavan (Krishna) and Arjuna is in fact the silent dialogue that goes on between the human and the Divine in the 'cave of the heart' of every person." S. Painadath, "Bhagavad Gita's Vision of Liberative Action," in P. Puthanangady (ed.), *Towards an Indian Theology of Liberation*, ITA & NBCLC, Bangalore, 1986, (49-65), p. 49.
14. Rayan, "Theological Education in the Social Context of India Today," in F. Wilfred, *Theological Education in India Today, the Statement, Papers & Proceedings of the Eighth Annual Meeting of the Indian Theological Association, Pariyaram* Kerala, Dec 28-31, 1984, ATC, Bangalore, 1985, (12-32), p. 29.
15. Rayan, "The Churches and Justice to Christians of Scheduled Caste Origin," in *Word & Worship* 11 (1978), pp. 227-239.
16. S. Rayan, "Decolonization of Theology," in *Jnanadeepa: Pune Journal of Religious Studies* 1 (1998)140-155, p. 154.
17. Rayan, "The 'How' of Third World Theologies," in J. R. Chandran (ed.), *Third World Theologies in Dialogue: Essays in Memory of D. S. Amalorpavadass*, EATWOT, Bangalore, 1991, (42-66), p. 62.
18. See K. Kunnumpuram, SJ, (ed.,) *Selected Writings of Samuel Rayan, SJ Vol 1: Jesus: The Relevance of His person and Message of Our Times*, St. Pauls Mumbai, 2011, p. 12; K. Kunnumpuram, SJ, (ed.,) *Selected Writings of Samuel Rayan,*

SJ Vol II In Spirit and Truth: Indian Christian Reflections on Spirituality and Worship, St. Pauls Mumbai, 2012, p. 10).

19. RAYAN, "Third World Theology: Where Do We Go from Here?," in *Concilium* 199 (1988) pp. 127-140, pp. 136-137.
20. J. B. CHETHIMATTAM, "Response to 'Church Journeying with Other Religious Groups,'" in K. KUNNUMPURAM & E. D'LIMA *et al.* (eds.), *The Church in India in Search of a New Identity,* NBCLC, Bangalore, 1997, (pp. 327-329), p. 329.
21. "Statement of Research seminar on Non-Biblical Scriptures," in D. S. AMALORPAVADASS (ed.), *Research Seminar on Non-Biblical Scriptures,* (663-699), p. 668.
22. F. WILFRED, *Beyond Settled Foundations: The Journey of Indian Theology,* Jothi, Trichy, 1993, p. 155.
23. RAYAN, "People's Theology," in *JD* 22 (1992), pp. 175-202, p. 201.
24. RAYAN, "Early Christianity as Counter-Culture," in P.MATHEW&A. MURICKEN (eds.), *Religion, Ideology and Counter-Culture: Essays in Honour of S. Kappen,* Horizon, Bangalore, 1987 (113-143), pp. 128, 123-129 respectively.

12

The Missing Child
The Contemporary Relevance of Samuel Rayan's reflections on Children

Kuruvilla Pandikattu, SJ

"The process by which we rid the world of economic depravity and excess is surely the same one by which we organise to end the suffering of the children who die of want and of their parents who must bury them. That will be the process by which the present economic system based on exploitation, violence and environmental destruction will be replaced by one in which human well-being, neighbourliness, friendship and nurture of the earth will flourish".[1]

Rajini Kothari

The Nobel Prize for Peace jointly awarded in 2014 to Kailash Satyarthi and Malala Yousafzai invites us to reflect on the missing children in our hearts. The brutal murder of 145 people, including 132 innocent and helpless children, in Peshawar on 16 December 2014 challenges us to dwell on what is missing in our heart.

Christmas, one of the central feasts of Christianity, is basically the feast of a helpless child. The Bible gives us a sign for joy and fulfilment: "And this will be a sign for you: you will find a baby wrapped in swaddling clothes and lying in a manger". One of the main hymns of Christmas ends with these words, "The eternal God was born as a little child". It equates the child born in a Bethlehem cave with "the eternal God".

As the Russian thinker and priest Alexander Schmemann writes that the message of Christmas can be summed up as: "The Child as God, God as Child". Why does joyful excitement build over the Christmas season as people behold that unique, incomparable sight of the young mother holding the child in her arms, and around them the "wise men from the East", the shepherds fresh from night-watch in their fields, the animals, the open sky, the star? Why are we so certain, and discover again and again this beautiful and joyful sight in spite of our daily tragedies. We return to this sight whenever we have nowhere else to go, whenever we have been tormented by life and are in search of something that might free us.

It is the words "child" and "God" which give us the most striking revelation about the Christmas mystery. Truly this is a mystery "directed toward the child who continues to secretly live within every adult, to the child who continues to hear what the adult no longer hears, and who responds with a joy which the adult, in his mundane, grown-up, tired and cynical world, is no longer capable of feeling". Yes, Christmas is a feast for children, not just because of the tree that we decorate and light, but in the much deeper sense that children alone can accept a God who comes to us on earth as a child.

This image of God as child continues to shine on us through many symbols and gifts that Christmas brings. The most essential and joyful in Christianity is found precisely here, in this eternal childhood of God. Adults, even the most sympathetic to "religious themes", desire and expect religion to give explanations and analysis; they want it to be intelligent and serious. "What are adults missing, or better, what has been choked, drowned or deafened by a thick layer of adulthood?" asks Schmemann. Above all, is it not that capacity, so characteristic of children, to wonder, to rejoice and, most importantly, to be whole both in joy and sorrow? Mostly adulthood chokes our ability to trust, to let go and give one's self completely to love and to believe with all one's being. And finally, children take seriously what adults are no longer capable of accepting: dreams, everything that which breaks through our everyday experience and our cynical mistrust, that deep mystery of the world, which is usually revealed to children, saints and poets.

Thus, only when we break through to the child living hidden within us, can we inherit as our own the joyful mystery of God coming to us as a child. The child has neither authority nor power, yet the very absence of authority reveals him to be a king; his defenselessness and vulnerability are precisely the source of his profound power. The child in that distant Bethlehem cave has no desire that we fear him; He enters our hearts not by frightening us, by proving his power and authority, but by love alone. He is given to us as a child, and only as children can we in turn love him and give ourselves to him. Not by fear, authority or domination. The child God desires from us our love, freely given and joyful; all He desires is that we give him our heart. And we give it to a defenseless, endlessly trusting child.

Through the feast of Christmas, the Church reveals to us a joyful mystery: the mystery of freely given love imposing itself on no one. A love capable of seeing, recognizing and loving God in the Divine Child, and becoming the gift of a new life.

Can we collectively listen to the tragic cry of the 132 missing children of Peshawar? Can we discover the missing child in our heart? Can we recognise God in a world where love and peace are missing?

This article reflects on Samuel Rayan's contemporary relevance. First we deal with what Rayan wrote about the younger ones already in 1989. Then to situate ourselves in the contemporary context, we elaborate on the Peshawar tragedy and similar tragedies afflicting children in our world. This takes us to a brief experience of the last year's Noble laureates Kailash Satyarthi and Malala Yousafzai, as signs of what we can collectively do to give childhood back to children. We look on the childhood and what we can learn from children. In conclusion, we see the significance of the missing children – missing children in India and the missing child in our own hearts. Through this article, inspired by Samuel Rayan, we hope to show that only if we can listen to the cry of the child and pay attention to its smile, can we celebrate Christian life in general and Christmas in particular.

1. Samuel Rayan's Theological Reflections on Children

"Serve the younger"

Besides being a good movie Salam Bombay speaks to "every mind and heart which has some measure of humanity left in it". The young boy who is abandoned by his family in the streets of Bombay accompanies the thieves, drug pedlars, prostitutes and pimps. The story concerns all the boys and girls of India. "It concerns India's honours, India's conscience, India's economic, political and judicial systems. It concerns the honour of India's religions, cultures and ethical values. It concerns the honour and the future of humankind".[2]

The rights of children declared by United Nations is also discussed by Rayan. He laments the fact that in India "a child dies every fifteen seconds from preventable diseases".[3] Then he takes up a typical situation of how summer and winter mean different things to the rich and poor children in Delhi. For the rich children summer is the time of lack of electricity and trouble with water. But for the poor ones, it is the only time when they can go out and play freely.

After analysing the situation of hunger and child labour, Rayan takes up the concrete issue of carpet weaving. Then he shows that the "present disgraceful situation is due to lack of political will".[4]

He recalls that according to the poor children, "Your waste is my living". One can listen to the agonising question: "Must I sweat till my blood runs to water".

Then Rayan relates the suffering of the children to the Bible. Rayan finds that the Bible retains stories and memories of cruelty to children. The divine election, blessing, rectitude and holiness and preference for the younger are the themes running through the Bible.

Finally coming to the specific qualities of the children and relating them to God, Rayan finds the Divine in them. "God has a child's capacity to wonder, for delight in simple things (which in fact are extremely complex) and in things common (which in truth are extraordinary and uncommon and unique, being children of God's will and word) like light, water... .".[5]

He concludes the article by asserting that "The growing child is the most important being in the world. Realise and work to nurture the flowers of the future".[6]He recalls that the child's laughter can be the best critique of our society. "The child's laughter continues. It is exposing and holding up for merciless scrutiny parents and educators and their claims to genuine concern and disinterested love".[7]

2. The Peshawar Tragedy of 132 innocent children

The Pakistani city of Peshawar is burying its dead after a Taliban attack at a school killed at least 132 children and nine staff.[8] "We targeted the school because army targets our families. We want them to feel our pain", the Taliban claimed.

On a chilly winter day in Peshawar, parents rushed to prepare their children for their last journey before sunset. School uniforms with green blazers and grey flannel trousers soaked in blood were cut off from young bodies brought home, before they were bathed and wrapped in white burial shrouds and put into coffins, which then headed for the local graveyards.

Tuesday, Dec 16, 2014, was examination day at the Army Public School in Peshawar when six militants of the Tehreek-e-Taliban stormed the premises and shot dead about 141 people, 132 of them students, going from classroom to classroom seeking their prey. Then the children who escaped saw their teacher being set on fire tied to her chair. As many as 250 lay wounded in a crime so heinous and horrific that within a few hours, most world capitals reached out to Islamabad.

Clad in the steel grey salwar kameez uniforms of the Frontier Corps, the militants entered the school around 10 a.m. through a graveyard at the back. Blowing up their vehicle, they sent a message that they were not returning. Survivors said the militants told them to recite prayers as they were going to be killed. What an irony of faith!

3. Other Tragedies with Children

Ashraf Engineer, "World watcher, ex-journalist, brand communication expert" reflects on saving children. He wonders if UNICEF Executive Director, Anthony Lake, watched the horror in Peshawar where Taliban gunmen massacred more than 130 school children, play out on 16th December, 2014. If he did, his words just eight days earlier would have seemed hauntingly prescient.[9]

"Children have been killed while studying in the classroom and while sleeping in their beds; they have been orphaned, kidnapped, tortured, recruited, raped and even sold as slaves. Never in recent memory have so many children been subjected to such unspeakable brutality," Lake had said on 8th December as the United Nations (UN) released a report on children and armed conflict.

The report termed 2014 a year "of horror, fear and despair for millions of children, as worsening conflicts across the world saw them exposed to extreme violence and its consequences, forcibly recruited and deliberately targeted by warring groups. Yet, many crises no longer capture the world's attention".

Attacks on schools, the report added, were on the rise. Engineer is convinced that it is not just Pakistan that has suffered. In Syria, where more than 7.3 million children find themselves in the midst of civil war, the UN verified at least 35 attacks on schools in the first nine months of 2014, which killed 105 children and injured nearly 300.

In 2014, hundreds of children around the world were kidnapped from school or on their way to it, while thousands were forcibly recruited by armed groups. As Jonny Cline, CEO of UNICEF Israel, observed: "This year, nightmares came true for too many children..."

It is in this painful context that Engineer invites us consider the following facts and numbers:[10]

- An estimated 230 million children are affected by armed conflict.
- Of these, nearly 15 million live in the Central African Republic, Iraq, South Sudan, the State of Palestine, Syria and Ukraine.
- In Gaza, 538 children were killed, more than 3,370 were injured, 1,500 were orphaned and 54,000 left homeless in the 50-day summer conflict.
- More than 1.7 million children in Syria are refugees.

- In the Central African Republic, 2.3 million children are affected by conflict; 245,000 live as refugees. In 2014, 432 children were killed or maimed--thrice the number in 2013.
- In South Sudan, the conflict has displaced 750,000 children and turned 326,000 into refugees. Around 12,000 have been recruited or used by armed groups. UN-verified data says that more than 600 children have been killed, more than 200 maimed and nearly 100 subjected to sexual violence.
- In Iraq, 2.7 million children have been affected by the internal conflict. Girls have suffered physical and sexual assault, sexual slavery, trafficking and forced marriage. Some have been sold in open markets. Children have been tortured and many forced to watch or participate in execution and torture. There are truly horrible tragedies told in cold numbers.

While children are the victims here, the solution to this problem cannot be found by focusing on the children alone, Engineer asserts, a view fully shared by Samuel Rayan."It requires a broader, holistic approach--one that tackles the social and political causes that are at the root of conflict", he adds.[11]

He takes the case of poverty. The prevalence of poverty--acute in many cases--is common to all the countries and regions mentioned above. Common sense suggests that poverty acts like a petridish for conflict, which in turn intensifies poverty further. Inequality--between, say, communities or races--would create an ideal environment for strife.

It follows that we need to ensure broader distribution of resources and make the right economic choices to ensure employment, keep inflation in check, focus development efforts on the poorest, and ensure universal education and healthcare. These would go a long way in reducing conflict, thereby making children safer.

While aid for schools, food, shelter, etc., is important, it is not the solution to the cause of the conflict itself. "If our children are to be safe, we'll need to tackle the larger issues," pleads Engineer.

Listening to his plea, we like to outline the lives of last year's Nobel Laureates, both of whom worked for the benefit of children.

4. The Nobel Heroes

Both the Nobel Laureates for Peace in 2014 are connected with empowering and liberating children. Let us briefly explore their stories.

a. Malala Yousafzai

Malala Yousafzai won the Nobel Peace Prize, along with Kailash Satyarthi, on December 10, 2014. She's the first Pakistani to win a Nobel Peace Prize. The 17-year-old joked during the ceremony, "I am pretty certain that I am also the first recipient of the Nobel Peace Prize who still fights with her younger brothers", she said. "I want there to be peace everywhere, but my brothers and I are still working on that".[12]

Jokes aside, here are some really inspiring excerpts from the speech she gave in Oslo during the Nobel prize-giving ceremony. These inspiring quotes speak of the power and passion in the child Malala.

"This award is not just for me. It is for those forgotten children who want education. It is for those frightened children who want peace. It is for those voiceless children who want change". She knows that she is awarded the Prize on behalf of all children. "I am here to stand up for their rights, raise their voice… it is not time to pity them. It is time to take action so it becomes the last time that we see a child deprived of education".

Reflecting on the choice she has made for herself, she says: "I had two options, one was to remain silent and wait to be killed. And the second was to speak up and then be killed. I chose the second one. I decided to speak up". Though she was attacked, the terrorists have not silenced her. "The terrorists tried to stop us and attacked me and my friends on 9 October 2012, but their bullets could not win.We survived. And since that day, our voices have only grown louder".

For Malala it is clear: "I tell my story, not because it is unique, but because it is not. It is the story of many girls".Though I appear as one girl, one person, who is 5 foot 2 inches tall, if you include my high heels. I am not a lone voice, I am many... I am those 66 million girls who are out of school.

Some other significant slogans and heart-breaking pleas from her speech:

- One child, one teacher, one pen and one book can change the world.
- In my own village, there is still no secondary school for girls. I want to build one, so my friends can get an education—and the opportunity it brings to fulfil their dreams... That is where I will begin, but it is not where I will stop. I will continue this fight until I see every child in school. I feel much stronger after the attack that I endured, because I know, no one can stop me, or stop us, because now we are millions, standing up together.
- It is not time to tell the leaders to realise how important education is - they already know it - their own children are in good schools. Now it is time to call them to take action.
- Some will say this is impractical, or too expensive, or too hard. Or even impossible. But it is time the world thinks bigger. She is emphatic: "the so-called world of adults may understand it, but we children don't. Why is it that countries which we call "strong" are so powerful in creating wars but so weak in bringing peace? Why is it that giving guns is so easy but giving books is so hard? Why is it that making tanks is so easy, but building schools is so difficult?
- As we are living in the modern age, the 21st century and we all believe that nothing is impossible. We can reach the moon and maybe soon will land on Mars. Then, in this,

the 21st century, we must be determined that our dream of quality education for all will also come true.

- So let us bring equality, justice and peace for all. Not just the politicians and the world leaders, we all need to contribute. Me. You. It is our duty.
- Dear sisters and brothers, let us become the first generation to decide to be the last. The empty classrooms, the lost childhoods, wasted potential—let these things end with us.
- Let this be the last time that a girl is told education is a crime and not a right.[13]

b. Kailash Satyarthi

Kailash Satyarthi won the Nobel Peace Prize along with Pakistan's Malala Yousafzai on December 10, 2014. He's the only Indian (i.e. born in India, and holding an Indian passport) to have won a Nobel Prize since Amartya Sen, who won the Nobel Prize for Economics in 1998. Here are some quotes from the speech he gave in Oslo during the prize-giving ceremony.[14]

- "Let's walk together. In the pursuit of global progress, not a single person should be left out or left behind in any corner of the world, from East to West, from South to North".[15]
- "Let's speak together, let our minds come together! Learning from the experiences of our ancestors, let us together create knowledge for all that benefits all".
- "I recall how thousands of times, I have been liberated, each time I have freed a child from slavery. In the first smile of freedom on their beautiful faces, I see the Gods smiling".
- "I represent here the sound of silence. The cry of innocence. And the face of invisibility. I have come here to share the voices and dreams of our children, our children, because they are all our children".
- "Twenty years ago, in the foothills of the Himalayas, I met a small, skinny boy. He asked me: 'Is the world so poor

that it cannot give me a toy and a book, instead of forcing me to take a tool or gun?'"

- "There is no greater violence than to deny the dreams of our children".
- "The single aim of my life is that every child is: free to be a child, free to grow and develop, free to eat, sleep, see daylight,free to laugh and cry, free to play,free to learn, free to go to school, and above all, free to dream".
- "I refuse to accept that the world is so poor, when just one week of global spending on armies is enough to bring all of our children into classrooms".
- "I refuse to accept that the shackles of slavery can ever be stronger than the quest for freedom".
- "Friends, the biggest crisis knocking on the doors of humanity today is intolerance".
- "I am afraid that the day is not far when the cumulative result of this failure will culminate in unprecedented violence that will be suicidal for humankind. Yet, young people like Malala, are rising up everywhere and choosing peace over violence, tolerance over extremism, and courage over fear".
- "Solutions are not found only in the deliberations in conferences and prescriptions from a distance. They lie in small groups and local organisations and individuals, who confront the problem every day, even if they remain unrecognised and unknown to the world".
- "Let us inculcate and transform the individuals' compassion into a global movement. Let us globalise compassion. Not passive compassion, but transformative compassion that leads to justice, equality, and freedom".
- "Whose children are they who stitch footballs, yet have never played with one? They are our children. Whose children are they who mine stones and minerals? They are our children. Whose children are they who harvest cocoa, yet do not know the taste of a chocolate? They are all our children".

- "We need collective actions with a sense of urgency. Every single minute matters, every single child matters, every single childhood matters".
- "I challenge the passivity and pessimism surrounding our children. I challenge this culture of silence, this culture of neutrality".
- "My dear sisters and brothers, may I ask you to close your eyes and put your hand close to your heart for a moment? Can you feel the child inside you? Now, listen to this child. I am sure you can!"
- "Let us march from darkness to light. Let us march from mortality to divinity. Let us march!"

After having listened to the heart-rending pleas of both the Nobel Laureates, it may be beneficial to look into our own hearts and see what is missing there, which we can learn from little children.

5. Six Things We Can Learn From Our Children

Rachna Parmar, Entrepreneur, Award-winning Blogger and Content Writer, recalls that when she became a mother, she had vowed to herself to protect the little one, teach him her wisdom, give him the best values and make him a child the world would be proud of. "Never once did I imagine in my parenting journey that both my kids would end up teaching me so much".[16]

Here are a few life's lessons they can teach us:

a. Forgive readily*:*

It is amazing how they fight and yell incessantly while playing yet make up easily. The signs of all acrimony completely wiped out by the end of the game. Why have we managed to hang on to every minor insult, grudge or regret and started burdening our souls? In fact children can forgive so easily and quickly and with all their heart? No wonder then that their minds are uncluttered and their souls devoid of any baggage. It does not matter if the culprit is a close friend, acquaintance or parent; they are always willing to give the benefit of doubt. Despite the disappointments, a few minutes back, some soothing words and promises from mommy is all it takes to put his anguish behind.[17]

b. Love easily:

Children find it easy to open their hearts to love. Rich or poor, fat or thin, young or old, they don't care. If there are any levelers in the world, they are our children. Irrespective of the social position, children can love each other spontaneously and freely. Children love without apprehension or judgment, unconditionally. Such an easy recipe for happiness!

c. Fear nothing:

Left to itself, child is not afraid of the unknown. Give the child a task, seemingly daunting, and you will find them approaching it with gusto. Their mind is free of conditioned fear and prejudices. Some children exasperate us with their little fearless experiments. Truly their spirit of adventure - it is something else and quite heartening as well.

d. Find beauty in everything:

For parents it was natural that they buy a lot of expensive toys and clothes. As the child grows older, he ditched the expensive toys and took a lot of pleasure in simple kitchen utensils. Sometimes they love playing with his car toys. Broken cars, those with missing wheels and old ones well past their prime are all lovingly played with. To them everything is beautiful, worthy of appreciation.

e. Notice the little things:

Often in the rush to see the bigger picture, we miss out on the little joys in life. A small child finds an anecdote hilarious and laughs a deep belly laugh. Children can derive great joy in seeing a butterfly take flight, in watching a spider weave a web, in seeing a flower bloom or in watching their pet dog come bounding to them -- activities that the adults have long stopped observing. As a multitasking people who works professionally, most of the time, we are missing the God in finer details. They make me resolve to *stop and stare* even as life rushes by.

f. Enjoy play:

Little children are delightfully active. From the time they learn to crawl, they waste not a minute. It is enjoyable just love watching the kids scamper around merrily. These little bundles of energy never get tired. Play is fun; our little ones ably teach us. On the other hand, for the adults, our beautiful bodies, the marvels of nature and the most fantastic machines around, are allowed to fall into disuse.

Childhood passes us by in a jiffy. And sometimes the unique qualities we had imbibed do as well. We can retain these wonderful attributes with some awareness and a little conscious effort. That is a call to rediscover the joy of living from our kids, something Samuel Rayan would highly appreciate.

Conclusion

a. The Missing Words: The Silence of Dawood Ibrahim

Dawood Ibrahim, lone survivor of the massacred class 9 in the Peshawar school attack.[18] His story may wake us from our theological slumber. Peshawar stands shocked and so does Dawood Ibrahim who is alive only because he attended a wedding on Monday night and his alarm did not work in the morning.

As reported by *The Express Tribune,* Dawood would have been another body in the pile, a plus-one in the death toll of the terrorist attack at the Army Public School on Warsak Road in Peshawar, had it not been for an incredible piece of fortune.

Fifteen-year-old Dawood, could not wake up on time and had to skip school. He is the only survivor of his school's ninth grade class. He has now buried six of his closest friends in one day. The shock has rendered him speechless and he is showing no emotion. "Dawood isn't talking to anyone, he isn't talking at all," his elder brother Sufyan Ibrahim said. "He is in judo and is a tough child but he is showing no emotion at all right now. He just attended funerals the entire day. No one from his class survived. Every single one of them was killed."

Sufyan also revealed the reason why his brother was not in school that day. "Dawood is lucky. He missed school today because we attended a wedding last night, and he overslept; it was fate."

Pakistan Judo Federation secretary Masood Ahmed added that Dawood is not the only one affected and all the athletes in the ongoing U16 national camp in Peshawar are ready to donate their blood to the injured. Pakistanis may be used to almost daily terror attacks against the security forces but an outright assault on children stunned the country, prompting commentators to call for a tough military response.

It may be noted: The silence of an alarm clock saved a life and the silence of Dawood now needs to serve as a wake up call for all of us. To move from the missing words to the missing children.

b. The Missing Children: Challenge to Ourselves

Finally the terrible statistics about children missing from our own midst: "In India, a child goes missing every eight minutes, according to data from the National Crime Records Bureau. Almost 40 percent of those children haven't been found." Wall Street Journal India Realtime.[19]

According to the National Crime Records Bureau (NCRB), almost 60,000 children were reported missing in 2011. Of these, 22,000 are yet to be located. However, according to a report by Bachpan Bachao Andolan (BBA), nearly 11 children go missing every hour, and at least, four of them are never found. According to BBA, the number of missing children could be as high as 90,000 per year. West Bengal topped the charts of missing children with 12,000 children missing in 2011. Madhya Pradesh followed with 7,797 cases, while Delhi had 5,111 cases. These are merely reported cases that discount those children who might run away due to various factors, ranging from abuse to dysfunctional homes, and exam stress, or some who might get lost while families travel. Majority of the missing children are just taken away. The statistics are scary – in 2011, 15,284 cases of kidnapping were reported. This was up 43 percent from the previous year.[20]

Between 2013 and 2014, at least 67,000 children in India went missing, of whom 45% were minors trafficked into prostitution. According to the National Crime Records Bureau, a girl is abducted every eight minutes in India. A US report on human trafficking states that India is one of the world's main hubs for child sex trafficking.[21]

True, the missing children – kidnapped, sold and even killed – must be traced and found. They cannot be left at the mercy of the kidnappers. Legal, social and preventive actions should be taken. We also need to recognise that the missing children are the reflection of the missing child within our own hearts. As grown-up adults, we have stopped to listen to the smile and the cry of children. The child within us feels suffocated. We need to rediscover the creativity, spontaneity, playfulness and love of the child and spread it to the larger world.

Then we can solve the problem, not by piecemeal approaches, but taking a holistic perspective. The tragedy afflicting our children calls for radical solutions changing our whole socio-economic and cultural understanding of the society. Otherwise our own lives are threatened. Let us, therefore, listen to the sane voice of Samuel Rayan and act accordingly: "To avoid collective catastrophe we must radically transform the underlying system of business to restore power to the small and the local... accomplishing the needed transformation will require the co-operative efforts of those within the system ... in addition to the efforts of citizen movements from outside".[22] For us Christians the celebration Christmas and the Joy of the Gospels urge us to rediscover the Child-God in our hearts and make children feel at home in our world!

The missing children (and girls) around us point to indicate that something is profoundly missing in our hearts – love, creativity and compassion. It further shows that the Christmas-Babe, the God-man, is missing in our hearts and lives. Poetically and symbolically we can say that the missing child indicates the missing God. With hope and joy Rayan will remind us that it is still not too late to discover the missing child and the spark of Divinity in our hearts and in the world around us!

Notes

1. Cited in Samuel Rayan, "God's Hope Becoming Visible in a Secular World," *God's Hope Becoming Visible: Collected Writings of Samuel Rayan, SJ, Vol. III*, Kurien Kunnumpuram (ed.) Delhi: ISPCK, 2013, p. 27.
2. Samuel Rayan, "Serve the Younger," in *God's Hope Becoming Visible: Collected Writings of Samuel Rayan, SJ, Vol. III*, Kurien Kunnumpuram (ed.) Delhi: ISPCK, 2013, p. 151. See also Kannan, K. P., and Indian Economic Association. Annual Conference. 2001. *Economics of Child Labour*. New Delhi: Deep & Deep Publications.
3. Samuel Rayan, "Serve the Younger", in *God's Hope Becoming Visible: Collected Writings of Samuel Rayan, SJ, Vol. III*, Kurien Kunnumpuram (ed.) Delhi: ISPCK, p. 153.
4. *Ibid.*, p. 156.
5. *Ibid.*, p. 174.
6. *Ibid.*, p. 176.
7. *Ibid.*
8. Baabar, Mariana. 2014. "132 Children Massacred in Attack on School - The Hindu." *The Hindu*. December 17. http://www.thehindu.com/news/international/south-asia/taliban-attack- peshawar-army-school-take-hundreds-hostage/article6697297.ece.
9. Ashraf Engineer, 2015 "Save The Children." *The Huffington Post*. Accessed February 28. http://www.huffingtonpost.in/ashraf-engineer/save-the-children_4_b_6345294.html.
10. *Ibid.*
11. *Ibid.*
12. AFP. 2014. "Malala Accepts Nobel Peace Prize with a Rousing Speech." *The Express Tribune*. December 10. http://tribune.com.pk/story/804655/live-nobel-peace-prize-ceremony-underway/. All the quotes in this section are from this Nobel Peace Prize Acceptance Speech.
13. See Indrani Basu. 2015. "Malala Yousafzai's Most Inspiring Nobel Peace Prize Speech Quotes 2014." *The Huffington Post*. Accessed February 28.

    http://www.huffingtonpost.in/2014/12/10/malala-yousafzais-most-in_n_6300800.html.
14. Indrani Basu. 2014. "Kailash Satyarthi's Most Inspiring Nobel Peace Prize Speech Quotes 2014." *The Huffington Post*. December 10.

    http://www.huffingtonpost.in/2014/12/10/kailash-satyarthi-nobel-p_n_6300316.html.
15. *Ibid.*
16. Rachna Parmar. 2015. "Six Things We Can Learn From Our Children." *The Huffington Post*. Accessed February 28. http://www.huffingtonpost.in/rachna-

parmar/6-things-we-can-learn-fro_b_6327412.html. These lessons from the children are adapted from this article.

17. *Ibid.*

18. Ibnlive. 2014. "Pakistan: The Lone Survivor of the Massacred Class 9 in the Peshawar School Attack." *IBNLive*. December 17. http://ibnlive.in.com/news/pakistan-dawood-ibrahim-lone-survivor-of-the-massacred-class-9-in-the-peshawar-school-attack/518519-56.html.

19. Kiran Manral. 2013. "Where Are Our Missing Children?" *Tehelka.com*. February 5. http://www.tehelka.com/where-are-our-missing-children/.

20. The missing girls or the killed daughters are another problem that contemporary Indian has to deal with. Under the motto "*Bhrun hatya paap hai* (female foeticide is a sin)"Prime Minister Narendra Modi flagged off awareness raths for the Government's new 'Beti Bachao, Beti Padhao' (BBBP) movement. Still more has to be done to save girl children from being murdered. See Sunaina Kumar. 2015. "The Missing Girls of Mahendragarh Open Magazine." *The Huffington Post*. Accessed February 28. http://www.huffingtonpost.in/open-magazine/the-missing-girls-of-mahe_b_6773976.html?utm_hp_ref=india.

21. Gary Craig. 2010. *Child Slavery Now: A Contemporary Reader*. Portland, Ore.: Policy Press.

22. Cite in Samuel Rayan. "God's Hope Becoming Visible in a Secular World," in *God's Hope Becoming Visible: Collected Writings of Samuel Rayan, SJ, Vol. III*, Kurien Kunnumpuram (ed.) Delhi: ISPCK, 2013, p. 27. This is Rayan's quote from John Desrochers, et al.

13

Transformative Spirituality

Response-Ability to Reality Search for a Relevant Spirituality in the Writings of Samuel Rayan

Stephen Chundamthadam, SJ

1. Introduction

Samuel Rayan has, through his writings and teachings, influenced, stimulated and challenged theologizing in India enormously. In this process he developed a relevant spirituality, i.e., a *transformative spirituality* which he practised in his personal life. For Rayan, God's creation and its struggle for justice and liberation is the basis of *transformative spirituality*. Rayan's spirituality is the result of his long association with youth, the religious, people of all religions and cultures. He had a clear perspective in his spirituality, i.e., from the point of view of the marginalized and the oppressed people and their struggle for liberation. So, his spirituality, like his theology, is living and relevant today. His writings are attempts to integrate the rich Indian spiritual traditions with the Christian traditions; they are a "harmonious combination of faith and praxis of theology and spirituality." Suffering (*dukkha*) of the people was the starting point of Buddha's search for liberation. Similarly, the starting point of Rayan's spirituality is the struggles of the people; struggle for equality, for justice, for fundamental rights and for total liberation.

The socio-political reality of India, the pluri-religious context, caste discrimination, oppression of women and children, ruthless exploitation of the earth and natural resources were the predominant factors which played a decisive role in shaping the transformative spirituality of Rayan. Spirituality, as he envisaged it, is a process leading to total liberation. For developing a new approach to spirituality he did not subscribe to the traditional Christian spirituality; nor did he accept the dominant Hindu spirituality as a model, but he drew inspiration from the liberative struggles of the people. This paper is an attempt to explore the defining characteristics of Rayan's Transformative Spirituality.

2. Discontent over the Conventional Spirituality

In his search for a relevant spirituality, Rayan was not satisfied with the traditional spiritualities which focussed more on pietistic practices oriented towards the other world. Organized religions are more concerned about the life in the other world, so the sufferings and the struggles of people are of no interest to them. Traditional religions developed a spirituality based on this world-view. Jordan Aumann defines spirituality from a traditional perspective:

> In its widest sense, spirituality refers to any religious or ethical value that is concretized as an attitude or spirit from which one's actions proceed. This concept of spirituality is not restricted to any particular religion; it applies to any person who has a belief in the divine transcendent power and fashions a life-style according to one's religious conviction. In this context, one can speak of Zen Buddhist, Jewish and Muslim Spirituality as well as Christian Spirituality.[1]

Aumann continues:

> Christian Spirituality is therefore a participation in the mystery of Christ through the interior life of grace, actuated by faith, charity and other Christian virtues. The life that the individual receives through participation in Christ is the same life that the Incarnate Word shares with the Father and the Holy Spirit.[2]

Christian Spirituality consists of "attitudes, benefits, practices which animate people's lives and help them to reach out towards supernatural realities".[3] According to Maria Teresa Porcile, spirituality is "a kind of homesickness for God, for silence, beauty, prayer, liturgy, chant, theology, which becomes worship". These definitions of spirituality, supported by rituals and ceremonies, focus more on the transcendental supernatural realities. Traditional spiritualities neglected the suffering of the ordinary people, their need for human dignity and liberation. These definitions accept a dichotomy between spirituality and physicality.

Genuine spirituality deals with the life and ethical values of a person as well as society which leads to transformation. Christian spirituality is partaking in the Christ event (life, passion, death and resurrection of Jesus) through personalization of Christ mystery. Spirituality is a life of total detachment lived in the awareness of the indwelling and all-pervading spirit. For Schmemann, Christian spirituality is as much for the body as for the soul, as much for society as for the individual. For prophet Micah, spirituality consists in acting justly, loving tenderly and walking humbly with the God of us all. (Micah 6:8). According to Thomas Merton, spirituality is a transformation of conscience from a self-centred state to another-centred condition. Spirituality for Jesus is to think as God thinks and love accordingly. For W. Pannenberg, spirituality is a progressive realization of the Gospel of transformative affirmation of the human person and human history by God's love.[4] Unlike the traditional definitions, these focus on individuals, love, justice and society and the need for transformation of conscience. Based on these insights, Rayan developed a spirituality taking into consideration the pluri-religious and spiritual context and the people's struggle for human dignity and liberation in Asia.

3. The Spiritual Context of Asia

Asia has a multitude of spiritual and religious traditions which are concerned about both the empirical and transcendent aspects of life.

3.1 Humanistic Spirituality

As a challenge to the ritualistic spirituality of the Mimamsakas; Carvaka, Buddhism and Jainism developed a humanistic spirituality based on ethical values and concern for nature and animals. Carvakas were the first ones who challenged animal sacrifice and the exploitation of the ordinary people by the priestly class in the name of gods and life after death. According to Carvakas, even the enjoyment of pleasures, which they accepted as the highest goal of life, should be based on certain ethical principles.

Buddha was least interested in metaphysical discourses or dogmas. He was concerned about ethical living, applicable to all sections of people: kings, princes, brahmanas, low caste, masters, servants, monks, ordinary people etc. He taught that the nobility of a person is not based on birth but on deeds. Compassion and love were his predominant characteristics. Hence, his philosophy can be rightly called the Ethics of practical Religion. Charity was the basis of Buddhist religion. The four Noble Truths are the essence of the Buddha's teachings, which he explained in his first sermon to his old colleagues at Isipattana. Buddhist spirituality is based on the four noble truths that is there is suffering in this world, there is a cause for suffering, there is an end to the suffering and there is a way to end the suffering. Buddhist spirituality has four stages *ahimsa* (not harming), *maitri* (loving kindness), *dana* (giving) and *karuna* (compassion).

Like Buddhism, ethical principles are the basis of Jain spirituality. Jains believe that the soul, which was originally pure, becomes impure because of its association with matter. Actions will only increase the impurity of the soul. In order to be liberated one has to have control over all actions. Ahimsa (non-injury) is an important mandate in Jainism. Everything in this world is to be treated with love and respect. Proper control over mind, speech and actions is an important aspect in Jain spiritualty. Austerities are practised in life, eating, sleep and dress. Right faith, right conduct and right knowledge are the three jewels.

3.2 Immanent Aspect of Spirituality

Hinduism stresses both the transcendent and the immanent aspects of God. For them spirituality is both a search and a life based on rituals and ethical values. The Second Vatican Council speaks about Hindu spirituality:

> In Hinduism the divine mystery is explored and propounded with an inexhaustible wealth of myths and penetrating philosophical investigation, and liberation is sought from the

> distresses of our state either through various forms of ascetical life or deep meditation or taking refuge in God with loving confidence.[5]

Two aspects are stressed in this description of Hindu spiritualty that is the divine mystery and the concept of liberation. The aim of a soul in this world is to attain salvation or *mukti* for which three ways are suggested. They are the way of action (*karma marga*), the way of knowledge (*jnanamarga*) and the way of devotion (*bhakti marga*).

3.3 Spirituality is Beatific Experience

Yogic spirituality is a unique way to beatific experience (*Kaivalya*) and supreme bliss.[6] Patanjali defines yoga as restraint of mental modifications, control of thought-weaves.[7] *Chitta* consists of three factors that is mind (*manas*), intelligence (*budhi*) and ego (*ahamkara*). *Dhyana,* Meditation is an unbroken flow of thought weaves towards the object of concentration[8] which leads to the final aim *Samadhi.* Practice of yoga is a spiritual pilgrimage towards the very foundation of a person. When, in meditation, the true nature of the object shines forth, not distorted by the mind of the perceiver that is absorption.[9] Absorbed in meditation, the seeker sees God within himself and all things in it.

3.4 Spirituality of Surrender

The spirituality of the Bhagavadgita can be understood from two perspectives, that is Ramanuja's qualified monism and Sankara's absolute monism. For Ramanuja, spirituality is total surrender to the Lord in love and service; for Sankara, it is enlightenment through knowledge about Brahman.

> The Yogi who has reached full illumination
> Contemplates through the eye of knowledge
> Everything in itself, and perceives that everything is himself
> And nothing else.[10]

The term 'yoga' stands for spiritual inquiry in the Bhagavadgita. Gita is the result of the existential agony of a sincere seeker in the person of Arjuna. The seeker finds himself in an acute crisis situation of life. His search for liberation from the existential agony is the main theme and the underlying dynamics of the text. *Sadhaka* experiences disharmony within and seeks harmony (yoga) with himself, with the world and the Divine. Gita represents a constant interaction between humans and God represented by Krishna and Arjuna. In this interaction, Indian spirituality emphasizes the uniqueness of the goal, single mindedness and a continuous pursuit. Moksa alone is the ultimate aim of life. Liberation can be attained through a qualitative change in the life and values of a person.

Islamic spirituality is based on the six basic principles i.e., reading of Koran, ritual prayer (*Salah*), legal alms-giving (*zakah*), fasting, pilgrimage to Mecca, *Jihad*. In Hinduism as well as in the Judeo-Christian tradition, the focus of spirituality is more on life in the other world, and not on the life here and now.

4. Transformative Spirituality of Samuel Rayan

There are two approaches in the history of spirituality in India: the humanistic spirituality represented by Carvaka, Buddhism and Jainism; and religious spirituality represented by Hinduism, Islam, Parsi, Sikh and Christian religions. Humanistic spirituality focuses on ethical living and the struggles of the people in the present life. But, religious spirituality is more concerned about religious observances, rituals and dogmas aiming at the after-life. Samuel Rayan was dissatisfied with the religious spirituality because it did not address the struggles and the need for liberation of the people. But he did not fully subscribe to the humanistic spirituality because the religious spirit in Rayan could not accept the atheistic spiritual traditions. Rayan, based on his experiences and involvement in the struggles of people, developed a spirituality which he thought would be an appropriate response to reality. The starting point of his spirituality is the earth, creation and the struggles of the people.

4.1 The Earth and Creation: The Starting Point of a Spiritual Journey

Rayan's spirituality is a response to the concrete reality in society. So, for him the journey to God has to be started from the earth which is His bride, because the earth and creation are God's self-manifestation, an on-going revelation of the word and God's attitude towards humans.[11] God lovingly takes care of the earth and his creation, Ps 65:7-14; Acts 14:17; 17:24-26. Creation is an act of love; it is God's delight and a sign of God's grace (Gen 1:2).Creation aims at a union with the Creator. Creation constantly communicates with God in silence and in eloquence.[12] God has entrusted his precious creation to the care of humans so that the earth and creation are ours (Ps 115). It is a common gift to all, it is our common home.

> This shared earth is both the basis and the sacrament of gentle human community... We are earth: bits of it which have come to develop a mysterious interiority, the capacity for reflexive thought and for freedom and love.[13]

The earth and creation proclaim the glory of God. Referring to the canticle of Francis of Assisi, tribal culture all over the world and Indian tradition in particular, Rayan considers created beings as sisters and brothers and the earth as Mother earth.[14] The earth and creation are precious both for God and for humans, they are to be treated with respect and reverence. An important aspect of spirituality today should be the care and concern for nature. This aspect of respect is there in most of the world religions; what we need to do is "to adopt simple lifestyles, to use things with mental maturity and responsibility to the community, to the earth, to future generations and to the Creator, ensuring that no plant or animal species is lost forever, and that nobody tomorrow is deprived of the blessing we know and enjoy today".[15]

Rayan, by placing the earth and creation as the launching pad of the journey to God has done away with the dichotomy between materiality and spirituality in the Christian spirituality. Moreover, Rayan is resonating with the tribal and the dalit traditions in India as well as with the Visistadvaita philosophy which considers the world and creation as the body of God.

4.2 Matter and Spirit two Aspects of the Same Reality

A world-view based on the dualistic understanding of reality will not help us to develop an authentic spirituality suited to the needs of the people in Asia. A dichotomy between spirit and matter is implied in the Western understanding of spirituality which despises matter.

Asians are confronted with abject poverty, exploitation of women, children and weaker sections in the society, under development, and caste discrimination. In such a situation the other-worldly spirituality will not change the situation. The Hebrew understanding of *ruah* which means the power or the breath of God includes matter, spirit and everything God created. "Spirituality is the sum total of one's loves and attitudes; it consists in the ordering of one's loves; it refers to the quality of one's heart and life".[16] Spirituality for a Christian is the following of Christ; it is a pilgrimage to the Absolute and a pilgrimage to the inner self which will transform a person.

There is spirituality in the life and struggle of the oppressed, in their suffering, in their celebrations, in their sharing. The Good Samaritan in the New Testament and the people rewarded in the Last judgement for doing good are examples of the spirituality of liberation. Dalits, tribals, women and other weaker sections of society participate in this kind of spirituality through their struggle for justice and human dignity. Charitable services and developmental works provide only temporary relief. Transformative spirituality envisages the elimination of the oppressive structures and systems[17] which will lead to the liberation of the peoples. Liberative and transformative aspects of spirituality are closely associated with the socio-political reality of the people.In this venture the spirit is not totally segregated from matter, matter and spirit together form one reality, they are inseparably connected with each other.

4.3 Spirituality is Openness to the Spirit

Spirituality is closely connected with the 'Spirit'. By the 'Spirit', Rayan does not mean the human psyche or soul but he means the Spirit of Jesus Christ. The Spirit of Christ which makes us children of God. "To be spiritual, then, is to be carried by the Spirit and be profoundly transformed by Her".[18] The Spirit is the medium of creation and creation remains united with each other and with the Creator through the Spirit. The Spirit ensures harmony in nature and creation. Ruthless exploitation of mother earth and natural resources creates disharmony leading to natural calamities. Eco-spirituality attempts to create awareness about various kinds of pollution and the destruction of harmony in nature. For Rayan, spirituality is not restricted to religious rituals and pious practices. Through the parable of the Good Samaritan, Rayan presents a new model of spirituality based on compassion, kindness and service.The aspect of compassionate service as a constitutive factor of spirituality is reasserted in the parable of the last judgement. The Son of Man accepts a large number of people into his kingdom because they were compassionate and cared for the poor, the hungry and the oppressed (Matt 25:31-46). Social justice and care for the poor and the oppressed (Isa 1:11-17), submission to the will of God (I Sam 13-22), justice and goodness were important factors in the spirituality of the prophets and not fasting, sacrifices and ritual observances.

4.4 The Prophetic Dimension of Spirituality

The spirituality of Jesus has a prophetic dimension in line with the Hebrew tradition in the Old Testament. Jesus asserts the need for reconciliation by the sacrificer as a necessary precondition for genuine sacrifice Matt 5:23-24. Reconciliation with one another and with the whole of creation is necessary for peace and harmony in the world. Peace and harmony among creation is the will of the Father which Jesus sought and fulfilled in his life. "God's will is mercy, love, compassion, solidarity and sharing of goods and of the knowledge of God among God's beloved children, God's dear family on earth".[19] Jesus' life is unique because he translated into action whatever he taught. Jesus' concern and compassion for the afflicted and the oppressed people motivated him to break the rules of Sabbath (Mk 1:14-3:6; Jn 5:9); to bring back to life the dead (Lk 7:11-17; Mk 5:21-43; Jn 11:33-34). Jesus' care for the people was revealed when he multiplied the bread for the crowd (Mk 6:30-44; Mk 8:1-9; Matt 14:13-21; Lk 9:10-17; Jn 6:1-13). His spirituality of compassion towards the woman who washed and kissed his feet in the house of Simon was a challenge to the legalistic spirituality of the Pharisees (Lk 7:36-50; Lk 15; Matt 9:10-13; 18:12-14). Jesus' spirituality did not prevent him from actively involving in the struggle of people in order to liberate them from oppressive structures.

Jesus was a Spirit-filled person, "his entire life is deeply rooted in and permeated by the Holy Spirit". "Jesus rejoiced in the Spirit, listened to Her voice and followed Her guidance". Even after his death he continued his mission through his disciples and apostles. He breathed on them and said to them, "Receive the Holy Spirit" (Jn 20:19-22). Early Christian communities were examples of people who lived together and shared bread and wealth among themselves guided by the Holy Spirit (Acts 2:42-47). The spirituality of Jesus was aimed at the total liberation of the human person by restoring her/his wholeness, human dignity and equality. "Jesus directed people's gaze to the Reign of God that was breaking in with His presence and services and to the beauty of life in the peace, love and solidarity of the Reign".[20] In spiritual journey we remain open to the Spirit and ready to respond to situations. Spirituality is openness to reality and creative response to the reality. In the parable of the Good Samaritan the Levite, the priest and the Samaritan responded to reality in different ways (Lk 10:37).

4.5 Spirituality Means Openness and *Response*-ability to Reality

In the modern world, to be spiritual means, "to hear the cry of the poor as God does, take their side in analysing and denouncing the subhuman system". In an unjust and exploitative world, spirituality has to resist and reject every form of violence and war. "To be spiritual is to be open and responsive to reality. Reality could be negative or positive". Openness to the negative reality means awareness of the presence of the destructive and dehumanizing forces and structures. This awareness should lead one to find their causes so that they can be eliminated. If the reality is positive the response is to welcome it to enrich and promote 'freedom, solidarity and the common good'. "Reality could be personal, familial, social-political, cosmic and transcendent-Divine".[21]

Spirituality is aimed at establishing God's Reign in the world today. The world in which we live is a broken world because of selfishness, injustice, violence and inequality. "We live in an era of incredible violence, massacres, bloodshed and destruction".[22] Spirituality should foster another world of "justice and peace, love and life, equality and solidarity. To be spiritual today is to stand with the millions of women and men in the World Social Forum and affirm that another world is possible and to strive together for its realization".[23] Economic and scientific developments are aimed at the full development of the human potentialities in their pilgrimage to the Absolute. The human is the centre of this new World where sharing and caring for the other becomes the very nature of people. The early Christian communities around the Mediterranean lived according to these principles for several centuries. Only when Christianity became the official religion of the Roman Empire the situation changed.

The Spirit is working in other religions and cultural traditions, so also in the peoples' struggles. If the Indian Church has to be spiritual it has to respond creatively to the Indian context. Rayan passionately argues, "Today's, therefore, will be a spirituality of involvement in the world of the people, in their concerns and hopes, their gropings and tears, and not a spirituality of flight from the world, mistrust of humans or retirement into cloisters".[24] The Church in India has to take a stand with the marginalized and the oppressed to participate in their struggle for dignity and freedom. The Church, then, will become a sacrament, and spirituality incarnational. If the Church in India goes through a process of self-emptying, *kenosis*, of the "pomp and prestige, institutional power, patronage of the great, security provided by the mighty," it can take a stand with the marginalized and the oppressed. Then the spirituality of the Church will become 'human and historical.' If the Church does not dare to self-empty, "it would amount to a denial of the Church's substance as an incarnate, redemptive presence".[25] 'The Spirit is urging us' to respond to situations in the way

> *She Herself* does: that is, eliminating the negative, wiping away the tears, binding up the wounds, lifting up the lowly; ending greed, hatred and violence, and fostering gently the beautiful and the loving- all for the common good, the welfare of all humankind, and for the greater praise and glory of God, the glory of God being the Human fully alive, whole and happy, flowering and fruitful.[26]

The Spirit is working in a special way in the Church, so too in other cultures and religious traditions. The Church to be a living witness to the Kingdom values, has to self-empty herself so that she can take a stand with the less privileged for the welfare of the humankind.

4.6 Christian Spirituality in the Indian Church

In the main stream Hindu tradition, spirituality and the way to the Absolute were strictly under the control of the priestly class which perpetuated class discrimination for their own benefit. Mimamsaka's ritualistic spirituality was a shrewd way of maintaining the monopoly on spiritual matters. People's struggle for spirituality from a different perspective was started in the beginning of the first millennium before the Common Era by Carvaka philosophy and continued during the Upanishadic period. Later this struggle was taken up by the Buddhist and the Jain traditions.[27] Christians in India need to approach other spiritual traditions with humility and openness. India being a land of plurality of cultures and spiritual traditions, the Church in India has to radically rethink "its heavy penchant for uniformity".

Christian spirituality in the Indian Church is limited to conventional religious observances and practices; whereas Indian spirituality is characterized by openness to various traditions and to the Absolute. The aspect of mystery is at the core of Indian spirituality. Rayan makes a clarion call for a new way of being spiritual in the Indian context: "Let its faith respond creatively to the diversity of the Spirit's charismata and the variety of life's situations and of peoples, and let a hundred flowers bloom, and a plurality of theologies, faith-formulations, worship-forms and ecclesial structures shape up and emerge".[28] When the Spirit is allowed to work the way She wants, there will be a transformation in the values and attitudes of people and society.

4.7 Transformation of Social Structures

Gandhiji responded to his context of colonial domination of India by a foreign power in a creative way. He equates Truth with God and argues that Truth liberates one. So the liberation of India from foreign rule became his life mission and his spirituality, a political spirituality. Non-violence, *ahimsa*, non-cooperation and civil disobedience to the imperial powers became the means of achieving Truth. In this struggle he "identified himself with the masses, emulated the simple life of the peasant," which helped him to win over their whole-hearted support and cooperation. His spiritual approach to the politics of colonial subjugation and non-violent resistance to aggression had a great impact on both his followers and on the aggressors. But, his spirituality was not based on the lessons of history and lacked a realistic approach to people and concrete situations.[29] Because of the unrealistic assessment of the situation, Gandhiji called off the civil disobedience movement in 1921 and 1930. The main reason he gave was that people were not yet ready for a non-violent disobedient movement. He 'urged the peasants to pay rent to the landlords and respect their legal rights'; because as part of the disobedient movement peasants refused to pay rent to them. These actions of Gandhiji reveal in a subtle way the class interest which influenced his policies and decisions, not the liberation of the oppressed and exploited classes. Rayan concludes, "Gandhiji, for all his greatness, seems to have been unable to step out of his metaphysical categories and class loyalties to meet the people in their upsurge and their unfolding history in its depths".[30]

Mother Teresa, Gandhiji and the Peasant, Tribal and Dalit movements represent three responses to reality based on three different spiritualties.The spirituality of social services or charitable activities presupposes an unchangeable social order and a clear-cut separation between the profane and the sacred. The spirituality of the developmental projects demands subservience to the developed donor countries and agencies so that they may continue to exploit the underdeveloped and developing countries through their technological, scientific superiority. These two approaches are not capable of effecting a transformation of the unjust and exploitative social structures.

People's movements and mass struggles are based on the insights from a careful social analysis and a sensitive response to the historical reality. "The spirituality at work here understands itself as prophetic with a word of liberation to proclaim, illustrate and live out...Its concern is not with going to heaven after death but with the coming of God's Kingdom on God's and our earth".[31] "God's outgoing and self-giving love in his creative and redemptive action" and the "outgoing or exodus love of Jesus Christ" are the best examples for an authentic spirituality today. Spirituality is the capacity of humans guided by the Spirit to go beyond human limitations and build God's kingdom in our earth based on love, compassion, sharing and caring. Quoting John Macquarrie, Rayan says, "Spirituality, then is the process of becoming a person in the fullest sense".[32] Mother Teresa and Gandhiji tried to achieve this aim without challenging the existing evil structures in society. People's struggles try to achieve the same goal by fighting against the unjust social structures. In the modern world it is not enough that individuals are spiritual, but larger groups and society as a whole has to undergo a transformation. The Church in Asia, in collaboration with other cultures and traditions, in the context of violence, oppression, slavery and exploitation, has a special role to transform peoples to create God's kingdom on earth. In spirituality we allow God to touch our hearts and transform them into hearts of compassion and love.

4.8 Compassion and Hope

A large number of people in India, because of centuries of oppression, exploitation, poverty, caste discrimination and humiliation, have lost their identity and human dignity.Citing the situation of Kolkata, a confluence of contradictions i.e., abject poverty and misery at the foot of enormous wealth and luxury, Rayan concludes, "We want a spirituality which can enable us to deal with such a reality in infinite compassion and anger and hope; and to work to transform it into a human place where children can grow up instead of dying".[33] Mother Theresa responded to the miserable situation in Kolkata and elsewhere in the world in a creative and challenging way. Her attempt at providing basic facilities, hope and love to millions of people all over the world was an expression of the spirituality of compassion. Social activists and liberation theologians severely criticised her works of charity for indirectly perpetuating the oppressive social structures and at the same time reducing the guilt conscience of the rich and the affluent. Rayan wished, "If Mother Teresa and her people were to do this (spelling out clearly in word and deed the dissent dimension) themselves, that would be excellent, and its impact would be tremendous".[34]

Spirituality is the life which Jesus lived in this world in its fullness. In that sense, spirituality in the world today is the life of the people in all aspects. In it "new dimensions of the Incarnation will begin to be revealed and realized, the Word of God descending ever more intimately into the heart of material, technological, political realities and lifting them to the sphere of the divine".[35] Spirituality cannot be limited to the ecclesiastical activities of the Church, nor to the activities of the priestly class – rites, rituals and ceremonies, or even to the monastic life of meditation and prayer in solitude. Spirituality is basically "a relationship of intimacy," a divine-human relationship. Human beings are endowed with a spirit capable of transcendence to the divine. The Church, as part of its renewal, has to undertake a two-way pilgrimage, an inward journey to its centre (*Lumen Gentium*) as well as an outward journey towards the other (*Gaudium et Spes*), then spirituality will remain no more neutral but experiential.

4.9 God-Experience as the Basis for Spiritual Authority

Spiritual authority in Indian traditions is based on God-experience and not on an organisational set up. Enlightened gurus are sought after by people because of the genuineness of their God-experience and transformed life and values. The Indian Church will have to replace authority based on ecclesiastical power structures with the authority of God-experience. Jesus received his power and authority from his intimate relationship with the Father. The Indian Church, instead of emphasising conformity and correctness, has to focus on justice, love and equality based on God- experience. Rayan speaks about three original spiritual traditions shaping the world: the *prophetic* (the Bible and the Quran), *the mystical* (Hinduism, Buddhism and Taoism) and the *symbolic* (African). The Church in India, to be more effective in proclaiming Jesus, has to integrate the mystical aspect of spirituality that is God being unravelled through dance, art, nature and daily experiences of people. "The Indian Church has to build more closely into its spiritual life the sacrament of nature and of ordinary daily human existence". Rayan, therefore, invites the Christians to learn from these three major spiritual traditions which will be enriching to each other. "Indian spirituality, then, is openness to the Ultimate

Absolute Mystery which is the ground of the cosmos".[36] Openness to the Absolute necessarily implies compassion for the other.

4.10 Liberative Potential of Spirituality

The liberative struggles and responses of the people take place in a cultural context. As a culture evolves, spirituality also undergoes change and growth. Spirituality in the Old Testament is the struggle for liberation from slavery, struggle for equality and justice. In that sense spirituality has a political dimension; it has to deal with 'the plight and destiny of the people'.

> Faced with the diabolical forces of militarism and oppression, the nature and process of spirituality would consist in awakening, conscientising, mobilizing, resisting, and envisaging alternatives and going ahead to create them, and marching forward to celebrate freedom.[37]

Rayan gives concrete examples of people who had the courage to think differently, to create alternative models of liberation. Quoting Ashis Nandy, Rayan argues:

> Gandhi tried to "draw upon the creative and innovative springs of local action at the grassroots". In Gandhi, as also in Martin Luther King, political action and profound spirituality were combined. Highly motivated people in touch with these springs constituted the real movement for equity, justice and human rights-that is, for authentic spirituality.[38]

Transformative spirituality demands that we take a stand with the poor and the oppressed to support the work of God to feed the hungry to clothe the naked and to take care of the widow and the orphan, to be with the people, to acknowledge that God is present and God cares for them. "Spirituality then is a large and complex reality which includes all the modes and modalities of living the life of the Kingdom restored through Jesus Christ".[39] When lived according to the Kingdom values, spirituality becomes the sum total of one's loves and attitudes, loving and compassionate relationship with God, with people and with creation.[40] Then it becomes a pilgrimage to the Father in and through the Spirit".[41]

5. Conclusion

Samuel Rayan started his search for a transformative spirituality from the concrete reality of the multi-cultural context in which caste discrimination, oppression of women and children, exploitation of earth and natural resources were rampant. Traditional spiritualities because of their preoccupation with rituals and ceremonies for life after, neglected the cry and suffering of the people and their struggle for equality, fundamental rights, human dignity and liberation. Spirituality of charitable or developmental activities is not going to make any change in the unjust social structures. Based on his experience and involvement, Rayan was fully convinced that a spirituality which is transformative in nature is the need of the time. A transformative spirituality guided by the Spirit has to start from the mother earth and creation. Kindness, compassion and openness to the Spirit etc., are the guiding principles of the new spirituality, and not rituals and pious practices. Like Jesus, we have to take a stand with the millions of the marginalized people and all those who work for establishing the God's kingdom on this earth based on love, compassion, human values, justice, equality and human dignity.

Samuel Rayan rightly argues for a spirituality of involvement leading to the transformation of persons and unjust social structures. For him retirement into cloisters and solitary places for God-experience is not genuine spirituality but solitude is to be experienced in the slums and in the struggles of peoples. "Today's, therefore, will be a spirituality of involvement in the world of the people, in their concerns and hopes, their gropings and tears, and not a spirituality of flight from the world, mistrust of humans or retirement into cloisters".[42] He gives Jesus as a model for involvement spirituality.

In the modern world, it is not enough that individuals are spiritual but society, peoples' groups and the Church have a greater role to play in establishing a just society. The Church in India, in order to take a stand with the oppressed, has to undergo a process of self-emptying; otherwise, it would be a counter-witness to the original mission entrusted to the apostles by Jesus. Spirituality for a Christian is a pilgrimage to the Father by following the life and values of Christ. It is an experience of transformation. Spirituality is the sum total of one's loves, attitudes, relationships with God, people and with the creation. Transformative spirituality is "living and walking in God's presence with body and mind and soul in the midst of the sufferings and struggles of this world".[43]

Notes

1. Jordan Aumann, *Spiritual Theology,* London: Sheed and Ward, 1979, p. 17.
2. *Ibid.*, p. 18.
3. Gordon S. Wakefield (ed.), *A Dictionary of Christian Spirituality*, London: SCM Press, 1983.
4. Samuel Rayan, "A Spirituality of Mission in the Asian Context," *Sedos,* Vol. 29 (1997), Nos. 6-7, also in *Selected Writings of Samuel Rayan,* Kurien Kunnumpuram (ed.), Vol. II, Bombay: St. Pauls, 2012, P. 85.
5. Vatican II, *Nostra Aetate* no. 2.
6. Patanjali. *Yogasutras* 4.33.
7. *Chittavrtti nirodhahyogah, Yoga sutras* 1.2.
8. *Tatrapratyayaiakatanatadhyanam, Yogasutras* 3.2.
9. *Tadevarthamatranirbhasamsvarupasunyamivasamadhihi, Yogasutras* 3.3.
10. Sankara, *Atma-Bodha*, 47.
11. Samuel Rayan, "The Earth is the Lord's," Vidyajyoti, 54 (1990), p. 116; also in *Collected Writings of Samuel Rayan*, Kurien Kunnumpuram (ed.), Vol. I, Delhi: ISPCK, 2013, p. 5.
12. *Ibid,* p. 117; *Collected Writings,* p. 6-7.
13. *Ibid,* p. 119; *Collected Writings,* p. 9.
14. *Ibid,* p. 121; *Collected Writings*, p. 9-10.
15. Samuel Rayan, "A Spirituality for Our Times," in Kurien Kunnumpuram (ed.), *Life in Abundance: Indian Christian Reflections on Spirituality,* Mumbai: St. Pauls, 2010 p. 234; also in Kurien Kunnumpuram (ed.), *Selected Writings of Samuel Rayan*, Vol. II, 2012 p. 32.
16. Samuel Rayan, "A Search for an Asian Spirituality of Liberation," in Virginia Fabella & Peter Fabella (Eds.), *Asian Christian Spirituality: Reclaiming Traditions,* Maryknoll, N Y: Orbis Books, 1992, p.18; also in *Selected Writings of Samuel Rayan*, Vol. II, 2012. p. 115.
17. Samuel Rayan, "Spirituality for Inter-faith Social Action," in Indian Journal of Spirituality, Vol. III (1990), No. 2; also in *Selected Writings*, Vol. II, p. 131.
18. *Ibid.*, p. 222; *Selected Writings*, Vol. II, p. 21.
19. *Ibid.*, p. 224; *Selected Writings*, Vol. II, p. 25.

20. *Ibid.*, p. 229; *Selected Writings*, Vol. II, p. 29.
21. *Ibid.*, p. 219; *Selected Writings,* Vol. II, p. 19.
22. *Ibid.*, p. 234; *Selected Writings*, Vol. II, p. 32.
23. *Ibid.*, p. 231; *Selected Writings*, Vol. II, p. 29.
24. Samuel Rayan, "Spirituality in the Indian Church Today," in Mathai Zacharias (ed.), *The Church: People's Movement,* Nagpur: National Christian Council, 1975; also in Kurien Kunnumpuram (ed.), *Selected Writings of Samuel Rayan*, Vol. II, 2012, p. 45.
25. *Ibid;* also in *Selected Writtings*, Vol. II, p. 47.
26. Samuel Rayan, "A Spirituality for Our Times," in Kurien Kunnumpuram (ed.), *Life in Abundance: Indian Christian Reflections on Spirituality,* Mumbai: St. Pauls, 2006, p. 237; also in Kurien Kunnumpuram (ed.), *Selected Writings of Samuel Rayan*, Vol. II, 2012 p. 33.
27. Samuel Rayan, "Spirituality in the Indian Church Today," in Mathai Zacharias (ed.), *The Church: People's Movement*; also in Kurien Kunnumpuram (ed.), *Selected Writings of Samuel Rayan*, Vol. II, 2012, p. 40.
28. *Ibid.*, *Selected Writings,*Vol. II, p. 40.
29. Samuel Rayan, "A Spirituality For Today," in Paul Vaz, *Basic Community Library Service,* Bombay: Seva Niketan, 1986; also in Kurien Kunnumpuram (ed.), *Selected Writings of Samuel Rayan*, Vol. II, 2012. p. 55.
30. *Ibid.,* also in *Selected Writings* Vol. II, p. 57.
31. *Ibid.*, also in Selected *Writings*, Vol. II, p. 64.
32. *Ibid.,* also in Selected *Writings*, Vol. II, p. 66.
33. Samuel Rayan, "A Spirituality for Today," in Paul Vaz, *Basic Community Library Service,* Bombay: Seva Niketan, 1986, also in Kurian Kunnumpuram (ed.), *Selected Writings of Samuel Rayan*, Vol. II, 2012. p. 49.
34. *Ibid*; also in *Selected Writings*, Vol. II, p. 53.
35. Samuel Rayan, "Spiritual Renewal in the Light of Vatican II," in Religion and Society, 15 (1968) I, p. 51; also in *Selected Writings of Samuel Rayan*, Vol. II, 2012 p. 74.
36. *Selected Writings,* Vol. II, p. 43.
37. Samuel Rayan, "Local Cultures: Instruments of Incarnated Christian Spirituality," in *Sedos*, Vol. 29 (1997), Nos. 6-7, p. 212; also in *Collected Writings,* Vol. III, p. 299.
38. *Ibid.*, p. 212; also in *Collected Writings,* Vol. III, p. 299.
39. Samuel Rayan, "A Spirituality of Mission in the Asian Context," in *Sedos*, Vol. 29 (1997), Nos. 6-7, p. 112; also in *Selected Writings*, Vol. II, p. 107.
40. Samuel Rayan, "A Search for an Asian Spirituality of Liberation," in Virginia Fabella & Peter Fabella (Eds.), *Asian Christian Spirituality: Reclaiming*

Traditions, Maryknoll, N. York: Orbis Books, 1992, p.18; also in *Selected Writings of Samuel Rayan*, Vol. II, p. 115.

41. *Ibid.*, p. 19; also in *Selected Writings*, Vol. II, p. 116.
42. *Cfr.* no. 32.
43. Samuel Rayan, "A Search for an Asian Spirituality of Liberation", in Virginia Fabella & Peter Fabella (Eds.), *Asian Christian Spirituality: Reclaiming Traditions,* Maryknoll, N Y: Orbis Books, 1992, p. 20; also in *Selected Writings*, Vol. II, p. 117, taken from the Statement of the World Council of Churches, Iona, 1987.

PART THREE

APPROACH TO THE BIBLE

14

"Stand Upright and Hold your Heads High, Because your Liberation is Near" (Luke 21:28) Samuel Rayan's Approach to Scripture

Jacob Prasad

1. Preamble: Theologian: A Listener to the Word of God

A theologian is one who listens to the word of God with reverence and proclaims it in faith (cf. *DV* 1). Theology, as an act of clarification, explanation and argument, implies attentive listening to the proclamation and instruction that come from the theologians of Israel like the Deuteronomist and Second Isaiah, and apostolic theologians like Paul and John. Indeed Scriptures are the source of wisdom and formative instruction as the author of 2 Timothy, standing in the Pauline tradition, put it at the end of the apostolic age in 3:15-17.[1] When drawing from this great source, a theologian engages in two kinds of activities: (i) of retrieving the distinctive meaning of the particular texts in their original context of communication between the biblical authors and their initial hearers or readers, and (ii) of pursuing the potential fecundity of texts to express a developed meaning in the further contexts, such as the whole Bible or the life of the church, that differ from the original setting of individual biblical documents. In fact interpretation is an oscillating movement between the exegesis that seeks to recover what the text originally meant and an understanding of what the Bible now means to say.[2]

It is in this perspective I would place Samuel Rayan's contribution as a theologian and his approach to Scripture. Rayan's main concern can be said to be two: (i) the interpretation of the Christian faith or the word of God in the multi-religious context of India and (ii) the development of a theology for the creation of a just and more humane society.

2. Rayan's Methodology in Theology

Rayan's approach to Scripture stems from his methodology in Theology itself which is evident in his many an article codified by Kurien Kunnumpuram in six volumes: *Selected Writings of Samuel Rayan* (2011, 2012, 2013) and *Collected Writings of Samuel Rayan* (2013 [three vols]). In several of these articles Rayan explains his methodology in doing theology. The articles, "Theological Education in the Social Context of India Today"; "Re-conceiving Theology in the Asian Context"; "The Irruption of the Third World – A Challenge to Theology"; "The 'How' of Third World Theologies"; "Commonalities, Divergences, and Cross Fertilization among Third World Theologies"; and "Third World Theologies: Where Do We Go From Here?"[3] are some of the examples in this regard.

In the 1984 meeting of the *Indian Theological Association* Rayan delineated his methodology for theological education in seven steps as follows:[4]

i) It begins with siding with the oppressed, sharing their suffering and participating in their struggles.
ii) Then it involves acquiring a fairly comprehensive and scientifically valid analytical understanding of the social reality. This is because if theology should be able to discern where God is present and what God is doing in history, and thus inspire, support and participate in social transformation, some in-depth grasp of social reality is essential.
iii) The response to the situation by the Churches and other religions has to be surveyed and carefully studied and it has

to be critically evaluated. Here one asks as to how qualitative and how adequate the response has been, the particular services offered, the policy followed, in preference to one or more other possibilities. Making use of J. L. Segundo,[5] Rayan thinks of the need to utilize the art of suspicion, for he thinks that Freud taught us to suspect influences from the personal subconscious and Marx to suspect those from the social subconscious; he holds that both are to be used for the sake of clarity and liberation.

iv) For a final evaluation and for further guidance in action, the orientations of the biblical faith are sought in order to listen to the Word of God and to accept it as judging our options and our practices. Here Rayan insists on three things:

  a) In ascertaining the meaning and message of the Bible, the best results of modern biblical scholarship have to be pressed into service so that one may not fall into fundamentalism or fanciful interpretations.
  b) This is because the Word of God and our faith-response must be seen as partners in dialogue with the actual socio-political context. Only then can the Word of God be welcomed as addressed to us and lived in the actual situation.
  c) Both the Bible and the situation have to be viewed and read from the place of the people, from below, through their eyes, their sufferings, struggles and aspirations. That is the way to detect the mechanisms of oppression and to release the liberational power of the faith.

v) It is in the reciprocity and the dialectic between the biblical "text" and the socio-political "context" that the flame of living theology emerges.

vi) Enriched with these insights and experiences one turns to the realm of practice. Practice can now be weighed afresh in the light of the Word heard in and through the mediation of historical reality.

vii) Yet the journey does not end. As history moves on, the theological pilgrimage will be made again and again, each time on a new plane with fresh insights emerging.

3. The Liberationist Approach

Obviously it is in Rayan's methodology in doing theology that his approach to Scripture emerges. His approach can rightly be posted within the contextual approaches to biblical interpretation as indicated by the Pontifical Biblical Commission's 1993 document, "The Interpretation of the Bible in the Church".[6] The Commission is generally positive about the new methods and approaches which have emerged besides the historical-critical method. It states:

> No scientific method for the study of the Bible is fully adequate to comprehend the biblical texts in all their richness. For all its overall validity, the historical-critical method cannot claim to be totally sufficient in this respect.... It is not surprising, then, that at the present time, other methods and approaches are proposed which serve to explore more profoundly other aspects worthy of attention.[7]

The document's survey and evaluation of the methods of and approaches to biblical interpretation includes also a consideration of contextual approaches (liberationist and feminist), in which the document acknowledges that "the interpretation of a text is always dependent on the mindset and concerns of its readers".[8] Hence, Rayan's insistence on the need for the analysis of social reality prior to the scientific reading of the biblical text stands.

After presenting the principles which guide the liberationist approach, the Commission's evaluation begins on a strongly positive note:

> Liberation theology includes elements of undoubted value: the deep awareness of the presence of God who saves; the insistence on the communal dimension of faith; the pressing sense of need for a liberating praxis rooted in justice and love; a fresh reading of the Bible which seeks to make of the Word of God the light and nourishment of the People of God in the midst

of its struggles and hopes. In all these ways it underlines the capacity of the inspired text to speak to the world of today.[9]

This appreciation, however, as noted by J. P. Ruiz, is tempered by the document's attention to the risk it can entail. Yet the overall evaluation of the liberationist approach is deliberately tentative:[10] "Since, liberation theology is tied to a movement that is still in a process of development, the remarks which follow can only be provisional".[11]

The in-depth study of the social reality or the context is seen in all the major works of Rayan before he goes in for a study of the biblical text. Articles like, "People's Theology" (1992), "Theological Priorities in India" (1983), and "Analysis of Society and Indian Theology" (1987)[12] are typical examples of this approach. In this last article mentioned here Rayan states, "The starting point of theology is the struggles of the people. That is the primary *locus theologicus*: the point where God acts and speaks in history here and now. All the rest, exegesis, analysis, archaeology etc. are meant to enable us to commune with historical reality and with the Divine that constitutes the Depth of the reality, and to take our stand at God's and people's side".[13] Here Rayan addresses the possible question as to how Karl Rahner could produce significant modern theology without bothering about the second world war or the Nazi regime or the Jewish Holocaust and how Thomas Aquinas, already centuries before Rahner, could construct a theological edifice without being disturbed by the problems of feudal system, the domination of Christian serfs by Christian lords etc. He responds by saying that these theological traditions have kept themselves away from reality, due to their abstract language and esoteric idiom which baffle an ordinary believer and that is the reason why we hear the lament from the lay faithful that our answers sound sublime but that they do not respond to their questions. Their problems are at once human and spiritual, economic and political; they are historical. Theological traditions, however, have been generally ahistorical, idealistic and metaphysical.[14]

Several stories of siding with the oppressed, sharing their suffering and participating in their struggles are told in "People's

Theology". In the article "Re-conceiving Theology in the Asian Context," as part of reading the context a number of challenges like material poverty, religious poverty, the aftermath of colonialism, etc. are treated at length.

Again in tune with the Biblical Commission's observation that liberation theology is tied to a movement and still is in the process of development Rayan concludes his article on "Theological Priorities in India Today", saying, "We are convinced that our theology will remain an unfinished endeavour, open-ended and hopeful of correction, improvement, and growth. Because, historical reality keeps evolving and changing, and because we are all conditioned by our situation and class position, we recognize the need for ongoing criticism and relativization of our approaches to theology".[15]

4. Feminist Approach

The Pontifical Biblical Commission notes that the goal of the feminist approach is the liberation of women and the acquisition on their part of rights equal to those enjoyed by men. The Commission tells of the three forms of feminist approach: (i) the radical form which denies all authority to the Bible, because it was composed by men and seeks to dominate women;[16] (ii) a neo-orthodox form which accepts the Bible as prophetic and recognizes that it at times sides with women; this then results in a "canon within the canon"; (iii) a critical form which uses a subtle methodology which seeks to discover the equal status of women among the disciples of Jesus, and other signs contradicting patriarchalism and androcentrism. This third form even as it uses the current methods of exegesis, especially the historical-critical method, adds two criteria of investigation. The first criterion involves a "hermeneutic of suspicion" which means that since history has normally been written by victors, one cannot trust texts as they stand and so one has to look for signs that reveal something different. The second criterion is sociological: the study of societies in biblical times reveals their social stratification and the place accorded to women.[17]

Rayan's approach is to be collocated with the critical form, which employs the hermeneutic of suspicion and the sociological criterion. These criteria are verified in Rayan's treatment of the stories of the five daughters of Zelophehad and of Queen Vashti. The former is told in Num 27:1-11 and 36:1-12. Zelophehad had no sons but only five daughters. When Zelophehad died his name was going to be lost since he had no sons; the daughters had no right of inheritance according to the Israelite law till then. If a man died without sons his nearest male relative got his property. The reason that Rayan postulates for not assigning property to a woman is that the woman herself was considered a possession; she was someone else's property. That is the reason why the Decalogue enjoined not to covet a neighbour's wife even as the goods of the neighbour were not to be coveted. Rayan goes into the larger background of Israelite community, where girls could be sold as slaves or bought back (Exod 21:2-11). It is against this background that the five girls appeared before Moses and the leaders of the community and pleaded for the right of inheritance of the property of their father. It was a revolutionary request, which eventually Moses and the leaders had to concede. Rayan employs the "hermeneutic of suspicion" in the refusal of Queen Vashti to appear before the king (Esther 1). He says, "Queen Vashti refused to come. She refused to become a show-piece, a toy in the hands of the king, a mere prop to his vanity and a pleasure object for the gratification of male eyes. She maintained her womanly dignity and debunked patriarchy".[18]

In narrating the story of Hagar in Genesis, taking the cue from Phyllis Tribe (*Texts of Terror* [1984]), Rayan sees a transformation taking place even in God. He says:

> God intervenes at three points in the story. In the first two instances we can scarcely recognize him. The God who orders an oppressed girl to return to her mistress and submit to her ill-treatment hardly resembles the Yahweh of Exodus and of the Prophets. Is not Yahweh who does right "always on the side of the oppressed"? (Ps 103:6). Obedience to a God who prescribes submission to oppression does Hagar little good... In the wilderness too it is not the exiled woman's bitter weeping that God takes note of; it is the male child crying that God hears. But that is something, for now God begins somewhat to resemble Yahweh the liberator of the oppressed and the hearer of the cry of all who are wronged. Hagar's defiant love of

> freedom seems to have done everyone good, including God! In her suffering, in the strength of her character, in her pride and her sense of dignity and in the courage with which she finally took charge of the child, Hagar belongs with the liberative history of women.[19]

The Biblical Commission observes positively that when applied to the New Testament the feminist approach has uncovered the normal situation of women in the first century of Jewish and Greco-Roman society and the innovation that the praxis of Jesus and the Pauline churches effected, in making the Christian disciples a community of equals, to which Galatians 3:28 bears witness.[20] Rayan brings forth powerfully in his reading of the New Testament this innovation that it brought about and how it stands for the emancipation of women.[21] He thinks of those texts, mainly post-Pauline, which enjoin submission, as having succumbed to the pressure of the larger society, and the intention of avoiding frictions within the Christian community at the expense of the radical freedom and egalitarian community character of the Jesus movement.[22]

5. The word of God

Rayan has a very open and broad understanding of the word of God. He does not limit it to the Bible. He acknowledges its presence in the scriptures of other religions and even in the non-scriptural religious traditions and in the events of history. He writes:

> Some of the old religions have their own and ancient scriptures. Asia speaks of the Bible as one among many sacred books, one of several revelations, and asks: Could a live historical process and spiritual quest be ruled forever by fixed texts born of particular, limited experiences of one ancient group of people? Are non-scriptural religious traditions necessarily inferior to those with scriptures? In the dialogue with these old religions, we are challenged and we raise new questions for ourselves. Is it not the witness of the scriptures that God is present not in books but among the people and in their struggles for justice and dignity? Should we not be converted from books and from oppressing one another with texts to the Spirit of the living God and of the questing people? How do sacred texts relate to

one another, and to God's presence and word and activity in the human heart, in significant events, in the signs of the times, in the unfolding of history?[23]

Rayan sees humans as God's word for "what the law requires is written on their hearts" (Rom 2:15). Their inner reality is identical with the written law. The promise of the new covenant stresses this identity and interiorises the law. God would be putting his law within humans, and writing it upon their hearts (Jer 31:31-34).[24] In this regard Rayan interprets the parable of the Good Samaritan. He says that the priest of the story must have known the Torah and the Nebiim thoroughly and must have been searching the scriptures in which he thought he had eternal life (John 5:39), but had never encountered the living and liberating word of God, laying there bare and red on the roadside; the Samaritan had recognised it.[25] Rayan further asserts that since God speaks in a human being, he speaks also in human decisions and in the activities and movements they give rise. Accordingly, the indignation in the heart of Moses, kindled by the burning historical situation of his people in Egypt, and the escape, made possible by a series of events, were God's work and word. So too the victorious advent of Cyrus of Persia on the scene of Israel's captivity was God's doing and an evangel of liberation (Isa 40:1-11; 45:1-8; 48:14-16).[26]

Of events and struggles for justice and dignity representing the word of God is all the more evident in Rayan, in his meditation on Gandhiji. He writes in a poetic format, as a meditation on the Beatitudes (Matt 5:1-12):

This is the word of God.
God's word comes not only in human language,
But in human life as well.
Gandhiji's life was a word of God addressed to us;
Bapu himself is God's word to our world.
What a prophetic word he is;
one that spells hope, and
pronounces judgement on our lives;
a word of power and of love;
a deep word, and mysterious too,
that vibrates within, and stirs the spirit.

A great word
of challenge, invitation, and benediction...

Bapu is a word of God;
a new version of the Sermon on the Mount;
translated into our common language,
into the life of the common man/woman,
the idiom of the loin cloth and
the bare body and
the emaciated frame and
the voluntary fast and the humble prayer
and honesty.[27]

By this understanding Rayan does not in any way reduce the importance of Jesus Christ as the Word of God. He says, "The word of God in nature, in the human being and in history – all come to a culmination and climax in Jesus Christ, his life and deeds, his experiences and relationships".[28]

Rayan's understanding of the "word of God" is in keeping with the conception of the same by Carlo Maria Martini who thinks that it can refer to (1) the events of salvific history because Hebrew *dābār* means, "word, event, reality"; (2) the spoken message of divine emissaries, especially of the prophets and Jesus; (3) the person of Jesus who is the Word of God (especially John 1,1); (4) Christian preaching; (5) God's general message to human beings; (6) the Bible.[29]

6. Bible and Non-Christian Scriptures

It is Rayan's broad understanding of the word of God that lets him take non-Christian scriptures almost on a par with the Bible, in his theological discussion. He thinks that in re-conceiving and re-expressing theology the Asian non-Christian scriptures will be sacred to us and at our disposal as sources. He says that the *Bhavavd Gita*, the poem cast in the form of a dialogue between God and humankind will be liberationally significant. Humans may question, object to, debate with God and only thus, critically and creatively, move toward faith and obedience. God is with us amid the struggles of life and not only or principally in the solitude and quiet of forests and caves and monastic peace. He points out that during the struggle of India for political liberation, the *Bhavavd Gita* had become a source of inspiration to the nation and that it is not without significance that half a dozen of the leaders of the struggle wrote commentaries on this text.[30] From the perspective of liberation, putting the Bible and *Bhavavd Gita* together Rayan observes, "God is on the side of the oppressed as the Bhavavd Gita and the Exodus show, as the prophets and Jesus claim. God intervenes to suppress adharma, to re-establish justice, to liberate the oppressed, lift up the lowly and fill the hungry with blessings (Gita 4; Exod 3; Isa 61; Lk 1 and 4)".[31] As for understanding the word of God in this regard Rayan asks: "Why only Christian scriptures? Other scriptures too carry the memory of an encounter with the Divine in the human heart, in history, in combats for life and freedom. They too contain the Word of God. That makes our (Third World) collection of Holy scriptures much larger than that of Western Christians".[32] At the same Rayan does not in any way give up the culminating character of the incarnate Word in Christ Jesus. To the question as to whether he means to say what the scriptures of other religions is also part of the story of Jesus he replies, "The Word of God has been there eternally, and it is through the Word that God has created the world. Through the Word and the Spirit God has been guiding every individual and all human groups that they may become more authentically human in love and justice. This is part of the story of Jesus".[33] If that is so, to the question then why should we tell the people of other religions the story of Jesus, Rayan responds, "It is perfectly right for us to communicate the incarnation of the Word of God, because that is the ultimate origin. Our very existence is in and through the Word. The Word, Jesus, is the basis and origin of human history and destiny. That story has to be communicated to as many people as possible".[34] Here Rayan's thoughts seem to concur with theologians like Claude Geffré who think that if there are "seeds of the Word" (*Ad Gentes* 11) in other religions and human history has always been a history of salvation that never ceases to be the place of illuminations by the Word and visitations of the Spirit, then there should be a certain "word of God" in the writings of other religious traditions.[35]

7. Ecological Concerns

Rayan reads the biblical texts with an eye for the conservation of this earth, that is, with planetary concerns. Beginning with the assertion of Ps 24 that "the earth is the Lord's" he goes into the explanation of similar texts as Exod 9,29; 19,5; 1 Sam 2,8; Ps 2,8; 8, 6-9; 47,8; 50,10-12; 65,6-14; 89,12; 95,4-5; Act 14,16-17; 17, 24-30). More is implied in this assertion than legal and juridical titles and rights, for the earth is constituted by being God's own. God's Breath and bits of earth united to give birth to human beings, to women and men, to women and men fashioned in God's own image of the Earth which in its turn is an image of the Heart and Womb of God, where it was first conceived and nurtured. Equally "the earth is ours" for as Ps 115:16 "heaven belongs to Yahweh, but earth he has given to the children of Adam". The Earth is interior to human existence. Multiple relationships to the earth in the shape of work, food, knowledge, contemplation and gift-giving are constitutive of the human. Thus, the Earth is God's provision for his entire family on this planet. Therefore, private ownership which excludes others, concentration of land and accumulation of wealth, which leaves others dispossessed and impoverished, involves fraud, robbery, plunder, and radical injustice. In the midst of the poor the wealthy are thieves. The early church had striven for community and sufficiency as is clear from Acts 2 and 4 and from the praxis of equality in the Breaking of Bread (1 Cor 10 and 11). But as it is today there is a gross injustice and imbalance in the distribution of the Earth. The population of India, China and Japan, comprising forty percent of the human race, is confined to ten percent of Earth's surface, while Canada, Australia and New Zealand, with one percent of the world population among them, occupy thirteen percent of land space. Hence, a planned and peaceful re-allocation of land to people is a basic necessity... It should be on the world agenda. Therefore, conviviality which recognizes the earth is humankind's common table laid by God for her terrestrial family and friends. Around that table we gather, not in competitive scramble but in joyful fellowship, nurturing and sheltering one another.[36]

In several of his articles Rayan presents the ecological crisis facing the planet.[37] As a solution he proposes the re-reading the Bible which cannot but impel one to action. He says:

> To meet the planetary crisis we need (among other things) a different kind of relationship to nature, a different view of the earth, a different perception of its meaning for and before God, a different estimate of nature's role in the salvation of the world and an adequate vision of the destiny of the cosmos. I submit that at this point the Bible could be a great help. The biblical view of nature and nature's relation to humans is not confined to nor exhausted by the single Genesis word about dominion. There is much more and much else in the Bible which is to the point. The meaning of dominion and mastery is itself to be determined within the total texture of relationships between earth, human beings and God.[38]

Rayan then interprets a host of biblical texts like Rom 1:19-20; Acts 14:17; 17:24-29; Isa 40:26-28; Jer 5:24; Rom 1:19-20; Gen 1; 9:8-17; Ps 19:1-4 and Ps 148 to come to conclude that the whole cosmos is divine revelation, God's self-disclosure, that nature, like the Bible, needs interpretation, the criteria and hermeneutical principle in either case being growth and dignity for all God's creation, that nature is something which God loves and that the Bible views and treats the earth as co-worshipper with humans.[39] He comes to the conclusion that what is being pleaded is for a mystical view of nature and a reverential approach to it; for a sacramental vision of the world; and for a culture of gentleness and poetry which can also act as a corrective to and a source of resistance against the kind of scientism and technology which have landed us in the present critical mess and brought us to the brink of annihilation.[40]

8. Incantatory Power of the Bible

Rayan is a poet and he enjoys the poetry and the power of the word of God. He is artistic in his expressions and his linguistic ability is enchanting. One stands with amazement at the numerous poems he recites and stories he narrates. There is a narrative sweetness and beauty in his expressions. He stands in admiration of poets like Rabindranath Tagore (1861-1941), Richard Crashaw (1612-1650),

Hildegarde of Bingen (1098-1178), Elizabeth Browning (1806-1861), William Blake (1757-1827) and particularly by the singers of the Bible.[41] He even translates into English the Malayalam poet O.N.V. Kurup's, "Requiem for the Earth".[42] Rayan thinks that if theology has to be more and deeper it has to be artistic.[43] He views the Bible as a gallery of icons. The Bible uses poetic language and imagery to express its faith interpretations of events and experiences involving Israel and God. Its theology is entirely bound up with the art of poetry, metaphor and symbol, myth and parable. The book is full of verbal icons of God and of the people.[44] Rayan tells with great passion how the beauty of the nature in Kerala and the fascination of faith that had conquered his young heart when at the age of 9 he came by a copy of the four gospels in his hands and how he read through the whole in the course of two afternoons and how the name of Jesus, which stood out in larger characters there, became decisive for him, how His story went home to him and how he was fascinated by His parables and how nature had become inseparable from the memory of Jesus and from his own experience of rural life. He also tells how the poetry of Kumaran Asan, one of the greatest poets of Malayalam, had influenced him after reading an essay written about his poetry which reflected nature's loveliness, society's problems, and which contrasted and clashed and reflected each other and interpreted one another.[45] Looking at the Gospels Rayan sees a birds and flowers theology (Matt 6:26-30). He says that John in his Gospel creates scripts of playlets with conflict, climax, denouement etc. ready for the stage, such as the Wine scene of Cana, the Attack on the Temple, the Cripple at the Temple, the scene of the Shared Bread etc. The conclusion that he wants to draw is to take theology as art rather than science, art because it will permit myths and symbols, even as John tried to do.[46] The meditations and reflections in the first volume of the *Selected Writings of Rayan* are fine ways in which Rayan approaches the mystery of Jesus, whom Rayan identifies as the Flesh Translation of Divine Compassion.[47]

9. Using the Best Results of Exegesis

Rayan is not an exegete. However, as he himself advises in his methodology, presented above, in ascertaining the meaning and message of the Bible, he has made use of the best results of modern biblical scholarship in order not to fall into fundamentalism or fanciful interpretations. This is very clear when in his interpretations, for instance, he makes use of modern authors like U. Luz, E. Ellis, G. M. Soares-Prabhu, D. Patte, C. Barth, D. Marguerat, E. Farahian,[48] Luke T. Johnson, Martin Hengel, Redmond Mullin and P. H. Davids.[49] The article, "Early Christianity as Counter-Culture",[50] is a typical example of how the findings of modern exegesis is pressed into the service of his theological reflection. In this article Rayan makes use of the historical-critical method. He asserts that Jesus was murdered. He holds that the powerful of Jesus' society had killed him; they included the Pharisees and the definitive sentence was passed by Pontius Pilate, the representative of the colonial power, Roman Imperialism.[51] Today's scholarship also holds that Pontius Pilate, with the co-operation of some Jewish officials, was responsible for the death of Jesus, although of course there is little or no mention of the Pharisees in the passion narratives.[52] Contemporary scholarship also believes that women played important roles in Jesus' public ministry,[53] a fact insisted on by Rayan, of which we have spoken above.[54] Rayan makes use of the findings of the historical-critical method in presenting the socio-historical background of the first century Palestine. Roland de Vaux, Joachim Jeremias, Norman Gottwald are some of the authors he makes use of in this regard.[55]

10. Critical Appraisal

Rayan is a theologian of exceptional calibre. He writes by way of meditations, reflections and as studies. In every piece of his writing there is a certain degree of uniqueness. All his writings are innovative and inspirational. Rayan does not write purely for academic reasons. He believes in writing for praxis. Listening to the Second Vatican Council's directive "... that theological investigation must be stirred up in major socio-cultural area..." (*Ad Gentes* 22) Rayan tells that the Council is calling for a fresh scrutiny of Sacred Scriptures in the context of India's religious and cultural traditions, and hopes for new insights and interpretations to emerge.[56] He, as a theologian, has taken this to heart. His investigation is also against the background of the socio-economic situation of India and of the so-called Third World. He conceives God's word as always alive and creative. He thinks of God speaking to us his word and into our situation in liberative judgement and gracing us with a view to fashioning our future.[57] Having investigated the present context, as Rayan's method is, he reads the Scriptures against their own background and sees how the word comes alive in our life-situations, disclosing new depths and possibilities which could have surfaced only in this particular concrete context. This is also the story of a text meeting another context, for every biblical text arose in a context, and context is the unwritten part of the text. Rayan's approach to Scripture is not that of *dicta probantia* (proof texts), citing the biblical text to confirm theological positions. As everybody knows, in 1893 there came forth from Pope Leo XIII the first encyclical relating to modern biblical studies, *Prodientissimus Deus,* in which the Pope said, "And therefore it is greatly desirable and necessary that the use of the sacred Scripture dominate the whole of the theological science and be as if its soul".[58] *Dei Verbum* modified or developed this teaching of Leo XIII, when it said that the "the study of the sacred page should be the very soul of sacred theology" (*DV* 24). The difference implied is important, for while the encyclical speaks of the "use" *Dei Verbum* speaks of the "study" of the sacred Scripture as the soul of theology. It is not enough to "use" the Scripture in theological discussion but it is necessary to study the Scripture systematically for it.[59] Rayan does it rightly well. Rayan's approach is mainly liberationist and feminist, which suffer, of course, from the drawback of dwelling more selectively on the narrative and prophetic texts to the neglect of the other parts of the Bible, with the possibility that it be one-sided.[60] As for Rayan the Exodus is a constant paradigm and even the death of Jesus outside the camp (Heb 13:13), which has semblance to every person who is oppressed, downtrodden and marginalised. However, the slant to one side is a demand of the context in which the text is read and the exigency of the context cannot be overlooked by a prophetic reader and creative thinker like Rayan. His approach, sometimes of putting the biblical text and the non-Christian Scriptures apparently on a par is also not without difficulty, especially as *Bhagavad Gita* would not desist from advocating just war nor would promote love of enemies. Given all these, Rayan's approach to the Bible and its interpretation is one of hope and can always inspire people to stand erect, hold their heads high and believe that their liberation is near.

Notes

1. Cf. Jared Wicks, *Introduction to Theological Method* (Casale Monferrato: Piemme, 1994) pp. 42-43. 2 Tim 3, 15-17 reads, "You have known the sacred writings that are able to instruct you for salvation through faith in Christ Jesus. All scripture is inspired by God and is useful for teaching, for reproof, for correction, and for training in righteousness, so that everyone who belongs to God may be proficient, equipped for every good work."
2. Cf. Wicks, *Theological Method*, pp. 58-59.
3. These articles are to be found in Kurien Kunnumpuram (ed.), *Collected Writings of Samuel Rayan, SJ* (Delhi: ISPCK, 2013) Vol. II, pp. 222-238; 241-262; 263-285; 286-312; 313-334; 335-348.
4. See "Theological Education in the Social Context of India Today," F. Wilfred (ed.), *Theological Education in India Today, The Statement, Papers and Proceedings of the Eighth Annual Meeting of the Indian Theological Association*, Pariyaram, Kerala, Dec 28-31, 1984 (Bangalore: ATC, 1985) 12-32: Kunnumpuram, *Collected Writings*, II, pp. 222-238.
5. J. L. Segundo, *The Liberation of Theology* (Maryknoll, NY: Orbis Books, 1976) ch. 1.
6. The Pontifical Biblical Commission, *The Interpretation of the Bible in the Church* (Vatican City State: Libreria Editrice Vaticana, 1993). Joseph A. Fitzmyer, *The Biblical Commission's Document, "The Interpretation of the Bible in the Church".* Text and Commentary (SubBi 18; Rome: Pontifical Biblical Institute, 1995).
7. The Pontifical Biblical Commission, *The Interpretation of the Bible in the Church*, I. B.
8. The Pontifical Biblical Commission, *The Interpretation of the Bible in the Church*, I. E.
9. The Pontifical Biblical Commission, *The Interpretation of the Bible in the Church*, I. E.1.
10. Jean-Pierre Ruiz, "New Ways of Reading the Bible in the Cultural Settings of the Third World," *Concilium* (1995/1) pp. 73-84, here p. 78.
11. The Pontifical Biblical Commission, *The Interpretation of the Bible in the Church*, I. E.1.
12. In Kurien Kunnumpuram, *Collected Writings of Samuel Rayan, SJ* (Delhi: ISPCK, 2013) II, pp. 79-103; 104-117; 156-164.

13. Kunnumpuram, *Collected Writings*, II, p. 161.
14. Kunnumpuram, *Collected Writings*, II, p. 223.
15. Kunnumpuram, *Collected Writings*, II, p. 117.
16. For instance, see M. Daly, *The Church and the Second Sex* (New York – Evanston, IL: Harper & Row, 1968) pp. 32-42, 138-149. See for further Bibliography Fitzmyer, *The Biblical Commission's Document,* 97, n. 129.
17. Fitzmyer, *The Biblical Commission's Document,*nos. 96-99.
18. "Five Girls Ask, Why? And a Woman says, No! The Revolution of Mahlah, Noah, Hoglah, Milcah and Tirzah, and of Queen Vashti," *Vidyajyothi* 57 (1993) 306-313: Kunnumpuram, *Collected Writings,* I, pp. 101-108.
19. "In Christ: The Power of Women," *Stree Reflect Series* 4 (All India Council of Christian Women Publication, 1986): Kunnumpuram, *Collected Writings*, I, pp. 109-147, here pp. 113-114.
20. Fitzmyer, *The Biblical Commission's Document,*n. 99.
21. "In Christ: The Power of Women",: Kunnumpuram, *Collected Writings*, I, pp. 128-141.
22. *Ibid.*, pp. 142-143.
23. "Commonalities, Divergences, and Cross Fertilization among Third World Theologies," in K. C. Abraham (ed.), *Third World Theologies:Commonalities and Divergences* (Maryknoll: Orbis Books, 1990) 195-213, here no. p. 58; Kurien Kunnumpuram, *Collected Writings of Samuel Rayan* (Delhi: ISPCK, 2013) II, pp. 325-326.
24. "The Word God," *Jeevadhara* 1 (1971) 95-106: Kunnumpuram, *Collected Writings*, II, pp. 273-281, here p. 279.
25. "The Word of God", Kunnumpuram, *Collected Writings*, III, p. 279.
26. *Ibid.*, p. 280.
27. "Gandhiji: A Meditation," *Together* 36 (1970) pp. 5-9: Kurien Kunnumpuram, *Selected Writings of Samuel Rayan, SJ*, (Mumbai: St. Paul's 2012) II, pp. 210-215, here pp. 210-211.
28. "The Word of God," Kunnumpuram, *Collected Writings*, II, p. 280.
29. Carlo Maria Martini, *La Parola di Dio alle Origini della Chiesa* (Rome, 1980) 56-58, as presented by Raymond F. Collins, "Inspiration," in R. E. Brown – J. A. Fitzmyer – R. E. Murphy (ed.) *The New Jerome Biblical Commentary* (London: Geoffrey Chapman, 1992) 1023-1033, here p. 1033.
30. "Re-conceiving Theology in the Asian Context", in Kunnumpuram, *Collected Writings*, II, pp. 252-254.
31. "Liberative Struggles in a Violent Society," in J. Vattamattam – V. Theckanath (eds.), Liberative Struggles in a Violent Society: Proceedings of the Workshop on the Dynamics of the Liberative Struggles of the Poor and the Oppressed (Hyderabad, 1990) 183-191: Kunnumpuram, *Collected Writings*, III, pp. 240-247, here p. 242.

32. "The 'How' of Third World Theologies" in Kunnumpuram, *Collected Writings*, II, p. 301. See also "The March has Begun" in Kunnumpuram, *Collected Writings*, III, pp. 38-60, here p. 38.
33. "Telling the Story of Jesus in Asia. Theme of Asian Mission Congress," The interview given by Samuel Rayan to UCA News and published in *New Leader* (November 2006) 2006: Kunnumpuram, *Selected Writings of Samuel Rayan*, III, pp. 55-63, here p. 56.
34. "Telling the Story of Jesus in Asia": Kunnumpuram, *Selected Writings*, III, p. 57.
35. Claude Geffré, "The Word of God in Other Religious Traditions and the History of the Nations as a Divine Narrative," *Concilium* (2010/2) pp. 22-31, here pp. 22-26.
36. "The Earth is the Lord's" *Vidyjyothi* 54 (1990) pp. 113-132: Kunnumpuram, *Collected Writings* I, pp. 3-23.
37. For example, "Ecology and Faith: The Mystery of the Earth," *Dr. Kunchala Rajaratnam Endowment Lectures delivered at Gurukul, Madras on March 29, 1990*: Kunnumpuram, *Collected Writings* I, pp. 24-36, esp. pp. 27-28; "Ecology and Theology: A Theology of Nature, A Theology of Life," *Mangalore University Journal* 3 (Sept 3, 1991) pp. 1-38: Kunnumpuram, *Collected Writings* Vol. I, pp. 46-77, esp.pp. 46-53.
38. "Ecology and Faith": Kunnumpuram, *Collected Writings*, I, pp. 28-29.
39. *Ibid.*, pp. 29-32.
40. *Ibid.*, p. 36.
41. *Ibid.*, pp. 54-56.
42. "The Earth is the Lord's" in Kunnumpuram, *Collected Writings*, I, pp. 20-21.
43. "Art and Theology," *Sahrdaya* 2 (1994) 3-7: Kunnumpuram, *Collected Writings*, II, pp. 145-515, here p. 145.
44. "Art and Theology," in Kunnumpuram, *Collected Writings*, II, pp. 146-147
45. "Ecology and Faith" in Kunnumpuram, *Collected Writings*, I, p. 26.
46. "Theology as Art," *Religious Studies* 26/2 (1979) 77-90: Kunnumpuram, *Collected Writings*, II, pp. 3-15, here esp. pp. 5-7, 14.
47. "Jesus: A Flesh-Translation of Divine Compassion", in *Jeevadhara* 26 (1996) pp. 212-229; in Kunnumpuram, *Selected Writings*, I, pp. 79-96.
48. "With Us – With Whom – Is God?"in Francis X. D'SA, *The Dharma of Jesus. Interdisciplinary Essays in Memory of George Soares-Prabu, SJ* (Pune: Institute for Study of Religion, De Nobili College & Anand Gujarat Sahitya Prakash, 1997) pp. 37-83: Kunnumpuram, *Selected Writings*, I, pp. 157-195.
49. See "Jesus Our Daily Bread," *Jevvadhara* 25 (1995) pp. 235 251; Kunnumpuram, *Selected Writings*, I, pp. 249-265.

50. In Philip Mathew – Ajit Muricken (eds.) *Religion, Ideology and Counter-Culture* (Bangalore: Horizon Books, 1987) pp. 113-143: Kunnumpuram, *Collected Writings*, I, pp. 208-235.
51. "Early Christianity as Counter-Culture": Kunnumpuram, *Collected Writings*, I, pp. 208-210.
52. Daniel J. Harrington, *Witnesses to the Word: New Testament Studies Since Vatican II* (New York: Mahwah, NJ, 2012) pp. 41-43.
53. Harrington, *Witnesses*, pp. 40-41.
54. "In Christ: The Power of Women" in Kunnumpuram, *Collected Writings*, I, pp. 128-131.
55. "Early Christianity as Counter-Culture" in Kunnumpuram, *Collected Writings*, I, pp. 217-222.
56. "The Responsibility of the Church in India Today," *All India Seminar on the Church in India* Today, Bangalore, May 1969, *Orientation Papers* (New Delhi: CBCI Centre, 1969) pp. 231-260: in Kunnumpuram, *Collected Writings*, I, pp. 319-343, here p. 331.
57. "Theology of the Church," *Do It Yourself: Vidyjoythi Correspondence Course, Lesson VI*: in Kunnumpuram, *Collected Writings*, I, pp. 284-318, here p. 291.
58. *Enchiridion biblicum* (Naples, ^{2}1954) § 114.
59. Cf. Albert Vanhoye, "Dopo la *Divino afflante Spiritu*. Progressi e Problemi dell'esegesi cattolica," in Pio Laghi – Maurice Gilbert – Albert Vanhoye, *Chiesa e Sacra Scrittura. Un secolo di magistero ecclesiastico e studi biblici* (Subsidia biblica 17; Rome: Pontifical Biblical Institute, 1994) pp. 35-51, here p. 42.
60. Fitzmyer, *The Biblical Commission's Document,* nos. 95-96, 100-101.

15

Face-To-Face with Jesus

Samuel Rayan's use of the New Testament

M. Paul Raj

1. Introduction

This short paper is a humble attempt to understand Samuel Rayan's use of the Bible, especially of the New Testament, in his systematic reflections. This is done by studying two of his articles found in the book "Jesus: The Relevance of His Person and Message for our Times - Selected Writings of Samuel Rayan vol. 1, edited by Kurien Kunnumpuram.

At the outset I would like to make a clarification as to how the Sacred Scripture is generally used for theologizing. In fact using Scripture as ***anima theologiae (soul of theology)*** or as ***ancilla theologiae***[1] ***(maidservant of theology)*** is one of the controversies in the history of biblical interpretation which concerns the way how theology 'makes use of' Scripture for its systematic reflection."The study of Scripture is the soul of sacred theology" is a statement we find in many Church documents starting from *Providentissimus Deus* of Leo XIII, in *Dei Verbum* 24 of Vatican II and in *Verbum Domini* (31 and in 47). All of us are well aware that the Fathers of the Church such as Origen, Augustine, and John Chrysostom were first and foremost commentators of Holy Scripture and every modern exegete would admit that their commentaries are a treasure even to modern exegesis. They still serve as the best examples of theologians who kept the Scripture as the *soul* of their theological reflection.

However, in Old Scholasticism, Scripture was mostly or even exclusively used, along with Tradition and Magisterium, to provide proof for a given theological thesis (*probatur ex Scripura, ex Traditione, ex Magisterio*). Rather than being the "soul of theology" Scripture was rather taken, like philosophy, as *ancillatheologiae*, an ancillary discipline. Remnants of a similar attitude seem to have survived even in modern-day theologizing. Using the Scripture (as a maid-servant is expected to serve her master) to serve the purpose of substantiating or explicating theological theses, would lead to "pulling out" individual verses out of the correlation, coherence and the context of the text.

The statement that Scripture is the soul of Sacred Theology has influenced and revived the theology of the 20th century which is reflected in the principle of "returning to the sources", adopted in the process of theologizing. Evidently Scripture forms the main component of the "sources" to which theologizing has returned[2] while the other components consist of materials such as Patristic traditions etc. This new approach exercised a great influence on Vatican II which also emphasized a return to the sources. One of the greatest achievements of Vatican II is that the Council has succeeded in rediscovering and reestablishing the central role of Scripture in the life of the Church. Samuel Rayan makes use of the Bible not as *ancilla* but as *anima* in his theological reflections. As Kurien Kunnumpuram remarks Samuel Rayan is radically committed to the person of Jesus, his familiarity with the Bible is amazing and he has gained deep insights into the biblical texts.[3]

Before I make my remarks on Samuel Rayan's use of Scripture in his theological reflections, I thought it better to present a summary of the two articles of study.The points 2 and 3 of this essay contain the summary of the articles and point 4 the different features of Rayan's use of Scripture for his theology.

2. Summary of the Article "Jesus: A Flesh-Translation of Divine Compassion"[4]

This article contains twelve statements about Jesus which delineate how Jesus represents the compassionate face of God turned towards the people, how Jesus has communicated this compassion of God through a boundary-breaking ministry and through the new relationships he established and how Jesus has become a challenge to all his followers to continue this ministry of compassion. In the following I attempt to synthesize the twelve statements:

2.1 Though the books of the New Testament present **different portraits** of Jesus based on their Jesus-experience and shaped by their historical situations, still we recognize some common features in Jesus. The predominant among them is that Jesus configures the compassionate face of God especially to the downtrodden and the broken, which causes his rejection, betrayal and finally his killing.

2.2 Jesus' **solidarity-compassion** with the people is demonstrated at his baptism through which he identifies himself with the conversion movement of the people (Mk 1:4-9), which reveals something of the Divine compassion (Mk 1:9-11) and which is followed by a period of testing (Mk 1:12-13). This testing is representative of all later temptations (Peter's protest in Mk 8:11-33; Jesus' family's attempt in Mk 3:20-21, 31-35; pressure to seek publicity in Jn 7:2-8; Pharisees demanding for heavenly signs in Mk 8:11-13 par; to be made king in Jn 6:14-15; to descend from the cross in Mk 15:29-32). Jesus' solidarity with the sinners is theme also elsewhere in the New Testament (see Rom 8:3; 2 Cor 5:21; Gal 3:14; [cf. Deut 21:23; Is 53] and Heb 2:9-18 and 5:7-10).

2.3 Against the prevailing domination of the establishments such as the temple with its priests and the empire with its Caesars, Jesus proclaims the **Reign of God** as a life-affirming reality through his words and deeds. Particularly, the miracles (cf. Mk 1:21-28, 32-34, 40-45; 3:1-6 and par) demonstrate the urgency with which Jesus expresses the compassion for the disabled and lifts them up and the Sabbath controversy stories (cf. Matt 12:1-8; Mk 2:23-28) which illustrate that mercy-compassion and justice precede over sacrifice and clerical claims (cf. Matt 9:13; 12:7; Is 1:10-17).

2.4 Jesus preaches the Reign of God through promoting **life** especially through the healing and feeding miracles which serve as privileged locus of his compassion. There is a personal care and concern expressed in all his miracles. He calls the woman with haemorrhage 'my daughter' (Mk 5:25-34), expresses his motherly concern by asking the child's parents to give her something to eat (Mk 5:21-24, 35-43), touches the blind and the dumb before healing them and does not hesitate to express his emotions (at the raising of widow's son in Lk 7:11-17 and at the raising of Lazarus in Jn 11:28-44). Jesus also shows his emotional involvement in weeping over Jerusalem (Matt 23:37-39; Lk 13:31-35) and when children come to him (Mk 10:13-16).

2.5 Jesus' rich humanity gets extended in eating together and sharing **bread**. In all feeding miracles the initiative comes from Jesus and he gets personally involved by forbidding the disciples from having recourse to other sources (Mk 6:30-44 par; Jn 6:5-6). Jesus' table fellowship with outcasts (Mk 2:15-17 par), his invitation to the disciples to 'come and have breakfast' (Jn 21:1-14) and his last supper could be seen as further moments of this sharing.

2.6 **Forgiveness** is central and decisive in Jesus' compassion. He forgives two women in Lk 7:36-50 and Jn 8:1-11 and teaches that his disciples should appropriate this attitude of forgiving others in the Our Father (Matt 6:12) and in the parable of unforgiving servant (Matt 18:21-23).

2.7 Jesus' deeds of compassion are further illumined by words of compassion and **mercy**. We see this in the story of the Good Samaritan (Lk 10:29-37) and in the three parables of Lk 15 which are told to counter the complaint that Jesus was welcoming sinners and eating with the outcasts and was associating with the dregs of society. The point is well made in the speech on Good Shepherd (Jn 10) who is different from robbers, thieves and hired men and in his invitation to those who labour and are overburdened (Matt 11:25-30).

2.8 This compassion expressed in the proclamation of the good news of the Kingdom and in healing people forms the centre of the **summary statements** (**in brief**) found in Matt 4:23-24; 8:16-17 and in 9:35-36.

2.9 Revealing his **identity** Jesus declares that his teaching and his deeds are from his Father who sent him (cf. Jn 7:16-17; 8:26-28; 12:49-50; 5:19; 10:25.37-38). Not just his word and deed but his very Self and Person spring from the depths of God and remain rooted there (Jn 10:25, 37-38; 7:28-29; 12:44-45 and 14:8-11). Thus, Jesus' compassion is a concretization of his Father's compassion.

2.10 From their experience of Jesus the Early Christians formulated their faith in **metaphors**. One such metaphor is that Jesus is the *Word of God* (Jn 1:1-3) who communicates God's Self, his love and forgiveness, compassion and peace to them. The other metaphor is that Jesus is the *Image of God* (Col 1:15; Heb 1:3) who is the All-merciful Father (2 Cor 1:3-4), who raises the dead (2 Cor 1:9), who is incarnate Compassion (2 Cor 7:4-7), who loved the world so much as to give his only Son (Jn 3:16-17), who gives sunshine and showers rain seeing the humans' need and not their merit (Matt 5:43-48), who cares for the birds and the wayside flowers (Matt 6:25-34), who protects a sparrow and the hair (Matt 10:28-31), who comforted Israel (Hos 2:14-25; Is 40:1-11; 54:1-17) and who clothed infant Israel in his own splendour (Ezek 16:1-14).

2.11 The Hebrew word for compassion and mercy, *rehmamim* which is the plural of *rehem* primarily refers to the internal parts of sacrificial animals and later to the **womb** (**heart**) of a mother. Thus, the compassionate God is to Israel father/parent (Hos 11), mother (Is 49:15-16) and husband (Is 54:4-48; Hos 1-3). Thus, God welcomes back the rebellious child and faithless wife. In the New Testament the compassion of Jesus is expressed through the word *splanchnizomai* (**σπλαγχνίζομαι**) which means to be moved in one's bowels/womb/inward parts (Matt 9:36; 14:14; 15:32; 20:34; Mk 1:41; 6:34; 8:2; Lk 7:13).

2.12 Jesus as the incarnate compassion of God is the most persuasive representation for Christology for our time. The Cross is compassion because it reveals the broken heart of God who makes his own the pain of his earthly family. And the Resurrection is also compassion because through this Jesus redeems the situation of hopelessness by making a breakthrough. It is above all a realization of God-with-us. Such an interpretation is also relevant for India. The power and presence that can transform human suffering is the 'quality of compassion' which is a **challenge** to every follower of Christ.

Thus, the twelve statements focus on the **solidarity-compassion** of Jesus as the most important of the **different portraits** we find about him in the New Testament. This solidarity-compassion is further expressed through Jesus' proclamation of the **Reign of God,** promotion of **life,** sharing of **bread,** and his emphasis on **forgiveness and mercy** expressed in the **summary statements** which sum up multiple healing stories. The total **identification** of Jesus with the Father which is the content of the **faith metaphors** formulated by the Early Christians reveals that Jesus' compassion is actually an embodiment of Father's compassion expressed in the symbolic language of **womb** and **heart.** And Jesus as the incarnate compassion of God poses the biggest **challenge** to every follower of Christ.

3. A Summary of the Article: "Prophet and Poet in One"[5]

This article presents Jesus as one who has perfectly integrated the qualities of a prophet and a poet by making a study of two texts from the New Testament (Jn 12:24 and Matt 6:25-34/Lk 12:22-23).

3.1 The first text Jn 12:24 contains a metaphor of a grain of wheat which contains a brief but a poignant expression of the theme: *new life through struggle*. The grain of wheat is a reference to Jesus himself and the whole metaphor symbolises the Paschal Mystery which is a struggle unto death in which Jesus is engaged in order to give birth to a New Humanity and a New Earth. Here it should be noted that just as the grain leaves the hope of being transformed into a new plant to the Creator God, so also is the plight of Jesus who has to die on the cross hoping that through his death new life will dawn upon the whole of cosmos.

3.2 The second text Matt 6:25-34 which occurs in the context of Sermon on the Mount serves the purpose of consecrating *hope*. This hope is demanded from and required of those whose resources are meagre, whose hearts are small, and who tend to shrink and settle down to their little life and succumb to the nagging of daily life's small worries about a change of clothes and morrow's breakfast. Without such a hope it is not possible to stand at God's side by collaborating with relentless trust in the effort to create the New Humanity and the New Earth envisioned by the Sermon on the Mount.

3.3 Quoting M. D. Goulder (Midrash and Lection in Matthew, London: SPCK, 1954, 70-97) Samuel Rayan concludes that the two texts under scrutiny reflect a mind of a poetic and imaginative cast and as the author of these texts Jesus must have been an inspired man, living and speaking under the Breath of the rejoicing and thrilling Spirit (Lk 3:21-22; 4:1.14-18; 10:21; Mk 1:12). For Jesus Nature-poetry was anthropology and theology because nature was the place of the revelation of God's mind concerning humans and poetry on nature revealed to men and women their greatness as God's beloved children, their future as placed in their hands and their present privileged task to shape that future and celebrate it. Above all Jesus is peoples' poet who through his poetry and stories upset the values and narrow visions of the existing social order and thus became himself a song of revolt and a revolutionary poem in which God challenges the earth by singing to it his own Humanity. The stories and imageries of Jesus which come in the form of a short, crisp and pungent utterances, which are often allusive, even cryptic, laden with irony and paradox are about farms, animals, the country and the cosmos as well as of religion, crime and punishment, economic life and the home / household.Thus, these two texts which are studied as samples of a number of other texts in the New Testament portray Jesus as a prophet in their content and as a nature-poet in their style.

4. Features of Samuel Rayan's Use of the Bible (NT) in his Systematic Reflections

4.1 Unity in Diversity: At the beginning of his article on "Jesus: a Flesh-Translation of Divine Compassion", Samuel Rayan identifies some of the common features found in the multiple portraits of Jesus presented in the different books of the New Testament. He affirms that the different portraits bring the Jesus-experience of the Christians, which consisted both of the authors of the New Testament books and of the members of the Christian community, "face to face"with their concrete historical conditions. Thus, he rightly leads the diversity of Jesus-portraits of the New Testament back to the community situations which consisted of the conflicts and suffering they had to face, of the transformation of their vision of the world and of the attempts made by them "to live their faith in diverse contexts with distinct predicaments and problems".

However, Samuel Rayan does not stop with affirming the diversity of the New Testament books, but goes on to recognize their unity in the common features of Jesus described by them such as "a friend of the common folk," "a suffering Son of Man", and "a face of God's own wondrous compassion".[6] This reminds us of what Irenaeus of Lyon (ca. 130-200 AD) wrote in his *Adversus Haereses* 3.11.8 (written ca. 180 AD) on the four Gospels in the New Testament. Against the contemporary tendencies both to reject the four Gospels as arbitrary and to integrate all of them into one, he affirmed that the four Gospels are four-fold in form but held together by one Spirit. Then he goes on to explain that this four-fold form is similar to the four faces of the Cherubim (lion, ox, human and eagle). Thus, Irenaeus defended the fundamental unity of the many Gospels. In the same way, while identifying the different portraits of Jesus present in different books of the New Testament, Samuel Rayan is taking a cumulative and integrated approach by insisting on the fundamental unity of all the books by focussing on the common features of Jesus, rather than accentuating the distinctions which would lead to a kind of exclusivist reading.

Similarly, while discussing the presence of various images but a similar handling of them in the New Testament (in the second article titled "Prophet and Poet in One"), he concludes that here we find evidence of one Mind behind all the synoptic teaching which is the mind of the Lord.[7]

4.2 Single-minded Commitment and Conscious Option for the Poor: Diverse methods of reading the Bible have been developed in the post-modern era and it is actually supposed to be a great strength for biblical scholarship. However, many a time it happens that the biblical scholarship tends to justify every convenient reading of the Bible which then amounts to a kind of an intellectual exploitation of the polyvalent character of the biblical text. Such attempts fail to identify and comply with the so-called semantic axis of the text. This semantic axis, in the case of the Bible or at least of the New Testament, is provided by the Death-and-Resurrection of Jesus Christ and is directed towards proclaiming it as a good news to the poor. In his reading of the New Testament Samuel Rayan remains faithful to its central message. He too identifies the death and resurrection of Jesus as central to the Gospels. This is seen in his understanding of Jesus primarily as "a friend of the common folk, especially of the downtrodden and the broken" and as "a suffering Son of Man". According to him Jesus is the "configuration of God's own wondrous compassion" and he reveals the "lineaments of God's face and hands and heart" in and through his words and deeds which result in his death and resurrection.

4.3 Inter-textual Analysis: One of the ways we can establish the probability of the biblical events is by searching for *multiple attestation* of the same event in more than one part or author. In order to discover such manifold evidence one has to work with many texts simultaneously which is technically called the *inter-textual analysis*. While making his point on the solidarity-compassion of Jesus with the sinners Samuel Rayan does not restrict himself to the study of the Markan text on baptism, but also gets the same point attested by the parallel texts from the Synoptics and by the epistles to the Romans, Corinthians, Galatians and Hebrews and by a few Old Testament quotations from Deuteronomy and Isaiah. This principle of *multiple attestation* is followed by him in all the statements he has made in these two articles.

4.4 Principle of Priority: He follows the principle of giving priority to Mark. As we know that the priority of the Gospel of Mark is an already established fact in the biblical scholarship. He also seeks to support his foundations from the authentic epistles of Paul which he probably considers as contemporary to Mark if not prior. At the same time he also emphasizes the special characteristics of individual authors. For example, while making a relatively long list of the miracles he draws the attention of his readers to Luke's special interest in women (Lk 7:11-17; 13:10-17) and John's emphasis on Jesus' special relationship to the family of Lazarus (Jn 11:28-44).

4.5 A Contextualised Reading: Samuel Rayan reads the biblical texts with the context of the reader in mind and attempts to make suggestions as to the application of the same texts in the life of the reader. In particular he also refers to the Indian context by way of comparison and suggestions.

While talking about the feeding miracles of Jesus, he interprets Jesus' demand on the disciples that they have to feed the people with their own resources with the following comment: "No recourse to the market and its Multinationals. Manage with your own resources".[8] Such a reading is encouraging for those readers who fight for the cause of the marginalised which goes against the interests of the profit-oriented and market-based multinationals. Another contextual reading of the text becomes clear when he comments on the story of a woman who had been caught committing adultery. In this story Jesus refrains from every kind of condemnation of the woman. Samuel Rayan comments on this and states, "if we fix our gaze on yesterday's sins and yesterday's laws, we shall have little to offer the guilty except death; and that would be neither religion nor humanity (2 Cor 3:6). If we fix our eyes on the heart of God and see the sinner there, as Jesus does in the story … we can make a fresh offer of life. God's eye does not get glued to the dead past or the dead law. His view soars to the virginal future which even this adulteress can have through his forgiving grace".[9] An appeal to the reader to be as compassionate as Jesus!

Further, talking about discipleship, Samuel Rayan demands that to be a follower of Jesus, one should enter by compassion into Jesus' experience of the divine and of the human. Quoting

Monika Hellwig, he concludes that whenever suffering becomes an unnecessary burden of unjust structures in society, the compassion shows itself as effective **challenge.**[10]

While contrasting the model of society envisaged by the Sermon on the Mount (Mt 5-7) with the contemporary one, Samuel Rayan describes the present society as consisting of the "ugly mess humans have made, compounded of squalor, oil, blood and war, affluence for the few, and capitalism and torture, and discarded plastic and discarded men and women".[11] Though, it sounds pessimistic, it contains a lot of truth about the world we live in.

While talking about Jesus' boundary-breaking proclamation of the Reign of God he includes the caste-barriers and observes that Jesus sympathised with the *paraiahs* of the society.[12] While claiming that a Christology which understands Jesus as the incarnate compassion of God, Samuel Rayan asserts that such a Christology is **relevant for India** and Asia where God's compassion has already been communicated through Gautama the Buddha, Gandhiji, Mother Teresa, Medha Patkar and others.[13] Samuel Rayan's Indian perspective becomes clear also in the context of his interpretation of Mt 6:25-34. Here he affirms that Jesus, as an Asian and a Mystic, "would boldly speak of the unity of nature and humans and the unity of these and their Maker".[14] Does it not reflect the Indian understanding of reality as interrelated and interconnected, as a *cosmotheandric* unity?

4.6 An Involved Dramatization: Samuel Rayan does not read the biblical texts merely with his dry intellect but with his involved heart that leads to a dramatization of the events. While talking about the man with a crippled hand in a synagogue in Mk 3:1-6, he comments: "we watch Jesus' eyes begin to glow with anger; we watch his face suffuse with sorrow for a people so stubborn, so wrong".[15] Such a comment evokes such an involvement that a reader begins to experience Jesus in close proximity.

Further, while discussing the way Jesus instituted the Eucharist, Samuel Rayan sees the love and concern of a mother in Jesus' invitation to eat his own body and drink his own blood, thus identifying mother language, motherly imagery and motherly gestures in those of Jesus. The same is expressed also in his invitation to the disciples to "come and have breakfast" (Jn 21:1-14)[16] and in the motherly invitation to all who labour and are overburdened to "Come to me, and I will give you rest" (Matt 11:25-30).[17] Again the motherly character of Yahweh is highlighted when Samuel Rayan speaks of Israel as an infant who "lay in the field on the day she was born, in her blood and dirt, unwashed, unwanted, uncared for", and to whom God in his great pity said "Live" and saw to it that she grew and developed, became rich and beautiful, clothed in His own splendour (Ezek 16:1-14).[18] Thus, it is only natural for Jesus to be like a hen seeking to gather her chicks, or a woman in labour, or like bread which like a mother becomes food for the children (Matt 23:37; Lk13:34-35; Jn 16:20-22; 6:15.50-58; Lk 22:19-20).[19] All these examples demonstrate that Samuel Rayan's comments on the biblical texts have the power to evoke the same experience in the readers.

4.7 Typological Reading of the Old Testament: A number of Old Testament categories are considered to be 'types' or 'prototypes' or even 'anti-types' of the New Testament categories. Samuel Rayan seems to believe in this. He sees Jesus as the fulfilment of the promises of the Old Testament. For example while talking about Jesus' incarnation and his identification with the sinful humanity he refers to Deuteronomy 21:23 and Isaiah 53.[20] Again he sees the people of Israel as a type for the Christians who are now the New Israel. And not just that, he goes further and extends this 'infant Israel' to 'frail humankind'.[21] By doing so, he frees the Old Testament from a 'nationalistic' interpretation and recognizes its 'open' character and its eternal validity as the Word of God.

4.8 Language as Key: In our post-modern world language is seen as a constitutive element of reality itself. The world we live in with its concepts and convictions is a linguistically constructed world. There is no such a thing as language being a transparent medium which communicates the reality objectively but every communication is also essentially influenced by the language. If language constitutes or creates that which it represents, discourses are far from being value-neutral.[22] In Samuel Rayan's understanding of Jesus' speeches, he focuses on the meaning given to language by Jesus. According to him Jesus deliberately uses the symbolic language of poetry and imagery which is rich in poetic suggestiveness "like the Wine of Cana, the Cleansing of the Temple, the Dialogue with Nicodemus, the Woman of Samaria, the Feeding of the People, the Healing of the Cripple and of the Man Born Blind, and the Raising of Lazarus".[23] Here, poetry is not defined as a piece of literature which is governed by regulations concerning alliteration, assonance and metre. Here, poetry is understood as an appropriate literary form which apprehends the wonder and beauty of nature and speaks of the unity of nature and humans and the unity of these and their Maker.[24]

4.9 Not Just the Meaning but the Meaningfulness: One can arrive at the 'meaning' of a biblical text if one is capable of reading the text in its context and say what it meant for its first readers. By doing this, one has not yet really understood the text. A more complete understanding of the text raises the questions of hermeneutics and seeks to understand the meaningfulness of the text for the context of the reader. When Samuel Rayan reads the biblical texts he does not get stuck with the above mentioned first level but moves on to the second level of interpreting the text for the contemporary context.

At the end of his first article he draws the conclusion of the whole reflection which results in the challenge every follower of Christ has to take upon oneself to be able to share in the compassion of Jesus Christ. He invites all the followers of Christ to get involved by saying, "We are most devout and closest to Jesus not when we avoid involvement in public and conflictual situations, but when we find ourselves drawn into the divine compassion in practical and effective ways wherever there is suffering of whatever kind".[25]

While outlining the Sermon on the Mount vision of New Humanity in his second article, Samuel Rayan comments that such New Humanity consists of replacing whole systems of grabbing with new movements of giving, replacing selfishness with love, oppression with justice, and classist fragmentation of humanity with a gentle community of brothers and sisters breaking bread to one another in tenderness. He adds further that members of this New Humanity will not go to court, will not take revenge, will not exploit one another but will deploy an exceptional and surprising quality of love which will reach out to the unlovable and the hurtful, will rejoice to go a second mile of service beyond all laws and compulsions, and will know how to light and salt the earth to keep it from stumble and decay and sustain it unto fresh flowering.[26] Thus, Samuel Rayan's reading of the biblical text does not stop with delineating the meaning of the text. He goes on to uncover the meaningfulness of the text for today.

5. Conclusion

The different features of Samuel Rayan's use of the Sacred Scripture, particularly of the New Testament, in his theological reflection reflects the view-points of a modern and progressive thinker. The fact that they come from a theologian who had a pre-Vatican II theological training is unbelievably wonderful. It tells of the person's diligence, vigilance, energy, vitality and attentiveness.

Secondly, his reading and reflection on the biblical texts express the power of the Word of God which is sharper than a double-edged sword. Without making false assumptions and exaggerated claims, Samuel Rayan is able to bring out the real power of the Word of God, thereby evoking a sense of awe and wonder in the heart of the reader.

And finally, in biblical studies the third-world readers adopt a discourse of resistance by which they use their own cultural identities to examine biblical texts.[27] This is in line with the spirit of Jesus who also showed resistance to the existing social order which is recaptured beautifully by Samuel Rayan in these two articles. As Kurien Kunnumpuram has already commented these two articles reflect the special love Samuel Rayan has for Sacred Scripture and the fact that the theological insights he draws are actually fruit of a creative reading of the Bible.[28] By doing so, Samuel Rayan makes a thorough study of the Scripture, especially of the New Testament and takes us to encountering Jesus face to face ridding off all the cultural and colonial remnants that have been added to the Bible down the centuries.

Notes

1. This distinction between the *anima*and a*ncilla Theologiae* is taken from a talk given by Fr. Lucien Legrand on "Scripture and Theology: A Gap?" at the annual meeting of the CBAI in Bangalore on 17 October, 2014.
2. For instance, the influential books of Hans Kueng on *Structures of the Church* and *The Church* are based on a study of the charismatic nature of the Church in 1 Cor.Later on, the *Theology of Liberation* which emerged in the South American context, the *Black Theology* of Africa and the *Dalit Theology* of India are results of a sociological and communitarian readings of the Bible. While giving the Bible its foundational place in the process of theologizing, they have also rediscovered the importance not just of Jesus Christ of the New Testament as liberator and redeemer but also of the Old Testament, particularly of the liberative thrust of the Exodus event and of the prophetic literature.
3. Kurien Kunnumpuram (ed.), *Selected Writings of Samuel Rayan, Vol. 1: Jesus: The Relevance of His Person and Message for our Times*, Mumbai, St. Pauls, 2011, p. 12.
4. Samuel Rayan, "Jesus: a Flesh-Translation of Divine Compassion," in *Selected Writings of Samuel Rayan, Vol. 1,* pp. 79-96.
5. Samuel Rayan, "Prophet and Poet in One," in *Selected Writings of Samuel Rayan, Vol. 1*, pp. 97-104.
6. Samuel Rayan, "Jesus: a Flesh-Translation of Divine Compassion", in *Selected Writings of Samuel Rayan, Vol. I*, p. 180.
7. Samuel Rayan, "Prophet and Poet in One", in *Selected Writings of Samuel Rayan, Vol. 1,* p. 101.
8. Samuel Rayan, "Jesus: a Flesh-Translation of Divine Compassion", p. 86.
9. *Ibid.*, pp. 87-88.
10. *Ibid.*, p. 96.
11. Samuel Rayan, "Prophet and Poet in One", p. 99.
12. Samuel Rayan, "Jesus: a Flesh-Translation of Divine Compassion", p. 83.
13. *Ibid.,* pp. 95-96.
14. Samuel Rayan, "Prophet and Poet in One", p. 99.
15. Samuel Rayan, "Jesus: a Flesh-Translation of Divine Compassion", pp. 83-84.
16. *Ibid.,* pp. 86-87.
17. *Ibid.*, p. 89.
18. *Ibid.*, p, 93.
19. *Ibid.*, p. 94.
20. *Ibid.*, p, 80.
21. *Ibid.*, p. 93.

22. W. Randolph Tate, "Postmodern Interpretation", in *The Oxford Encyclopaedia of Biblical Interpretation*, ed. Steven L. McKenzie (Oxford: Oxford University Press, 2013), pp. 135-137.
23. Samuel Rayan, "Prophet and Poet in One", p. 98.
24. *Ibid.*, p. 99.
25. Samuel Rayan, Jesus: a Flesh-Translation of Divine Compassion, p. 96.
26. Samuel Rayan, "Prophet and Poet in One", pp. 98-99.
27. R. S. Sugirtharajah, *The Bible and the Third World: Precolonial, Colonial, and Postcolonial Encounters* (Cambridge: Cambridge University Press, 2001), p. 7.
28. Kurien Kunnumpuram (ed.), *Jesus, The Relevance of His Person and Message for our Times*, p. 10.

16

Yes Indeed He is with us

An Appraisal of Samuel Rayan's Biblical Exegesis and Hermeneutics

Henry Pattarumadathil, SJ

In 1987, I got a golden opportunity to attend an introductory course on Liberation Theology offered by Fr. Samuel Rayan at the Jesuit Socio Religious Centre (SRC) in Calicut. It was, in fact, a Bible study rather than a theology course. I still remember the kindling eyes of Fr. Rayan as he spoke of the liberation project of God in the book of Exodus, and Jesus' option for the oppressed and the marginalized in the gospels. Later, I was fortunate to have him as my theology professor and community member at Sameeksha, Kalady. I heard him saying several times that he had a desire to do his higher studies in Bible, but his superiors sent him to study Systematic Theology. It was a blessing in disguise, I believe. Thus, we obtained a theologian who is literally possessed by the word of God. Though his superiors could not allow him to go for biblical studies, Fr. Rayan never gave up his desire. I remember that, when I was preparing to come back to India after my licentiate at the Biblical Institute in Rome, I received a letter from Fr. Rayan requesting me to obtain for him a copy of the Introduction to Biblical Hebrew by Thomas Lambdin. I gladly did it and he was very happy. It was in 2000 and Fr. Rayan had already celebrated his 80th birthday. His passion and fascination for the word of God can easily be seen in his writings. Explaining a theological concept, or expressing his opinion on an environmental issue, or raising his voice against the maltreatment of women or the Dalits or tribals, whatever may be the subject, the foundation of his deliberations has always been the Bible.

I attempt here to highlight the exegetical method and hermeneutical approach that Fr. Rayan follows in his writings. To be more concrete and precise, I am presenting my observations based on an article that Fr. Rayan wrote in 1997 entitled "With Us - With Whom - Is God?" in honour of the late Fr. George Soares Prabhu.[1] This article, which Fr. Rayan humbly qualifies as "an unscientific footnote to Soares-Prabhu's work", is indeed a masterpiece of his exgetical and theological genius. I hope Fr. Rayan will forgive me for dissecting this poetic piece and analyzing his approach more than the content.

A comprehensive study of a biblical passage or theme consists, in my opinion, normally of five basic elements, namely, *Investigation*, *Information*, *Interpretation*, *Inspiration* and *Integration*. We will use these parameters to review Fr. Rayan's article and come to appreciate its exegetical and hermeneutical profundity.

1. Investigation

Identification of the exegetical and the hermeneutical issues and problems is fundamental to any scientific study of a scriptural text. In this article, Fr. Rayan takes up the name 'Immanuel' (God with us) attributed to Jesus in Matt 1:23, and explores how this theme is presented in the gospel of Matthew and to whom the pronoun 'us' refers. The title of the article clearly presents the basic question of his investigation: "With us - with whom - is God?". Throughout this 48 page long article, this question is raised again and again and a brave attempt is made to respond to it with a profound analysis of the text in its context.

2. Information

"More than anything else, what an exegete needs is sharp eyes", said one of my professors at the Biblical Institute. Normally a text contains a lot of useful information - lexical, structural, cultural, historical, theological etc. - needed for its interpretation. The beauty of Fr. Rayan's exegetical conclusions is that they are founded on his sharp observation of the text. He connects various observations intra-textually and inter-textually and brings out further conclusions. Let me highlight some of the observations and conclusions that he makes in the first section of the article under the subtitle 'Immanuel':[2]

- "Matthew's Gospel is to be read from start to finish as the good news of God's saving presence and solidarity with "us". It is on this note of divine presence-solidarity that the Gospel opens and closes".

He substantiates this general observation further with a few concrete observations:

- "In Matthew 1 a genealogy and a birth narrative culminate in the naming of Mary's Son".
- "Two names are given, both having reference to the mission and the meaning of the Child".
- "Mary's Child is to be called Jesus "because he will save his people from their sins" (1:21). He will also be called Immanuel, "a name which means 'God-is-with-us' (1:23)".
- "This second name, ..., reappears in 28:20 as the concluding and crowning good news Matthew has for us. The Risen Jesus, as he sends his disciples on a world mission, gives them the assurance of his companionship "to the end of time (28:18-20)".

His eyes go beyond these framing texts (1:23 and 28:20), and they find many other passages in the gospel which revolve around the semantic axis of 'divine presence and solidarity'. See the intra-textual observations he makes on page 160:

- If, however, the Gospel as a whole is considered, and the strategic position and function of the doublet 1:23 and 28:20 is remembered, the name Immanuel might appear quite basic. It is a torch to take up as we set out to explore Matthew's message, and the point to retain and remember when the journey, if ever, is over and we close the book.

> A point which keeps emerging again and again in various forms as, for instance, in 3:17 the Voice from Heaven; 5:45 the Giver of sunshine and rain; 6:26 the Feeder of birds and Clother of flowers; 9:15 the Bridegroom with his friends; 10:19-20 and other 'worry not' and 'fear not' passages about a Strengthener; 18:19-20, Presence where two or three meet in his name; and 25:31-46 the King in solidarity with the needy. The two names, Jesus and Immanuel, together, then, are a theological statement concerning the identity and the mission of Mary's Son, and concerning God's role in both.

A primary level intra-textual observation alone is not enough to understand any gospel passage. The evangelists, in their attempt to present Jesus and his identity, have drawn much from the Old Testament. In fact, the OT was the only authoritative source that the evangelists had and used to communicate the divine project that was fulfilled in the life and mission of Jesus. So it is important also to explore the inter-textual connections of a passage or a theme with the OT. Similarly, the views of the other NT authors on the theme are to be examined. In his exposition, Fr. Rayan journeys through the OT and the NT and identifies several texts (Exod 3:12; 33:14-16; 34:8; Isa 6:7,14; Jer 1; Ezek 1–3; Dan 7:13-14; John 1:14; 2 Cor 5:19; Col 2:9) which allude to the theme of 'Immanuel' in Matthew.

3. Interpretation

Fr. Rayan does not mention the use of any particular exegetical method for his analysis and explanation. In fact, in his introductory paragraph, he expresses his distaste for "the tangled web of biblical sciences" and "sundry critical methodologies". However, one can identify the use of several modern exegetical approaches/methods in this so- called 'unscientific footnote'.

3.1 Synchronic Approach

Fr. Rayan applies a synchronic approach in his study of the Gospel. He works with the canonical text of Matthew. He follows the narrative flow of the final text with the basic conviction that "Matthew's Gospel sprang from Jesus' ministry of *good newsing* the poor". With this approach and conviction he examines several texts from Matthew [e.g. the Genealogy (1:1-17), the Visit of the Magi (2:1-23); the Proclamation of John the Baptist (3:1-12), the Temptation of Jesus (4:1-11), the Beatitudes (5:1-12), the Lord's Prayer (6:9-13), the Mission Discourse (10:1-42), the Last Judgement (25:31-46), the Passion and Resurrection Narrative (26-28) etc.] and shows how the reality of Immanuel pervades the Gospel.

3.2 Structural Exegesis

On page 160 in footnote 7, Fr. Rayan quotes from the commentary of Daniel Patte.[3] This commentary is unique as it follows a structural approach to interpret the Gospel of Matthew. In biblical exegesis, the structural approach helps the reader to identify the interconnected elements in a text. Fr. Rayan, taking insights also from Ulrich Luz,[4] J. D. Kingsbury[5], and Peter Ellis[6], identifies several interconnected texts and themes structured logically and strategically in the Gospel. Thus, he observes a number of *inclusions*[7] in the text and develops his reflections based on them. The following table shows the different inclusions that Fr. Rayan observes in the first four (1-4) and the last three (26–28) chapters of the gospel:[8]

Matt 1–4	Matt 26–28	Observations
1:23: The angel announces to Joseph that the child to be born will be called Immanuel – 'God with us'.	28:20: The Risen Jesus promises his disciples that he will be with them till the end of the ages.	The Immanuel theme. The article further shows how this theme is linked to many other texts and presented as the major theme in the gospel, e.g. in 3:17; 5:45; 6:26; 9:15; 10:19-20; 18:19-20; 25:31-46.

2:1-12: The Gentile Magi confess their faith in the Jewish Messiah.	27:54: The Roman centurion and his companions confess their faith in the 'Son of God'.	This aspect of the "non-ethnic character of the Gospel and grace" is discussed again referring to 8:10-13; 15:21-28; 21:28-32:40-43.
In Matt 2, Herod seeks to destroy the child, and the chief priests and scribes of the people are around (2:4-6).	In Matt 27, Herod's masters, the imperial power, execute Jesus, and the chief priests and scribes are around (27,1.20.41).	The inclusion that chapter 2 makes with chapter 27 is seen as an interpretative frame of reference within the larger frame made of 1:23 and 28:20 as Jesus' character as the Immanuel cannot be properly "grasped without regard to the passion and resurrection of Jesus (Matthew 27 and 28) and to Jesus' radical doctrine of life through death".[9]
In Matt 3 Jesus is found standing with the common people to be baptized by John the Baptist.	The narration of the passion and death of Jesus (26–27) - which is symbolically mentioned elsewhere as 'baptism' - forms an inclusion with chapter 3.	A link between the baptism and death of Jesus is not explicit in Matthew as it is in Mark 10:38; Luke 12:50; Rom 6:3-4. What is highlighted in the article is Jesus' being with the ordinary people at the baptism and his sharing of their plight in the passion.

In 3:17 the Father declares the divine identity of the Son.	In 27:54, a Roman centurion and his companions confess the divine sonship of Jesus.	These two texts are beautifully presented as the "second basic Christological inclusion".[10]
In chapter 4 Jesus is tempted to "walk the ways of the vain and the wealthy, ways of conceit and control, of sensationalism and domination".[11] He triumphs over that temptation (4,1-11) and walks with the despised people living in darkness and in the shadow of death (4:12-35).	In chapters 26–27 Jesus becomes like one of these despised people: "spat upon, struck, whipped, stripped, mocked, crucified and done to death (26:67; 27:26-44)".[12]	Thus the baptism scene and the temptation scene are seen as "metaphors of Jesus' and his people's humiliation-exaltation, incarnation-glorification, death-resurrection".[13]

3.3. Interdisciplinary and dialogical

It is quite amazing to observe the way Fr. Rayan integrates various disciplines in his writings. His theological and biblical reflections are not abstract, but deeply related to the life situations of the people, especially of the poor. He uses insights from the social sciences, Marxism, cultural anthropology, aesthetics, ecological studies, feminist studies etc. to decipher the meaning of a text that was written 2000 years ago. Thus, he makes it intelligible and relevant to the current generation. The frequent use of the studies of R. A. Horsley[14] and M. R. Tripole[15] and the reference to the works of T. Eagleton[16] and D. MacLaren[17] in the present article clearly reflect Fr. Rayan's interdisciplinary approach to biblical exegesis. No doubt, his interpretation of the Genealogy of Jesus (1:1-17) from a feminist perspective, and the Visit of the Magi (2:1-23) from a sociological perspective and the Beatitudes (5,3-12) and the Last Judgement (25:31-46) from a liberation perspective are characteristic examples of his interdisciplinary and contextual hermeneutics.

Besides George Soares-Prabhu, the names of twenty biblical/ theological scholars appear in the endnotes of this article.[18] Fr. Rayan's dialogical approach - sometimes agreeing with the position of these scholars, sometimes modifying them, and sometimes challenging them and departing from them - makes his article rich in content and profound in insights.

3.4. Contextual, Post-colonial Exegesis

Fr. Rayan's approach is dialogical, at the same time he is very critical of the exegetes who are slaves of their cherished methods, and whose analysis and conclusions remain distant from the living context of the people. Since the biblical texts are written to bring good news to the people, especially the ordinary people, their interpretation too should serve this purpose. Therefore, when we have to choose from two or more possibilities of interpretation, we should go for the one that corresponds more closely to the living reality of the people. This view of Fr. Rayan's is reflected very well in his interpretation of the 'poor in spirit' in the first beatitude (Matt 5:3) and the 'least of my brethren' in the Parable of the Last Judgement (Matt 25:31-46).

Ever since the time of the Fathers, there have been several authors who 'spiritualize' Matthew's 'poor' saying that the ones who are called 'the poor in spirit' are the ones who put their trust in God. Such an interpretation may delight some rich people who trust in God or the religious who pronounce a vow of poverty, but it neglects the pains and sorrows of the deprived mass who may not even be able to raise their head to call God in their distress.

Fr. Rayan, who is not an alien to the struggles of the poor, is convinced that this beatitude is given primarily to the poor people whose spirit may even be crushed by the reality of poverty. Fr. Rayan shares the view of Soares-Prabhu, who took an uncompromising stance for the cause of the poor in his writings:

> All through the Bible the poor are a sociological rather than a religious group. Their identity is defined not by any spiritual attitude of openness or dependence on God, but simply by their sociological situation of powerlessness and need. This need is not necessarily economic need... The poor of the Bible are all those who are in any way...deprived of the means or

> the dignity they need to lead a fully human existence; or who are in a situation of powerlessness which exposes them to such deprivation. The poor of the Bible are thus "the wretched of the earth", the marginalized, the exploited, all those who are actually or potentially oppressed.[19]

Who are 'the least of these (brothers of mine)' in Matt 25:40-45? Many are of the opinion that it refers to the disciples or to the Christian missionaries.[20] Such an interpretation may be justified as it attempts to link the teaching of Jesus with that in Matt 10:42. But it overlooks the universal dimension of Jesus' teaching in 25:31-46. Fr. Rayan's reaction is exceptionally strong against such a narrow view:

> Indeed the view that the eternal destiny of all men and women will depend upon their treatment of Christians is essentially immoral. And profoundly ridiculous. It is funny to suggest that the disciples are the centre of world history; and comical to affirm that Jesus sent out his disciples in order to pose to be served rather than to serve. What the opinion undermines is the universality and uniqueness of the Gospel and the love-commandment, and the mysticism of faith, and the depth dimensions of the history which God is making with us.[21]

Further, Fr. Rayan explains the implications of such an interpretation in contemporary society. He challenges readers to look at the world around and its history before they favour such a view. Referring to Christian missionaries who were sent by the colonial powers with their political agenda rather than religious zeal, Rayan writes:

> They belong with a 500-year old history of world conquest, and systems of enslavement and total plunder. If it is to them that the text primarily refers, and exclusively, it has ceased to have meaning. They are not hungry nor thirsty nor naked; they do not need to be served, and they have largely incapacitated us to render services to anyone.[22]

Certainly, Jesus never imagined colonial conquests or crusades when he sent out his disciples as missionaries. Perhaps, in its original context Matt 25:40-45 might have had some link with Matt 10:42, and the term 'least of my brothers' might have referred to the disciples of Jesus. But Fr. Rayan refuses to interpret the text in that line today, in the post-colonial era, as it would justify the atrocities of the colonialists done also in the name of Missions. Moreover, a disciple-centred interpretation of Matt 25:31-46 completely ignores the reality of "global poverty and suffering" and the "struggles of concerned men and women to secure justice for the victims of world-wide exploitation".

Fr. Rayan argues that this passage of the Last Judgement "echoes the ancient west-Asian view that the role of the king is to defend the weak and take their side. It is thus a revelation of the kingship of Jesus. That is the only kind of kingship Jesus would admit and claim. The pericope is a call to everyone to identify with the oppressed and to struggle for justice".[23] In fact, this parable of the Last Judgement could be seen as the sum and substance of the teachings of Jesus in the gospel of Matthew. Even structurally, it is presented as the climax of all the discourses of Jesus. Immediately after this parable, the evangelist begins the Passion Narrative. According to Fr. Rayan, the passion and death of Jesus is "undergone in order to bring about the social transformation and the new earth envisaged in the new economic-social relations and concerns of Matt 25".[24]

3.5. Liberation Hermeneutics

The phrase 'the gospel's liberational potential' that Fr. Rayan uses in this article (p. 182) is, in my opinion, the key to understanding his hermeneutical stance. The gospels are the written account of the faith expressions of the Christian community which embraced the good news of the arrival of God's reign in and through Jesus in their lives. In him and in his words the people experienced God's salvific project which invited them and led them to an integral liberation from all sorts of bondage that prevented them from realizing and living their true identity as the children of God. The early community decided to write the gospels in order to share their faith experience with successive generations and to help them experience this integral liberation that God offered to human beings through Jesus. That is why it is said that the gospels have 'liberational potential'. To men and women of every generation the gospels have the same message, the message of God's acts of liberation. Though the context changes, the purpose of the gospels remains the same. Such a hermeneutical stance treats the gospels (or any other book in the Bible) not as a set of ancient codes that should be deciphered in the academic laboratories, but as the word of God that is to be heard in the living context of the people. We will see several examples of Fr. Rayan's liberation hermeneutics in the next section.

4. Inspiration

Obviously, inspiration is basically a subjective experience. Something that is inspiring to one person need not be inspiring to another. However, exegetes and theologians can play a vital role in this regard. They can, through their interpretation, help people to experience the power of the Word of God in their daily lives. On the scope of biblical interpretations Fr. Rayan says, "The test of authenticity is whether a suggested interpretation moves us to commitment, always 'to think the things of God', 'be on God's side' (Matt 16:23), and adopt God's values as these are embodied and disclosed in Jesus of Nazareth".[25]

How can one 'be on God's side'? Fr. Rayan would say, 'by being on the side of the poor'. How can one 'think the things of God'? The answer would be 'by thinking the things of the poor'.

After establishing the 'Immanuel' (God with us) promise as the fundamental message of the gospel of Matthew,[26] Fr. Rayan begins to ask the question: "To whom is the Lord present? Who is or are the 'us' of God-is-with-us? With whom is God-in-Jesus *solidary*, and whose cause and concerns does he make his own? Or, in whose life-situation does God immerse himself in order radically to transform it?"[27]

Fr. Rayan argues that the God whom Immanuel reveals is not the so-called 'omnipresent God' of the philosophers who is seen everywhere and who moves with everyone. He is a God who sides with the poor and the marginalized. Challenging the neutral stance of some exegetes and theologians Fr. Rayan comments: "Scholars discuss the structure and unity of the Gospel; and take it for granted that the identity of the 'us' is obvious: the 'us' are the people. But which people? for people are many interests, many sectors and classes.

To have some clarity concerning the identity of the 'us' is vital to the understanding of the Gospel since the Immanuel theme enfolds the work and acts as a term of hermeneutical reference".[28]

Analyzing different episodes from the gospel Fr. Rayan shows who 'the people' are with whom the Immanuel is and to whom he brings the good news of salvation. Let me quote some of his inspiring affirmations.

1. 'Us' in the historical context of the Immanuel prophecy (Isa 7:14).

> The 'us' in that historical context comprised not the whole world, not the entire Hebrew people, not at all those who planned aggression, but Ahaz and his realm, the threatened and frightened people of Judah, out of their wits for fear and powerless, and placed unjustly in the shadow of imminent invasion and destruction. Their resources are inadequate to cope with the situation. Therefore, God takes their side. He does so not because their faith is anything wonderful, but because they were being victimized and oppressed.[29]

2. With women

> "In the 'us' Matthew includes women who in traditional Jewish religion and society were marginal and secondary".... Women, uncircumcised, had no official part in worship, no obligation of pilgrimages, no debt to Sabbath rules (Ex 4:24-26; 12:44-49; Josh 5:2-9; Ex 23:17; 20:10; 34:23). Jesus rejected and subverted this tradition of discrimination, and Matthew walks in his steps by including names of four women in Jesus' genealogy (1:3, 5, 6).... By naming these women in the ancestry of Jesus Matthew is saying that Immanuel is solidary not only with men, not only "with his mother Mary", the Virgin, (2:11) but with those who are despised and abused and relegated to the outskirts of religion and society. He is saying that the blood of these women flows in the veins of the Saviour".[30]

3. With gentiles

> "It [*the story of the Wise Men from the East looking for the newborn king of the Jews*] represents the writer's deliberate refusal to restrict the 'us' to Israel or to any particular ethnic group. It

> affirms that God is with all who seek the truth and strive to follow what light they see, and long to meet God's King as he steps into our history. It is meant to include the 'Gentiles', represented by the Wise Men, whom Jews of the time tended to despise as godless and refer to as dogs (Mt 15:27-28; Eph 2:12)".[31]

4. With the victims of every age

> "Hanging on the cross he cried, My God, why have you forsaken me? (27:46). That was complete solidarity with the experience of the destroyed children and with all the stripped, the scourged, the mocked, the tortured and the crucified of history".[32]

> "The ultimate reason why the poor are blessed is that they are He, Jesus, his Body, which God raises and fills with light and life. A great part of their blessedness consists in that they, the oppressed, can meaningfully call Jesus Immanuel, God-is-with-us, right within our misery, challenging us to action and enabling us".[33]

In short, the Immanuel is one with the sorrowful, the defenceless, the mocked, the imprisoned, the stripped, the naked, the thirsty and the poor, done to death.[34]

5. Integration

The principal mission of exegetes and theologians is to help people to engage in an ongoing discernment in their life keeping God's word as the frame of reference. They interpret the word of God, written twenty centuries ago, making it relevant to the lives of people today. They enable people to experience God in their lives and respond to his invitation to journey with him. Naturally, such an experience should lead people to *metanoia*, a change of mind, a change of perspective, a change of lifestyle, and a change of stance. Fr. Rayan is quite faithful to his mission as an exegete and a theologian. He does not exhort his readers with 'dos and don'ts'. Rather he accompanies the reader and helps him/her to develop a proper understanding of God revealed through the scripture, through the person of Jesus, through history, and through various events happening around them. Let us see some of his theological convictions expressed in the present article.

He presents God as the liberator who makes a definite option for the oppressed and the marginalized, who cannot be possessed by the exalted and the eminent. "God's heart is disclosed not to the learned and the clever, the dominant class, but to little children, the small and simple folk who do not matter in the councils of the great".[35] About God and his ways Fr. Rayan says:

> God is always Immanuel in his gifts and promises, in creation and the wonders of nature, in his redeeming action and in all liberative events of history, in his re-educating wrath and chastisement, in his gentleness and concern and tender compassion, in all oppressed peoples, in the person of Jesus, in Jesus' wounds and tears and the joy of his resurrection, and in his sharing of our human condition, and in his pursuit of justice and friendship.[36]

> God was never a private limited concern for Israel of strict observance, but the Mystery that enfolds our history's brokenness and gathers our tears. Immanuel means that God-in-Jesus is with the despised peoples and cultures, and with all who know their place in the order of things and their need for mercy.[37]

> God makes life sprout from the heart of death suffered for his sake (16:21-23; 17:22-23; 20:17-19). God subverts human power and raises to life and glory those whom the mighty oppress and kill. This is the faith and hope of Jesus even when he cries his Why to God.[38]

> God is not so much with the 'first', the top-dogs, the possessors of economic, social or political power, as with the 'last', the under-dogs who have little or no status or power. (19:30; cf. 20:16 and 11:25). The lost and the lowliest are God's first concern.[39]

Fr. Rayan assists the readers to discern whether God is present or absent in their life situations and to distinguish between the agents and structures of life and those of death. He challenges them to examine their value systems and to see where they stand: with God and Jesus or with anti-God powers. Jesus, in his view, is not a neutral divine figure, but God's Son who desires and demands mercy more than sacrifice.

> But what Jesus brings is not cheap peace or superficial reconciliation. He brings the sword of discernment, of renunciation of false values and of side-taking in the cause of justice and on behalf of the victims of brutal power 10:34-36). The final assurance is that "anyone who loses his/her life for Jesus' (and the Kingdom's) sake will find it (10:37-39; 16:24-25).[40]

> The truth of Jesus was sensed and his person was experienced as Immanuel as people and relationships were remade in his ministry of healing the sick; appreciating the finer faith he found outside Israel (8:10-13); recognizing the humanity and dignity of publicans and sinners (9:9-13); acknowledging the faith and freedom of the woman who took his healing touch (9:18-22); placing this woman and others beyond the range of pollution laws and purity prejudices: setting aside thereby life-restricting socio-religious taboos: and assigning primacy to mercy over sacrifice and to human beings and their needs over all laws and ascetical practices (9:10-17).[41]

He defines the Kingdom as God's sovereign rule where everyone experiences equality and justice and lives as God's children. Everyone is called to labour with God and Jesus to make God's reign a reality in this world.

> Food for the hungry and liberation for the indebted, making for fellowship, freedom and equality, are God's will for human life on earth. They are essential dimensions and experiences of the Kingdom as it realizes itself in our history. The Kingdom is the theological horizon and the compelling reason of this insistent concern for the impoverished masses. The Kingdom is God's redeeming activity. Its purpose and goal is newness of life in a new social order in re-shaped local communities which would be a new family for those who joined it (19:27-29).[42]

> The Kingdom and its blessings do not come on the wings of repeated religious words, but in the heart of faith which consists in doing God's will about caring for one another, sharing of

> goods, cancellation of debts, and making justice a prime and passionate concern (5:6; 6:33; 7:21-27). The kingdom comes when together we build a new house, a new world, on the truth-rock of Jesus words.[43]

A call to commitment, especially to the cause of the poor and the marginalized, permeates Fr. Rayan's writings.

> The 'us' comprise the victims of the Herods of all ages, and of the presidents and managers of wars and owners of vast killer-power such as has been exhibited in Auschwitz and Hiroshima and Bhopal and Chernobyl and in the Gulf region and in Central America and South Africa.[44]

> Those who care for the wretched of the earth and struggle on their side to secure (a human measure of) justice for them also belong with the poor and with the Kingdom which is theirs.[45]

Conclusion

To conclude this short appraisal of Fr. Rayan's article, I would like to respond briefly to three questions. What do we, the readers, see in the article? What does it tell us? What does it ask of us?

We see a highly scientific and systematic analysis of some of the passages from the gospel of Matthew which directly or indirectly deal with the theme of Immanuel. The arguments are well substantiated with sufficient data, and critically examined in conversation with the prevailing scholarly views. The analyses of the passages are interconnected; the flow from one text to the next is so natural, and together they appear like a collage. We also see a profound reflection on the significance of these texts in our context, challenging our faith and our life. In this article, one cannot escape hearing the prophetic voice of a committed theologian speaking on behalf of God's people, the poor and the marginalized.

The article tells us the story of our God who is 'Immanuel', who makes his presence felt in our lives through his Son Jesus. It underscores the good news of liberation that God proclaims through Jesus for the underprivileged of society. It also tells us where we should seek the Immanuel, where he can be found, whom he identifies with and what worship he desires. Where agents and structures of death plot against the helpless and the lowly God cannot be present. He cannot be worshipped in such situations. He keeps company with the "companionless among the poorest, the lowliest and the lost".

Pointing out, in myriad ways, God's preferential option for the deprived and the destitute, the article challenges us to examine our images of God, faith expressions, understanding of the Church and the sacraments, interpretation of the word of God and, more than all, our lifestyle. It invites us to recognize the Immanuel's presence among the 'least and the lowliest' and to labour with God in his project of human liberation.

> The work of Jesus and his disciples is not meant to pacify and domesticate people and integrate the victims neatly into the existing system which the powerful create and keep for their own benefit. The mission would mean the disruption of existing structures and old wine-skins, both mental and social, and the shaping of new ones that are free and human (10:34-36; 9:14-17).The work of renewal is conflictual, and those who take it up must be ready to have relationships sundered, and enter into new ones mediated by their own cross and the crosses of the poor.[46]

Notes

1. So, this article was originally published in Francis X. D'Sa (ed.), *The Dharma of Jesus, Interdisciplinary Essays in Memory of George Soares-Prabhu, SJ,* Pune: Institute for the Study of Religion, De Nobili College &Anand: Gujarat Sahitya Prakash, 1997, pp. 37-83. But in the present article I am referring to the version published in K. Kunnumpuram SJ (ed.), *Selected Writings of Samuel Rayan, SJ, Vol. I: Jesus: The Relevance of His Person and Message for our Times,* Mumbai St. Pauls, 2001, pp. 157-195.
2. See pages 158-161.
3. D. Patte, *The Gospel According to Matthew. A Structural Commentary on Matthew's Faith,* Philadelphia: Fortress Press, 1987.
4. U. Luz, *Matthew* 1-7 *A Commentary,* Minneapolis: Augsburg Fortress, 1989.
5. J. D. Kingsbury, *Matthew: Structure, Christology, Kingdom,* Minneapolis: Fortress Press, 1989.
6. P. Ellis, *Matthew: His Mind and Message*, Collegeville: Liturgical press, 1974.

7. 'Inclusion' (Latin *inclusio*) is a literary device where the writer places similar material (an idea, a theme, a phrase etc.) at the beginning and end of a section with the intention of forming a thematic frame.
8. The references given here are only a sample. Fr. Rayan refers to several other inclusions in the article.
9. Page 169.
10. Page 173.
11. Page 174.
12. *Ibid.*
13. *Ibid.*
14. R. A. Horsley, *Sociology and the Jesus Movement,* New York: Seabury, 1989.
15. M. R. Tripole, "A Church for the Poor and the World: at Issue with Moltmann's Ecclesiology", in *Theological Studies* 42 (1981) 4, pp. 645-659.
16. T. Eagleton, *The Ideology of the Aesthetic,* Oxford: Blackwell, 1990.
17. D. MacLaren, "Solidarity - Beyond the Clichés: A Theological Perspective" in *New Blackfriars 72* (Nov 1991), pp 489-496.
18. They include U.Luz, J. D. Kingsbury, D. Patte, C. Barth, G. Stanton, P. S. Minear, P. Ellis etc.
19. Page 176, quoted from the article of G. Soares-Prabhu, "Class in the Bible: The Biblical Poor, A Social Class?" in *Vidyajyoti* 49 (1985), p. 331.
20. See Page 178 for a long list of authors who take such a position.
21. See Page 179.
22. Page 179.
23. Page 181.
24. *Ibid.*
25. Pages 157-158.
26. This is stated clearly in Page 161 with a quotation from Kingsbury: "In the person of Jesus Messiah, His Son, God has drawn near to abide to the end of time with his people, the Church, thus inaugurating the eschatological age of salvation".
27. Page 162.
28. *Ibid.*
29. Page 164. While making this affirmation Fr. Rayan does not ignore the fact that Ahaz was a cowardly king. See page 165.
30. Page 165.
31. Page 167.
32. Page 169.
33. Page 175.
34. Page 181.
35. Page 182.

36. Page 190.
37. Page 167.
38. Pages 169-170.
39. Page 183.
40. Page 170.
41. Page 188.
42. Page 185.
43. Page 187.
44. Page 172.
45. Page 175.
46. Page 189.

PART FOUR

THEOLOGIZING IN INDIA

17

Exploring the Realm of Implicit Theologies

Reflections on Samuel Rayan's Method of Theologizing

P. T. Mathew, SJ

Introduction

This paper is a tribute to my Guru, Fr. Samuel Rayan. The theological insights I gained from his lectures and writings became a valuable resource in my later involvement among the coastal people, and in my teaching and guidance work at the Regional Theology Centre at Kalady, Kerala. The focus of this paper is on the basics of the theological method that Rayan seemed to be engaging in his writings. Rayan provides us with some valuable bricks for building an Indian Christian theology in and through his writings that span a period of four decades. He doesn't aim at building a theology or a system; that has never been his intention. So his thoughts lie scattered in his numerous articles. My task is only to bring those bricks together for us to work with. I will try to make Rayan speak for himself, as far as possible; my words will have neither the power nor the splendour of his theological and linguistic imagination.

One's Understanding of Theology Embodies One's Method

Why do we want a theology at all? What does it do to life and our existence? What form of a theology should we aim at?.... Rayan does not hesitate to ask disturbing questions. Questions and answers merge into each other in a harmonious symphony emitting sparks of theological insights in the process. He is concerned with what theology does and what theology is meant to do. So, he writes with clarity: "We want theology to be a service to life and to human wholeness. It should be service to life at all levels – from the tiny blade of grass to the singing bird, to the growing baby, to the heights of rigorous thought and warm friendships, to the depths of mystic joy and divine darkness.... Our theology will be at the service of those who work, suffer and hope, those who struggle for justice and human dignity for all women and men".[1] The concrete human person struggling for dignity and wholeness is at the centre of Rayan's theological enterprise. His theology is humanistic to the core. The human reality in the concrete context of India/Asia becomes his point of reference. That is why he affirms that all theology is local and contextual – a running theme in all his writings.

"The theology we do in India is Indian, local, and contextual", he states emphatically. Theology takes every concrete historical situation seriously. "The fact is that theology anywhere, anytime, is born of two interlacing experiences: of the faith and of the reality of life". The two are brought together "to face each other and to dialogue, questioning and critiquing each other, challenging each other. Theology is the spark that leaps up at the point of their encounter".[2] The imagery is fascinating: **theology is a spark** that emerges from the encounter of life and faith. "Where faith and social reality (thus) meet *theology sparks*: a theology which can uphold both the transcendental dimension of God's Reign and the New Person on the one hand, and their historical and political dimensions on the other, without the reductionism to which Marxism and traditional theology have both succumbed".[3]

Every bit of Rayan's theological writings emphasizes the local and the contextual. 'The' context for Rayan is primarily the Indian context, we may say. It is to be understood in two senses: one, it is concerned about the vital issues in the Indian societal context; two, it draws from the Indian context as its theological resource. While remaining thus rooted, his reflections have a pan-Asian and cross-cultural quality about them; he is aware that the Indian context cannot be grasped adequately unless it is placed within the wider Asian context, and still more, in the global Third World context. His long term association with EATWOT and his theological contributions to its thinking reflect this dialectics well. He thus emphasizes the need for cross-fertilization of various contextual theologies and for inter-continental contacts (that is radically different from the colonial contacts of the past). The twin term 'Indian/Asian' is used in this paper to denote this cross-cultural character of 'context'.

Taking the 'context' seriously leads Rayan to consciously reject imposition of any uniformity in theology, and to emphasize the inevitability of theological pluralism. "Pluralism is a grace. No one person, race, culture, language or religion can grasp and express exhaustively the riches of God's self-communication. The nuances that one misses, some others experience and articulate to the benefit of all".[4]

Decolonization of Theology: Precondition for Doing Theology in India

The colonial context of India/Asia comes in as a key variable in Rayan's theological articulation. He observes that in the early phase of Western expansion the Churches were allies in the colonial process, and benefited from the expansion of the empire. In return the Churches legitimized imperialism. "No wonder, colonial theology failed to call in question, to critique and resist the colonial plot as contradicting the Gospel and basic Christian and human decencies. Colonial theology failed to see that the subjugation and exploitation of peoples effectively annulled the Gospel of freedom and divine filiation".[5] Taking a broader view of history he considers the traditional theology with its accent on Latin or Syriac in liturgies and devotions, as basically colonial. God gets presented as a foreigner and stranger to our land. He calls into question the use of foreign languages as an act of contempt for the people and their culture. Reflecting on Paul's letter to the Corinthians he observes: "There are any number of different languages in the world…, but if I am ignorant of what the sounds mean, I am a savage to the man who is speaking, and he is a savage to me" (1Cor 14:12).

How to decolonize theology? The first step in decolonizing theology and in building an authentic Indian theology, he says, is "to re-examine the colonially obtained/imposed definition of theology and to re-understand it, if need be, and re-describe it".[6]

Re-describing Theology in terms of Discipleship

Rayan makes various attempts at re-describing theology, and he keeps adding nuances as he moves on. He gives the clearest description of theology in an article published in 2001. "Theology has been defined by St. Anselm as *Fides quaerens intellectum*, 'faith seeking understanding'. But, what understanding? The Aristotelian kind of understanding? The intellectual, cerebral understanding? Should we not rather think of theology as 'faith seeking justice', 'faith seeking the dignity and honour of every woman and man', 'faith seeking social transformation', 'faith seeking the transformation of humankind into the family of the Father of Jesus Christ',....?"[7] These questions point to the direction in which Rayan's theological project proceeds.

Classical theology, built on Anselm, is tied up with philosophical speculation directed to the construction of a perfect system. Looking from the Indian context theology has to be concerned with people and their quest for meaning and their will for freedom. "In the concrete context, then, of our life today, theology would be faith seeking justice and equality, love and responsibility, resource-sharing and community, and peace and wholeness for our world. That precisely is discipleship".[8] Yes, he makes theology and discipleship face each other. He dwells at length on the parable of the Good Samaritan (Lk 10:25-28) to elicit the difference between a theologian and a disciple. The two questions that the lawyer puts to Jesus makes him an excellent theologian. But he goes away sad since he was not prepared to be a disciple. In contrast the Samaritan shows what it means to be a disciple. Rayan's vision of theology involves the theologian and the disciple walking hand in hand, supporting each other and sharing insights. The Samaritan's deed is a confession of his faith in a God who is Father of us all, and "a rich and sturdy theological affirmation, a finer God-talk than any elaborate conceptual fabric could have achieved. It means that in the Samaritan of the story the theologian and the disciple meet and unite. The parable is a pointer to the unity of the two provided they are duly grasped and fathomed".[9] Theology's task cannot be separated from the call to discipleship. Jesus "calls them/us to a new vision of the world, to new patterns of living and relating and to a close following of Himself, walking in His footsteps, sharing His concerns, appropriating His values and participating in His struggles and sufferings".[10]

Rayan's Reading of the Indian/Asian Context

Construction of an Indian theology that is capable of resonating with and responding to the Indian context remained a core concern for Rayan. It presupposes a proper understanding of the Indian context, and he doesn't hesitate to utilize other disciplines, especially the social sciences, in this task. He sees the question of society and its structures as intimately connected with theology. He considers scientific societal analysis an inevitable ingredient in grasping the structures and hidden forces at work. The myths and stories of people become effective tools for cultural analysis. Could not these stories give guidance in discerning what structures and forces are at the service of death, and what are at the service of life?[11] He is convinced that a theology capable of serving the wholeness of life will be ever springing forth at the meeting point of faith and the reality of our country.

In an article titled "Re-conceiving Theology in the Asian Context" Rayan uses the framework he is fond of in his theological inquiry. It begins with the *challenges*, moves on to list the *resources*, and then discusses the *prospects*.[12]

i. The Challenges

The first challenge is the teeming millions of human persons in India/Asia which is home of more than five-ninths of the world population. They belong to various colours, cultural traditions and language systems. Their questions concern their role in the making of an Indian/Asian theology, and the contribution that would make to their lives. The rich religiousness and spiritual traditions, with most scripture religions born in Asia, present another challenge; they ask: What account will you take of us in your theological striving, and what role are we expected to play? The third challenge comes from the reality of poverty in the Indian/Asian context. The sharp contrast between the crushing poverty of the masses and the great wealth of the elite does challenge any theological project. The European colonization made it more sharp. Will this state of 'enforced poverty' be a central source and locus of theology? Will there be a clear break with the past colonial mode of theology? Will theology bring to light the socialist dimensions of the gospel faith and sacramental practice? The socio-political realities with the various contradictions ruled by class and caste interests, values and attitudes pose another challenge. Disillusionment of the masses finds expression in protests and struggles. Will theology be prophetic enough to bring the good news to the poor?

These challenges demand that our theology discerns God's presence in them and Sheds light on reality, arôuses consciousness and Denounces all that is dehumanizing and unjust. It is a call to reconceive theology in the Indian/Asian context. It is the vision of the kingdom of God that guides this process.

ii. Resources

Rayan presupposes the sources common to Christians the world over, viz., the faith, the Judeo-Christian scriptures, and the historical experience of the churches. He discusses in detail the resources that are specific to the Indian/Asian context; they are, in his own words, "our people, the sacred writings of the other Asian religions, the spiritual history of the people, and the liberative potential of their traditions".[13]

The people of India/Asia are the primary resource. "The courage and the strength that have enabled Asians to survive, despite material destitution and great physical and mental suffering, in the midst of death;... their struggles; the hope that sustains them and the hope that they sustain – these are theological loci.... There is, therefore, an implicit, unspoken theology in human lives and relationships.... There is an implicit theology in their will to change, in their vision and dream, however vague, of a just society and their readiness to achieve it and pave the foundations of a new society".[14] Rayan considers the Asian non-Christian scriptures – Hindu, Buddhist, etc. – as valuable resources at our disposal for re-conceiving theology. The world of spiritual experience and vision symbolised in these writings has been, for centuries, the word of God for the Asian peoples, guiding them and nourishing life and sustaining hope in a hopeless world. And we are heirs to this large body of holy scriptures. The spiritual history of Asians is the history of "a relentless quest for truth, meaning and freedom". Particularly significant is the Bhakti tradition that has been nourishing the masses for many centuries.

iii. Prospects

Rayan doesn't attempt at a systematic presentation of the prospects of an Indian/Asian theology; he only indicates some directions and possibilities. These would pave the way for us to work on.

- It is from the experience of the poor that theology comes to birth. It is in the poor and the oppressed of Asia and in their struggles for dignity, justice and freedom that theology has to seek and find the living God. It is to the simple and to children, not to the learned and the clever, that God discloses the saving truth and grace (Matt 11:2-6, 25-27).
- Since, the poor of Asia belong mainly to other religions, to meet God in the poor is to meet him in the poor of those religions. It would mean theology has to take their religiousness seriously – their beliefs, hopes and symbols.
- God is to be conceived not as absolute and impassible, but is discovered in the process of committed action to build history, the struggle of a people for justice and freedom.
- God approaches us not merely in our situations of despair, but in our responsible initiatives that may imply wrestling with God as Jacob did (Gen 32:23-33) or challenging God as Job did (Job 9:2-4, 11-35), or questioning God as the Psalmist did (Ps 44:18-26) or as Jesus did (Mk 1:34).
- Theology has to pay more attention to the subversive dimensions of God's interventions, not as the protector of the status quo. This would require theology to undergo radical conversion – from a god of the conquerors and the

killers to a God who identifies himself with the broken and the humiliated.

- Theology concerns with a God who speaks to all peoples, not only to Christians and in their churches. God reveals himself both in creation and in history, even the secular events of human history.
- Theology will remain open, for "God is known only in the measure in which the kingdom of God comes and we become it".[15]

Latent Theology is as Important as Academic Theology

One recurring theme in Rayan's writings is that of *latent theology*. Even though he spent the major part of his life in a theological institute, moving around academic circles, he was fully aware that real theology is lived by men and women in various spheres of life, in their struggles for dignity and their hope amidst threats to life and livelihood. He was a keen observer of various movements of people – the Dalits and tribals, the coastal fisher people, women; he kept up his contacts with them all through, and it had its impact on his theological outlook. His reflections on latent theology deserve close analysis.

After indicating that our God-speak begins with listening to what God is saying to us through nature, events, people, their struggles, etc., Rayan states: "In all such responses, struggles and hopes a theology lies latent, even when those who respond are not aware of it, even when they do not explicitly believe in anything transcendent or divine. Their faith is, as the liturgy declares, known to God alone".[16] The imagery of 'seeds of theology' is insightful; "faith inspired insight into historical realities carries significant seeds of theology", he writes.[17] That is how we discern the cross of Jesus in the cross of the people, and the power of his resurrection in their struggles against oppression.

The basic assumption here is that "the secular anthropological is the matrix of the theological". "Where there is faith there is (at least some incipient) theology. Where there is implicit, latent faith, there is latent, implicit theology. There is implicit theological faith in whatever is marked by an authentic anthropological or human faith.

Such human faith is not only the test and criterion of theological faith but its mother, and its incarnate historical form".[18] He extends this reflection to affirm that the people are the subjects of theology. "Hence, it is that people who fight for freedom and struggle for justice are the subjects of theology. It is they that call it into being. They construct it.... People are already theological, and are the doers of theology, interpreting the Divine to the world... Professional theologians and experts... are welcome to be servants of the theology of the people by helping them to organize and articulate it".[19] Here, he is helping us to clarify the role of academic theologians vis-a-vis the people who are the real makers and doers of theology.

One theological notion that influenced me deeply during the years of my social engagement and my later academic research among the coastal fisherpeople was that of latent theology. This notion is especially useful as a tool in the study of religious identity and dynamics of any faith community on the margins.[20] Every religion at the latent level implies a latent theology and a proper method, and the religion of the fisherpeople is no exception. At the latent level they become real subjects, not mere consumers, of religion and theology. The story of the fisherpeople illustrates the two sub-processes that are at work, viz. to be *interpreters* (of the Christian tradition from their world of experience) and to be *creators* (of a theology that would sustain them). The ongoing process of encounter and dialogue between the pre-Christian *neithal*[21] religiosity and the Christian tradition is proof enough. This has been taking place for the past five centuries, largely unnoticed by the mainstream theology.

On Theological Method

For Rayan method is the way theology, as disciplined knowledge, is done. "Methodologies are not principles to be applied to reality; they are a guide to clarify our commitment and praxis. Our aim is not new doctrines, but new relationships and lifestyles. Method implies a direction, and liberation is the direction".[22] Unlike the academic theology which starts reflection from above, from the academy and from unchangeable data furnished by scriptures and magisterium's definitions, Rayan asks us "to start from below, from our life's realities, from the 'profound and enriching questions' which these realities pose", and to proceed to a "re-reading of scriptures and doctrines, in view of action to humanize the situation further". His concern is with today (Ps 95; Heb 3 and 4; Matt 6), with the Now and Here, with this Earth and its promise, with the social order we build.[23] He borrows extensively from liberation theology in articulating his method.

An article Rayan wrote in 1981 exemplifies his theological method. It is titled "Outside the Gate, Sharing Insults", and is an amazing meditation on the issue of caste and untouchability (an age-old curse of the Indian society).[24] He begins by dissecting the reality of caste from various socio-political and religious angles, and relates it with caste-like formations worldwide. He leads us to the social order in Palestine in the time of Jesus to take note of similar traits. Then he explores the Gospels to educe the mind of Jesus: his parables of inversion, demolition of the myth of purity of race or nobility of birth, his miracles aimed at breaking the culture of silence, and submitting himself as an outcaste to be sacrificed outside the gate. Then he moves on to the task that we Christians are invited to take up: conversion of heart, action for transforming the social order, and upholding the language of the cross in solidarity with the victims of caste ideology. "It is the Cross of the outcaste that bears the promise of the new earth and the new India with a human heart, a heart of flesh, full of karuna, sensitive to the all-encompassing Brahman, and realizing advaita and brotherhood and sisterliness at all levels of life and relationships".[25]

For Rayan *commitment* is the first act of theology. "We are convinced that an academic type of theology divorced from action for change is irrelevant. With our oppressed brothers and sisters elsewhere, we are prepared for a radical break in theological methodology, in order that commitment to the oppressed and to their struggle for freedom, justice and fellowship be the first act of theology. This commitment is, we hold, implied in and demanded by our faith-commitment to God in Jesus Christ".[26] In his methodology "practice and theory, action and reflection, discussion and prayer, movement and silence, social analysis and religious hermeneutics, involvement and contemplation constitute a single process".[27]

If to theologize is to interpret the present reality in the light of God's Word and Action, the question arises: who is to do this? Rayan's answer is unambiguous: "It is the community that theologizes; the professional *theologian* speaks for the community. The *theologian's* presence within the community saves *theology* from the danger of becoming academic on the one hand and the danger of becoming over-populist on the other. It must be rigorous but not divorced from *life*; it must be a people's *theology* but not uncritical".[28] This focus on 'community' reflects an age-old principle in Christian theological tradition: that of *sensus fidelium*. It says that "the body of the faithful as a whole, anointed as they are by the Holy One, cannot err in matters of belief".[29] It further adds that this supernatural sense of faith characterises the People as a whole. This principle is easy to grasp since Vatican II presents the Church primarily as the 'People of God'. And that is very much in line with the biblical understanding as articulated so well in the letter of Peter (1 Pet 2:9-10). (The term 'community', however, remains vague and amorphous, open to diverse interpretations. A more effective use of the social sciences may be needed to remedy it.)

Rayan refers to Jesus' own way of doing theology as illustrated in his reply to the followers of John the Baptist (Matt 11:1-4). The accent is on the invitation to see and hear and touch what is present, and to understand and to interpret. "Theology, then, is the interpretation of seen events – the blind re-covering their sight, the lame walking, the dead rising to life, and the poor hearing good news that is hope-giving".[30]

People's Struggles and Movements as the *Locus* (Place) of Latent Theology

Rayan's theological method has a symbiotic relationship with people's struggles and people's movements. He is convinced that "the starting point of theology is the struggles of the people. That is the primary *locus theologicus*: the point where God acts and speaks in history here and now". He explains the reason: "Theology... is made, done, lived before it is spoken or written. Theology is born of theopraxy, right action. All struggles for liberation, justice, dignity, and community are right action, theopraxy".[31] People's theology "comes to birth when people wake up to the truth of their condition, develop a critical consciousness, discern between justice and injustice, between true peace and the calm of structural violence, recognize their own dignity and their vocation to live as God's friends and co-workers in the fashioning of the New Age, the New Earth".[32] This method affirms the primacy of historical events over the primacy of texts, unlike in academic theology. "In the biblical tradition the founding events are Abraham's migration, the Exodus from Egypt, the Cross of Jesus and his Resurrection. These originating events are made to interact with the events of people's organized revolts and liberation movements...."[33]

I came to understand the in-depth meaning of these prophetic words during my involvement in the fisher people's struggle in Kerala in the mid 1980s. It was a struggle the fisherpeople undertook to ensure their means of livelihood and to protect the sanctity of Mother Ocean, their life support. More than a political act it was an expression of coastal solidarity, not only among themselves but also with Mother Ocean, and an expression of their undying hope in a future that would provide for all God's children. The official church took many years to grasp the deeper meaning of this struggle and its theology.

Why does Rayan stress so much the struggles and movements of people? He himself tries to answer it. "To theologize is to know that God is active in our day, in our history, in all the struggles for justice, freedom and fellowship; and to join the significant movements and work at God's side".[34] Further, there lies embedded within the people's life and struggles an implicit theology as well. "In fact that is where real and relevant theologies of liberation and life sprout and grow. The praxis of and the struggle for life and liberation come first. Theology lies in solution as it were within that struggle and becomes crystallized through reflection".[35] In an article published in 1999 Rayan dwells at length on this theme. He shows the vital link between Jesus of Nazareth and peoples' struggles anywhere in the world, and suggests that these struggles are inspired and sustained by him in mysterious and hidden ways.[36] Referring to the various peoples' struggles on the Indian soil over a period – peasant struggles, women's struggles, Dalit struggles, tribal struggles, working class struggles and environmental struggles – he concludes that work for these means work for the Kingdom of God and everything Jesus stood for.

If struggle is the starting point of theology, then the question arises: who is a theologian? The subject and author of theology in the first place is undoubtedly the poor and oppressed who struggle. Then what role do the professional theologians or theological experts have? "They too are doers of theology in the measure in which they participate in the struggle against forces which dehumanize and in the effort to build the new earth. The people can use the experts' skills in articulating, arranging and systematizing, if need be, the theology which shapes up in the womb of historical praxis. Experts are theological midwives".[37]

Theology, for Rayan, is no mere cerebral exercise an academician engages in. The vital link of theology with the transformation of the world we live in runs through all his writings. What gives credence to this passion for transformation is the Christian symbol of the Reign of God. "What faith in the Kingdom can offer is an orientation and a vision, a sense of direction and of values, motivation and the assurance of a hope that wins. It can enable us and sustain our courage. It can commit us to sustained efforts to bring about transformation in a particular direction. But, the tools of analysis and action must come from the sciences".[38] Here, Rayan is realistic about the scope and the limitation of theology, and shows his conviction about the interdisciplinary character of any theological project.

I would add a word of caution about the one-sided emphasis on 'people's struggle'. The term 'struggle' is increasingly being used in today's socio-political context, but not necessarily at the service of love or justice. It is being exploited to promote selfish or divisive goals, as we often observe at the Jantar Mantar in Delhi. A more critical view of 'struggle' is necessary.

Broadening the Meaning of Scripture as a Source of Theology

The primary sources of the Christian theology are always the Christian scriptures and the tradition. Rayan affirms the core principle that the Sacred Scripture is 'the soul of theology' (*DV* 24). "God is experienced as a partner in every striving against forces of death and domination.

Concern for life is the key to the theological process. 'I have come that they may have life and have it in abundance' (John 10:10), said Jesus. Was it not his sensitivity and commitment to live at all levels beginning with the basic and the physical that made him such a master of God-talk?"[39] Rayan consciously and insightfully broadens our understanding of 'source'; he brings in as active ingredients the Indian/Asian scriptures, spiritual history, mythical narratives and ritual traditions in his theological project. Indian spiritual texts like the Upanishads and the Bhagavad Gita frequently enrich his reflections.

A referral to scriptures is certainly the identifying mark of any theology. But why only Christian scriptures?, asks Rayan. "Other scriptures too carry the memory of encounter with the Divine in the human heart, in history, in combats for life and freedom. They too contain the Word of God. That makes our (Third World) collection of Holy scriptures much larger than that of Western Christians. And why scriptures only, when there are scriptureless primal religions and spiritualities whose followers also reflect in faith in their struggles for dignity and living space? .... The Word meets us in events and experiences which are distinctly secular and are never considered *religious*".[40]

Here we see the insight of Vatican II taken to its logical end. It says that all religions "often reflect a ray of that truth which enlightens all men", and directs us to "acknowledge, preserve and encourage the spiritual and moral truths found among non-Christians".[41] The FABC articulates it still better: "We accept them (the Great religions of Asia) as significant and positive elements in the economy of God's design of salvation... over many centuries they have been the treasury of the religious experience of our ancestors, from which our contemporaries do not cease to draw light and strength".[42] This area deserves further exploration.

The importance of the broader view of scripture became clear to me again in the coastal context of fishing communities. The coastal people embraced Christianity with the arrival of Francis Xavier in the 16th century, but the efforts of the missionaries to weed them away from their pre-Christian past hardly succeeded. Studies indicate the existence of a unique coastal culture, the *neithal* culture, and religious expression that harmonised with their geo-social environment and occupation. Coastal lore, myths and rituals, often centred on the Mother Ocean, depict the faith tradition of a people in a pre-literate society. Embracing Christianity didn't do away with their *neithal* past; what indeed happened was a superimposition of the Iberian Christian tradition over the age-old *neithal* religiosity.[43] Where to draw the dividing line between the Christian scriptures and the pre-Christian heritage of the coastal Christians? Here lies the significance of Rayan's insights on 'sources of theology'. It may raise disturbing, at times destabilizing, questions; but these need to be addressed sooner or later.

Call for a New Language and Grammar

Rayan's theology may be categorised as more narrative or poetic than conceptual. He guides us insightfully through the parables that Jesus narrated, through the mythic narrations of the Indian epics, through the stories of Gandhi and Mother Theresa, through the death-bed poems of a young girl Gitanjali. He is fond of quoting from Gerald Manley Hopkins, the Jesuit poet, and Ravindranath Tagore, the Indian bard and mystic. His poetic and mystical approach to theology has certainly evolved from a deep communion with the Master himself. He is convinced that Jesus is a marvellous story-teller, and tries to draw from that wellspring. He takes out a story at a time dissecting it with refreshing originality guiding us through profound meditation. One would miss the profundity and beauty of Rayan's theology if approached with a rational mindset.

Rayan tries to move away from an absolutizing language, and often pleads passionately for a new language of theology. "The new language will integrate the music of the different dialects into a rich symphonic composition. It will be a concrete language, a historical and committed idiom". It is the language of the poet and the artist. A poet is "a shaper and singer of our destiny", and would evoke the "mystery that has appeared in flesh, flower and fruit, the mystery that is at work in the heart of every man and woman".[44] Bible's "theology is entirely bound up with the art of poetry, metaphor and symbol, myth and parable. The book is full of verbal icons of God and of people". Theology is more and deeper than merely scientific; it has to be artistic. Art enables us to see the world more truly and more deeply. "Beyond and within the commonly observed surface reality of things lies the realm that science tackles. Further or deeper still glows the sphere of meaning with which the artistic is concerned. In the inmost depths of all this throbs the mystical, the divine touch, the great Presence.... The function of art and religion is to equip people to see with the heart instead of with the eyes; to see with 'the divine eye' which the Lord gifts to people".[45] Here Rayan sounds more like a mystical theologian in the great tradition of Christian mystics. Theology's task is to help people see with the heart, to look at the human context through the divine eye.

Unity of Theology and Spirituality

Theology, for Rayan, is far from a cerebral exercise; it engages the whole human person and every human faculty. He narrates in his trademark poetic style: "In theology we need to use the language of the heart, of the hands, of the womb; a body language, an embodied language like stories and parables and myths and metaphors. The language of folk song and dance, popular celebrations and festivals, picture and sculpture would be fine media for the articulation of the faith as it is lived and grasped in depth within our concrete situations. God is love; the appropriate language of God-talk will be the language of love and silence, and the language of symbols".[46] Here the separation between theology and philosophy, theology and art, theology and spirituality, etc. fades away. There emerges the unity of all these. He writes: "Our methodology has restored us to the ancient unity of theology and spirituality, which had flourished before theology moved out of the warmth of (monastic) piety into the cold halls of academic rationality. 'Theology is spiritual activity, a function of our faith in Christ, interior to our faith union in God.... By the same token we have come to discover the close relatedness of spirituality and politics, contemplation and commitment, our understanding of God and the conflictual process of becoming human".[47]

Rayan's fascination with *apophatic* (or negative) theology comes through in his reflections, though never developed fully. This is most evident when he discusses the book of Job. After discussing the two phases in Job's own theological journey Rayan concludes: "Apophatic theology is welcome back. Our ancestors, the Seers and Rishis, faced with the real beyond name and form, kept repeating *Neti Neti* (*na iti, na iti*), 'Not thus, Not thus', but always other and greater, and greater still".[48] He seems to imply that the *apophatic* method of theology, rather than the western *cataphatic* (or affirmative) method, contributes to the making of an Indian Theology. It would resonate better with the Indian mode of thinking. He concludes that "mystics are uncompromisingly apophatic".

Philosophy, Theology, and Imagination

An article which Rayan wrote in 2001 with the title "Philosophy and Theology" is a bold attempt at articulating the contours of his theological method. Classical theology incorporated philosophy as its handmaid; but philosophy is understood primarily as the Aristotelian Greek model which became the foundation for much of modern western philosophy, and hence of theology. Rayan takes a critical look at the whole framework and asks the question: "which philosophy do we have in mind? There are many philosophies, and each may relate to theology in a different way". He makes a global survey of philosophies - East Asian, South Asian, West Asian, Western as well as various forms of modern and contemporary philosophies - in order to prove his point.[49]

The point he wants to make is this; there is no one philosophy that theology interacts with in all times and places. Each culture has given rise to its own philosophy. He emphasizes the rich philosophical traditions in India and the different *margas* or ways of salvation, and states: "In the Asian context, especially in South Asia, there is no clear division between philosophy and theology, or theology and spirituality and spirituality and mysticism. They feed into each other and may never be separated. Spirituality, theology, mysticism, philosophy – all are interrelated".[50] Here he joins the company of many Indian theologians who struggle to clarify the Indian way of thinking vis-a-vis the Western. Amaladoss quotes A. K. Ramanujan to clarify the contrast: the western way of thinking is context free, while the Indian way of thinking is context sensitive. Amaladoss concludes: "The Asian way of thinking is holistic and integrated, experiencing reality as one and interdependent. It uses symbols that seek to seize reality imaginatively in its lived complexity.... A narrative method is more suitable to speak about life than a logical network of concepts.... It is praxis-oriented rather than merely theoretical".[51] Rayan's theological venture has to be understood against this Indian/ Asian way of thinking.

While admitting the value of reason and of being reasonable, he affirms that "we are not simply a bit of reason". He laments the tendency to marginalize other human faculties like intuition, emotion and imagination. "Without intuition reason could be lame, even dangerous. A great deal of truth is attained through intuition.... Poetic souls, feminine spirits especially, work with intuition.... Faith and reason, yes! But 'Faith, Reason and Intuition' should be better. And better still if emotion too is taken into account.... Moreover, there is imagination, without which theology, even philosophy, would be lame".[52]

Conclusion

George Gispert-Sauch, a long time associate of Samuel Rayan, insightfully writes that his writings "contain a passionate call for solidarity with the poor, and a strong critique of colonialism, various policies of the Catholic Church, and capitalist culture".[53] That is a skilful way of presenting Rayan's approach to theology in a nutshell. Rayan is deeply rooted in the Indian soil, yet his theological concerns span through countries and continents. The perspective, however, remains the same – that of the poor and those who struggle in hope. Here we can see clearly a theologian trying passionately to give wings to some basic insights of the Vatican II from an Indian/ Asian standpoint. There are obvious loose ends, sure. He was not well equipped to base his exploration of implicit theologies on sound empirical data; but that is the task left to us. The possibilities opened up provide us with hope – and responsibility.

In the concluding section of one of his articles Rayan writes: "I have provided you with some bricks with which you could possibly build something beautiful".[54] Looking back at the end of this study I too would say, yes, Rayan has provided us with some bricks or building blocks, and it is up to us to put them to effective use in the construction of a theology that is rooted in our Indian/Asian context, and capable of responding to the human quest for the good news of salvation and fullness of life. This study may add in a small way, I hope, to that collective task awaiting us.

Notes

1. Samuel Rayan, "Re-conceiving Theology in the Asian Context", in Kurien Kunnumpuram, (ed.), *Collected Writings of Samuel Rayan, SJ, Volume II: Doing Theology: Indian Christian Reflections on Theologizing in India Today*, Delhi: ISPCK, 2013, p. 241.
2. Samuel Rayan, "Doing Theology in India", in *Doing Theology*, p. 16.
3. Samuel Rayan, "Irruption of the Poor: A Challenge to Theology", in *Doing Theology*, p. 182.
4. Samuel Rayan, "Decolonization of Theology", in *Doing Theology*, p. 42.
5. *Ibid.* p. 30.
6. *Ibid.* p. 35.
7. Samuel Rayan, "Philosophy and Theology", in *Doing Theology*, p. 178.
8. Samuel Rayan, "Theologian As Disciple – Disciple As Theologian", in *Doing Theology*, p. 49.
9. *Ibid.* p. 50.
10. *Ibid.* p. 49.
11. Samuel Rayan, "Analysis of Society and Indian Theology", in *Doing Theology*, p. 157.
12. Samuel Rayan, "Re-conceiving Theology in the Asian Context", in *Doing Theology*, pp. 241 ff.
13. *Ibid.* p. 250.
14. *Ibid.* pp. 250-51.
15. *Ibid.* p. 261.
16. Samuel Rayan, "Doing Theology in India", in *Doing Theology*, p. 20.
17. *Ibid.* p. 21.
18. Samuel Rayan, "People's Theology", in *Doing Theology*, p. 100.
19. *Ibid.* p. 103.
20. For further details on this, see P. T. Mathew, *We Dare the Waters – The World and the Worldview of Mukkuvar*, Chennai: University of Madras, 2011, Ch. 7.
21. *Neithal* refers to the coastal tract, one of the five geographical and cultural zones mentioned in the *Sangam* poetry.
22. Samuel Rayan, "Commonalities, Divergences, and Cross-fertilization among Third World Theologies", in *Doing Theology*, p. 319.

23. Samuel Rayan, "The 'How' of Third World Theologies", in *Doing Theology,* pp. 288-89.
24. Samuel Rayan, "Outside the Gate, Sharing Insults", in Kurien Kunnumpuram (ed.), *Selected Writings of Samuel Rayan, Vol 1: Jesus – The Relevance of His Person and Message for Our Times*, Mumbai: St. Pauls, 2011, pp. 266 ff.
25. *Ibid.* pp. 293-294.
26. Samuel Rayan, "Theological Priorities in India Today", in *Doing Theology,* p. 104.
27. Samuel Rayan, "The Irruption of the Third World – A Challenge to Theology", in *Doing Theology*, p. 279.
28. Samuel Rayan, "Theological Priorities in India Today", in *Doing Theology,* p. 110.
29. Vatican II, *Lumen Gentium,* no. 12.
30. Samuel Rayan, "Theological Priorities in India Today", in *Doing Theology,* p. 112.
31. Samuel Rayan, "Analysis of Society and Indian Theology", in *Doing Theology,* pp. 160-61.
32. Samuel Rayan, "People's Theology", in *Doing Theology,* p. 101.
33. *Ibid.* p. 102.
34. *Ibid.*
35. Samuel Rayan, "Analysis of Society and Indian Theology", in *Doing Theology,* p. 159.
36. Samuel Rayan, "Jesus and the Struggles of the Masses in India" in *Jesus,* p. 234.
37. Samuel Rayan, "Analysis of Society and Indian Theology", in *Doing Theology,* p. 160.
38. Samuel Rayan, "The Kingdom of God – A Blueprint for a New Society", in by Kurien Kunnumpuram (ed.), *Selected Writings of Samuel Rayan SJ, Vol. III: The Mission of the Church – Christian Reflection on Evangelization in India Today,* Mumbai: St. Pauls, 2013, p. 231.
39. Samuel Rayan, "Commonalities, Divergences and Cross-fertilization among Third World Theologies", in *Doing Theology*, p. 326.
40. Samuel Rayan, "The How of Third World Theologies", in *Doing Theology,* p. 301.
41. Vatican II, *Nostra Aetate,* no 2.
42. "Evangelization in Modern Day Asia" (Statements and Recommendations of the 1st Plenary Assembly of the FABC, Taipei, 1974), in *For All Peoples of Asia*, Vol. I, Manila: IMG Publ., 1984, p. 30.
43. For details see P. T. Mathew, *We Dare the Waters*, Ch. 2.
44. Samuel Rayan, "Theological Priorities in India Today", in *Doing Theology,* p. 116.

45. Samuel Rayan, "Art and Theology", in *Doing Theology,* pp. 147-48.
46. Samuel Rayan, "Analysis of Society and Indian Theology", in *Doing Theology,* p. 163.
47. Samuel Rayan, "Third World Theology: Where Do We Go From Here?", in *Doing Theology*, p. 339.
48. Samuel Rayan, "Wrestling in the Night", in *Doing Theology,* p. 58. *Apophatic theology* is an attempt to describe God by what cannot be said of Him. This method was popular among theologians such as Tertullian, St. Cyril of Jerusalem and the Cappodocian Fathers, and continues to be influential in some Eastern churches. *Brihadaranyaka Upanishad* describes Brahman as 'neti-neti', or 'neither this nor that', and it is as an example of *apophatic theology.*
49. Samuel Rayan, "Theologian As Disciple – Disciple As Theologian", in *Doing Theology*, p. 47.
50. Samuel Rayan, "Philosophy and Theology", in *Doing Theology,* p. 166.
51. Michael Amaladoss, "Asian Theological Trends" in Felix Wilfred (ed.), *The Oxford Handbook of Christianity in Asia*, New York: Oxford Univ. Press, 2014, p. 105. See also his *Quest for God – Doing Theology in India*, Anand: Gujarat Sahitya Prakash, 2013, pp. 135ff.
52. Samuel Rayan, "Philosophy and Theology", in *Doing Theology*, pp. 176-7.
53. George Gispert-Sauch, "Asian Theology", in David F. Ford (ed.), *The Modern Theologians,* Cambridge: Blackwell Publ., 1997, p. 460.
54. Samuel Rayan, "Philosophy and Theology", in *Doing Theology*, p. 180.

18

The Art and Science of Theology

Keith D'Souza, SJ

Should theology be more of an art than a science? This is a theme question which is central to the writings of Samuel Rayan. Rayan seems to plump for theology being more of an art, as compared to a science. He has numerous reasons in support of this conviction, some of which will be presented in this essay. Moving beyond the writings of Rayan, we will explore the implications of this question, arriving at a nuanced and mediatory position with regard to the identity or nature of theology, in relationship to the disciplines or nature of art and science.

1. The nature of theology: The problematic

At first glance, the word theology connotes a discipline which has to do with the scientific examination (*logos*) of data related to the divine dimension (*theos*) of life. However, unlike other regular sciences which have the appendage *logos*, theology is unique in that the subject matter—or the objective data under consideration—is not as empirically or tangibly available for public scrutiny.

Theology is clearly different from the 'hard' or natural sciences, which are comparatively more objective, neutral and universal in their approach. Thus, it hardly makes sense to talk of a Christian biology or a Christian geology, but it is quite normal to speak of a Christian theology. Theology is apparently more akin to the soft or human or social sciences, where it is indeed possible to speak of a Christian anthropology or a Christian psychology. However, it is more appropriate to place the discipline of theology within the humanities or the 'arts', because it is primarily a discipline which has to do with literature—in this case, religious literature—or records of events, experiences and reflections which are expressed or articulated in literary form. In this preliminary sense, then, theology is more of an 'art' than a 'science'.

The word 'art' is derived from the "Latin *artem* accusative of *ars* skill. The Latin *ars* is related to *artus* joint, *arma* tools, weapons, and is cognate with Greek *arariskein* to fit, *artyein* arrange, prepare, and Sanskrit *rta* fit".[1] The word 'science' is derived from the "Latin *scientia* knowledge, from *sciens* (genitive *scientis*), present participle of *scire* to know, perhaps originally meaning to separate, divide, related to *scindere* to cut, split".[2] The distinction between the sciences and the arts into two separate fields of knowledge arose only in the modern period of Western history, with the ascendency of the age of reason.[3]

While both art and science are skills, from the root meanings of the words above it clear that art is considered to be more of a practical skill derived from human labour, as opposed to science which is a theoretical skill applied to the world of nature—including, by extension, human nature. Etymologically and historically speaking, the active nature of art may be easily contrasted with the relatively passive nature of science, as in the latter one does not create the object of one's labour, but relative to the arts, dispassionately observes and explores its nature and dynamics. However, beyond the etymological and traditional understanding of art and science, there have been significant shifts in the way these disciplines have been understood over time. As a result the aesthetic world cannot be said to be entirely without objective standards or criteria of judgement.[4] Similarly, the world of scientific investigation has progressed much beyond the passive nuances associated with its objective and empirical character. Contemporary philosophy of science has elucidated the active role of theoretical or conceptual production—the creation of intellectual frameworks or paradigms—which influences the way in which data is experienced and processed.

Within the history of theology itself there have been significant shifts in understanding the primary locus of the discipline along the wide spectrum from art on the one hand to science on the other. Thus, the question as to whether theology is an art or a science cannot easily be given a trans temporal or trans contextual answer, as factors such as time, context (location and situation) and agency or authorship all come into play while attempting an answer. Also, the specific type of theology undertaken will lend itself more towards a science or an art, depending on its subject matter and orientation. Historical, biblical, liturgical, moral and juridical theology would lend themselves more to description, explanation, elucidation, exegesis, validation, etc., while foundational, systematic and spiritual theology would allow for more of a focus on understanding, application, inspiration, etc., and thus feature comparatively more literary flourish.

One of the better known major differences in theological method was that between the Alexandrian and Antiochian schools. Beyond the specific Christological controversy—about the nature of Christ—with which the distinction between these schools is emphasized, in general, the Alexandrian school, influenced by neo-Platonism, was more oriented towards speculative, symbolic (allegorical) and mystical theological interpretations, whereas the Antiochian school was more oriented towards abstract, reflective and literal interpretations. The latter school gradually gained ascendency, and by the time of the high Scholasticism of the thirteenth and fourteenth centuries, theology came to be understood more as a scientific—methodical, abstract, systematic—discipline rather than as one more aligned to the creative, speculative, symbolic literary arts. However, as Wolfhart Pannenberg points out, before this time of Scholastic prevalence, "Christian teaching, under the influence of Augustine, had been regarded as *sapientia*, in sharp distinction from *scientia*".[5]The former approach was more wisdom-oriented while the latter became more discipline-oriented, with the emergence of theological schools, systems and compendiums, such as Aquinas' *Summa Theologiae*.

Engaging with Rayan's corpus of works entails both a scientific and an artistic approach. The scientific approach entails a systematic and critical analysis of the works of Rayan. This objective process may throw up both areas of insight as well as blind spots and limitations in Rayan's thinking. The artistic approach entails a sympathetic appreciation of the contribution of Rayan's aesthetic manner of theological composition, as well as the unique and creative style of the critic or author. What follows, then, is on the one hand an objective, systematic and critical representation of the framework and trajectory of Rayan's theological contribution, and on the other, an assessment of this contribution featuring a preferred style of argumentation, from within a particular perspective.

2. Samuel Rayan on the nature of theology

There is a perceptible ambivalence in the writings of Samuel Rayan with regard to the nature of theological expression. On the one hand, he wants to propose a programme of theological articulation that is clearly aesthetically oriented, with many dimensions of art forms involved. On the other hand, there is an equally strong critical theological agenda that he wishes to pursue, with many dimensions of social critique involved. He seems to be equally passionate about both of these theological interests and projects, thus implying that for him theology entails both artistic as well as scientific dimensions.

2.1 An aesthetic programme

Perhaps the most seminal of Rayan's works with respect to the nature and typology of theological discourse is the article titled, "Theology as Art".[6] In this he systematically argues that theology be considered more as an artistic or intuitive enterprise rather than a scientific or rational one: "In our hands the Word-Become-Flesh has become fleshless words, thin, flat words, distinct, clean and cold".[7] In contrast to this he prefers a theology that uses "myths, images, fables and legends... poems and parables, sayings and songs".[8] Besides these, "Paintings, sculpture and dolls no less than dance, music and poetry could also be theological statements".[9]

Rayan is impressed with the artistic mode of theological presentation in the Gospels, and asks, "Could we someday decide to produce some Birds-and-Flowers kind of theology?",[10] keeping in mind Matthew's Sermon on the Mount (Mt. 6: 25-34). He is likewise in favour of "Mark's Gospel that speaks in theatrical terms", and

John's Gospel, which "tends to fall naturally into a dramatic mould". He follows up with a programmatic question: "How is it that though John has always been acclaimed as a theologian of rare power and appeal; we have not cared to pause and consider his approach as suggestive and challenging for our own theology?"

In keeping with this aesthetic criterion for theologizing, Rayan's canon of theologians does not only include those at the centre of theological discourse, but even those who live at the periphery, and who may arguably be considered marginal or merely popular theologians. Among these number painters like Jyoti Sahi, poets like Tagore and Gitanjali Ghei[11] and literary composers like G. K. Chesterton.[12] While pointing out these many examples of alternative forms of theological communication, he asks plaintively, "Why don't we express our theology in art form, in poetry, in drama? And why do we exclude dance from our theology and our worship? Some rethinking could be done at this level".[13] His question springs from his conviction that, "Art... is sacramental, and that precisely is what theology is meant to be and hopes to become".[14]

Rayan is opposed to an "a priori, doctrinal, abstract"[15] approach, and prefers an approach which "starts from the concrete reality" of experience, which is "subversive of abstract principles".[16] He highlights two phases within the experience-based approach: "The first phase raises questions, seeks to criticize and to unravel, to speak and to formulate. It then deepens into the second phase, which is one of contemplation, adoration and silence".[17] The first phase would entail reflective mechanisms, but these mechanisms need not be restricted to Western philosophical and theological categories, rooted in a particular cultural framework. Rayan contends that the root of the problem of non-aesthetic theological expression may lie in its heavy reliance on Greek philosophical categories. While commenting on John Paul II's *Fides et Ratio*, he argues that while "the use of Greek philosophy by the Greek and some Western fathers is providential", by implication, "Christianity, the Christian faith and grace, brought to this earth by an Asian, a West Asian named Jesus of Nazareth", needs similar articulation with the help of Asian categories and ways of thinking. Thus, while in the West, much is made about the binary opposition between faith and reason, Rayan wants to include other neglected human epistemic features into the faith-reason dynamic: "along with reason, then, we must think about intuition, imagination and emotion, which can make positive contributions to the understanding and restructuring of reality, especially of social reality".[18]

Besides the use of intuition, imagination and emotion, Rayan adds a few more methods, concerns and criteria which are more central to the Asian way of philosophizing and theologizing. Among these is attention to the mystical dimension, which has received marginal treatment in Western theology. Also, rather than employ philosophical energy in exploring the nature of reality in terms of ultimate causes, he asks, "Should not philosophy be redefined as search for humanisation and meaning? In which case, there is an immediate and direct relationship between philosophy and theology".[19] This earthy approach that he advocates is best communicated via the many means of visual, plastic, dramatic, and literary art forms pointed out above. By advocating an emphasis on experience, intuition, imagination and emotion—and the artistic means through which these may be communicated—as a complement to faith, Rayan hopes to circumvent the unnecessary opposition between faith and reason that has resulted from the culture wars in the West over the past half millennium.

Rayan ends his article, "Theology as Art", with a plea, viz., "that we begin to treat theology as an Art rather than as a science".[20] Rayan does not have a problem with science itself as a legitimate intellectual discipline. In fact, he appreciatively points out that, "Whether it is the science of archaeology, chemistry, botany, physics or astronomy, theology is glad that the human being has the call to investigate, to follow and find the truth".[21] However, Rayan is clearly unhappy that the discipline of *theology* has gradually metamorphosed into a science.

2.2 A critical programme

While Rayan is well-known to accentuate the aesthetic programme of theological articulation, he is equally eager to introduce key critical themes into his theological programme. While he does not seem to use the word, his theological locus is a subaltern one, in dialectical tension or opposition with a socially or theologically antagonistic position perceived as Western, colonial, patriarchal, hierarchical, clerical, supremacist, racist, capitalist, elitist, individualistic and scientifically and rationally driven, i.e., "other-worldly, abstract and discarnate".[22] In contrast to this seemingly dysfunctional social or theological orientation, the alternative theological framework that he attempts to develop is Asian, Indian, contextual, postcolonial, gender-sensitive, participatory (democratic), egalitarian, socialist, popular, liberationist, communitarian, practical, aesthetic and mystical.

To begin with, Rayan brings in the heavily relationship-oriented consciousness central to Asian theological concerns when he ponders over Anselm's well-known definition of theology as "faith seeking understanding". According to Rayan, "The 'understanding' which this faith-love seeks has little to do with conceptual abstractions and academic systematization... It is like a friend's understanding of his friend, appreciating, respecting and supporting his person and his options. Or, it is like a father's understanding of his children with their needs, fears, fancies and sorrows".[23]

Besides this foundational Asian emphasis on relating more than knowing, perhaps the most obvious Asian theological concern is that of social justice, given the many types and layers of social inequality that persist in Asian countries. Accordingly, Rayan asks, "Should we not rather think of theology as 'faith seeking justice', faith seeking the dignity and honour of every woman and man', faith seeking social transformation', 'faith seeking the transformation of humankind into the family of the Father of Jesus Christ'."[24] However, for Rayan, "liberation theology is not the only theology in the Third World. Here is among the poor a theology of the beautiful in creation and in human relationships; a theology of hospitality and solidarity; a theology of joy and celebration even in the midst of oppression and suffering".[25]

The practical and social dimensions of theology necessary for an Asian and an Indian mode of theologizing are then evident: "In doing theology the primacy of praxis over theory is affirmed, and the primacy of social analysis and involvement over detached philosophical speculation".[26] It is clear, then, that Rayan does not only advocate a benignly aesthetic approach to theology, but also sees the wisdom in employing the historical and critical approaches adopted by rigorous social scientific investigation.

2.3 Critique of Rayan's position

Samuel Rayan is perhaps one of the clearest theologians I have ever read. He sets us all an example as to how abstruse notions can be expressed in simple terms. Even though he is averse to the quest for clear and distinct ideas—because of its Cartesian presuppositions and implications—he himself is very clear and distinct in his articulation.

Rayan's heavy use of symbolic expression in his writings supports the validity of the proposal of theology being more properly an art rather than a science. To have a greater impact on contemporary society, the use of artistic means is extremely expedient. While Pope John Paul II's—or even Pope Benedict XVI's—stylistic approach is in general very scientific and erudite, Pope Francis' communicative actions seem to have a much wider appeal, and thereby a much wider influence. The social and pastoral responsibility of the theologian must not be forgotten at the altar of academic excellence and acceptance in the exclusive world of the theological guild. Thus, besides aspiring for peer review for academic excellence, there needs to be a simultaneous public review for pastoral and social effectiveness. In this regard, those communities in which faith is alive offer a salubrious and potent working condition for the exploration of newer and more insightful theological ideas. A living faith is a good testing ground for theological insight and ingenuity. Those communities in which faith is lax or has lapsed would be arguably better served and revived by theological contributions which stir the heart rather than the head alone—a task eminently more suitable via artistic rather than scientific means.

With regard to his content, Rayan may be described as a polemical theologian, and more specifically, an aesthetic or critical apologist. He seems to have a clear sparring opponent in mind, whether he is advocating an aesthetic or critical theology. This is because, like most theologians, he is a child of his times. He lived through the pain of the Second World War and the agony of colonization. He is witness to the visible misery of the masses, the mindless insensitivity towards nature in the name of scientific and material development and various forms of discrimination. Small wonder, then, that for him theology may not resort to an intellectual or subliminal escape into the world of an abstract matrix of ideas. Theology needs to address the pain and anguish of a broken world, through a scathing critique of those conditions and circumstances which lead to this brokenness and anguish.

The post-Vatican II sensitivity of and openness towards both the secular world and a trans-European and trans-Christian world seemed to influence theologians like Rayan, who took this opportunity to express theology from within a perspective that was hitherto considered subaltern to the grander Eurocentric and ecclesiocentric narrative. This is why Rayan supported theological inculturation—theologizing which takes a particular locus or context seriously—as a happier regional alternative to universal and abstract theological speculation.

Rayan likely went through a philosophical and theological formation which was heavily cognitively biased, and probably featured the abstract, conceptual, foreign, system-based theological articulation which he militates against. It is an over accentuation of these more cognitively-oriented metaphysical and clinical approaches to theology that was perhaps one of the reasons that led him to stress the more affectively-oriented symbolic and mystical approaches and the volitionally-oriented critical and practical approaches that he later advocated as a methodological alternative.

What is Rayan's unique contribution to theology? Between Rayan the critical theologian and Rayan the aesthetic theologian, the aesthetic contribution would seem to feature as a more unique one, for the primary reason that critical theology has innumerable advocates, whereas aesthetic theology has comparatively very few, both nationally and internationally. Rayan would be more like an Indian version of Hans Urs von Balthasar—both of them sharing a minority position—who similarly stands out strongly in favour of a more aesthetic, practical and spiritual approach to theology as opposed to the dominant cognitive, scientific, historical and critical approaches employed. However, unlike Balthasar, Rayan is more expressive of historical and critical analyses from a subaltern position. Rayan could have, however, attempted to bridge the gap between the aesthetic and the critical, by demonstrating how the former could be used in favour of the latter. This is what Jesus does in numerous places in the Gospels, by providing metaphors and parables which are often counter cultural and aimed at enhancing personal and social sensitivity. A more recent example may be found in the teachings and writings of Anthony De'Mello, which featured powerful messages critical of a rigid, exclusivist or xenophobic mindset, via the apparently innocent medium of stories.[27] While Rayan sometimes mentions the link between the aesthetic and the critical dimensions of theology, he does not seem to systematically develop or employ it in his own works. The development of this theme could feature as one of the more promising contributions of Asian and Indian theologizing.

A contentious feature in Rayan's works is an apparent conflation of theology with spirituality. For example, he poetically states that, "somewhere in the caverns of the heart, the sources of artistic and theological activity meet and mingle".[28] Also, in one of his many definitions of theology he nominates the discipline as "a religious-spiritual activity".[29] Furthermore, he often presents the Gospels as theological texts,[30] rather than the more widely accepted understanding of them as spiritual or inspirational or revelatory texts. By considering theological literature in a similar vein to spiritual literature, he risks the loss of objectivity that one usually associates with scholarly, objective and scientific approaches in theology. In Paul Ricoeur's terms, this approach would result in a lack of sufficient 'distanciation' of the text from its author or reader.[31] Within the hermeneutical spectrum from understanding on the one hand to explanation and critique on the other, Rayan seems to place this 'spirituality-theology' more along the lines of understanding, rather than making sufficient space for explanation and critique. His position is akin to that of Hans Georg Gadamer, who in his magnum opus, *Truth and Method*, proposes that the social sciences and the humanities need to be understood more along the lines of intuitive, inter-subjective and tradition-based processes, rather than objective and methodical processes more proper for the natural sciences.[32]

Yet another contentious approach proposed by Rayan is to reduce theology to a practical project, and thereby minimize its value in terms of theoretical analysis and speculation. In one text, Rayan criticizes Aristotle for being a successful metaphysician who is able to thoroughly examine the root causes of the material world, but is unsuccessful as a social philosopher, as he seemed to justify slavery and gender inequality, rather than likewise successfully examine their root causes.[33] But, Rayan seems to be in the exact opposite camp: he seems to successfully examine the root causes of social anomalies, but is reluctant to engage in traditional theological or metaphysical speculation. However, the link between practical action and its metaphysical moorings could also feature as a wholesome theological pathway to tread. This is because praxis involves not just social and pastoral engagement, but a change of perspective that arises as an ongoing and cumulative result of this engagement. This change of perspective comes not just from experience, but largely from reflection over experience, guided by an undergirding set of presuppositions and assumptions. Thus, reflection has to do not only with proximate causes, but also with universal final and formal causes—the meat and substance of speculative activity, which may be found, for example, in the technical working out of the dialectical and historical materialism espoused by Marx.

Rayan's preferred starting point for theologizing is connected with this practical import. He is right in claiming that theology should not only be conceptually focused but needs to also have practical goals, e.g., "to enable people live authentically and joyfully as human beings and believers".[34] But the claim that follows, viz., that "That is why our starting-point is not concepts but reality, life and history"[35] may be justifiably disputed.If the term 'starting point' simply refers to a preferred methodological point of departure on a theological project, this may be quite legitimate. But, one suspects that Rayan wants to privilege "reality, life and history" over the theological worldview or perspective through which one encounters these phenomena. However, one does not view reality, life and history from the perspective of a *tabula rasa*, but phenomenologically speaking, there is already a cultural and personal experiential and ideational framework through which all of these are encountered and articulated. The many faith presuppositions—or subconscious affirmations—which Rayan had cumulatively developed over the years would qualify as equal parameters or vectors in terms of theological starting points, whether he was aware of them or not. In fact, as has been demonstrated earlier, Rayan views reality not neutrally, but via the powerful prisms of his aesthetic and critical perspectives. Here traditional thinkers like Gadamer are right in affirming the role of the past in cumulatively forming our consciousness. Part of this past is indeed born of experience, but a large part of it is the 'effective historical' intellectual residue which we share with members of the multiple communities to which we belong and with which we are connected.

Finally, Rayan often seems to subscribe to radical binary oppositions based on substantial generalizations, and in so doing, perhaps falls into the same trap he advises against, viz., modernist hegemony, which favours one extreme position over the other, without easy admittance of nuances in between. This may amount to a form of reverse theological discrimination. Admission of nuances between extreme positions would have perhaps made Rayan—and his theological project—more acceptable to both Indian and international readers. Preferential options need not—and ought not—blind us to the gray areas of life, or worse, result in ideological sloganeering, which is sometimes the bane of positioned theologizing.

3. Theology as art and science

To ascertain whether theology is either an art or a science—or to adjudicate over the issue without introducing some form of nuance—would be to subscribe to an unnecessary binary opposition which contemporary postmodern thought precisely and quite justifiably militates against. It is more helpful, rather, to consider a range or *spectrum* of possible positions with regard to theological articulation between scientific expression on the one hand and artistic or aesthetic expression on the other.

The issue becomes even more complex when one considers the very nature of the sciences and the arts themselves. Here too, arriving at a clear and specific delineation between these two fields is not so easy. There are different professional views regarding what constitutes genuine science and what is genuine art. Science as a deductive enterprise following the ancient and medieval formal and final cause oriented approach is long gone. Science has become more inductive and also 'softer' over the years, both in its theoretical and in its empirical certitude. Speaking specifically about the relationship between theology and the sciences, David Munchin points out that, "the fact that natural science is constantly changing, sometimes in a way which repudiates previously strongly held theories, should serve as a warning to those who criticize theology for not having an easily identifiable and unshifting core paradigm, by demonstrating that change and revision is always a product of the scientific method".[36] Accordingly, discussions in the philosophy of science—dealing with the nature and scope of science—over the past half century have much to contribute to the progressive development of the understanding of the nature of theology.

The 'arts' too have undergone significant shifts in understanding over the centuries, far beyond the limited range of literary, visual and plastic creativity with which the word is more generally associated today. The 'arts' is an umbrella term within which non-empirical axiomatic systems like mathematics as well as the soft sciences take refuge at the professional level. The conception and execution of many art forms demand methodical attention, rigour and expertise—traits which one usually associates with the scientific enterprise. As in science, reputation and recognition concerning proficiency in the arts is also a matter which entails common and public social processes and social acceptance.

Given this contemporary scenario, to put up a fight against the notion of theology as a science—and preferring, as Rayan would, to propose it as more of an art—would amount to engaging in a bout with a straw man. Douglas MacIntosh argues that theology can indeed be legitimately considered a science:

> The question to be faced is as to whether theology, understood thus as description of the divine reality, can be made truly scientific. And what we mean by "scientific" is not merely logical in the older deductive sense, i.e., consistent with presuppositions. Ancient and mediaeval science, modeled upon the geometrical method, was essentially abstract, *apriori*, unempirical. With its formal, deductive

logic it was an instrument of criticism and discovery within but narrow limits. It was the lesser organ of exact knowledge. Modern science, with its concrete, empirical, inductive method, is an instrument of criticism and discovery within limits set only by human experience itself. It is, as Francis Bacon called it, the *novumorganum*, the new and greater organ of exact knowledge.[37]

Many of the terms which Rayan associates with a wholesome theology features in this description of modern science as presented by MacIntosh: concrete, empirical, inductive, experience-based—as opposed to the abstract, *apriori*, unempirical and narrow approach of the older scientific method. Having said this, a distinction may still be made with regard to the dominant styles and purposes or intentions of scientific and artistic representation. On the one hand scientific modes of representation aim to clarify, explain, expose, illustrate, enlighten, argue, invent, etc., while artistic modes of representation aim to express, inspire, energize, reveal, move to action, etc. The former employs distinctively cognitive and argumentative means of presentation while the latter employs primarily emotive, affective and volitional means of presentation.

Two types of questions may be asked with respect to these two broad modes of theological expression. The first is a descriptive one, viz., has theology historically adopted largely a scientific style of discourse or an artistic one? The second is a normative or prescriptive one, viz., should there be a preferential option for one style over the other? As we shall see, the answers to both of these questions involve significant nuance.

Historically, there has been a wide spectrum of theological writing, from the very scientific and abstract on the one hand, to the very artistic and symbolic on the other. The scriptures themselves—if they are accepted as theological literature, as Rayan does—bear witness to the variety of styles within this spectrum, from more historical and prescriptive pericopes to more metaphorical and inspirational ones. The style of Augustine is less discursive or didactic and more inspirational, as compared to the style of Aquinas, who writes from a more philosophically developed and sophisticated perspective. Nearer to our times, the encyclicals and public discourses of Pope Francis and Pope John Paul II may serve as good exemplars of these two quite different styles and emphases of theological appeal—the former artistic and literary; the latter more scientific and discursive.

Thus, both artistic and scientific styles have been employed in the history of theological composition. This brings us to the second question, viz., should a theologian or a particular community make a theological option vis-à-vis scientific or artistic representation? While answering this question, one needs to keep in mind that theology is largely articulated from within a particular cultural context, and to satisfy a particular cultural need. Whether it is scientific or artistic is thus secondary, as compared to many preliminary or prior questions, viz., what are the literary abilities of the theological agent, what is the audience under consideration, what is the social situation that needs healing, etc.? Perhaps the most important consideration concerns the salient features of the context within which the text is composed.

While addressing an Asian or Indian audience, there are several cultural features or factors that need to be considered while composing theological literature. Firstly, the language used needs to be simple and direct. This is especially important in an oral tradition, in which the subtleties and convolutions permissible and even expected in a written tradition may be considered excessive and even dull.[38] Secondly, the use of illustrations by way of analogies, examples, narratives, anecdotal testimony, etc., all help to bolster the relevance and import of the theological message. Asian and Indian psychology is largely intuitive and 'right-brained'. Hence, long and abstruse argumentation often seems pompous and unnecessarily verbose, if not supplemented by these helpful illustrations. Thirdly, theological communication would need to have a clearly relevant and practical dimension to it. Indian philosophy in general has a practical orientation, striving to overcome ignorance so as to attain the higher good of spiritual enlightenment and eventual liberation. Speculation and argumentation for the sake of engaging in theological niceties or for excellence in academic performance alone would be considered to be a waste of human resources, an exercise in pride, or at best an intellectual luxury. The primary metaphysical categories within ecclesial circles in India has come to be becoming and doing, so *praxis* (reflective action), *poiesis* (creative production) and *phronesis* (practical wisdom) have come to be better valued than *theoria* (theoretical reflection) and *scientia* (demonstrable knowledge). This is understandable, given the tremendous need for social transformation in the Southern global hemisphere in general, and India in particular. Fourthly, the theological agent would need to match words with deeds, as personal authenticity is greatly valued, especially in the worlds of religiosity and spirituality. Philosophical and theological argumentation may limp and be considered effete, if not matched by an appropriate mentality, behaviour pattern, and set of personal beliefs and life options of the author.

Given all of these local features, it is understandable that theology should take on more of an artistic or aesthetic style and content. However, it is also important to make a distinction between a popular style of theological expression and a more scholarly one. Rayan's preferred mode seems to be popular, but it is not legitimate to universalize this mode of theological expression, even in an Asian or Indian context. This is because there is also a need for a more scientific approach to theologizing. In this approach, both systematic method and critique need to be given due importance. One needs to have recourse not only to soft critique, through the use of symbols, but also a hard critique that is logical, rational and argumentatively challenging. This is especially important if one is to expose serious social inequities and fissures which are in need of theological, religious and spiritual redressal. Christians and others living in the Indian subcontinent would clearly benefit from such methodical and critical analyses from a theological perspective. This becomes especially significant and beneficial when the problems and solutions discussed can also be articulated on a more neutral and inclusive platform, using a common, secular language.

Ideally, then, theologians need to fulfill two vocations: one is to engage in scholarly, technical and insightful research work, and the other is to make theological learning available to common folk in a language that is reader-friendly or listener-friendly, as well as inspiring and motivating. The scientific and inductive temperament of post-Enlightenment Western culture has had its impact on ecclesiastical programmes of philosophy and theology—making them extremely rigorous disciplines in their own right. This impact and rigour is not as prevalent in India, because of the many factors listed above.

Engagement in practical matters has taken precedence over the often hard, lonely and unrewarding work of scholarship and intellectual production. Small wonder, then, that the scientific dimension of theology in terms of the systematic articulation and propagation of ideas is not taken as seriously. This lacuna at the level of a collective ecclesial will to correct this lopsided emphasis needs to be seriously addressed if Indians are to substantially contribute to global theological exchange and influence. While it is indeed important to bolster the faith of believers with a more popular style of writing, it is equally important for at least some theologians, who are more adept, to engage with the larger global community of theologians at a more sophisticated level of scholarly work, if Indian and Asian thought is to contribute towards wider circles of theological exchange.

4. Theology at the service of '*recta relatio*' (right relationship)

Whether theology is an art or a science is subsidiary to the more fundamental issue of the goal of theological writing itself. The primary role of faith—and by extension, of theology—is to bring about a *just or harmonious relationship* within our cosmotheandric reality.[39] This is rooted in the spirituality we have inherited from the Hebrew people, for whom the primary theological concern is the quality of the relationship between their community and God, and not speculation regarding the nature of God and material reality. The primary metaphysical category for the Hebrews was relating, not being.[40] The Christian community expanded this focus on communitarian relationship to include the whole human family.

Traditionally oriented theology tends to privilege the significance of orthodoxy, while a large part of the theology of the South understandably tends to cultivate orthopraxis. While both orthodoxy and orthopraxis are important and necessary theological axes, an even more fundamental concern in Scripture and in the Christian tradition is *ortho-koinonia* (right communion or participation), or in Latin, *recta relatio* (right relationship). More than ever before, this is seen to include a right relationship with the natural environment as well.

What was once considered theologically appropriate and adequate in terms of leading to right relationships may not be considered apposite in later times and in different contexts. Hence, an ongoing development of theological reflection over the years and in different contexts is necessary. Thus, the need for creative fidelity on the part of those responsible for the understanding, articulation and transmission of the faith—to continually reinterpret and deepen the faith, so that it may never lose its relevance and challenge. The issue of whether theology is an art or a science then becomes secondary. The deeper issue and concern is about the sustenance of the vitality and depth of faith at personal and community levels, and the creation of whole some spiritual, social and ecological relationships at local, global and cosmic levels. If a theology helps to achieve these goals, it is immaterial whether it is expressed more in terms of an art or a science.

Notes

1. *Chambers Dictionary of Etymology*, ed. Robert Barnhart (New York: Chambers, 1988), p. 52.
2. *Ibid.*, p. 968.
3. *Ibid.*
4. One of Immanuel Kant's major treatises first published in 1790 attempted to provide the systematic and objective foundations of the understanding of the aesthetic world of experience, viz., *The Critique of the Power of Judgment*, ed. Paul Guyer, trans. Paul Guyer and Eric Mathews (Cambridge: Cambridge University Press, 2000).
5. Wolfhart Pannenberg, *Theology and the Philosophy of Science*, trans. Francis McDonagh (London: Darton, Longmann and Todd, 1976), p. 7.
6. Samuel Rayan, "Theology as Art," in *Religion and Society*, 26/2 (1979): pp. 77-90.
7. *Ibid.*, p. 78.
8. *Ibid.*, p. 79.
9. Samuel Rayan, "Doing Theology in India," in Jacob Parappally, ed., *Theologizing in Context: Statements of the Indian Theological Association* (Bangalore: Dharmaram Publications, 2002), p. 19.
10. *Ibid.*, p. 80. The other quotations in this paragraph are from pp. 80-81.
11. Gitanjali Ghei died of cancer at the age of eighteen in Mumbai (in 1977). Her powerfully moving poems were published posthumously in a collection titled, "The Gitanjali Album" (Anand: Gujarat Sahitya Prakash, 1992).
12. See Samuel Rayan, "Philosophy and Theology Relation," in *Vijnanadeepti* 4/1 (2001),p. 48.

13. *Ibid.*
14. Rayan, "Theology as Art," p. 84.
15. Samuel Rayan, "Wrestling in the Night," in Kurien Kunnumpuram, SJ, (ed.), *Doing Theology: Indian Christian Reflections on Theologizing in India Today—Collected Writings of Samuel Rayan, SJ, Vol. II* (Delhi: ISPCK, 2013), p. 57. This article was originally published in M. H. Ellis and O. Maduro, (eds.), *The Future of Liberation Theology: Essays in Honour of Gustavo Gutierrez* (Maryknoll, NY: Orbis, 1989), pp. 450-69.
16. *Ibid.*, p. 58.
17. *Ibid.*
18. Rayan, "Philosophy and Theology Relation," p. 44.
19. *Ibid.*, p. 46.
20. Rayan, "Theology as Art," p. 90.
21. Rayan, "Philosophy and Theology Relation," pp. 40-41.
22. Rayan, "Doing Theology in India," pp. 17-18. Rayan gives a complete list of "the main traits . . . of this imperial-colonial-colonized theology" in Section 2.9 of his, "Decolonization of Theology," in *Jnanadeepa* 1/2 (1998): pp. 47 ff.
23. Rayan, "Theologian as Disciple, Disciple as Theologian," in *Third Millenium* 4/4 (2001), p. 103.
24. Rayan, "Philosophy and Theology Relation", p. 46.
25. Rayan, "The How of Third Word Theologies," in J. R. Chandran, ed., *Third World Theologies in Dialogue: Essays in Memory of D. S. Amalorpavadass* (Bangalore: EATWOT, 1991), p. 53.
26. Samuel Rayan, "Decolonization of Theology," in *Jnanadeepa*, 1/2 (1998), p. 142.
27. Even though De Mello was not a theologian, his publications nevertheless came under the scrutiny of the Congregation for the Doctrine of the Faith, and prompted the then Cardinal Ratzinger—the Prefect of the Congregation—to issue a 'Notification' in 1998 indicating certain aspects of De Mello's works which were not in consonance with traditional Catholic doctrine. See http://www.vatican.va/roman_curia/congregations/cfaith/documents/rc_con_cfaith_ doc_19980624_demello_en.html.
28. Rayan, "Theology as Art", p. 85.
29. *Ibid.*, p. 88.
30. See the section titled, 'Birds and Flowers Theology,' in "Theology as Art", pp. 79-81.
31. See Paul Ricoeur, "Phenomenology and Hermeneutics," in his, *From Text to Action: Essays in Hermeneutics, II*, trans. Kathleen Blamey and John B. Thompson (Evanston, IL: Northwestern University Press, 1991), p. 42.

32. See Hans-Georg Gadamer, *Truth and Method*, 2nd rev. ed., trans. revised by Joel Weinsheimer and Donald G. Marshall (New York: Continuum Publishing Company, 1989).
33. Rayan, "Philosophy and Theology Relation", pp. 37-38.
34. Rayan, "Doing Theology in India", p. 18.
35. *Ibid.*
36. David Munchin, *Is Theology a Science?* (Leiden: Brill, 2011), p. 2.
37. Douglas Clyde MacIntosh, *Theology as an Empirical Science* (New York: Macmillan, 1919), p. 2.
38. Indians have inherited an oral tradition which revels in speaking and listening. This tradition does not easily lend itself to written and systematic theological articulation. For this, one needs to live in a written tradition, in which people revel in writing and reading.
39. The term 'cosmotheandric' has been coined by Raimundo Panikkar to draw attention to the intercommunion yet distinctiveness of the three primary dimensions of reality: the cosmic, the human and the divine. See Panikkar, *The Cosmotheandric Experience: Emerging Religious Consciousness* (Maryknoll, NY: Orbis, 1993).
40. Likewise, for the Hebrews, 'truth' (*emeth*) is understood more in terms of an ontological category (being faithful, firm (constant), stable, reliable, etc.) rather than an epistemological one.

19

The Impact of Indian thought on Samuel Rayan's Theology

Sebastian Painadath, SJ

Samuel Rayan is acclaimed as the most perceptive advocate of liberation theology in the Indian context. Definitely he has been considerably influenced by the theological perspectives and insights of the Latin American Liberation theologians, most of whom he personally met in international conferences. But, the liberative perspectives which Rayan developed in theology did have a clear Indian taste. For him the sources of theologizing in India have been the spiritual heritage of the country, the resistance movements of the past, the contemporary secular cultural trends as well as peoples' movements. The characteristic of a Liberation Theology born on the Indian soil – unlike in Latin America – is that it evolves in an ongoing dialogue with the past heritage and present culture of a multi-religious society. "God encounters us in the faith and devotion of the followers of religious traditions other than our own, and in their saints, sacred Scriptures, symbols and artistic creations."[1] In this paper a few sources of Indian thought used by Rayan are highlighted.

Bhagavad Gita

Of all the classical sources of the Indian thought it is the Bhagavad Gita that has contributed significantly to Rayan's theological paradigm. He often makes reference to this spiritual classic in his writings, most conspicuously in the article: "Indian Theology and the Problem of History", published in the book, R. W. Taylor (ed), *Society and Religion: Essays in Honour of M. M. Thomas*, CLS Madras, 1976, pp. 167-193.[2] Here he theologically addresses the widespread allegation that Indian thought lacks the sense of history, and hence respect for the dignity of the human person and also social responsibility. "The idea seems to be common that India's interest is in metaphysics and mysticism rather than history; Indian thought and religions tend to naturalize history rather than historicize nature. Historical values such as the affirmation of the person, involvement in situations, building up of social relationships, creativity and freedom and concrete action to change and improve conditions of human existence are said to be minimized in favour of passivity and contemplation, and an other-worldliness which neglects matter and time and evades sustained struggle. Time moves in cycles, and salvation is said to be from history and not of, in and through history".[3] Rayan quotes serious Indian theologians like M. M. Thomas, S. J. Samartha, R. H. S. Boyd, Bishop Appasamy and K. Dockhorn who seem to subscribe to this sweeping judgement on Indian thought.[4] In the book, "The New Directions in Faith and Order", published by the WCC in 1968, p. 10, he finds a terse statement: "In ancient religions history is naturalized; in Israel nature is historicized".[5] This apparent discrepancy is a fundamental problem in Indian theology. We shall examine how Rayan addresses this key issue with a rereading of the Bhagavad Gita:

> The very opening words of the Gita, '*in the field of Dharma, in the Kurukshetra field*', are suggestive of the way the spiritual and the secular are inseparably linked up one to the other throughout the work".[6] Here, history with all its ups and downs is affirmed, society with its ambivalences is confronted and the human person addresses a situation of acute crisis in life. Instead of being overcome by momentary passions and evading social responsibility, one is asked to pay heed to "the call to meet the crisis, the summons to decision and action, the commitment to the cause of what is right"[7] (Gita, 2:3,5). Mere loyalty to caste duty is ambiguous, greed for personal gain is disruptive, running away from the battlefield of life is not liberative (Gita, 2: 31-38, 39). What then is the way out? Here Gita proposes a new

> ethos of life-affirming and life-transforming work: *nishkama karma*, work without greed, work with inner freedom, work as participating in the divine work, work for the integral welfare of the world (*lokasamraha*) (Gita, 3: 20-25).[8] Rayan observes that "Gita introduces salvation into the stream of history, and into the heart of our struggle to become a human community".[9] "*No doer of good will ever be destroyed nor tread the path of woe*" (Gita, 6:40). We humans can affirm life and transform history because God is the Lord of history, not somewhere far away from us, but deep within the heart of all (Gita 3:30-32). "*Those who commune with me in loving devotion abide in me and I abide in them*" (Gita 9:29). Rayan comments on this text: "Here time and space become personal through relationship to the Lord. Time is saved from its cyclic quest and brought home to its Lord".[10] "*The deepest secret, the ultimate word, is this: I love you intensely!*" (Gita, 18:64)– this revelation of the divine Lord is the salvific confirmation of an inter-personal relationship with the Divine, with its consequence for a compassionate inter-personal relationship among humans (Gita, 12:13-14).

Rayan detects four important hints for the Gita conception of time and history: "Time is open to God's action (i) through the revelation given at the beginning, (ii) through His present word, (iii) through his coming in, being on the earth from age to age to establish dharma, and (iv) through his love for the human person (Gita, 10:20, 13:17, 15: 15,16: 18, 18:61). These are movements of salvation, *Chronos* or mechanical time becomes *Kairos,* salvation time, and we stand summoned to decision...History is time open to God and on the move, maturing towards its own wholeness which is already present in the presence of its Lord within its heart".[11] Gita does not advocate a metaphysical image of the Absolute totally unconcerned about human history, rather it presents the loving God who brings about spiritual and material prosperity (*yogakshemam,* 9:22), the Lord of history who intervenes when the dharma-oriented process of human destiny is in peril (Gita 4:6-8) Our history is God´s own history with us "It is the *Dharmakshetra* where crucial battles are fought and won or lost".[12]

Time does not make a historical process if it rolls on in pre-destined cycles. It is human freedom and creativity that fashion history (Gita 18:63). "It is when a human being rides it that time becomes history. The central message of the Gita is that the recurring consequences of Karma can be overcome, and mechanical time can be led to a meaningful personal goal and thus redeemed by relating in faith to the Lord who loves us. At the end time ripens into life with the Lord".[13] The liberated souls do not return to this samsara (Gita: 8:15-16); they enter into a divine mode of being (Gita: 8:5, 18: 53). This means that time is not an endless cyclic process.

Here, Rayan asks the question: "If liberation is for individuals, does not history still remain bound and unredeemed?"[14] His study of the Gita offers him the following insight: "With the divine Lord something new has entered the arena of life, changing the texture of history. In the divine Lord the Ultimate Reality has become present and involved in life making and sharing a common destiny. That God loves the world and in this love is salvation, is a new revelation. The situation of the world is now different, and salvation is for the first time available to all. The most sinful of people who worship the Lord with undivided devotion must be regarded as holy for he/she has rightly resolved, he/she will quickly become righteous and obtain everlasting grace"[15] (Gita: 9:30-32). When the assurance is given that God shapes history with us our history becomes salvation history. "God is with us amid the struggles of life and not only or principally in the solitude and quiet of forests and caves and monastic peace. It is there that we are guided by God, the charioteer of our lives".[16] The assurance that "*no devotee ever perishes*" (Gita: 9:31) is not without historical repercussions and social consequence.[17]

Gita proposes a liberative and integrative path of action, commitment to the welfare of all. Caring for this world is seen as a divine work, for one participates in the caring concern of the divine Lord. "*Brahmanirvana* is only for those who rejoice in, engage in, and strive to secure the weal of all contingent beings. The bhakti which makes a human being the Lord's beloved, which thus enters into the texture of liberation, requires that we hate no one, that we be to all beings friendly and compassionate, and entertain no thought or feel of *I and mine*, of *ahamkara* of being a private individual, that we do not shrink from people nor cause them to shrink from us, and that we learn to deal equally with friend and foe"[18] (Gita, 9: 30-32, 18: 68-70,

5:25, 12:4). With the self-revelation of the Divine as personal Lord Gita affirms the personal dignity of the human person, the ethical integrity of human community and the creative process of history. Rayan concludes his reflections with an observation of Richard De Smet SJ, a renowned scholar of Vedanta: "By considering the whole trajectory of India's religious development,...it has dawned upon me that it reveals itself to the eye of a Christian as a *Holy History*.[19] C. F. Andrews spoke of the *higher religious history* of Indian traditions.[20]

If the Indian mind were to have no sense of history and social responsibility how can we account for the creative endeavours and social projects of Indians across the centuries, Rayan asks: "India's exuberant secular and religious activity, its far flung land and sea trade to the East and the West, its textile industry and advanced metallurgy, its cultural and spiritual missions to East and South-East Asia, its elaborate organization of society, the development of complete systems of law and medicine, the remarkable achievements in the sciences of human anatomy, medical botany, acoustics and architecture as well as grammar and poetics, the glad expression of is inner life in a riot of artistic imagination and artistic production in music, dance, painting, poetry, plays, fables, legends, epics, sculptures and temples and in feasts and celebrations full of light and life and brimming with vitality and vigour...roads and shade trees along the roads under which the weary traveler could rest from sun and heat, the free provision of drinking water along the high ways,..."[21]

In an other article Rayan explores convergences and divergences of the plights of Job and Arjuna.[22] Both have been going through a dark night of the soul, tossed in the storms of life's struggles. Flight from the struggles of life is denied in both the texts. "The Lord finds Arjuna's way of resolving the crisis is too simplistic".[23] The experience of God's gratuitous love as the means of overcoming suffering is the theme of both the books. "From spiritual trauma and paralysis there is no exit via reasoning and argument".[24] It is the inter-personal encounter with a caring divine master that liberates Job and Arjuna from their predicament.[25] "Both are reestablished in freedom, and enabled to walk in love, and work for the liberation of the victims of greed and of self-regarding religion, which uses God for private gain".[26] In the Gita this experience paves the way to commitment to society with inner freedom (*nishkamakarma*).[27] "Both Job and the Gita bear witness to the truth of God's liberating presence in the midst of life's struggles and history's vicissitudes: a presence that does not tranquillize us but challenges and urges us to act against *adharma* and create a new world that could reflect and respond to the world of grace".[28]

Myths and Symbols

In reflecting on Theology as art, Rayan dwells on the meaning of myths. Myths evolve from the deeper levels of the unconscious, articulating a lot of archetypes emerging from the collective unconscious. "Myths unite and hold together the sacred and the profane, for our fantasies are ultimately rooted in the Wondrous and Shared Ground of our Self".[29] As Indians our psyche should well resonate with the myths and symbols of this country. "Then we shall be able to enter into and explore theologically the wealth of wisdom and vision, the depth of experience of the Real which stand embodied in such great myths and symbols of our land as the Dance of Siva, the Siva Lingam, the Descent of the Ganga, the Churning of the Ocean Nectar, the Figure of Kali, the Dialogue of Krishna and Arjuna, Krishna's Flute, the Repose of Vishnu on Ananta, the theme of Arthanareeswara, and a hundred others and the numberless puranic stories. We need these tales, this rich heritage of creativity and creative fantasy, their inspiration and their challenge".[30]

Bhakti Movements

A living source of India's spiritual heritage is the rich world of popular devotions. Though most of these devotional forms have taken to extreme ritualism and sectarianism, there have been sages and traditions of strong prophetic protest in India. Rayan looks into the liberative potential of some of the bhakti saints and their resistance movements. One of the classical sources of the bhakti movement is the Bhagavad Gita. "The Upanishads, Buddhism and the Gita, each in its time and its turn, are voices of dissent and protest, and path-breakers in new directions for the journey of the free spirit of the human person. An entire history could be traced of the people's struggles for new patterns of living and relating, from Vedic ritualism and Brahmanic domination to Upanishadic experience, to Buddhist humanism with a secular-social accent, to the Bhakta's untrammeled joy in the discovery of God's great and tender love relativizing the past with all its traditions, opening up new visions for the future and setting concrete tasks for the present".[31] Since, the bhakti movement sprang spontaneously from the lower strata of society, "it has been the religion and spirituality of the Indian masses for over two thousand years".[32] In fact these popular forms have their origin in the pre-Vedic Aryan times for they are nonconformist vis-à-vis classic Brahmanism. There are basically two basic streams: worshipping Vishnu or Siva.[33] Rayan considers them as a rich source of theological reflection in India. "The Bhakti traditions are rich in liberation potential. They have been described as the most creative upsurge of the Indian mind, which has inspired several social and political revolts. This religious current has helped many low castes to bear their social status with courage or to seek release from it".[34] The poems of the North Indian bhakti sages and the hymns of the South Indian Alwars and Nayanars resonate well with the religious psyche of the common people for they find in them spiritual elevation and social courage.

"The deepest vein in the history of India is the story of its struggle to win spiritual freedom. And what was won proved to be a responsible freedom; faith in God and prayer, religious observance and ethical striving have in large measure continued among the masses without a central authority".[35] Authority in the spiritual heritage of India is not a matter of power and position but a fruit of genuine spiritual experience. "It is grounded not in any external appointment but in an inner attainment and quality, in a personal experience of truth, meaning and love. The spiritual authority is the Guru, the one who has seen, touched and suffered the Divine, and realized Brahman".[36] Rayan believes that the Christianity has a lot to learn from this Indian experience.

One of the popular forms of devotion practised all over India is the *Namajapa*. Rayan reflects on the spiritual power of the devotional chanting of the name of the divine Lord. "The immediate effect of the uninterrupted practice of *Namajapa* may be a sense of spiritual upheaval, an intense burning sensation in the body, a feeling that the name is circulating along all the intra-organic channels of the physical frame. But the ultimate fruit of this practice is the transformation of the *sadhaka* into the glory of the name itself, finally the fountaining forth of ineffable joy in the purified and liberated self".[37] The chanting of the name gives the devotee the inner experience of the abiding presence of the divine Lord and the courage to accept oneself as accepted by the Lord, and to transform oneself and society as desired by the Lord. This gives also the inner energy to raise a protest against divisive forces in society.[38]

Gandhi and Tagore

Two persons of recent Indian history having a significant influence in the theological reflection of Samuel Rayan are Mahatma Gandhi and Rabindranath Tagore.

Gandhi impressed him for what he said and did, and much more for what he was. There is an authentic integration between the thinking, acting and the way of life in Gandhi. "Gandhi identified himself with the masses, emulated the simple life of the peasant, spoke their language and thus won their heart and their support".[39] He was a relentless seeker of Truth. "For Gandhiji, the decisive, central, overarching reality is Truth. Life is only authentic and worthwhile inasmuch as it is a quest for Truth," because "God is Truth…Truth is God." (*Young India*, 1.12.1931, pp. 427-8)".[40] Since colonial imperialism is untruth political commitment to the liberation of the masses is participation in the divine work. "This fusion of religion and politics, this integrated way of life, is the characteristic of Gandhiji's spirituality".[41] The path of Truth is ahimsa. "Truth reached through ahimsa is itself life and love".[42]

Rayan admires Gandhi's efforts to achieve political independence, but he notes too Gandhi's failure in bringing about the liberation of the masses from the grips of religious communalism, casteism and corruption. "With the high idealism and lofty motives Gandhi did not respect the dynamics of history".[43] "He pursued an imaginary Hindu-Muslim fraternity, completely ignoring the fundamental differences between the two rooted in history and culture".[44] Though he said, "I abhor with my whole soul the caste system that reduces the masses to a level less than that of beasts," (*Removal of Untouchability*, Navajivan, 1954, p. 6) he did not address the economic basis of caste nor did he question the unequal relationships of production; he was a consistent opponent of any class struggle of the landless labourers.[45] "As a result we have had transfer of power without a social evolution; and a simple continuation of the status quo to the advantage of the bourgeoisie".[46] Still Rayan writes on Gandhi with great respect and admiration. Relating Gandhiji to the vision of the Sermon on the Mount Rayan wrote a beautiful meditation:

> "Gandhiji's life was a word of God addressed to us; Bapu himself is God's word to our world, a word of power and of love, a deep word that stirs the spirit... In Bapuji God has once more asserted and vindicated the sovereign freedom of his grace against all narrow Churchism...May I call him a saint?"[47]

Tagore has been a spiritual inspiration in the life and thought of Rayan. He enjoys reading the poems from *Gitanjali* during the Eucharistic celebrations and prayer services. He could resonate well with the mystical insights and eco-sensitivity of Tagore. Quoting Tagore's words "*Silence, my soul, these trees are prayers,*" Rayan writes: "Tagore has a spiritual understanding of trees and of the earth. Trees are earth's prayers, the lifting up of her spirit to God, her hands raised in worship. The trees are the earth dancing out her praise and thanks, her joyous fruit-rich religiousness and her flowering devotion".[48] Tagore gives wings to the imagination of Rayan: "Not only trees, but streams as well, and the winds too, and the mountains and the beasts that roam in them, and the birds that sail the blue expanse of the sky, and the sky and the sea and the stars and all the fish..."[49]

The influence of local culture on Samuel Rayan's theology is very conspicuous in his writings in Malayalam, his mother tongue. He did graduation in Malayalam and loves the language passionately. He could present theological reflections in a lucid and poetical Malayalam. The social reformers and peoples' movements of his homeland Kerala appear significantly in his vernacular writings.[50] In an article on 'Kerala culture and theology' he describes the liberative potential of the social involvements of Sree Narayana Guru, Ayyankali, Kumaran Asan and Sahodaran Ayyappan.[51] They all gave a sense of self-esteem to the downtrodden and marginalized sectors of the Kerala society. In their commitment Rayan discovers the emergence of the Kingdom of God that evolves beyond all religions and castes.

One could cite many other persons and elements of India's spiritual heritage, which have become like building stones of the theological edifice of Samuel Rayan. He integrates them critically with his theology centred on the person and message of Jesus. He uses them with great respect for he believes that the divine Spirit touches and transforms the hearts of millions of our people through these sages, symbols and scriptures. As with the great *rishis* of India a relentless search for *the Beyond* always motivated Rayan to go beyond the trodden religious paths and familiar theological categories. This makes his theology ever fresh and explorative. With this he advocates not only a theology of liberation, but also a liberation of theology from traditional jargons and symbols.

Notes

1. "Doing Theology in India", 2002, *Collected Writings, Vol.* II. p. 18.
2. *Collected Writings II*, pp. 192-221.
3. "Society and Religion: Essays in Honour of M. M. Thomas", 1976, *Collected Writings, Vol.* II. p. 195.
4. *Ibid.* pp. 193-4.
5. *Ibid.* II, p. 194.
6. *Ibid.* p. 198.
7. *Ibid.*
8. *Ibid.* pp. 198-202.
9. *Ibid.* p.199.
10. *Ibid.*
11. *Ibid.* p. 200.
12. *Ibid.* p. 216.
13. *Ibid.* pp. 200-201.
14. *Ibid.*, p. 201.
15. *Ibid.* pp. 201-202.
16. "Re-conceiving Theology in the Asian Context", 1983, *Collected Writings*, Vol. II, pp. 253-254.
17. "Society and Religion: Essays in Honour of M. M. Thomas", 1976, *Collected Writings, Vol.* II, pp. 201-202.

18. *Ibid.* p. 202.
19. *Ibid.* p. 203.
20. *Ibid.* p, 203.
21. *Ibid.* pp. 195-196.
22. "Wrestling in the Night", 1989, *Collected Writings, Vol.* II. pp. 53-78.
23. *Ibid.* p. 61.
24. *Ibid.* p. 67.
25. *Ibid.*
26. *Ibid.*
27. *Ibid.* p. 63.
28. *Ibid.* pp. 67-68
29. "Theology as Art", 1979, *Collected Writings,* Vol. II. p. 12.
30. *Ibid.* p. 12.
31. "Indian Theology and the Problem of History", 1976, *Collected Writings,* Vol. II, p. 197.
32. "Re-conceiving Theology in the Asian Context", 1983, *Collected Writings,* Vol. II, p. 257.
33. *Ibid.* p. 257.
34. *Ibid.* p. 258.
35. "Spirituality in the Indian Church Today", 1975, *Selected Writings,* Vol. II, p. 40.
36. *Ibid.* p. 41.
37. Naming the Unnameable, 1985, *Collected Writings,* Vol. II, pp. 129-130.
38. *Ibid.* p. 128.
39. "A Spirituality for Today", 1986, *Selected Writings,* Vol. II, p. 54.
40. *Ibid.* p. 53.
41. *Ibid.*
42. *Ibid.* p. 54.
43. *Ibid.* p. 55.
44. *Ibid.*
45. "Outside the Gate, Sharing Insults", 1981, *Selected Writings,* Vol. I. p. 267.
46. "A Spirituality for Today", *Selected Writings,* Vol. II. p. 57.
47. "Gandhiji, A Meditation", 1970, *Selected Writings,* Vol. II. pp. 210-215.
48. "Ecology and Theology", 1991, *Collected Writings,* Vol. I, p. 54.
49. *Ibid.*
50. Samuel Rayan, *Naleyilekkoru Neelkazcha,* in Michel Tharakan & S.Painadath SJ (eds), Cochin: St. Pauls.
51. *Ibid.* pp. 249-267.

20

Historical Existence as Praxis Samuel Rayan's Understanding of History

Isaac Padinjarekuttu

The following reflections are based mainly on two articles of Fr. Samuel Rayan, "Indian Theology and the Problem of History" in volume II[1] and "Models of History" in volume III[2] of the *Collected Writings of Fr. Samuel Rayan, SJ*.[3] In them Fr. Rayan discusses several points which are important for theology in general and Indian Christian theology in particular. I shall concentrate on two: the first is to challenge the commonly held view that a sense of history is absent in India's traditions and show that India has nearly the same idea of history as the West. Secondly, he shows what genuine historical sense means, why a sense of history is essential for the Christian faith and how it can help a contextual and praxis-oriented Christian theology in the Indian context.

1. Rayan's Understanding of History

In his article "Models of History", Rayan spells out his understanding of history. He begins by giving a description of the common models of history: the cyclic, the linear and the spiral. The cyclic model which is said to be characteristic of archaic men, pre-modern generations, primitive cultures, oriental peoples, agricultural civilizations and the popular masses in general, is the way the world process was seen in ancient times, and according to Rayan, even today by all, but an elite minority.[4] Time and history are experienced and represented as periodic and repetitive, and moving cyclically. There is a periodic regeneration of life which points to a periodic regeneration of time. The result is the idea of the eternal return of what has been before. No event is irreversible and no transformation is final. In a certain sense, it is even possible that nothing new happens in the world, for everything is but the repetition of the same primordial archetype.[5] Neither the objects of the external world nor the products of human activity have any intrinsic reality or autonomous validity. History in itself is meaningless. Hence, it is periodically abolished. The succession of aeons and *yugas* represents a decadence from the Golden Age but it is at the same time the condition for regeneration and of the new cycle, to the return to the Golden Age. Persons, events and situations are sooner or later shorn of their historical particularities and uniqueness. Nothing that happens in the world, neither the rise and fall of civilizations nor the wars and sufferings of peoples nor the conquests and social injustice is arbitrary or contingent. All events and catastrophes are seen as necessary and inevitable. They are caused by the cosmic rhythm or the Will of God. So there is what Mircea Eliad calls the "terror of history" among traditional peoples and resistance to the novelty and the irreversibility of history. They refuse to situate themselves in concrete historical time. Rayan asks: are they afraid of movement and spontaneity? Are they terrified by the risk of freedom and the dangers of the historical situation? There is no clear answer to these questions. But he tells us at the same time, how nearly all organised religions and churches closely respond in their attitude to liturgies, dogmas, structures and authority, to this description of the cyclic conception of time.[6]

When we come to the linear model of history, there is no repeated return of the same world to the same starting point. History is conceived as creative advance towards a goal. It is moving towards fulfilment and some day will come to an end. Time is not reversible, uniform or static; it is structured, dynamic, and forward-moving. It is a one-way reality. Novelty is a characteristic of history. According to Mircea Eliad, the Hebrews were the first to make this discovery. It began with Abraham who introduced the category of faith, which means freedom from the natural law of cyclic movement, a creative freedom which has God for its source and support. Trusting in God, the people move forward, through what happens in history, through victories and defeats, ultimately going back to God. This understanding was taken up by the Christian writers tracing a straight line for humanity's course from the "Fall" to Final Redemption. For the Christians, history also came to be seen as possessed of unique meaningfulness because at its heart stood the incomparable event of Jesus Christ.[7]

The third model, the spiral model of history, is an unfinished model of history in which we see cyclic fluctuations and periodic crises. There is a dialectical movement in history, but ultimately moving towards an ever more authentic human history (Karl Marx). But progress occurs not in a straight line but along a spiral of struggles against alienating forces. As long as such forces exist, history is in process of becoming – becoming more human. The final stage of history is one in which men and women will have unhindered possibility of endless creative advance and personal self-realization as free individuals in an equal community. Human beings shape history and are shaped by it. There is no submission to nature and to the past as in archaic conceptions; nor is there a break with them as in the linear model of history. History is a dialectical spiral process of creative advance necessarily overcoming the contradictions and alienations present in history at any given time.[8]

Then Rayan addresses some specific issues that are common to all these models. What is the role of God in history? For some, he is outside the historical process, not affected by it. It is the position of classical theology. But others, for example, proponents of Process Theology, would see God as part of history: "God is in this world or he is nowhere" (Whitehead). He is passionately involved in our history and deeply affected by it. The second question is what is the role of nature in history? There are those who exclude nature from history because nature repeats itself while history is marked by novelty. But others maintain that we belong to and are one with our environment. "We are organic to nature. We ought not to attempt to separate human experience and history from nature, but rather see that nature itself is historical – by which I mean that it is processive, with movement and change" (Norman Pettinger). Another issue is the end of history because the understanding of history also depends on the way the end of history is envisaged. Since the end is not yet there, all our understanding and interpretations of it are provisional. What is known is the individual's history and that gives a clue to the historical process. The next issue is looking at history from above and from below. A history from above is the history of the rulers and the powerful and a history from below is the history of the ruled and the powerless. Much of history is a truncated one because it is a history from above, but from the second half of the 20th century, there is recognition of the fact that nothing can be written off as irrelevant. The role played by social position and class interest in the understanding and portrayal of history must not be overlooked. And lastly, what is the subject of history? Is the subject of history the individual person or society as a whole? Depending on the answer to this question, history will be seen as sum total of personal achievements or failures or the collective struggles of human beings to overcome alienation and injustice.[9]

Although there are different models and understandings of history, in general, history is divided into linear and cyclic. The linear is attributed to the Christian West and the cyclic to the other societies of Asia, Africa and America. The economic and technological progress in the West and the lack of it elsewhere has often been attributed for a long time to the difference in understanding history, indirectly implying that all must adopt the linear view. Rayan is of the opinion that this calls for critical assessment. According to him, the linear view is not a fully accepted view of the West. History as creative advance is the vision of an elite minority. The great majority, he says, "continue, down to our day, to preserve themselves from history by ignoring it and by tolerating it." From the beginning, there were supporters of both views among Christian writers and thinkers.[10] For over a thousand years, Christian theology was framed with Platonic and Neo-Platonic philosophies which were basically philosophies of changeless permanence and eternal return. The modern times, described as the time of the historical people, have expressed nostalgia for the cyclic view of time. In the writings of Octavio Paz, Carlos Fuentes, Friedrich Nietzsche, T. S. Eliot, James Joyce, etc.

one sees this longing for the past. According to Karl Marx, historical linearism reduces history to a succession of actions by the powerful and the elite. So there is always nostalgia for return to the paradise lost.[11] In fact, the cyclic does not seem to be quite so primitive and meaningless, nor incompatible with Christian faith and thought as it is often made out to be. It is rather a way of living in history which includes nature, and of relating to nature which constitutes the history-making process. We belong with nature and the cosmos and our existence is bound up with their rhythm. To pretend otherwise would be unrealistic and unwise. Even the most linearist historical person performs repetitive gestures like breathing and walking. Further, archaic primitive cultures which are said to resist and abolish history by an escape into endless cyclic time have nonetheless been inventive and innovative, changeful and progressive when they were not subject to oppression. After all, modern linearist people did not invent the fire or the wheel or food grain or agriculture, or city life, or the idea of tools, or language, or the art of writing, weaving, cooking, domesticating animals, building houses, and a thousand other things which make up the basic fabric of human life today, asserts Rayan. A cyclic understanding of time does not necessarily mean the abolition of history or its rejection and such an understanding is not limited to a particular culture as shown above.[12]

2. History and the Indian Tradition

It is rather commonplace to say that historical writing or even historical mindedness, at least as it is conceived in the West, seems to have been lacking in India prior to the beginnings of Muslim conquest in the central Middle Ages: "Historical writing was one of the least developed areas of ancient Indian culture. The mythological texts, the *Puranas*, did, however, include dynastic lists which contained rudimentary material for political history. A few Sanskrit texts from the Hindu 'middle ages' also record the achievements of individual monarchs or the history of regional dynasties ... systematic chronicles of political events, especially wars, conquests, succession of dynasties and the like, really begin with the Muslim chroniclers".[13] So the impression is that particularly Hindu India lacked a strong tradition of historical writing because for the Hindus, time is supposed to have been 'fuzzy' or 'cyclical'. These statements are dubious at best. Hindu India, it is true, expressed its historical memory through legends and ballads, a true representation of popular constructions of the past. Yet even Hindu kingdoms had elaborate records, genealogies and annals which could be as precise as those found in other early modern societies.

Others would go a step further and even say that history in its modern form came with the colonial rulers. Against this it must be pointed out that the Indo-Muslim tradition of historical writing, drawing on the precision and concern for correct testimony of Arabic and Persian exemplars developed under the patronage of the Mogul and other Indian Muslim courts. This tradition continued to flourish during the late seventeenth and eighteenth centuries. Persian histories of dynasties and religious teachers, biographical dictionaries of writers and poets, local histories of landed clans and small towns were written in great numbers, often by the Hindus of the scribal classes who had taken Mogul service. While one of the main themes of these histories was the evanescence of human might in the face of God's greatness, other more 'secular' themes emerged too. Eighteenth century indigenous historians were deeply concerned about the corruption of Mogul public office and the decline of virtue. Such writers were by no means innocent of an historical explanation. It is simply that their explanations differed from twentieth century predilections, though not necessarily from eighteenth century European ones. These themes were quickly adapted to the new conditions created by the rise of British power. Persian histories chronicled the gradual British takeover of the Mogul domain by stealth. They sometimes lauded the stability the 'Franks' brought, but often denounced their brutality and incivility. These historians wrote of a revolution in power which had brought the 'drunken and licentious butlers' of the English to power. In the early nineteenth century grand chronicles were matched by large numbers of local histories, often produced by the old literati under British direction. Without these histories, the 'modern' British and Indian historians who produced their numberless volumes on India would be literally left high and dry as far as sources for their works are concerned.[14]

Such ideas are held also by Indian Christian theologians. So S. J. Samartha wrote: "That classical Hinduism did not give sufficient importance to the historical dimensions of human life is generally conceded...There was always in Hinduism a tendency for the historic to be swallowed up in the cosmic".[15] The tendency in Hindu thought has always been to emphasise that aspect of human freedom which enables man to rise above the flux of time. Individuality is not asserted in action and commitment within the social context; it is rather realized through detachment from history than through involvement in its conflicts and tragedies. According to Samartha, the quest for the ground of Being culminating in the Brahman has resulted in minimising the significance of the world of history and consequently in neglecting social realities and group relations. Insufficient attention is paid to the freedom and responsibility of the individual person, the social and historical dimensions of human life, the possibilities for the emergence of the new both in nature and in history, the fact of tragedy and evil within human spirituality, the persistence of sin, guilt and death in human existence, etc.[16] R. H. S. Boyd concurs with this view saying that the most important theological issues to be faced by the Indian church are the meaning of history, personality and community, and the meaning of body and matter. These tend to dim and disappear in the Hindu view which stresses the universal, timeless and cyclic rather than the particular, the purposive and linear.[17] The cyclical view of time stands out powerfully in the doctrines of reincarnation, *karma-samsara* and in the tables of *yugas, mahayugas, and kalpas*. According to Bishop Appasamy, the Hindu concept of *Avataras* is docetic, and does not regard history as important. They do not act by making decisions in history, but by creating harmony and restoring concord between man and the cosmos.[18]

Christianity, on the other hand, is **the** historical religion, **the** religion of history. According to Wilhelm Dilthey, the historicity of man was discovered by Christianity. According to Gregory Dix, Christianity is the only religion which actually depends entirely upon history. According to Mircea Eliade, the conceptions of history outside Israel were caught in a cyclic view. In ancient religions history is naturalistic; in Israel, nature is historicized.[19]

These ideas are not Christian prejudice against Hindu religious culture. According to Vivekananda, in religion, historicity is not a strength, but a weakness. Disprove the historicity of the man and the whole fabrication tumbles to the ground. In Hinduism, one's allegiance is to principles and not to persons. Gandhi confessed that he was not interested in the historical Jesus. The Sermon on the Mount would be true for him even if Jesus did not exist.

Thus, the idea seems to be common that India's interest is in metaphysics and mysticism rather than history; Indian thought and religions tend to naturalize history rather than historicize nature. Historical values such as the affirmation of the person, involvement in situations, building of social relationships, creativity and freedom and concrete action to change and improve the conditions of human existence are said to be minimized in favour of passivity and contemplation and other-worldliness which neglect matter and time and evade sustained struggle. Change is supposedly devalued, little room is left for the new, time moves in cycles, and salvation is said to be from history and not of, in and through history.[20]

Is this view correct? According to Rayan, a second look at the thesis that Hindu traditions lack nearly all the dimensions of the historical is in order. Quoting M. P. John, Rayan says: "The type of historiography that developed during the last century in Europe is certainly not found in ancient India... And yet there is a link with, a reverence for, the past which is certainly a form of historical living. The great importance given to the chain of teachers and students, the emphasis on genealogy and caste, the monuments raised and many other similar items are expressions of a concern with history though they are inadequate and disappointing in a modern historian's quest for sources".[21] Hindu India's exuberant secular and religious activity, its far flung land and sea trade to the East and the West, its textile industry and advanced metallurgy, its cultural and spiritual missions to East and South East Asia, its elaborate organizations of society, the development of complete systems of law and medicine, its remarkable achievements in the sciences of human anatomy, medical botany, acoustics and architecture as well as grammar and poetics, the glad expression of its inner life in a riot of artistic imagination and artistic production in music dance, paining, poetry, plays, fables, legends, epics, sculptures and temples and its feasts and celebrations full of light and life and brimming with vitality and vigour, are they not expressions of historical existence and concerns?[22]

The concept of the four *asramas* reveal an experience of time which is not cyclic or amorphous but progressive and structured. It conveys a sense of movement towards a consummation, the sense of a process of maturation. This articulation of life is not a datum of nature but a construction of the human being. While the *asramas* testify to a view of individual existence as history, the theory of *yugas* and *kalpas* conceive the life of the cosmos in historical terms. But they have a human quality which depends upon human decisions and relationships. Basing himself on the Hindu scriptures and epics, Rayan proves that time is never at a stand still or moving in cycles nor is it a thing in itself. It has its substance in human decisions and actions, and steadily inclines towards a goal. The realism of traditional India's approach to life becomes crystallized in the four *purusarthas*: *Mukti*, *Dharma*, *Kama* and *Artha*. Admittedly *Mukti* is the goal, but it matures within a life of *Dharma*. And *Dharma* governs *Artha* and *Kama*.[23]

The thoughts of ancient India were not always conformist or repetitions of the past. The *Upanishads*, Buddhism, and the Gita are voices of dissent and protest and path-breakers in new directions for the journey of the free spirit of the human person. An entire history could be traced of the people's struggle for new patterns of living, from *Vedic* ritualism and *brahminic* domination to *Upanisadic* experience, to Buddhist humanism with a secular social accent. These open up new visions for the future and set concrete tasks for the present. There are so many examples of new movements in India which sprang from the interaction and conflict of historical-social forces and needs, and gave rise to new socio-economic structures and redistribution of power. Religious thought and life in India intertwine root and branch with concrete situations and movements of history.[24] There is a mutual embeddedness of history and religion in India. All Hindu reform movements were attempts to give a spiritual force for political and social action without any sense of a break with or violation of orthodoxy, and in this the Gita is particularly important. That is why many modern leaders of India have written a commentary on the Gita in terms of its political and social relevance.

According to Rayan, the very opening words of the Gita, "In the field of *Dharma*, in the *Kurukshetra* field" are suggestive of the way the spiritual and the secular are inseparably linked up one to the other throughout the work. From the start we are placed in a particular historical situation of political conflict, clash of philosophies and ideals, and intense mental perplexity. A deliberate, reflective decision is to be made before God and humans in dialogue with God in worship and prayer, face to face with people and the possibilities of the future, giving weightage to moral considerations and to compassion. It is in a fully historical situation that revelation is given. Time is not amorphous and uniform. Sometimes *Dharma* is strong, and at other times *Adharma*. As there are crises, there are also opportunities. There is a call to meet the crisis and summons to decision and action, to commitment to the cause of what is right. What is relevant to humans' real life before God is discussed – the problem of work as at once necessary for life and dangerous for salvation. Work was felt to affect adversely the quality of human life and remove it far from its fulfilment. The answer is, work cannot be unwholesome in itself since God himself works; but he remains free because his work is not selfish. What should be shunned, then, is selfishness, not work. One should work without any selfish desire and imitate God's *niskamakarma* for the welfare of all, *lokasamgraham*.[25]

The point to note here is the keen awareness of historical existence from which the dilemma itself arose, and especially the position of the Gita in almost identifying *Mukti* or wholeness with selfless action for the welfare of all, thus introducing salvation into the stream of history, and into the heart of our struggle to become a human community. Selfless action is good and no doer of good will ever be destroyed nor tread the path of woe.[26]

Many important hints for the Gita's conception of time are found in its fourth chapter. Time is open to God's action: first through revelation given at the beginning; second, through His present word; third, through his coming into being on earth from age to age to re-establish *Dharma*; and fourth, through his love for the human person.[27] These are moments of salvation, and we stand summoned to decision. But time is open not only to God but also to anti-God powers. Time is *Kurukshetra* where conflicting forces confront each other. Time becomes for us summons and opportunity for life or for death, depending on the response we choose to give.

Time rolls on in cycles like the wheels of a vehicle, but time understood as mere days and nights and seasons following one after another in rotation, is not history. It is when a human being rides it that it becomes history. The mechanical time can be led to a meaningful personal goal and thus redeemed by faith in the Lord. The possibility of a definite end to *samsara* is "not a rare possibility nor a hard one". Even a little of *dharma* will save a man from recurring death.[28] The road of death is *samsara*, cyclic time, while the path of life is history, time open to God's love and ripening into life with him. The liberated do not return to any form or process or experience of death. The Gita does not rule out a new *kalpa* but it will be a new set of relationships and a new complex of action and reaction, opportunities and responses.

So there is place for community concern in Hinduism. The ascetic tradition of withdrawal from the world and from works is set aside not mainly on grounds of personal perfection, but in view of *Lokasamgraham*, the unity and well-being of the world. Commitment to action has basis in the longing to bring about the welfare of all. Caring of this kind will also blaze a trail for others just as God's own caring for the world is a model for us. The ideas of renunciation, world welfare, selflessness, concern for all beings, etc. provide the basis for a social ethic and social gospel which the Buddhist tradition and several branches of Hinduism have sought age after age to make operative in actual life.

According to Rayan, the historical dimensions of Gita are remarkably profound. So the idea of history was not brought to India by Western colonizers. The author of the Gita shows a keen awareness of history which is a holy history. A basic fact of India's culture is the clear awareness that the whole of existence is holy being rooted in God and continuing to be in and through him. The very structure and composition of his work, the way he makes all previous religious thought and tradition – the *Vedas*, the *Samkhya* system, Buddhist concepts and the whole world of the *Upanisad* – converge on Krishna and serve the revelation of Krishna, after they have come under his judgement for correction and discernment, show his grasp of India's holy history as something moving towards Krishna. There is a sense of direction, of past and future, of *Kairoi*. The author sees the different views as stages in a growth, within each of which he is ready to see God's hidden presence.[29] History is congenial to India's spirit and belongs to the structure of its inner life. What we meet in India is not anti-historical and negative attitudes but a religious culture that is very much open and sensitive to the historical.

But having the same idea of history is not the same as having the same experiences in history. There is actual diversity in the experience of history in different cultures and even within the same religious-cultural milieu, as for example, the time of the Bible and modern Europe. But one common understanding about history today is that it should take sources seriously and analyse them critically to arrive at the truth. It is an understanding that emerged with the Enlightenment. But the claim of the grand old man of "Enlightenment History", Leopold von Ranke that it is possible to know something from the past as it actually was (*wie es eigentlich gewesen ist*) through historical research is abandoned today as unachievable. The essential element of history now is not its pastness but its meaningfulness, its responsibility to the human now.[30]

Even in Christian theology there are diverse understandings of the notion of history and its importance for theology. Rayan proves this from the writings of three Western Christian theologians: Rudolf Bultmann, Wolfhart Pannenberg and Hans Urs von Balthasar. Rudolf Bultmann, for example, is emphatic in saying that history cannot be the basis of faith. Faith rests on the Word alone. Basing faith on history is historically impossible and theologically illegitimate. History is intensely personal; for the believer, the problem of universal history no longer exists. The end of history has come in the Christ-event and in one's experience of the Christ- event.[31]According to Rayan, such an understanding of faith and history would find ready acceptance by the Hindus. The Gita holds not that one reaches Krishna when *samsara* comes to an end but that *samsara* ends for everybody who reaches Krishna. The Indian position is that something happens to the structures and processes of history when the very goal of history becomes present within history and we respond to it in faith. Another ancient Hindu belief is that faith cannot be made dependent upon scientific history. Our faith existence is already above history and time; our freedom is limited because we are chained by our past. It is therefore necessary for one to become free from oneself through faith.[32] Bultmann's transcending of the historical through faith is very much in line with that of the Gita's.

Wolfhart Pannenberg agrees with Bultmann that in Jesus indeed the "End" or the finality of history has appeared within history but it does not end history. It is only an anticipation of the end of history. It rather makes history possible, giving it meaning and coherence.

For Pannenberg, the individual is not the centre and bearer of history, but God and his actions. When the individual is the centre of history the unity of history is dissolved. The unity of history is in God who grounds it, embraces the contingencies of history and is ever faithful. Hence, the concept of God is indispensable for the historian. The history of humans cannot be told apart from the history of God. History is a totality comprising creation and redemption, the inner world as well as the outer. Revelation is not a plus added to history, but it belongs to the historical itself. Only on the presupposition of a universal historical horizon can one meaningfully raise the question of whether God has revealed himself at one or in several places and times in history. According to Rayan, Pannenberg's position rejoins cherished Indian convictions concerning the unity of history and the presence of the God of salvation to all people everywhere. The Hindu will be appreciative of the truth that the history of the human being cannot be told without the history of God and that God has a history with the whole of his creation. He will also point out that this conception of history as the unity of the secular and the redemptive, of humans and God with Jesus as the centre is no longer linear.[33]

Hans Urs von Balthasar maintains with Bultmann that the human being, thinking, loving and spiritual, is not a particular reality limited by and tied down to concrete time and space. Each one has a universality, a comprehensive character and an expansion to the ultimate boundaries of the universe and to the last frontiers of reality. His historicity, therefore, is not only in being in space and time but in making history in his or her decisions, choices, struggles, all of which have a universal reference. With Pannenberg he holds that there is actually no distinction between a particular, historical salvation history and a universal secular history. This distinction is annulled with the Christ-event. World history and salvation history practically coincide. This is exactly the point the Hindu makes when he raises difficulties about the historical Jesus. Nobody wholly immersed in the limiting particularities of space-time history could have universal saving significance. In their religious thought and spiritual experience both coalesce.[34]

So there is no single conception of history nor a uniform theology of history. There is no common stand on the relation between Christ and time and on what happens to history when the End of history appears right within it. There is no clarity about whether history is linear or cyclic; rather it begins to appear that neither model is adequate to describe the complex reality we call history. None of the theologians mentioned above seems to say categorically that history is linear, which has been the first principle of Western understanding of the historical process. The principle was allegedly derived from the Bible, though the biblical idea of history is not quite linear either.

The biblical idea of history is based on captivity and liberation. The cycle of "sin-calamity-repentance-liberation-sin-calamity" keep rotating. The Ecclesiastes finds nothing new happening under the sun. If history is understood in terms of the new, or defined as humanity making itself, or as human beings' increasing mastery over nature, the Bible has little of that. Nearly always the agent is God alone; the human person is not making himself, but is being made, liberated, led, carried, punished, rejected, taken back, and so on. When God begins to have a history along with us, not only secular and sacred history begin to coalesce, but both cyclic and linear are also surpassed. History obtains a new multidimensionality, depth and breadth. This is what Vatican II affirmed when it said that any person at any point of time may become present to and be ruled by the Paschal Mystery, which, although understood as a particular historical event, is salvifically present to the totality of the historical process. The conclusion is that history lies beyond linear and cyclic thought patterns and must be described in non-geometrical, positively personal terms. That is why the Bible does not understand history in the modern Western sense with dates, names, places, chronology or sequences, nor gives importance to exact reporting of what was said or done. The concern is for meaning, for the message and for the personal dimensions within the context of God's saving action. What the Bible presents are theologies of history. And this is true in its measure of India's traditions as well.[35]

3. Relevance for an Indian Christian Theology

It may be interesting to note that in the wake of the Modernist Crisis a century ago, the clergy were not allowed to study in Universities without explicit permission, and the two most dangerous courses to be avoided were philosophy and history. The Church had for a very long time shunned a historically conscious approach. A historically conscious approach sees the Church as a divine-human reality. What has taken place in history is very much human but it can also point beyond the human, to the presence of the divine in the world. In other words, being historical does not deny the "Mystery" of the Church. But that does not free the Church from human limitations and errors. The Church is a living, changing and ever adaptable organism whose life and structures are never to be identified with one culture, social system or period of time. Often there was resistance to historical research because it was embarrassing to the Church. But, that does not free the Church from the obligation to follow a strictly historical method. But being historically conscious is something more than following a strictly historical method. According to Rayan, "when we are committed to and involved in the making and up-building of history, we shall come to know history's true shape and face, and we shall know its real enemies and their way of effectively abolishing it".[36] History does not just happen by the passing of time. Time can pass mechanically and such time is not history. Real time is "human time", time as experienced by humans and that makes history. When time is humanized it is historicized and then it is given a new content and a meaning. Here time begins to be purposeful and forward looking. Time begins to have a face. It is in and with such moments and actions that history is made. It is not made by moving forward but moving deeper into reality and life. History is a matter of relationships and this relationship also includes God and it is in this sense that history is also salvation history. God encounters us in history on this earth, the totality of the universe and in ourselves. God makes history by creating the cosmos, by creating human beings and in his interventions on behalf of the human which all religions proclaim. For Christians it has culminated in Jesus Christ. Human beings make history, when they imitate God and his actions, for freedom, dignity and justice – "Action to bring good news to the poor, and liberty to captives, action to restore to the dispossessed masses their land and their power over their own future, action to end imperialism of every kind and to liberate people from political, economic and cultural colonialism and action to set the downtrodden free and build a new social order in which justice shall dwell".[37] The making of history and its progress are, therefore, to be understood not in geometrical terms of the linear and the circular, but in ethical and spiritual terms of the coming of the Kingdom on our earth. Temporality is only a condition for authentic existence. History is made or unmade in the measure human beings create conditions for authentic existence. History is made or unmade in the measure people wake up to the reality and struggle for freedom and justice. Whatever is not fostering freedom and justice is not genuinely historical, it is non-history. According to Rayan, the vocabulary of the linear and cyclic, vertical and horizontal, is a diversionary tactic to distract us from the tasks of the moment and the demands of history. The Bible traces the advance of history in terms of justice and freedom through concrete struggles. But it is possible to dehistoricize the Bible and reduce its historical message to general spiritual principles with no teeth to bite into the hard realities of earthly existence. It has been possible to dehistoricize Christ, too. We have been given a Christ who was very much God but the historical Jesus was reduced to an irrelevant incident. What mattered were the eternal truths. Orthodox theology does not deny the historical humanity of Christ. It simply disregards it. It is concerned with Christ's eternal 'human nature', but not with the contingent event of his human life in the world, nor with the fact that Christ belongs totally to history.

The key to a theological understanding of time and history seems to lie in the fact that the end of history is already present within it. If history is one unity, the end or the Eschaton is present within the tissues of history and is active in it from start to finish. For Christians, the risen Jesus is the Eschatological reality and the fulfilment of history. His Resurrection and Ascension are not a withdrawal from history but fuller, deeper involvement in it by being present within the totality of space and time and in the heart of every person. The resin Lord is the depth of history. The final reality is God's and is God himself. God continually transforms the world and the movements of history which are full of promises and risks. History is the relationship God establishes with humankind. It is a matter of chosen relationships and not of chronological advance. Wherever a human being existentially responds to God in faith, time matures and comes to ripeness and history reaches its end. Since God is love, love is the Eschatological virtue. Wherever people love truly, they are in a movement to the Eschaton, to the end time and the completion of history. Love binds people together and humanises them. Love unites past, present and future. Love is the ultimate historical virtue. The human being is the central reality on earth, the centre of history. Time is for the human person; he is its meaning. It is the arena of his decisions and actions. He, through his humane actions in time and history, gives meaning to them, transforming himself and the earth and creating a community.[38]

Truly historical choices are actions by which humans become increasingly more human. The way to the human is not the way of domination, conquest or violence, of enslavement, exploitation or brute strength. Such actions do not spring from a truly historical perspective and a genuine sense of history. Every decision and movement detrimental to humans and creative of unfreedom, suffering and misery render time futile, empties it of historical content and turns its course backward in the direction of initial chaos. Any fanaticism and militancy can only be understood as a lack of historical configurations and a sense of time and space. Rayan quotes Karl Marx who defines every age in which all men and women are not free, in which not all men and women are decision-makers and shapers of their own destiny, in which some are masters and others slaves, in which a few are affluent and the rest are wretched, in which antagonisms and contradictions exist within productive relationships, as pre-history, where people are not yet human, no one is properly human. Human history proper will begin only when humankind's brokenness is healed and a society without classes and contradictions has been achieved. Every effort and movement towards authentic human life is of historical significance; what moves away from this ideal of the human is historically negative and preventive of our evolution into the historical age.[39]

What we need for the making of history is not mere technology and the control of nature but a new humanity with foundations laid deep in new hearts and new structures. And this can happen only with God because everything human is incomplete and deficient. We need God to work with us. In that way history is always salvation history in that God is active in the events of our life and struggles. He is the starting point of our history, its driving force and the end of history. The theological problem of history is, therefore, the problem of the inward history of each person, of his heart's experiences, struggles and decisions. It is also the challenge to change the old world and build a new one. But it is a partial view of history to describe it exclusively in terms of external action. History is also a matter of the heart and of faith.[40]

Therefore, religions cannot be but praxis, and true theology is a theology of praxis. Theology has to spring from the theologian's involvement in actual life situations of the concrete history of one's own nation or group, so that a theology may emerge capable of responding to actual needs and possibilities. Praxis means, further, that theology must make its contribution to remake the world and humanise history, so that God's rule may come. As education is praxis of freedom, so theology is the praxis of salvation, of human a wholeness and of ultimate meaning. All aspects of our faith can become dynamics of social change and of the evolution and rebuilding of history. It will not do merely to assert that the consciousness of world history is the contribution of Christianity or that Christianity is a historical religion. Is the universality of the Christian idea of God clear and beyond question in praxis? In a situation of injustice and oppression God does not exist. There is no faith, no universal and historic idea of God and no God except in the praxis of justice and compassion. Faith lives by building history. Universal history, all history is a task to fulfil and a mission to accomplish. It ismade in the measure in which we love and build up one another to shape a better world.[41]

Notes

1. Hereafter, *SR II.*
2. Hereafter, *SR III.*
3. Kurien Kunnumpuram, SJ (ed.), *Collected Writings of Samuel Rayan, SJ*, 3 Volumes, ISPCK, Delhi, 2013.
4. *SR III*, p. 342.
5. *Ibid.*
6. *Ibid.*, p. 343.
7. *Ibid.*, pp. 343-344.
8. *Ibid.*, p. 345.
9. *Ibid.*, pp. 345-348.
10. *Ibid.*, p. 349.
11. *Ibid.*, p. 350.
12. *Ibid.*, p. 352.
13. T. Raychaudhuri, "Indian Historiography", in J. Cannon et al. (eds.), *The Blackwell Dictionary of Historians*, Oxford, 1988, p. 205.
14. C. A. Bayly, "Modern Indian Historiography", in Michael Bentley *(ed.), Companion to Historiography*, Routledge: London and New York, 1997, pp. 678-680.
15. *SR II*, p. 193.
16. *Ibid.*
17. *Ibid.*
18. *Ibid.*
19. *Ibid.*, p. 194.
20. *Ibid.*, p. 195.
21. M. P. John, "The Problem of History in the New Testament: A Discussion in the Indian Context", *Indian Journal of Theology* 16 (1967) pp. 9-10.
22. *SR II*, p. 196.
23. *Ibid.*, pp. 196-197.
24. *Ibid.*, p. 197.
25. *Ibid.*, pp. 198-199.
26. *Ibid.*, p. 199.
27. *Ibid.*, pp. 200.
28. *Ibid.*, p. 201.
29. *Ibid.*, p. 203.

30. J. M. Patrapankal, "Is there a Scriptural Approach to the Knowledge of Christ?" in *Indian Journal of Theology* 16 (1967) p. 88.
31. *SR II*, pp. 206-207.
32. *Ibid.*, p.207.
33. *Ibid.*, p.208.
34. *Ibid.*, pp. 209-210.
35. *Ibid.*, p.211.
36. *Ibid.*, p.353.
37. *Ibid.*, p.354.
38. *Ibid.*, pp.212-213.
39. *Ibid.*, 214-215.
40. *Ibid.*, 216.
41. *Ibid.*, 216-218.

21

Prime Path-Finder of Dalits

A. Kulandaisamy, OFM Cap.

It is a privilege for me to critically comment on the writings on the dalits by Samuel Rayan, the well-known Indian theologian. He indeed apprehended the existing unjust society in which the subaltern people, especially dalits are insuperably struggling for extricating themselves from bondage. The one who is unable to analytically understand one's own societal situation cannot think of and work for the radical transformation of the unjust society in which one is immersed in. Contrary to this, the author emphatically affirms his comprehensive knowledge of his society in his writings on dalits. His profound knowledge of society persuades him to take sides with the subaltern groups like dalits, tribes, women, and the poor in the society. As a result of taking sides with the subaltern he thinks of, writes about and supports the theologization process of the subaltern or doing theology by decolonizing theology from the western constructs and concepts. He distinctly claims that colonization engenders exploitation, precipitating the swift corrosion of the freedom, dignity, life and culture of the subaltern people.[1] On account of the colonial domination, the creativity and resourcefulness of the subaltern deteriorate and they eventually become dependent at all levels of life and in all areas of existence. That is why they struggle against what is oppressive and inhuman and fight for a fuller life of dignity, finer justice and integral liberation. This ethical fighting against social evils and oppression for the establishment of a just society is doing theology or theologizing. That's why the author rightly stresses that the starting point of theologizing is not concepts but concrete reality, life and history.[2] Thus, theologizing of the subalterns is an emancipation from the oppressive reality, the empowerment of the vulnerable and the enrichment of all those who are broken. It should be noted that this process of liberation happens within the very textures of oppression. Hence, my concern in this essay is about the dalits who are struggling for justice and liberation in the writings of Samuel Rayan. This article focuses on the understanding, approaches and inevitable constituents of dalit theology as propounded by the author in his writings. The first part of this article deals with his perception on dalits and the second part emphasizes his ideology.

His Perception

Dalitness: The Demand of Justice

There is a tradition, with an unwritten law, which is not uncommon today in many of the remote villages, that only non-dalits can name dalits at their birth. The names given by the non-dalits convey two significant implications: first, the dalits have no right to give a name to themselves; second, these names carry within them the virus of a binary opposition of 'we- the pure' and 'you-the impure'. As against the names[3] given by the non-dalits, the dalits choose to call themselves dalits. The name 'dalit' identifies their oppressors and the cause of their dehumanized situations. This name 'dalit' connotes the consciousness of the existence of slavery and oppression. The name 'dalit' also indicates certain militancy and stands as a symbol of change, confrontation and revolution. That is why, the author rightly points out that dalit literally means brokenness, oppression and dehumanization. The name 'dalit', therefore, makes the dalits realize the truth about themselves and to identify their own victimhood. Hence, this naming of themselves, which is a social reality, is the beginning of the process of theologizing.[4] Hence, this naming precisely portrays the dehumanized and oppressed condition of the dalits or their dalitness.

According to the author, dalitness is often bound up with myths of purity and pollution. To substantiate this affirmation, he quotes from the Bible that the Jews would not associate with Samaritans or with Gentiles (Jn 4:9; Acts 10:28; Mk 7:26-28; Lev 11-15).[5] However, in the creation story we read that God finds that everything is good (Gen 1:1-26) and God never calls anyone as profane or unclean. This indicates that the mythical stories on purity and pollution are concocted by human beings for providing a justification of their oppressive hierarchical structures. Therefore, the author clearly points out that dalitness is a human creation, particularly the creation of the so-called high caste people. In the beginning, there was no dalitness, no oppression and no brokenness. All creatures are created by God who is a God of justice, equality and brotherhood. It is the oppressors who on account of their vested interests and selfish intent, systematically discriminate against dalits and bring untouchability into existence. Therefore, dalitness, that is, loss of dignity, rights, humanness and freedom is also the fact of being oppressed by the high caste.

Dalitness, the consequence of the injustice perpetrated by the so-called high caste people, does not mean a fatal resignation to constraints or loss of the nobility of one's heart. Dalitness, instead, sharpens the critical spirit, ferments the thirst for freedom and energizes the dalit community for the struggle for empowerment.[6] The author clearly states that dalitness enkindles the liberative spirit in the dalits for eradicating untouchability. Therefore, dalitness demands emancipation from all forms of enslavement, ethical commitment to justice and freedom, and moral indignation against human degradation. In the words of Marvin Ellison, dalitness breeds dalit theologizing for liberation that is born not in books but in communities of resistance that are deeply embedded in social relations of domination and subordination.[7] The goal of dalitness, therefore, is to radically bring about the transformation of the unjust society. For the author, dalitness is not only an outcome of bondage but also the cradle of acts of justice, struggles for freedom, and emancipation of life from degradation and the celebration of life with rights. Dalitness demands justice, which is the quintessence of dalit liberation. This justice can be formal justice (the impartial, consistent and fair application of principles themselves) and substantive justice (legitimate demand of justice). Dalitness demands that one has to be rooted in the realities of life and work towards the restoration of the dignity and rights of dalits.

Rootedness: An act of Faith

Those who sincerely want to work for the liberation of the dalits, first and foremost ought to immerse themselves in their struggles and dreaded situations. This immersion initiates a process of theologizing like the one that happened when Jesus stepped into the River Jordan. This immersion enlightens one to recognize the humanity of the dalits, acknowledge their dignity and affirm their worth. Like Jesus, this immersion moulds the dalit liberators to be one with the untouchables and outcastes of all times and everywhere. This "being-with" consciously animates the dalit liberators to meticulously search for the root cause of their oppression and dehumanization and to discover new ways and means of annihilating the existing oppressive structures. This "being-with" summons the liberator to go to the dalits outside their own camp to share their degradation or insult (Heb 13:11-13), to identify oneself with the dalits' defencelessness, outcastededness, fleshlessness and then empty one's life too in liberating action.[8] This efficacious identification like Jesus' table fellowship with societal and religious outcastes generates the hope of a liberated future to the hopeless people.

This immersion or "being-with" or identification paves the way for taking root in the socio-cultural, economical and political lives of the dalits. The liberators, by being rooted in the life of the dalits, come to know about the emancipatory dynamics found in cultures of the dalits and learn the human values envisaged in their ordinary existence. This rootedness in dalits' mind-set of death and triumphant injustice awakens a fresh hope and a new vision of a new community founded on equality, fraternity and love. Those participating in the liberative process of the dalits have been enabling the oppressed people to no longer see their plight as an intractable fate but as an artificial human creation, which they can tackle, use and forge into a sword, which severs the chains that hold them in bondage.[9] For the author, rootedness is the external manifestation of faith in a God of justice. That is why he obviously interprets Christian faith as going outside the camp and leaving the caste fortresses and prisons in order to forge solidarity with the oppressed. This solidarity is a constitutive element of Christian faith.[10] This rootedness, therefore, is an ethical demand of faith and stands out as the very core of faith. It remains as an essential component of faith and the axis of its growth. This rootedness is indeed painful but an effective process, because it provides an indispensable transition from security to insecurity. This faith-manifestation, which is demonstrated in rootedness, rescues the dalits and leads them to the world of freedom, dignity and creative living. This rootedness would be the right and justifiable response to the call, cry and demand of the dalits. To lead the oppressed to a just world, rootedness has to promote subversive as well as inversive activities, which are affirmative actions for justice and rights.

Inversion: Act of prophetic Revolution

Another act of rootedness is the readiness to critically study the reality and constructively analyze the existing oppressive structures of a society. Constructive criticism that vividly clarifies what is oppressive and what is liberative cleanses the corrupt society. In the process of cleansing, something unjust has to be either eliminated or subverted or inverted and something just and liberative has to be protected and promoted. Constructive criticism engenders subversion, which is a destabilization of the authority of any system that enslaves. For the author, subversion is a prophetic and messianic act. The author states that Jesus subverted the central socio-religious traditions like purity laws and Sabbath regulations (Jn 9:24-25; Matt 11:16-19).[11] Another example cited by the author is God enlightening Peter not to call anyone profane or unclean. Subversion depicts the liberator's comprehensive knowledge of the present society. Subversion is an act of discretion and an ethical act of the liberator. Subversive action is the first step for an integral liberation as well as for a radical transformation. Subversion empowers the dalits to regain or restore their mortgaged self from the oppressive elites. It is a sign of independent thinking or self-reflection. Unless and until dalits subvert the domination of the so-called high caste, the radical change of an unjust society becomes impossible. The repeated subversive activities lead to inversion.

The author mentions in his writing that inversion is a major theme of the New Testament. For example, the song of Mary expounds that God turns the social order upside down and puts the dalits in charge of history.[12] Inversion denotes putting traditional practices upside down or in the opposite order, position or arrangement. For the author, Jesus unmasked the myth of pure ancestry. Even if the biological purity of blood were true and demonstrable, Jesus profoundly states that anyone who does the will of God is my mother and my brothers. This reply of Jesus carries a profound challenge to everybody and impels the liberators to transcend biological-natural purity of race or nobility of birth. Jesus sets upside down the Jewish dietary rules by conducting table-fellowship with the outcaste, which is an indigestible act for the Jews. Like all forms of oppression, the caste system also creates and imposes a culture of silence.[13] Dalits neither complain of torture, exploitation and rape nor speak at all. They are kept in a sullen silence. The right to speech is intentionally denied to the dalits on whom silence is forced upon by the so-called high caste. For the author, dumbness is thrust upon the oppressed by the satanic social forces and their human agents. Now Jesus breaks into such situations and empowers them to speak, protest, claim their rights and affirm life.

The author also inverts the traditional understanding of the Eucharist. For him, the celebration of Eucharist is a promise to overcome oppression and division and to build a community of justice and equality.[14] The author emphatically states that to practise discriminations in the Eucharistic celebration is to convert the Eucharist into a ritualistic act and to numb its socially transformative thrust. Inversion is a revolutionary activity that eliminates the dehumanized structures. The author quotes the words of M. N. Sriniwas that the rebel or revolutionary sects reject the idea of brahminical supremacy, the performance of elaborate rituals and the punctilious observance of rules of pollution and purity. Instead, they emphasized the love of God and right conduct as indispensable to salvation.[15] Inversion that brings forth revolution will never accept blindly any hegemonial ideology, inhuman practices and colonized or enslaved structures. It always attempts to wittingly do away with them. Inversion, therefore, is not only elimination but also creation of a society based on egalitarianism. Therefore, inversion creates and prepares a space for the invention of newness and the writing of an alternative history or dalit history.

Historiography: An Inevitable Move for Liberation

When the author speaks of people's theology he strongly advocates that people's theology should recognize its foundations in the events of history in which people share their faith, work and life struggles for liberation. The word 'people' in Greek is λαικός (LAOS), which signifies the working class or subaltern people or people of inferior rank. That is why he wants theology to emerge from below, not to be enforced from above. In other words, theology should emerge from the subaltern or oppressed or dalits and not from the elites or ruling class or the so-called high caste. Dalit theology, therefore, emerges from the historical events of dalits without which there can no longer be theology. We should always remember that the history of the dalits is different from that of the so-called high caste. The following differentiations can obviously be observed:

First, the history of the so-called high caste considers dalits or subalterns to be objects or spectators or aliens of history, but the history of dalits considers the dalits the subjects of history or creators of history. Second, the history of the so-called high caste records only achievements of individuals and eventful ones associated with power and the throne, but the history of the dalits records their struggles, disappointments and failures which constitute the eventful history of everyday life. Third, the history of the so-called high caste is written in books, but the history of the dalits is an oral narrative. Fourth, the history of the so-called high caste is one-sided, fragmented and biased but the history of the dalits is erased by the ruling class from the surface of the earth. Fifth, the history of the so-called high caste is a justification of unjust slave-ridden society, but the history of the dalits is revolutionary and liberative and an inverse agent. Sixth, the history of the so-called high caste is unity and adopts a monolithical identity, but the history of the dalits is diverse and has overlapping of identities or multiple identities.

Observing the differences, we can say that the history of the dalits is not a history but historiography, that means the study of error in the history of the so-called high castes and writing a counter or alternative history to that of high caste. This writing of historiography is doing theology or subaltern theologizing. This historiography is the subaltern history that wakes up the dalits to the truth of their condition develops a critical consciousness, discerns between justice and injustice and distinguishes between true peace and the calm of structural violence. It recognizes the dignity of dalits and their vocation to live as God's friends and co-workers in the fashioning of the New Age and the New Earth.[16] For the author, the lower classes need not remain low and their squalor and servitude are not part of God's plan. Historiography provokes justice and makes the dalits know about the historical injustices done by the so-called high caste. One can never initiate a rightful process of theologizing without historiography. It is an indispensable prerequisite for liberation. One who understands the history of the dalits stands by them in the eradication of untouchability. The dalits can work as the children of God by throwing away the yoke imposed on them, because their historiography points out their enemies and the oppressive structures. Therefore, for the author, the essential element of historiography is not its pastness but its meaningfulness.[17] Historiography embedded with the alienated and the marginalized becomes meaningful to the dalits to extricate them from the history of enslavement. In this alternative, the history of the dalits finds sense, assurance and effective means for freedom and methods of evaluating their strength and weakness for the exodus march. As dalit liberators design historiography they become the defenders of their rights and dignity.

Defensiveness: An Act of Discipleship

The author states that all people are sacred because they are created in the image of God. In other words, nobody can ever subjugate others and all are equal. The community of men and women in equality is the place of life-giving encounter and communion with God. If the community observes caste distinctions, practises untouchability and discriminates in any way against the dalits, it lacks the elements of Christian community and the basics of Christian faith. In such a community, the dalit is found without the means required to meet human needs, without resources for creative action and participative life in society.[18] In a caste and class discriminated society, the ethical God always abides with the weak, the powerless and the socially humiliated and empowers the downtrodden by defending the inalienable as well as the constitutional rights of dalits. For the author, God is always on the side of the oppressed (Ps 103:6) to urge the dalits to reject and resist attitudes, acts and traditions of contempt.

The author wants the community of followers of Jesus to be the community of the disciples of Jesus. Our discipleship consists in opting out of an old order of wealth, privilege, popularity and security in order to follow Jesus who defends the rights of the marginalized and exalts the downtrodden. To be a disciple is to be a catalyst of a new human awakening, of a fresh awareness of the possibilities of the deprived masses, of effective organizing and a responsible dissenter of anti-human, unjust and demonic elements of the so-called high caste. A disciple of Jesus is to secure for the dalits constitutional rights like justice in social, economic and political life, equality in status and opportunity, liberty and fraternity. The disciple of Jesus resolves to defend the constitutional rights of dalits like article 38 of the directive principles[19], article 46,[20] article 16(4),[21] and article 338[22] assured in The Constitution of India. The disciples of Jesus constitute a living Church that continues the mission of liberation.

The mission of the Church is to free and enable dalits to be themselves first and then build their destiny and their future. The author reinforces that the ecclesial mission ought to liberate the dalits from ritual religion and morality; and from the meshes of legalistic religion and morality and the shallowness of externalism. The church must remove every sort of fear of gods and evil spirits from the dalits. The nature of the Church is to emancipate the dalits from all burdensome traditions and all oppressive powers symbolized in the caste system. To be a Church means liberating the subaltern from isolation and individualism. The liberated Church will never be a preacher of innocuous pieties, dealer in religious platitudes, and a traditionalist mouthing old words or quoting ancient authorities.

The silence of the Church amidst enormous atrocities perpetrated on the dalits is not an example of ambiguity but an example of support for the status quo, which has mechanisms of oppression built into itself.[23] Being silent makes the people of God to deeply get involved in the system of individualism and competition with a view to the maximization of profit. That is why the author consciously admonishes that the concern of the Church is not Christians but the poor; its struggle is not for itself but for the liberation of the captives.[24] Instead of being an instrument of oppression, the Church must be a catalyst of social change, defender of the weaker sections, and a movement of liberation and life of the lifeless. Therefore, the call of the Church for a redistribution of national resources will be heralded by a re-allocation of its own resources with a clear partiality for the poor and the downtrodden. The author expects that, like Jesus, His followers and the Church are to be defenders of the inalienable and constitutional rights of the dalits. For him, defending the rights against injustice is the life-breath of all the creatures in the world. Defending the weak is the manifestation of divinity and holiness. Defensiveness is an act of right conscience of society that demands discipleship. A true disciple has to be the voice of the voiceless, right of the rightless and hope of the hopeless. Therefore, the Church becomes secular in order to work for all the oppressed. Those who defend the rights of the weak are by nature secular.

Inclusiveness: The Nature of Secularism

The word 'secular' though having many layers of meaning is being analyzed in three levels. In the first level, in secularization what were once considered sacred are viewed and interpreted more and more in a worldly perspective. According to the author secularization is the activity and the process of thus distinguishing, separating and liberating the world and human affairs from the dictates of religious authorities and of turning people's attention away from the "other world" to this world. For example, the subalterns, particularly the dalits, unlike the so-called high caste, neither deify and make sacred something in the created world nor cause sacrilege to them but accept and respect everything as they are. In the second level, the words 'secular' and 'secularity' refer to a state of society resulting from this process of secularization. Secularity describes the characteristics of the free reality. For example, the dalits are not willing to be slaves to something but they are enslaved by the so-called high caste. They make up their minds to get rid of this bondage. Strictly speaking, they are free beings or secular. In the third level, secularism refers to the ideology and philosophy that support secularization and secularity. Secularism not only affirms the relative autonomy of the historical events but also rejects all transcendence and denies everything that is not measurable by empirical standards. For example, the dalits do not believe in a God, religion and sacred scriptures that enslave them, but do believe in humanism. However secularism in a pluralistic society has various contextual significances.

Firstly, secularism that is specifically a word of this present material world is the cradle of pluralism. The Latin word '*saeculum*' from which the English word 'secular' is derived denotes the temporal aspect of life and world realities. For the author, in a broad sense secularism refers to time, what belongs to this age, what is engaged in, cares for the present world, for the earth, for the temporal and the historical world.[25] Secularism deals with this present and existing world but not the other world of which nobody has an empirical knowledge. That is why the dalits do not believe in rebirth, salvation, dogmas, karma theory, theology of heaven and hell and the subtle doctrines of the other world. This existing world created by God is real and materially visible but not *maya* or illusionary. The dalits are believers of materiality and visibility that are highly envisioned by secularism. They are people of this world. This tangible world that is the source of life for the dalits is to be well protected. The dalits, who are an embodiment of secularism, really fight against ecological crises like deforestation, pollution, commodification of natural resources, global warming and industrialization. Thus, secularism is the principle of materiality and of present life. Materiality definitely entails particularity and contextuality. That is why every society finds its own forms of secularism according to its contexts and needs. Therefore, the concept of secularism is polyvalent, context-based, culture-specific and this world-oriented. Hence, secularism constitutes a living world of pluralism.

Secondly, another aspect of secularism is the principle of neutrality. In a society embedded with multiple cultures, languages, religions and races the state has to adopt a stance of neutrality in the mode of governance. When a state tends to favour one group and is prejudiced against another group it becomes anti-secular. This neutrality that eliminates favouritism eventually establishes an egalitarian society. Therefore, the author interprets secularism in such way that it includes sensible religious and sacred realities, meaningful spiritual activities and liberative ecclesiastical institutions, which are no less than everyday economic and political concerns.[26] It was with this sense of egalitarianism that the Constitution of India was framed to affirm the secular nature of Indian state. Privileging one religion or linguistic community has been avoided in order to treat all religions and minority communities equally. The secular orientation of the constitution goes against communal violence. The modern legal status of neutrality implies impartiality and equality that consider everything as equal. This equality emerging from secularism strongly thwarts dominance, oppression, slavery and the hierarchical system. In a context of inequality, secularism cultivates the sense of liberation in the hearts of secular people. The secular people like the dalits and women have a thirst for emancipation.

Thirdly, the implication of secularism is the principle of co-existence and human solidarity. It is the principle of regulation of inter-human relationships in equity. In India, secularism synthesizes religious harmony and tolerance. Sometimes secularism excludes various dogmas and beliefs tenaciously held by religions, superstitious religious practices and irrational traditions like caste system maintained and practised by religions. However, in fact secularism need not necessarily and in every case imply indifference or opposition to religion, because religions have great power and actually play a crucial role in constructing a just society. Therefore, the author writes that the religious and the secular are neither rejected nor ignored nor privatized but consciously included.[27] This inclusiveness that is the ethical principle of nature brings forth co-existence and tolerance. The issue of co-existence and tolerance becomes in practice an issue of inter-religious relationship. In the same way, religious freedom is as much a secular issue as it is a religious issue. For example, the queen of England is still the head of the Anglican Church in England and in the same way the monarch even today appoints the Archbishop of Canterbury. Secularism and religions basically work for the welfare of the society. Religions, castes, race, language, nature and people are by nature inclusive. Therefore, they co-exist and tolerate each other without dominating each other. For example, the civil religion spoken of by Rousseau is not opposed to secularism or detrimental to it. There is a give and take policy among them. Thus, secularism signifies inclusiveness articulated in the context of co-existence and tolerance.

His Emphasis

The author rightly understands the subaltern, particularly the dalit issues and underlines the root causes of oppression. However, his emphasis varies from that of dalit theologians in India. Firstly, it seems that the author in all his writings propounds the non-dalits as agents of liberation of the dalits. He substantiates his arguments with Jesus' model of working for the liberation. It can be a descending model. By participation in the struggles of the marginalized Jesus becomes a marginalized in order to extricate them. It can be self-marginalization that is willingly and voluntarily chosen by individuals. It is also very much required for the annihilation of enslavement. This kind of participation can be called descending or vertical participation that can make the subalterns, particularly the dalits, passive recipients of liberation from non-dalits. It can work for liberation without getting their co-operation or active and strenuous involvement. The oppressed may not feel the value and the ethical demand of liberation. It may lead to indifference to the construction of a just society. That is why Ambedkar admonishes the liberators to participate in the freedom-struggle already initiated by the dalits per se. Here the dalits become agents of their liberation that demands of them an active and significant role for liberation. It can be an ascending or horizontal method in which they fight against dehumanization with conviction till the end. They realize that their dalitness is imposed upon them by the so-called high caste. They whole-heartedly include the non-dalit liberators in their exodus journey. In such a context, the dalits disseminate that dalitness, which is not only a problem of the dalits but also that of the whole humanity. Therefore, it should be highlighted that dalit liberation is a liberation of the entire humankind of which the oppressed are the agents.

Secondly, the author focuses his attention on the weakness or impoverishments like untouchability, landlessness, dependence and powerlessness of dalits rather than on their strength and values like sharing, unity, hard-work, simplicity, humanness and frankness. There is a public opinion that non-dalits should sympathize with the dalits, because the dalits know nothing at all about themselves and so non-dalits should teach them everything. However, the non-dalits fail to learn from the life-struggles of the dalits. In such a context, non-dalits ought to breathe for the survival of the dalits. It is like spoon-feeding and possessiveness. In the words of Leo Tolstoy it is like a man sitting on the back of dalits making them carry, having pity on them, wishing to lighten their load by all possible means except getting off their back.[28] There prevails a cultural hegemony, which has been introduced by the so-called high caste on the dalits. Here non-dalits determine or decide the method and means of fighting for the liberation of dalits. Their creativity, potentiality, human values and thirst for liberation will go either unnoticed or undermined. This is not liberation but another form of bondage. However, the biblical God takes sides with the oppressed due to their strength, cultural values, humanism and sacredness. Liberators should learn from the dalits and put forth their cultural symbols as liberative instruments. This recognition of their strength or potentiality surely emboldens the dalits as liberators who are in search of a new cultural identity.

Thirdly, the author intends to affirm that theology is not faith seeking understanding but faith seeking justice, because justice is enshrined in faith. Here he speaks of orthodoxy or right opinion of theology, but not of orthopraxis or right action. Theory and action or thinker and activist are differentiated or considered as two separate entities, but they are to complement each other. In other words, they should emerge from one source, that is, the personal experience with the subalterns. The experience comes from the struggles for liberation of the dalits. The thinker or scholar must emerge in the context of the suffering and agony of the oppressed in which he or she has a personal experience and in a similar way the activist must think in the same above mentioned context. Otherwise, their theory and action would become out-modeled or they cannot be consonant with the actual oppressive situations of the dalits in order to liberate them from their situations. In other words, the proposed ways and means will no longer liberate the oppressed. One who has experienced or undergone repression by the so-called high caste can effectively think and do something for liberating oneself with the co-operation of other dalits and non-dalits. Today, the so-called scholars or thinkers who have no exile experience have only intellectual knowledge or volumes of books to their credit, mostly remaining futile, for liberating the oppressed. However, the activists who have experienced oppression speak and write a little and work more for liberation. Here experience that is the base for both theory and action becomes a source and efficacious means of emancipation.

As a conclusion, liberation theology that emerged in Latin American countries brought an epistemological break in the life of the entire Church. Indian theologians like Sebastian Kappen and M. M. Thomas attempted to articulate a liberation theology in the form of subaltern theologies. In the seventies and eighties, the author inverted ecclesial thinking and the mission of the church in India. He very systematically contextualizes the Word of God, the mission of the church, dogmas, theology and doctrines of church according to the dalit context of India. The liberation of the subaltern people is the central and pivotal theme of his writings. The author, however, according to my observation, lacks emphasis on the dalit as the agent of liberation, on the strength of dalits and the dalit experience as the source of theory and action.

I consider, therefore, this author as a prime path-finder but not the path of liberation per se like Jesus, Periyar, Nammazhvar, Narayana Guru, Jyotirao Phule, Oscar Romero, and Helder Camara. The path can only be found in immersion, participation and identification with the dalits, without which the path-finder remains in illusion. The path is the result of prolonged struggles, agony and toil found in the process of liberation, but the path-finder is an outcome of intellectual pursuits. The path emerges from personal experiences with the oppressed but the path-finding comes out of rationality. The path is verified and lived by the dalits and is very vivid but the path-finding is a not yet reality. It is very nebulous. The path demands emancipatory actions but the path-finder proposes different versions of enslaving theories. To be a path is to be practical, which is challenging indeed, but path-finding is a theoretical and rhetorical. In other words, the path-finder becomes alien to the path and can only allude to the path of dalit liberators. Here my intention is not to undermine his epoch-making contributions to the field of theology of the Church in India. Rather, I wish to underline that there has not been a tangible transition from the path-finding to being an inspiring liberative path. The subaltern communities in India are nevertheless very indebted to and ever grateful to this defender of the subaltern. He is one of the pioneers and defenders of dalit liberation.

Notes

1. Samuel Rayan, "Decolonization of the Theology", *Doing Theology*, ed., Kurien Kunnumpuram, Vol. II, (New Delhi: ISPCK, 2013), p. 26.
2. Samuel Rayan, "Doing Theology in India", *Doing Theology*, ed., Kurien Kunnumpuram, Vol. II, (New Delhi: ISPCK, 2013), p. 22.
3. The non-dalits call dalits avarnas, antyajas, panchamas, exterior castes, outcastes, depressed classes, scheduled castes, harijans and untouchables.
4. Samuel Rayan, "The Challenge of Dalit Issue: Some Theological Perspectives", *God's Hope Becoming Visible*, ed., Kurien Kunnumpuram, Vol. III, (New Delhi: ISPCK, 2013), p. 181.
5. *Ibid.,* p. 187.
6. *Ibid.,* p. 193.
7. Samuel Rayan, "The How of Third World Theologies", *Doing Theology*, ed., Kurien Kunnumpuram, Vol. II, (New Delhi: ISPCK, 2013), p. 286.
8. Samuel Rayan, "Outside the Gate, Sharing Insults", *Jesus: the Relevance of His Person and Message for our Times,* ed., Kurien Kunnumpuram, Vol. I, (Mumbai: St. Paul's Publication, 2011), p. 289.
9. *Ibid.,* p. 293.
10. Samuel Rayan, "The Challenge of the Dalit Issue: Some Theological Perspectives", p. 194.
11. *Ibid.,* p. 188.
12. Samuel Rayan, "Outside the Gate, Sharing insults", p. 280.
13. *Ibid.,* p. 282.
14. Samuel Rayan, "The Challenge of the Dalit Issue: Some Theological Perspectives", p. 196.
15. Samuel Rayan, "Outside the Gates, Sharing insults", p. 291.
16. Samuel Rayan, "People's Theology", *Doing Theology*, ed., Kurien Kunnumpuram, Vol. II, (New Delhi: ISPCK, 2013), p. 101.

17. Samuel Rayan, "Indian Theology and the Problem of History", *Doing Theology*, p. 206.
18. Samuel Rayan, "The Churches and Justice to Christians of Scheduled Caste Origin", *God's Hope Becoming visible*, ed., Kurien Kunnumpuram, Vol. III, (New Delhi: ISPCK, 2013), p. 203.
19. The state shall strive to promote the welfare of the people by securing and protecting as effectively as it may a social order in which justice–social, economic and political – shall inform all the institutions of the national life.
20. It enjoins promotion with special care of the educational and economic interests of weaker sections of the people, in particular of the Scheduled Castes and the Scheduled Tribes and their protection from social injustice and all forms of exploitation.
21. It provides for the reservation of appointments or posts in favour of any backward class of citizens which is not adequately represented in the service.
22. It provides for Presidential appointment of special officer for the Scheduled Castes and Scheduled Tribes to investigate matters relating to the safeguards provided for them under the Constitution and to report to the President.
23. Samuel Rayan, "The Churches and Justice to Christians of Scheduled Caste Origin", *God's Hope Becoming Visible*, p. 207.
24. *Ibid.*, p. 210.
25. Samuel Rayan, "The Catholic College in India and the Challenge of the Secular," *God's Hope Becoming Visible*, p. 249.
26. *Ibid.*
27. *Ibid.*, p. 251.
28. Antonyraj, *Children of a lesser God*, Madurai: DCLM Publication, 1992, p. 2.

22

Colonization, Erasure and Theologizing in India

Victor Ferrao

Thinking the unthought is authentic thinking. Often the unthought is that which remains forgotten. It thus remains an unsaid in all that is said. Within this world of the unthought, the history of colonization remains forgotten in theology. But today, the imperial face of theology is being examined and interrogated in several quarters. The Australian aboriginal painter, Lin Onu, in his painting, 'and on the eighth day' presents a visual satire of the biblical narrative of creation. He portrays that 'on the eight day' the English Angels arrive bearing sheep, fencing wire, a gun, a Bible and disinfectant, attempting to unravel how the colonized land was needed to be fenced-and the people to be subjugated with a gun, civilized with a Bible and disinfected of unwanted elements.[1] In a similar way, Claude Alvares and Norma Alvares in their provocative article ''The Christian and the Wild", forcefully manifest how Christianity that claimed to originate with the prince of peace exhibited deeds that were associated with the prince of darkness, particularly during the colonial era. They argue that the dark side of the project of civilization and Christianization was enslavement.[2] A complete demonizing of the interrelationship of Christianity with colonization would be crass reductionism. It would amount to simply forgetting that benevolent dimension embedded in the colonial project. Yet the complexities and the ambiguities associated with it pose challenges to our faith response in this modern era. Certainly, we can notice a discomfort to deal with these crucial, vital and critical terrains of Christian encounters with the colonized peoples. But this is our prophetic mission. We need to recover the original grace that is given to us through our faith that is entangled with the evils of colonization. We can trace this noble attempt of Samuel Rayan in his seminal article, 'de-colonizing theology' where he brings forth his quest for a liberating and liberated theology in India. Following the path pioneered by Samuel Rayan this study attempts to examine the relevance and importance of such a project. This project can free us as well as our country from the disastrous afterlife of colonization. Hence, we shall try to argue that colonization cannot be reduced to a tabula rasa and kept under erasure by theology in India. We shall attempt to inspire a new spring-time for theologizing in India that strives to respond to the complexities of colonization.

Ambiguities and Complexities that Face Christianity Today

Colonization has not really ended with its political end but continues to live on the borderlines of the present where we seem to find ourselves in a position of being 'in-between' as we experience an afterlife of colonization brewing among the people who were colonized. We can identify a metamorphosis of colonisation in the shape of multiple neo-colonial modes of domination in our society. The Christians who inhabit the once colonized societies have to negotiate their loyalties to Christianity as well as the newly independent, politically robust, and sovereign State in their respective societies. Often Christians are displaced, deprived, and discriminated against by their religious other despite the fact that they often have a shared biology, and a common history and memory of colonial experience. Hence, the claims for identities have become sites of innovative collaboration and contestation in the post-colonial societies like India, leading to profoundly antagonistic, conflictual and even incommensurable exchanges among communities marked as different on the basis of their religious orientation.

Alienation of Religious Minorities in Post-colonial India

Post-colonially, India exhibits both antagonistic as well as affiliative movements among communities that are othered by religious affiliation. The majority community that has emerged from various indigenous movements and religions during the colonial era and stakes claim for legitimate citizenry, while its religious other has to prove the same, although everyone is bestowed citizenship by virtue of being born in India. The tone and tenor of this cultural engagement are produced performatively. Hence, we cannot think of the antagonistic as well as the affiliative processes as being pre-given and set in the fixed tablet of tradition. This representation of sameness and otherness is a complex ongoing process that seeks to authorize and privilege the majority community and reinforce its position through the re-invention of tradition. One can see the consensual as well as conflictual lines along the borders that are continuously constructed and maintained to guarantee a sense of majoritarian identity. The mjoritarian Identity is reinforced through a production of demonized minorities that are thought to have been estranged from the cultural ethos of our country. The other side of the line of affiliation is the affliction of the religious other, but one cannot simply reduce these affiliative as monolithic and fixed processes. There is an inbuilt heterogeneity (like in every other community) in the majority community that refuses to dissolve into a monadic unity. Hence, it is clear that Christianity in India is in an interrogatory interstitial space where she has to continuously negotiate the forces and processes of de-territorialisation. This location into an interrogatory zone has opened up numerous possibilities of being both Indian and Christian. We can already trace the fact that Christians in India have responded primarily through inculturation and Dalit theologies. Yet the barriers seem to persist and linger synchronically on both sides of the divide, and we seem to be led into an in-articulable and un-representable terrain that has its roots in the colonial era.

The Synchronic Process of Territorialisation and De-territorialisation

The processes of minoritizing simultaneously becomes the processes of majoritizing. The self-presence of the majority is synchronous with its discontinuities, its inequalities and its minorities. This means that the majority territorialises by a simultaneous de-territorialisation of its minorities. By usurping of the enunciative space, a majority territorialises itself and silences a range of other dissonant and even dissident voices and histories. It thus constructs and maintains its power position in our society. This occupation of the enunciative space brings the minorities under the gaze of what is viewed as natural and normal by the majority and effectively puts the minorities into a mode of self-policing and self-surveillance. This means that the reigning cultural politics in our country produces its nationalism by disenfranchising its minorities. Within this milieu, Christians in India are totalized and disenfranchised. They thus remain as an exiled other in their own country. As Benedict Anderson effectively says, we can see that the current nationalism proposes an 'imagined community' rooted 'in homogenous empty time' of modernity and progress. Thus, the power elite in our country have assimilated the technologies of domination of the colonial masters and evolved as their clones or mimic men. These technologies of domination mimicked from the West ironically un-home Christianity in India. The power elite successfully use the technologies and architecture of domination to re-locate his home and thus mark out the world of un-homeliness which is viewed as the dwelling space of the Christians and other minorities in India. Although, the 'un-homely' was a common colonial condition of all Indians under colonization, the power elite as fractural image of the colonizer makes his home by un-homing the Christians and other minorities in a free India. Some might say that Christianity is facing the logic of reversal since it had already un-homed several religions and communities under the garb of colonization. All cultures recognize themselves through the projection of otherness, and Christianity and other minorities today become the other that produces a sense of stable sameness in the majority community.

The Second Colonization

It is an experience of post-colonial societies that something is beyond control but not beyond accommodation. The suffering, pain and trauma of the colonial era irrupt and disrupt our society producing an un-homing stirring in everyone. Feeling un-homed, dislocated and lost, there are movements of recovery, reclamation and restoration in post-colonial societies. Indeed, we can view a complex quest for healing of colonial trauma through its re-enactment. Perhaps Rene Girard's theory of mimetic desire might help us to arrive at some understanding of how the past lives in complex ways in our present. With the encounter with the colonizer, there sprang the desire to be like the colonizers. That is why we can trace mimicry/imitation of the colonial era in our modern society too; an imitation/mimicry that relocates the self and other relations and ends up repeating the colonizer/colonized relation and their tyrannical histories of domination. This is succinctly articulated by Fanon when he said 'the Negro is not any more than the white men'.[3]The re-enacting histories of domination in post-colonial India exhibit the naked incivility of the colonial condition irrupting again in our society. All Indians seem to be over-determined by the image and fantasy of the colonizers and have become the image and likeness of the one we hated most. This is clearly brought to the fore by Ashish Nandy in his book, *Intimate Enemy*: *the Loss and Recovery of Self under Colonization*, forcefully demonstrating that colonization was a colonization of the mind. He speaks of the second colonization that is surviving in our country long after the demise of the empire. The second colonization legitimated the first colonization and even those who resisted the first colonization guiltily embraced the second colonization.[4] In fact, the second colonization released forces in our society that have altered our cultural priorities, and which have transformed the concept of the modern West from a geographical and temporal entity to a psychological category. The West is now everywhere and there are many imaginations of the West in our minds. We are challenged to beat the West on the strength of our acquired Western-ness. That is why, like Albert Camus, we might state that the innocent is called upon to justify itself in contemporary India.[5] We might include Christians, Muslims and other minorities who are called to justify themselves under the new order of things in a post-colonial India. The West has produced its blind imitators, critical admirers, ornamental dissenters as well as circus-tamed opponents who are in the final analysis reproducing the oppressive technologies of the West in front of local appreciative Caesars.

Deciphering the Shared Culture of Colonization and the Space of Christianity in India

Colonization is primarily a relationship. It cannot be identified with economic gain and political power. Colonial relations continued even when there were economic and political losses.[6] Colonization is more a state of mind and a matter of consciousness. The psychological contours of colonization needs to be decoded so as to understand how colonialism is still alive and active in several sectors of our life in India even after the end of the Raj. The sources of colonization remain deep in the minds of the colonized people and continue to afflict them in post-colonial times. Colonization continued through the induction of socio-economic and psychological rewards and punishments. This still continues by way of a new garb of incentives and dis-incentives by the mimic men of the colonizers to their victims who are constantly trumpeted to fall in line with their imperial agenda.

Christians as not Indian Enough

Christians in India are subjected to a panoptical vision of domination that lays a clear demand to be a subject that is Indian but not quite. This subject produces a feeling of enough among Christians. Theology has tried to address this demand through the theology of inculturation, but not very successfully. This demand has its roots in colonization. In fact it mimics the colonizer who drew up the lines of difference and thus invited the Indians to be civilized by becoming like white men; creating a desire that can never be really fulfilled. Colonial mimicry is ambivalent. In order to be effective it has to continually produce its slippage, its excess, its difference. The colonized people never really qualify enough to be an exact image of the white men. What is interesting about this mimicry is that it generates self-policing or surveillance in the colonized. This in turn continuously reminds them that they are not Western enough and legitimates and normalises the colonial hegemony over them. Along with the mimicry, there is also mockery which constantly reminds the colonizers of their failed mimicry, thus reinforcing the fact that they are not yet quite there. The success of the colonial project depended on mimicry which at once became resemblance as well as menace. Indeed, Christianity was used by the colonizers to drive home the project of mimicry and consolidate colonial hegemony. In post-colonial India, we can locate the colonizer's strategy of mimicry in a new *avtara*. This time the coordinates of mimesis are identified, singularized, and craftily nationalized from our plural Indic tradition. This strategy generates a constant feeling of not being Indian enough among the Christians and legitmates a politics of outsidering, championed by some bigotry and exclusionary nationalist agenda. Thus, we have a complex mimicry that repeats the colonial hegemony and brings about the second colonization from within. This might be viewed as the way in which colonial trauma is seeking collective catharsis. The white presence and its brown Indian resemblance are repeated and re-enacted as Hindu Indian presence and its resemblance in the mimic practices of Christian and other minorities. All in all, a Christian remains a lacking or castrated subject who cannot be accepted as fully Indian. Hence, the theology of inculturation, though significantly important, seemed to bow down to the subjected position of lacking or castrated nature of Christianity in India, and is mimed in complex ways chiefly through the brahminical tradition.

Transgenerational Trauma

The colonial condition was a dehumanizing experience for the colonizers as well as for the colonized. It has a cumulative emotional and psychological wounding dimension that extends over communities and gets transmitted from generation to generation. This is called inter-generational transmission of trauma. Most of the studies that have been done on the transmission of trauma have concentrated on the survivors of the holocaust. Trauma breaks down the protective shield of the people; the shield that gives security and safety to them and brings great damage in their personal as well as social life. Trauma seeks healing through re-enactment and continues to afflict our people even after political independence. Certainly colonization was a disruption and invasion of the social, political, cultural, economic, religious and psychological life of the colonized people. Albert Memmi describes the colonial society as a diseased society. Scholars have evolved a category, 'Historical trauma', as a hermeneutical tool to understand the impact of the psychic damage inflicted by colonization. Within this perspective, we may understand how Christianity in India is looked upon with suspicion and may be even viewed as a disruptive force by some sections of our people. The growing pathologization of Christians and other minorities in our country can be seen as an indication of that complex trauma of the colonial past that is still afflicting our society even today. Hence, we need creative and therapeutic responses to the present condition as well as diverse ways to free Christianity which is entangled in the complex web of colonial history. Hence, Christian theology has to become therapeutic and should strive to free us from the karma of the colonial era that is still afflicting us even today.

Subjecting to the Foreclosed Boundaries

We have been able to rise beyond the natural common understanding of power which views power externally as something pressed upon the subject and embrace the understanding of power as one that forms the subject and forms the very condition of its existence, and thus nurses the trajectory of its desire. Becoming a subject requires submission to the process of subjection. This means that power doubles up as it simultaneously subordinates as well as produces us as subjects. The colonial condition has made us subjects in subordination. Hegel in his master-slave dialectics has pointed out that the master who first appears 'external' to the slave re-emerges in the slave's own consciousness.[7] Thus, power which appears as something external and pressed upon the subject into subordination acquires a psychic form that constructs the subjects' identity. Louis Althusser says that a subject is formed through linguistic interpellation. Moving forward in the same direction, Michel Foucault drives home the point that a subject is a construct of discursive production.[8] But there is something more profound that makes the subject remain attached to his or her own subordination. There is an ambivalence in the subjection of the subject who is at once formed and subordinated at the same time. We Indians experience this dependent subject formation like a child and hence are vulnerable to subordination and exploitation. These dependencies bore from caste oppression. At the same time, colonization conditions a passionate attachment to those who replicate and regulate the power structure in post-colonial India and continue to produce possibilities for being within foreclosed boundaries. Christians are also challenged to be in foreclosed boundaries. That means Christians are produced as subjects by a condition from which they are differentiated and separated. Julia Kristeva in *Powers of Horror: An Essay on Abjection*, theorises on how the subject is constructed by positioning of boundaries that bring about the dynamism of exclusion and inclusion.[9] Those that are excluded become the abject that ambivalently carry both fascination and horror within them. Hence, it is important to discern how Christians have taken to the foreclosed boundaries of being less Indian in India.

Discerning the Foreclosed Boundaries of Being an Indian Christian

There is space or site that is being construed for the Christians of India. It is a site or space which Christians are to occupy in the imaginary of India. It is a site of subjectification whereby the subjecthood of Christians is constituted in India. A Christian is a bound subject in India. The term subject in this context has to be primarily understood as a linguistic category, a kind of place holder where an Individual Christian comes to occupy the site. It is within this bound framework that Christians are understood in India. It is by subjecting to this dynamic, entangled socio-politico-psychological space that a Christian emerges as a subject. Hence, this socio-politico-psychological place holder exerts power and also becomes a site wherein a Christian submits to subjection and emerges as a subject in India. Thus, in some way, Christians collaborate and invest in the reproduction of the geography of closure that has been weaved to deal with the trauma of colonization.

Geography of Closure

The position of the boundaries of inclusion and exclusion is a fruit of the psychic life of power and is responsible for the dynamic construction of chora or the place holder for the emergence of a subject. The chora determines the boundaries of self and its other. The place holder/chora is discursively produced and is pressed on to subject who actively internalizes it. The chora simultaneously becomes a space through which the subject seeks closure of the colonial trauma. By assigning a place to its other, the colonially displaced subject attempts to seek to numb and tranquilize the discomfort of colonization. The loss of self under colonization is recovered through an active construction of the chora through which one seeks to insulate oneself from the pain of the past that afflicts the present. In the act of assigning a space for its other, the self appropriates its own space. The condition of subordination to the dynamic chora makes possible the assumption of power. This assumption of power is tied to its conditions of productions but in an ambivalent manner. This means that the power assumed may at once retain and resist subordination. From our discussion, we notice that a Christian is a bound subject whose legitimate existence is under interrogation, whereby the Indian-ness of a Christian is abjected. Thus, being under-interrogation brings a sense of being un-homed and there is a tendency to submit to the subjection position or chora imposed on them. Thus, the power not only acts on a Christian subject but in a transitive sense enacts him/her into being a subject. But a Christian subject is not merely an effect of power but can claim to incarnate power that a Christian as a subject effects.

Constricted Imaginaries

The dynamic chora that we have discussed introduces other foreclosures. It somehow constricts and tethers our imagination. This restricts our creative investments as our consciousness remains encaged and captive to limited possibilities that can be imagined by us. Of course, the constricted imaginaries reflect and signify a self-opted space of belonging which constitute a stable core and mark out and differentiate the inside from the outside. This brings to birth the imagined identities that foreclose our selfhood and restrict other possibilities of self-creation. This means that we become captive to arbitrary dividing lines that function on the social, cultural, religious, and psychic levels. We territorialize ourselves by defining our 'ins and outs'. The territorialisation of self brings about the de-territorialisation of its other through the foreclosure of the boundaries of selfhood. But, herein also lies the possibility of deconstructing the previously established boundaries that demarcate the self from its other. This is possible through the expansion of the imaginaries which allow border crossing of the self and its other. This process is more contentious than consensual because it attempts to reclaim the dislocated space of self. That is why we notice a high sense of awareness of location and position in post-colonial India. Within this struggle to reclaim the lost space of the self, we can understand the de-territorialisation of the Indian Christians despite their share in a relation of kinshipship and common Indian history. Often these imposed boundaries are appropriated by the Christians as they attempt to imagine and reclaim their space in post-colonial India.

DiscursiveTrauma

There are also self-imposed boundaries created either consciously or unconsciously by the Christians themselves. One such foreclosure is the entire experience of colonization. Colozination has been treated like a tabula rasa even by the theologians as they seem to have no faith response to this vital experience of our country. Can we really bracket the relationship with colonization? Can we treat it merely as a footnote in our theology? The more we attempt to forget it the more it seems to come back and haunt us. Thankfully, we can trace a glimmer of hope in the work of Samuel Rayan, SJ, particularly in his paper decolonizing theology. But the overall silence in our theologizing is disturbing. We seem to prefer silence rather than creative engagement and therapeutic dialogue with the afterlife of colonization. The colonial period cannot be put on the edge of the official history of our country. Humans are not merely shapers of history but are also shaped by history. Hence, there is an urgent need to develop a Christian response to the afterlife of colonization reigning in our society today. The debris of the colonial past is still afflicting our people as the past continues to live in the present. We need to understand the way Christianity inhabits the imagination of our countrymen and strive to actively work to loosen the chains that entangle and nail Christians to the colonizers. But, the fact that we seem to hesitate and experience a discomfort in dealing with the colonial cloud covering the face of Christ and the Church in our country reveals profoundly that colonization as well its afterlife in our country profoundly afflicts us. Colonization and its afterlife seem to have put us into a numbing silence. This anesthetization of our theological response may be viewed as a discursive trauma that keeps the unsaid like a ghost lingering in everything that is said. That is, colonial trauma forecloses and controls what is said in our theological discourse. But its remnants which are otherwise suppressed and hidden ooze out somehow as an unsaid in everything that is said in our theological discourses. Hence, the challenge is to hear the voice within the voice of our theological discourse, and allow the silenced tongue to speak.

Responding to Cultural Politics

The absence of recognition has un-homing effects on the minorities in our country. This de-recognition of the other is the politics of inferiorization that can be discerned where there are hegemonies of racism, casteism, and colonialism and politics of culture as it unfolds in our country. Within this politics of de-recognition, can we try and appreciate how Christianity as a signifier is entangled in the colonial era? Though our attempts at inculturation have tried to overcome this othering, an un-homing process somehow persists and continues to afflict us. The un-homing process unleashed by the politics of culture pulverizes our society and requires an urgent, critical and therapeutic response.

Re-imagining other ways of Belonging to India

Following Julia Kirsteva one might have to say that the erosion of capacity to adequately respond to politics of outsidering is a sign of depression.[10] But, this retreat into an imputed history by forgetting the colonial past only manifests a lack of responsibility on our part. Perhaps this retreat of Christianity from the shadow of the colonial era may be seen as a Freudian retreat into the law of the father. Hence, there is a need to bring about a transformation of the collective psychic space of the Christians community in India. One way of achieving this is through a creative use of narrative, memory, and testimony. This might then be able to destabilize the common understanding of nation as being a product of universal abstraction. Christians then might be able to freely participate in the hope and the promise of India as a nation. The abstract uniform national ideal fails to recognize the plural communities that inhabit our country and as such cannot be the benchmark of betrayal of our nation for every otherness that stands as an inassimilable difference in its view; it actually ends up banishing the freedom to be other in a plural India. Christianity and other minorities being other and different remind the majority of the failure of a national ideal which is essentially marked by the idealism of being a religious subject. The religious subject that is privileged being a Hindu, any difference inhabiting in the Christians and other minorities is viewed as not universalizable and therefore deemed as not part of the national ideal. This certainly is unjust to Christians and other minorities whose otherness is viewed as a betrayal of the promise of a nation. Hence, this subjection has to be contested by interrogating the social and political discourses that rule the roost in our country. This can begin by naming the process of cultural politics of identity that strips the minorities of legitimate belonging to our country and render them vulnerable to a disposable bare life. Hence, an obligation based on respect for otherness and accountability for the others' obligation can motivate resistance and might bring about new modes of belonging to our country. This can open up possibilities of re-imagining other ways of being Indian. This will disentangle the primary focus on viewing citizens as a religious subjects while we claim that we are a secular country.

Disentangling Christianity from the Relation of Coloniality

Colonization was not a unilateral process. Though it dehumanized both the colonizer and the colonized, it survived in terms of the creation and maintenance of colonial dominance. The requisite behaviour to produce and maintain colonial hegemony is referred to as relation of coloniality. The relation of coloniality produces a coloniality of power. Coloniality of power is a term coined by Arnibal Quinjno to name the structures of power and hegemony that emerged in an era of colonization and survive even in our days.[11] The coloniality of power depended on the creation of the colonial difference whereby the natives were inferiorized and rendered willing subjects of the colonial masters. Christianity to a large extent was used as a vehicle of coloniality of power by the colonizers to achieve their colonial hegemony. Hence, though Christianity is not reductively identifiable with colonization, it is entangled with colonization in the imagination of the natives in all post-colonial societies, particularly our society in India. Hence, the imperative to disentangle the colonial knots that entangle Christianity becomes a promise of healing and therapy to these societies. That is why we require a concerted effort to re-imagine the trajectory of theology in our country. To carve out a new path for theologizing in India, we need to dismantle the relation of coloniality that afflicts within as well as outside the folds of Christianity in our country.

Overcoming the Forgetting of Colonial History

The challenge to disentangle Christianity from the colonial past takes us to a disturbing aspect of our theology. It appears that there is a forgetting of history in our theology in India. We seem to have a certain discomfort when dealing with our colonial past. Unfortunately, this forgetting of history only reinforces the entangled hermeneutics of our fellow countrymen. The entangled hermeneutics views Christians through the trauma of the colonial past. The Indian plural Mythos is disrupted by the complex colonial pathos and Christianity is trapped within the boundaries of the colonial matrix. We can no longer occlude colonial history from our theology. Hence, there is a need for broadening the horizons of inculturation. Perhaps, Inculturation has to be viewed as overcoming alienation as taught by George M. Soares-Prabhu. Keith D'Souza succinctly draws Prabhu's path when he says "while for the West, Inculturation as a theological enterprise would entail aggiornamento within one's cultural stream, for us in India; it would entail a process of 'decolonization'.[12] Until we become fully aware of the colonial consciousness, we cannot necessarily work to disentangle Indian Christianity fully from the colonial baggage. India is yet to reach it's de-colonial moment and Christianity with its profound resources can bring about this process. Hence, an awareness of our colonial consciousness may be of therapeutic value for us and we might thus overcome our discomfort with the colonial past and thus prevail over this de-historicized condition of theology both in

Asia and in our country. Indeed, the treatment of the colonial past as a tabula rasa is afflicting us and our people. Hence, it is an imperative of faith that we as theologians in India bring our colonial past and it's afterlife to the feet of Christ.

Unmaking the Un-homing Habitus

Pierre Bourdie's notion Habitus[13] conceptualizes the way society gets deposited in the individuals in the form of lasting dispositions or trained capacities to think, feel and act. These dispositions are acquired without formal learning. There appears to be a habitus that seems to generate dispositions that leads a section of the people in our country to un-home the Christians, women, tribals and other minorities. Though a habitus is enduring and transferable it can also be changed. Hence, we have the challenge to unmake the un-homing habitus reigning in our country. I find that this noble task can be done from a marginal location like Goa.

Decolonizing Theology

The colonial entanglement of theology is succinctly brought out in the open by Samuel Rayan SJ. He courageously manifests how a triumphant subliminal messianism seems to have sanctified the colonizing drive of the Europeans.[14] The Church saw colonial expansion as a God-given opportunity to save souls. We saw the second coming of Constantine Christianity with the spiritual authority being given to the kings of Portugal and Spain by Pope Alexander VI, 1494.[15] As a result a potted Christianity or Western Church was transplanted in the newly discovered lands.[16] Theologies churned out in western academia began to be imported into these churches even in post-colonial times. These theologies were chiefly other-worldly and found favour among the colonizers. Thus, the theology that accompanied the colonizers failed to lead Christianity to become incarnate in the local cultures as well as to a large extent occluded the prophetic mission of the Church. There seemed to be no gospel for the poor in colonial times. Hence, there is the imperative to de-colonize theology so that we can have an authentically liberated and liberating theology. The project of de-colonization is complex and would become a way of the cross for us. This would also require a reinterpretation of Christian symbols tainted by the colonial era. Thus, for instance, the symbolism of the cross that has the stains of the colonial era has to be de-colonized so that we can overcome the alienation of Christianity in India. Among the early Christians, the cross was the symbol of the suffering Christ. With the conversion of Emperor Constantine, and Christianity emerging as the official religion of the Roman Empire, steadily the cross acquired new a signification that with the rise of emperor Charlemagne became a symbol of military victory and came to represent Christ the conqueror.[17] The Portuguese converted the cross into a symbol of their fatherland during their overseas mission in search of Christians and spices. The overseas mission of the Portuguese have been viewed as an extension of the crusades. This is because the moors constituted their chief rivals in the spice trade and were their hated religious enemies. This brought about a collapse of religion, politics and economics. Hence, drawing upon the symbolism of the suffering Christ can help us view Christ crucified in our society and thus re-interpret the Cross for our country.

Resisting the Neo-civilizing mission

The plural ethos of our country is in danger of being assimilated into a monocultured singularized culture and religion. Suddenly our plural past, geographies and anthropologies are made to look incompatible, incommensurable and irreconcilable with our India as a nation. The civilizing mission of the colonizer is now reproduced by the mimic men of the colonizers, the Hindutva fanatics. They produce the self of the colonizer in matter and form. The matter is replaced by the Hindu tradition while the monoculturing form remains congruent with that used by the colonizers. Goa can provide a critical space that can open another window to India. Unfortunately, Indian Intelligentsia are largely trapped in the discourses that have their basis in British orientalism. Goa can provide an alternate space to picture India even before the political and geographical boundaries of our country were fixed. The other orientalism and the different mode of colonization of the Portuguese that foreruns the British colonization of India by two hundred years can open new vistas. That is why to resist and respond effectively to the neo-civilizing mission unleashed by the Hindutva forces, we need to redeploy the other orientalism of the Portuguese and manifest how our plural geographies, pasts and anthropologies were steadily kept under erasure by the British. This will help us deconstruct the tendency to monoculture the dynamic and evolutionary pasts of our country and demonstrate that our country was not merely a kind of tabula rasa with Hinduism written all over it. This reductive vision of our country defines the relation of the self and the other and often throws up feelings of hate and disgust which lead the majority to treat the minorities as abjects that defile the self. The abject thus threatens the subject since it is perceived to be opposed to the 'I' and rival in the share of the common life promised by the nation. Hence, it is important to open the narrow narrative that conditions the way we live out our belonging to our country and one another. The expansion of the narrative is possible from Goa since Goa itself was not part of the narrow and frozen narrative (that puts on the mask of being national) that is being forced on the rest of us. Hence, a re-narrativization of the narrative of our country that will accommodate its plural ethos is the ethical imperative of the hour and we can creatively and prophetically attempt to do it from Goa.

Theologizing the Colonial Context

Theology cannot keep the colonial era under erasure. The colonial context is not a *tabula rasa* that does not affect the post-colonial condition of our country. It certainly afflicts us and our people. One might respond to it by theologizing colonialism from a pluritopical hermeneutical[18] position that remains open to the pluriversal. The universalization of universality was part of the imperial colonial project. In fact it was presumed that all civilization is based on the notion of universality as conceptualized in the West. Hence, we can trace how that which is universalizable is identifiable with the universalizing imperialism of the West and is unconsciously imitated in matter and form by the local elite who chooses to universalize a local history, culture, and religion for the rest of us in India. Hence, these power elites are cloning the imperial designs of their colonial masters in the local contexts of our country, homogenizing and universalizing reductively the pluriversal ethos of our country. Hence, theological response to our collective colonial experience cannot reproduce it in the image and likeness of colonial imperialism. Moreover, we have a pluralism of colonialisms in India and therefore we cannot posit universalized colonialism into one British era. Hence, a pluri-topical hermeneutics is an apt tool to develop a faith response to our complex colonial past that afflicts our living present. Pluri-topical hermeneutics is an entangled hermeneutics that is open to trauma, pain, as well as power differential that can affect our understanding. Hence, our theological matrix dwells in the colonial era and attempts to disentangle the reduction and identification of Christianity with colonization while responding to the complexity of the colonial past. Thus, a de-colonial thinking as well as de-colonial theologizing can be critically generated from Goa, since Goa has a colonial experience of four hundred and fifty years. The entangled hermeneutics is a kind of *senti-pensar* (a feeling-thinking) that is open to a pluri-logical dialogue with the past as well as the present. Such a pluri-logue would open a plural space of interpretation so that the multi-temporal heterogeneity of the post-colonial condition can be illumined by the light of revelation in the Jesus Christ. Hence, the pluri-logue that deals with the multiple pasts residing in the present of our country can be indeed therapeutic.

Therapeutic Dialogue

A pluri-logue is required to deal with the multi-layered and intensely multi-temporal and heterogeneous past that lives in the present of our country. The colonial past and its varied degrees of impact on diverse communities and their cultures and religions still afflict in multiple ways our society today. Hence, a therapeutic dialogue can certainly play an effective role in liberating us and society.

Understanding Multi-temporal Heterogeneity

We as beings-in-the-world experience a depth-dimension as far as time is concerned. Our lived time is intertwined with the past and the future. The past and the projected future are embedded and reside in the present. We humanize ourselves by historizing ourselves in our dynamic context. Our present is experienced as pregnant with multiple temporal layers that give us possibilities of being-in-the-world. Time is experienced as thick and dense while lending us the possibilities of making ourselves. The complex texture of time conditions the way we territorialize and humanize ourselves in our dynamic context. Indeed, time becomes figural and we experience multiple layers of meanings laden in time being released through the process of historization. The entangled, intertwined and embedded layers of time disentangle and resonate with living and dynamic contexts and condition in our life. Hence, we can trace among other things the colonial past dwelling in the present of our country. That is why we cannot oversimplify and linearize the flow of time. Time is not merely chronological but may be viewed as inundated with layers of temporalities that are complexly synchronous. This means that we encounter multiple temporalities intensely affecting the condition of our being in the world. Thus, time is bound to heterogeneous temporalities that are available for humanity to embark on the dynamic construction of the self and its other. Hence, we might understand why the colonial trauma continues to afflict our countrymen and how the colonial temporalities colour and condition the way we create ourselves and the other in society. Time being profoundly social, the unresolved colonial pain and sense of loss of self as well as sense of loss of *telos* of time under colonization generates a dynamism of recovery of the lost self and lost *telos* and continues to afflict us in our days as an unfinished business. We can clearly trace this dynamism in Post-colonial society in our country and Goa as we immerse ourselves in the ceaseless flow of multi-temporalities embedded in time.

Understanding the Kairological Intensity of the Paschal Mystery

We experience time bound to multi-temporalities in our everyday life. We experience time as chronos that is intertwined and intersecting with multi-temporalities that are synchronous and are experienced as interruptive, disruptive, irruptive and even corruptive. Besides time as inundated chronos we also experience kairos, the time concentrated by the presence and grace of God. This is fullness of time or what can be viewed as unbound time. As unbound time, we cannot objectify and describe it in our essentialist and positivist terms. It is dynamic presencing that happens all around us in the mode of absencing. The kairos carries within it the intensity of the Paschal Mystery that can cross the boundaries of our bound temporalities and bring about a wholesome healing of our selves, so that we are enabled to deal with the broken layers of temporalities in our life and our society. Thus, kairos intersects with the chronos and sets it free from everything that binds and nails it. As we historize drawing from our resourceful past and a promised future of possibilities, the grace emanating from the Paschal Mystery becomes available to illumine our path to a salubrious self-creation and its relations with its other. That is why it is an imperative for catholic faith to bring the web of multiple-temporalities that shape our life and our society in our country under the horizon of the Paschal Mystery. Hence, a pluri-loge with the multi-temporalities embedded in the experience of time in the power of our catholic faith becomes a way of letting the salvific power of the Paschal Mystery take charge of temporalities that bind and impede our self-creation and the relations with the other in society.

Fusion of Horizons

Pluri-logue being poly-logue can bring the horizons of multi-temporalities in dialogue with the horizons of the Paschal Mystery. This fusion of horizons is salubrious as is merges the saving and healing power of the Paschal Mystery with the fragmented and broken temporalities that afflict our society. Although, like all humans, we are embedded in the bounds of multi-temporalities of our experience, our Christian faith leads us to open ourselves to *kairos* which is synchronically presencing itself with the flow of our life. This openness to the Paschal Mystery becomes the driving force that leads us to interrogate the rendering of the colonial era as a *tabula rasa* and challenge us to break the walls that have successfully kept it under erasure as we theologize in our country. Hence, the pluri-logue that we have proposed in this study is an invitation to an authentic intra-logue that opens up possibilities that can allow the complex colonial era to come under the feet of Christ and disentangle Christianity from its inter-locked condition with the colonizers in our country. This intra-logue has the potential to re-invigorate a theologizing that will not keep colonization under erasure but strive to bring the light of revelation on it and attempt to bring wholesome healing to its afterlife that is afflicting our society in our country. This means that the intra-logue leads us towards an extra-logue that is at once complex and thus becomes a pluri-logue. The pluri-logue is a salubrious dialogue with the religions, pasts, cultures, aspirations, hopes, and traumas, etc., of the peoples of our country. It is one that will transform our theologizing into a language/*glossia* that will lead Christ to become all to all.

Conclusion

We have tried to understand how the colonial past afflicts the Post-colonial society in our country. We have seen that somehow, we are creating the self of the colonizers in matter and form. The matter is Indic while the form remains western. Hence, in complex ways we are entangled in the colonial trauma in our living present. This has produced a theological silence on the era of colonization. Somehow, Christians seem to have rendered the colonial era a *tabula rasa* and have tried to suppress colonial pain by keeping it under erasure. But, the complex and dynamic afterlife of colonization has come back to haunt us. Hence, we have an imperative of faith to dis-entangle Christianity from the colonial tangle. A new way of theologizing that will become a sensitive pluri-logue and to the multi-temporalities affecting our living present is the salubrious way ahead for Christians in India.

Notes

1. See Mark G. Brett, *Decolonizing God: Bible in the Tides of Empire* (Sheffield: Sheffield Phoenix Press, 2008), pp. 7-8.
2. See Claude Alvares and Norma Alvares, "The Christian and the Wild' in Teotonio R. de Souza (eds.), *Discoveries, Missionary Expansion and Asian Cultures,* New Delhi: Concept Publishing Company, 1994, pp. 19-31.
3. Homi K. Bhabha, *The Location of Culture,* New York: Routlege, 1994, p. 40.
4. Ashish Nandy, *The Intimate Enemy: Loss and Recovery of Self under Colonization*, Delhi: Oxford University Press, 1983, p. 11.
5. *Ibid*, p.1.
6. *Ibid.*

7. Judith Butler, *The Psychic Life of Power: Theories in Subjection*, Stanford: Stanford University Press, 1997, p. 3.
8. *Ibid*, p. 5.
9. Julia Kristeva, *Powers of Horror: an Essay on Abjection*, Leon S. Roudiez (tr.), New York: Columbia University Press, 1982.
10. Tina Charter and Ewa Plonowaska Ziarek, (Eds.), *Revolt, Affect, Collectivity: the Unstable Boundaries of Kristeva Polis*, Albany: State University of New York, 2005, p. 3.
11. https://www.ocf.berkeley.edu/~marto/coloniality.htm accessed on 4th December 2014.
12. Kieth D'Souza S. J. "George M. Soares-Prabu, S. J.: A Theologian for our Times", in Francis X D'Sa, *The Dharma of Jesus : Interdisciplinary Essays in Memory of George Soares-Prabu SJ* (Anand: Gujarat Sahitya Prakash, 1997) p. 10.
13. See Pierre Bourdie, *Physical Space, Social Space and Habitus* (Blindern: University of Olso, 1995), pp. 15-17.
14. Kurien Kunnumpuram, *Collected Writings of Samuel Rayan*, SJ, Vol. II (Delhi : ISPCK, 2013), p 29.
15. *Ibid.*
16. *Ibid.*, p. 30.
17. Rovena Robinson, *Boundaries of Religion : Essays on Christianity, Ethnic Conflict and Violence,* New Delhi: Oxford University Press, 2013, pp. 26- 27.
18. See Walter D. Mignolo, *Coloniality, Subaltern Knowledge, and Border Thinking: Local Histories/Global Designs*, New Jersey: Princeton University Press, 2000, pp.14-18.

Paper Contributors

Dr. A. Kulandaisamy, OFM Cap.
Queenship of Mary Church
1/8 Padavattamman Kovil Street
Chindatripet
Chennai 600002
Kulandaisamy68@yahoo.co.in

Dr. Francis Gonsalves, SJ
Papal Seminary
Nagar Road, Ramwadi
Pune 411014
fragons@gmail.com

Dr. George Pattery, SJ
Provincial of South Asia
225 Jor Bagh
New Delhi 110003
gpattery@gmail.com

Dr. Henry Patttarumadathil, SJ
Pontificio Instituto Biblico
Via Della Pilotta 25
00187 Rome / Italy
henrypatar@gmail.com

Dr. Isaac Padinjarekuttu
Oriens Theological College
Mawlai
Shillong 783008
padinjarekuttu@gmail.com

Dr. J. Charles Davis
Papal Seminary
Nagar Road, Ramwadi
Pune 411014
davischarlesj@gmail.com

Dr. Jacob Parappally, MSFS
Tejas Vidya Peetha
Kumbalgodu PO
Bangalore 560074
parappally@gmail.com

Dr. Jacob Prasad
Rector, St. Joseph's Pontifical Seminary
Carmelgiri, P. B. No. 604
U. C. College PO
Aluva 683102
jacprasad@gmail.com

Dr. Joseph Lobo, SJ
Jnana Jyothi
Attibele Road, Anekal
Bangalore 562106
jlobosj@gmail.com

Dr. Keith D'Souza, SJ
St. Pius College
Aarey Road, Goregaon East
Mumbai 400063
keith@jesuits.net

Dr. Kochurani Abraham
Karippaparambil
P. B. No. 7
Kanjirappally 686507
kochuabraham@gmail.com

Dr. Kurien Kunnumpuram, SJ
Papal Seminary
Nagar Road, Ramwadi
Pune 411014
kuriensj@gmail.com

Dr. Kuruvilla Pandikattu, SJ
Papal Seminary
Nagar Road, Ramwadi
Pune 411014
kurusj@gmail.com

Dr. M. Paul Raj
Papal Seminary
Nagar Road, Ramwadi
Pune 411014
maapaaraasaa1967@gmail.com

Dr. Mohan Doss, SVD
Ishvani Kendra
Matchwel Road
Pune 411014
mohansvd@hotmail.com

Dr. Nicholas Tharsiuse
Madre-de-Deus Church
Vettucaud, Thumba
St. Xavier's College PO
Trivandrum 695586
tharsiuse_nichi@yahoo.co.in

Dr. P. R. John, SJ
Vidyajyoti College of Theology
23 Raj Niwas Marg
Delhi 110054
jpudota@yahoo.co.uk

Dr. P. T. Mathew, SJ
Vidyajyoti College of Theology
23 Raj Niwas Marg
Delhi 110054
matpampa@gmail.com

Dr. Sebastian Painadath, SJ
Sameeksha
Kalady 683574
spainadath@gmail.com

Dr. Shalini Mulackal, pbvm
Presentation Sisters
Prernalaya
A/49, Priyadarshini Vihar
Delhi 110092
smulackal@gmail.com

Dr. Stephen Chundamthadam, SJ
De Nobili College, P. B. 3007
Ramwadi, Nagar Road
Pune 411014
sthadam@gmail.com

Dr. Victor Ferrao
Rachol Seminary
Rachol, Salcete
Goa 403715
victorferrao@yahoo.co.uk